Valuing Freedoms

Sen's Capability Approach and Poverty Reduction

SABINA ALKIRE

UNIVERSITY PRESS

OXFORD
UNIVERSITY PRESS

Great Clarendon Street, Oxford OX2 6DP
Oxford University Press is a department of the University of Oxford.
It furthers the University's objective of excellence in research, scholarship,
and education by publishing worldwide in

Oxford New York

Auckland Cape Town Dar es Salaam Hong Kong Karachi
Kuala Lumpur Madrid Melbourne Mexico City Nairobi
New Delhi Shanghai Taipei Toronto

With offices in
Argentina Austria Brazil Chile Czech Republic France Greece
Guatemala Hungary Italy Japan South Korea Poland Portugal
Singapore Switzerland Thailand Turkey Ukraine Vietnam

Oxford is a registered trade mark of Oxford University Press
in the UK and in certain other countries

Published in the United States
by Oxford University Press Inc., New York

© S. Alkire, 2002

The moral rights of the author have been asserted
Database right Oxford University Press (maker)

First published 2002
First published in paperback 2005

All rights reserved. No part of this publication may be reproduced,
stored in a retrieval system, or transmitted, in any form or by any means,
without the prior permission in writing of Oxford University Press,
or as expressly permitted by law, or under terms agreed with the appropriate
reprographics rights organization. Enquiries concerning reproduction
outside the scope of the above should be sent to the Rights Department,
Oxford University Press, at the address above

You must not circulate this book in any other binding or cover
and you must impose this same condition on any acquirer

British Library Cataloguing in Publication Data
Data available

Library of Congress Cataloging in Publication Data
Alkire, Sabina.
Valuing freedoms : Sen's capability approach and poverty reduction / Sabina Alkire.
p. cm.
Includes bibliographical references and index.
1. Welfare economics.   2. Poverty—Developing countries.   3. Sen, Amartya Kumar.
I. Title.
HB99.3 .A575   2002   339.4′6′091724—dc21   2001055463

ISBN 0–19–924579–7
ISBN 0–19–928331–1 (pbk)   9780199283316

1 3 5 7 9 10 8 6 4 2

Typeset by Newgen Imaging Systems (P) Ltd., Chennai, India
Printed in Great Britain
on acid-free paper by
Biddles Ltd., King's Lynn, Norfolk

To My Family

Preface

This is a book about Amartya Sen's capability approach—his proposition that the objective of development should be that of 'expanding the real freedoms that people enjoy'. The book is written for academics and practitioners in economic development who consider using the tools of their trade—whether these be econometric analyses or small non-governmental organization activities or monitoring and evaluation procedures—in order to expand people's real freedoms. They wish to think through, systematically, such questions as 'what are valuable capabilities in my areas?', 'how do I think through trade-offs', and 'who should decide what?' In short, they wish to consider how to operationalize Sen's approach—to put it into practice in uncomfortable, messy, compromised practical work at the microeconomic level. It is also written for sceptics (philosophical and economic) who claim there to be nothing value-added in the capability approach because it leaves too many values issues unresolved and thus is impractical.

These pages address, in a number of ways, the question: 'how do we identify "valuable" capabilities?'. This question contains a number of sub-questions, such as 'valuable to whom?' and 'how valuable?' and 'who are the "we"?'

Each chapter of Part I synthesizes Sen's position on one issue, the criticisms he has received, and shapes a way to operationalize the capabilities approach on these issues. It refers to the corpus of Sen's writing on capabilities and poverty but is by no means complete in its treatment of the discussions he has led others to undertake. It sketches the shape that further work in these areas may helpfully pursue. Part II sketches some methodologies of participation and qualitative ranking which identify capability changes that are not now considered. It does not purport to provide a complete analysis.

Anyone who undertakes to publish a sketch is bound to feel self-conscious, as it exposes so many roughnesses of knowledge and mind. However, there may be value in offering up a sketch to the public space, that others may adapt it, contribute to it, and above all improve it. It is to that end that this book has been devoted.

SA

Acknowledgements

Those writing theses and first books accrue kindnesses that can be acknowledged, but not repaid. On the practical side, I am grateful to the George Webb Medley Fund, for providing assistance for two periods of field research in Pakistan. I am very indebted to the Human Development Centre in Islamabad, and its founder the late Dr Mahbubul Haq and his wife Khadija Haq, for providing institutional support and desk space whilst in Pakistan, and for including me in their activities and conferences. Oxfam has been uniformly supportive. Oxfam House provided the subsistence costs of my second field stay and Chris Roche and Elsa Dawson guided me to practical problems; the staff of Oxfam Pakistan provided both practical as well as personal assistance for which I am truly grateful. I also owe thanks to the Sustainable Development Policy Institute and its director Tariq Banuri for characteristically stimulating seminars and conferences. I am extremely indebted to Magdalen College for many reasons, including for a hardship grant to replace a stolen laptop. The author would like to thank the following for permission to reproduce published materials: extracts from *Women and Human Development* by Martha Nussbaum reproduced by the kind permission of the author and Cambridge University Press, extracts from *Natural Law and Natural Rights* by John Finnis reproduced by the kind permission of Oxford University Press.

I am also intensely appreciative of those who have given so generously of their time, thoughts, and abilities as employees of these institutions, or as participants of the activities they support. Particular thanks are owed to Safia Ali Nawaz and Hidayat Narejo, the Oxfam programme staff who did the three case studies with me and whose friendship, wisdom, and translation to and from Sindhi was indispensable. I would also like to thank Nasira Habiba of Khoj, the family of Imam Zadi of RWWO, and Sugrah and Ashiq of Arabsolangi, for providing rich information, and facilitating the case studies. I owe a particular debt to Dadi Taja, whose example I return to again and again. Early in the research I spent five months visiting participatory development activities, and observing how their methods of participation tailored income generation activities to non-economic values. In this regard I am grateful to the Aga Khan Rural Support Programme, Idara-e-Kissan, Oxfam, and the United Nations High Commission for Refugee offices in Peshawar and Jalalabad, for supporting extended visits to study their participatory methods. Also, I spent several months with the Asia Foundation in Pakistan. The teaching and repeated application of the assessment methodology, and discussions with colleagues, especially Erik Jensen greatly deepened my grasp of its usefulness and limitations.

As to intellectual debts, my doctoral supervisors, Professor Frances Stewart and Professor John Finnis, guided and grounded the work on which this book is based, and the comments and criticisms from each have been deeply appreciated.

Conversations with Professor Finnis gave me a clearer understanding both of his own work and of the patient attentiveness that is necessary to apply it. Frances Stewart provided significant direction, and personal support. I learned from each far more than I have been able to reflect. I am also grateful to James Griffin and Paul Collier for soundly challenging the structure of this work early on, to my examiners Jerry Cohen and Meghnad Desai, and to two anonymous referees for their insightful comments. I am particularly grateful to Mozaffar Qizilbash, for steadily enduring and improving many early drafts, and to Martha Nussbaum whose immediate warmth and accessibility, as well as incisive suggestions, directly enhanced my own capabilities. Meeting Amartya Sen was one of those graduate student experiences of startled wonder, when a name turns out to be a person—and a warm one. I am grateful to him for ongoing support and direction.

I have been sincerely grateful to each of those who read and offered valuable comments on chapters or on early drafts of them: Tariq Banuri, Rufus Black, John Cameron, Dave Crocker, Severine Deneulin, Des Gaspar, Germain Grisez, Christian Illies, Martha Nussbaum, Caterina Ruggeri-Laderchi, Mozaffar Qizilbash, Amir Sadighi, Nicholas Sagovsky, Amartya Sen, Francis Teal, Mark Thompson, Rosemary Thorp, and Nick Townsend. Regarding the section that compares different authors' lists, I am immensely grateful to Robert Chambers, Robert Cummins, Manfred Max-Neef, Deepa Narayan, Martha Nussbaum, Mozaffar Qizilbash, Maureen Ramsay, and Shalom Schwartz for their corrections and to Bestami Bilgic for his cheerful and very Turkish research assistance. Finally, I am very indebted indeed to the friends who proofread different chapters, or who helped me with the writing style: Frank Fountain, Eric Greitens, Hilary King, Pamela Lowden, Anasuya Sengupta, Christiania Whitehead, Lucy Wooding, and most particularly Ann Barham, who also was a vibrant sounding-board.

Queen Elizabeth House generously provided desk space and computer support and a splendid environment. Magdalen College was likewise all one could wish for as a home, Chapel, library, and community. My supervisors at the World Bank allowed me to arrange time off for completion of the manuscript.

Above all, thanks are due to my family—my grandmother, my father and his wife, and my sister and her family—who are a source of strength and joy, and to whom this book is dedicated.

For all the support which I have received in writing this book, its inadequacies remain very much my own.

Contents

List of Tables	xi
Abbreviations	xii

1. Introduction: Capability and Valuation — 1
1. Overview of the problem — 1
2. Sen's capability approach — 4
3. Criticisms — 11
4. The need for a framework — 14
5. Finnis's approach — 15
6. Terms and structure — 18
7. Conclusion — 22

PART I

2. Poverty and Human Development — 25
1. Identifying valuable capabilities — 25
2. Central human capabilities: Nussbaum's approach — 32
3. The practical reasoning approach — 43
4. Other accounts of dimensions — 59

3. Range, Information, and Process — 85
1. Multidimensionality and evaluation — 85
2. Ethical rationality in poverty reduction — 89
3. Sen's informational pluralism — 94
4. Sen's principle pluralism — 102
5. Finnis's principle pluralism — 105
6. Ethical rationality reconsidered — 113
7. Operational considerations — 115

4. Participation and Culture — 125
1. Introduction — 125
2. Participation: means, ends, debate, and identity — 129
3. Subsidiarity — 143
4. External assistance — 144
5. Conclusion — 152

5. Basic Needs and Basic Capabilities — 154
1. Absolute poverty and capability — 155
2. Basic capabilities or basic functionings? — 166
3. Development: 'equality' or 'expansion' of capabilities? — 177

    4. Indicators and basic capabilities   181
    5. Conclusion   195

PART II

6. Assessing Capability Change   199
    1. Introduction to Part II   199
    2. Cost-benefit analysis   206
    3. Capability set analysis   218
    4. Conclusion   232

7. Three Case Studies   233
    1. Loans for goats   235
    2. Literacy and community development   255
    3. Rose cultivation   271
    4. Comparison of activities   277
    5. Relating Part I and Part II   287
    6. Conclusion   296

Appendix   297

References   299

Index of Names   327

Index of Subjects   329

List of Tables

2.1. Nussbaum: central human functional capabilities	35
2.2. Finnis: basic reasons for action	48
2.3. Max-Neef: four expressions of the human need for understanding	61
2.4. Max-Neef: criteria for generating a classification of human needs	62
2.5. Narayan et al.: well-being according to the voices of the poor	64
2.6. Shalom Schwartz: universal human values	66
2.7. Doyal and Gough 1993: intermediate needs	69
2.8. Inglehart values	71
2.9. Qizilbash: prudential values for development	72
2.10. Finnis et al.: criteria for dimensions of human flourishing	74
2.11. Dimensions of human development	75
2.12. Thirty-nine lists of dimensions of human development from different disciplines	78
3.1. Alternative evaluative spaces	95
3.2. Finnis's principles of practical reasonableness	110
3.3. Menu of informational categories relevant for choosing between actions	118
4.1. Agency as an intrinsically valued dimension	132
5.1. Criteria for capability indicators	184
5.2. Needs and commodity requirements	187
5.3. DAC indicators	192
6.1. Criteria for women's participation	230
7.1. RWWO financial flows	237
7.2a. Estimated benefits from one female goat	238
7.2b. Goat owners' aggregate financial benefits	239
7.3. Projected financial benefits for goat owners	240
7.4. RWWO net discounted benefits	241
7.5. Unremunerated costs of goat activity	241
7.6. RWWO running costs and present values under various assumptions	244
7.7. RWWO projected NPV and IRR at various rates of unskilled labour	246
7.8. Additional RWWO costs and benefits	249
7.9. Rankings of RWWO human impacts	253
7.10. Financial costs of Khoj	260
7.11. Khoj staff and salaries	260
7.12. Internal rates of return under varied wage and benefit estimations	263
7.13. Additional Khoj costs and benefits	265
7.14. Rankings of Khoj impacts by different groups	271
7.15. Rose project expenses	274
7.16. Wages from rose garland production	275
7.17. Income and profit-sharing from roses	276
7.18. Rose cultivation internal rates of return	276
7.19. Comparative efficiency indicators	280
7.20. Qualitative ranking of impacts by facilitators	282
7.21. Qualitative ranking of participation	284

Abbreviations

AKRSP	Aga Khan Rural Support Programme
BA	beneficiary assessment
B.A.	Bachelors of Arts
BNA	basic needs approach
CA	capability approach
CBA	cost-benefit analysis
CBO	community-based organization
DAC	Development Assistance Committee
EIA	environmental impact assessment
GNP	gross national product
HDI	human development index
HDR	*Human Development Report*, annual (of the UNDP)
HPI	human poverty index
ILO	International Labour Organization
IRR	internal rate of return
LE	life expectancy
NGO	non-governmental organization
NGORC	NGO Resource Centre
NJ	non-compulsive judgements
NPV	net present value
OECD	Organization for Economic Cooperation and Development
PPA	participatory poverty assessment
PRA	participatory rural appraisal
QEH	Queen Elizabeth House
RERR	re-estimated rates of return
Rs	Pakistani rupees
RWWO	Rural Women's Welfare Organization (Senghar, Sindh)
SA	social assessment
SCBA	social cost-benefit analysis
SIA	social impact assessment
SPO	Strengthening Participatory Organizations (a national NGO)
SVJ	Substantive and valuational judgements
Tanzeem	organization; may be male or female
UNDP	United Nations Development Programme
UNESCO	United Nations Educational, Scientific and Cultural Organization
USAID	United States Agency for International Development
VO	Village Organization (VO members are male unless otherwise stated)
WDR	*World Development Report*, annual (of the World Bank)
WIEGO	Women in the Informal Economy Globalizing and Organizing
WO	Women's Organization

1

Introduction: Capability and Valuation

> Poetic Justice, with her lifted scale,
> Where in nice balance truth with gold she weighs,
> And solid pudding against empty praise.[1]

1. OVERVIEW OF THE PROBLEM

In 1995, a women's organization in the village of Arabsolangi, Pakistan, requested funding from Oxfam for an income generation activity in their village.[2] Together, the male and female social organizers and one Oxfam programme officer invited eight of the poorest persons in the village to participate with them in this initiative. Whether poverty is measured in absolute or relative terms, whether in income or calories per day or literacy or life expectancy or social exclusion, these eight people in interior Sindh—widows and landless heads of households—were poor. After considerable discussion, meetings, and technical input, the group decided to cultivate roses. They leased land and planted the first rose field in the area. The roses grew well, and after experiments with rose-water and rose paste, the group found that rose garlands were the most lucrative, and began to produce these. Two adult male members and the small sons of two women from the group sold the garlands in a nearby market town. During the first year and a half, by all accounts, changes occurred. Dadi Taja, a widow, became, quite literally, able to 'walk about without shame'[3] and reported, 'People in the village now respect me'.[4] Dadi Taja explained that she values the income the rose project produces, but this is not its only benefit. She also mentioned her delight that the fragrance of roses permeates her clothing, her satisfaction from working together in a group, and her inner peace because the garlands are used in saints' shrines and to decorate the Qur'an Sharif. Other members valued similarly diverse changes. The social organizer, for example, said that her capacity and confidence have been greatly strengthened through this activity, and she has now marshalled funds from various donors for additional development initiatives, and has helped train other social organizers for Oxfam.

Changes occurred, but how should they be valued? How could they be measured? How does Oxfam decide if their scarce resources have been optimally used in the rose

---

[1] Alexander Pope, *The Dunciad*, bk. i, l. 52.
[2] Details of this case study are found in Ch. 7, Sect. 3.
[3] Sen (1981a: 18) referring to Adam Smith (1776: 351–2). For a further discussion of this as an aspect of absolute poverty see Ch. 5, Sect. 1.   [4] Dadi Taja, May 1996; see Ch. 7, Sect. 3.5.

cultivation project in interior Sindh? Oxfam Pakistan's *1995–1996 Annual Report* stated that one way of framing its progress was to ascertain whether Oxfam activities had reduced poverty *more* than if the Oxfam Pakistan budget (about £300,000 per year)[5] was simply handed out to a group of the absolutely poor. 'Thus the question is, did we achieve impact on poverty equivalent to one time consumption assistance for between 4,000–10,000 people, or to a sustained increase in monetary income for between 200 and 500 people?'[6] In the case of the rose cultivation activity, the increase in monetary income in 1996 seemed marginal: each rose group member received just over 300 Rs that year, which is roughly one man's labouring wage for five to seven days—and the future income stream was unpredictable. Had the rose cultivation grant been handed out to each member, each would have received 2,365 Rs. Dadi Taja's 12 year old son fared slightly better. He earned about 2,500 Rs in 1996 from selling the garlands in the market town, and was able to pay his own school fees and buy trainers. If Oxfam acted on the basis of these assessments, it would reinvest scarce resources in alternative activities that generate more income.

But analyses of income generation alone exclude benefits such as empowerment, knowledge, and meaningful work which, though difficult or impossible to price accurately, were highly valued by participants.

The capability approach will be introduced very shortly and revisited often. But the fundamental insight of this approach is remarkably simple. It argues that the goal of both human development and poverty reduction should be to expand the capability that people have to enjoy 'valuable beings and doings'.[7] They should have access to the positive resources they need in order to have these capabilities. And they should be able to make choices that matter to them.

According to the capability approach, we could not say *definitively* that poverty reduction has occurred simply because income per capita had increased in Arabsolangi. Nor could we necessarily conclude that poverty reduction has occurred if we were to have information that people were meeting more of their basic needs than they had in the previous term (because this could be coerced). But if we knew that the rose cultivators could realistically choose to enjoy a greater set of valuable activities or ways of being, then we would conclude that poverty reduction had occurred.

The capability approach avoids some of the pitfalls and omissions of alternative ways of conceptualizing development. But leaving these aside for now, already we have enough information to become curious how to apply it. We ask, what are these 'valued beings and doings' for the rose cultivators? Are they the same for everyone in the world? Who is to choose focal capabilities of the rose cultivation initiative—Oxfam? The rose group? Economists or politicians?—and on what grounds? Which capabilities and whose are to be given priority?

---

[5] This does not include funds for emergency and relief work, nor grants from other donors.
[6] Oxfam Pakistan (1996: 1).
[7] (1999*a*: 75, 1992*a*: 39). See also Sen (1990*a*). Henceforth all footnotes that do not specify an author either in the text or in the footnote, refer to Sen's writing.

Introduction: Capability and Valuation

These are common enough questions and Sen's capability approach does indeed, as we shall see, provide some answers. By and large these answers either describe how to use limited consensus to create a partial ordering of options, or they are quite general—they raise all possible considerations but leave it up to (unspecified) agents or political communities to make the value judgements necessary to interpret and use the capability approach. Yet those who are working at a microeconomic level and amid value conflicts also need something more concrete.

These chapters represent an attempt to 'operationalize' the capability approach—to describe how it can be put into practice in microeconomic poverty reduction initiatives. Sen has not specified how the various value judgements that inhere in his approach, and that are required in order for its practical use (whether at the micro or macro level), are to be made. His reason for this is that there are a number of competing ways in which this specification may take place, each of which would be coherent with the capability approach. To choose one might be to rule out others and therefore compromise the 'incompleteness' and 'pluralism' of the capability approach.

But without some specification—and simplification—the capability approach cannot be used efficiently. The challenge is to simplify it without introducing significant distortions in the process. Hence this book will explore one broad way of identifying the information and judgements required to apply the capability approach, and the appropriate location of these.

I have taken as a focal problem the need for a methodology by which Oxfam field staff in Pakistan could identify which 'valuable'[8] capabilities a development activity (such as rose cultivation) had expanded or contracted. Such a methodology is needed by both local and international institutions that assess activities (and ultimately allocate resources)[9] according to heterogeneous considerations—such as how participatory an activity was, how much it had targeted the poor, empowered women, built capacity, strengthened institutions, improved the environment, catalysed local government, mobilized communities to undertake collective action, deepened cultural life, or generated sustainable social services. The methodology developed here represents an explicit attempt to explore the operational strengths and limits of the capability approach.

In order to develop and articulate the linkage between the capability approach and an operational methodology, some foundational work on value judgements was necessary. To clarify the identity and nature of the value judgements in the capability approach I have drawn on Sen's own work on rationality, and on other approaches that support pluralism, incompleteness, and freedom of choice, and acknowledge the wider implications of possible actions, especially John Finnis's.

---

[8] Capabilities are valuable by Sen's definition, so the adjective is formally redundant. I none the less sometimes employ the term 'valuable' simply because much of this book is concerned with singling out what people value. Furthermore, if valuable 'beings or doings' are chosen by a value judgement (and if so chosen are capabilities) then what do we call 'non-valued' beings and doings, or beings and doings 'of disputed value'?

[9] This assumes that development institutions are concerned to maximize the effectiveness of their loans or grants in expanding capabilities.

I have also drawn on Martha Nussbaum's work, as hers is the most well-developed active proposal of how the capability approach should be put into practice; and on the methodologies of 'participation',[10] because value issues arise in many participatory exercises. I have used these sources to construct a framework for specifying valuable capabilities in a way that seems consonant with Sen's capability approach taken as a whole. I am aware that many will disagree, and hopefully will find other practical methods for specifying the capability approach.[11] I am also uncomfortably aware that simplification and operationalization seems, inevitably perhaps, dissatisfying or even discourteous to those who have worked out far sharper accounts of component concepts. Yet by making the simplifications explicit, one is better able to invite criticism and modification of them.

Having sketched roughly the topic of this book, the remainder of this chapter identifies the problem more precisely. Sen's capability approach is introduced, and several salient criticisms of it are reviewed. Then the key terms and sources are introduced, and the relation of each chapter to the overall topic is outlined. The chapters that follow are tethered to the problem of how to identify, obtain, and process the information that is required to implement the capability approach in the assessment of poverty reduction initiatives at the microeconomic level.

2. SEN'S CAPABILITY APPROACH[12]

In the monograph *Inequality Reexamined* Nobel Laureate Amartya Sen argues that social arrangements should be evaluated according to the extent of freedom people have to promote or achieve objectives they value. Sen argues that if equality in social arrangements is to be demanded in any space—and most theories of justice advocate equality in some space, such as that of liberty, income, primary goods, resources, or utility—it is to be demanded in the space of capabilities.[13] Rather than aiming to equalize the income of an elderly farmer and a young student, for example, policy-makers should aim to equalize the capability each has to enjoy valuable activities and states of being. Sen uses the metaphor of 'space' to bracket off the area in which different theories of justice require equality, or impartial treatment of persons. Because of the fact of human diversity, equality in capability space—the space of freedom to promote or achieve valuable objectives—will, in fact, go along with inequality in other spaces.

The following four sections will introduce Sen's capability approach through four of its core concepts: functionings, freedom, pluralism, and incompleteness.

---

[10] See e.g. Bamberger (1988), Chambers (1992, 1993, 1994*a–c*, 1995, 1997), Narayan (1995), Norton and Stephens (1995), Paul (1989), Rietbergen-McCracken and Narayan (1997), Stiefel and Wolfe (1994), University of Stockholm (1991), Vivian and Maseko (1994), World Bank (1996*c,d,e*; 1998*b*).

[11] For some practical examples see Chakraborty (1995, 1996), Pattanaik (1997, 1998), McKinley (1998), Qizilbash (1997*b*, 1998*a*).

[12] For the main texts developing the capability approach see Sen (1980*a*, 1980/1, 1985*a,b*, 1987*b*, 1988*a*, 1990*a*, 1992*a*, 1993*a*, 1994*b*, 1996*a,e*, 1997*a*, 1999*a*).

[13] (1992*a*). See also Sen (1996*g*).

2.1. *Functionings*

Sen argues that functionings—that is, 'the various things a person may value doing or being'[14]—taken together create a better conceptual space in which to assess social welfare than utility or opulence. Functionings are 'beings and doings', such as being nourished, being confident, or taking part in group decisions. The word is of Aristotelian origin and, like Aristotle, Sen claims, significantly, that 'functionings are *constitutive* of a person's being'.[15] So when Oxfam undertakes to evaluate an individual's or group of persons' well-being (in the course, perhaps, of assessing their quality of life, standard of living, social welfare, or level of poverty), Sen would argue that it must have in view their functionings. How did the 'beings and doings' of the rose growers expand and contract?

The focus on functionings sets the capability approach off from other approaches to the evaluation of well-being. For example many would evaluate well-being in the space of psychic utility or preference fulfilment (the capability approach has been developed during a period when welfare economics has been dominated by fulfilled preference formulations of utilitarianism). Others would evaluate it in terms of income per capita, or in terms of the commodities persons were able to command. Still others, following Rawls, would assess well-being in the space of primary goods (which include commodities and other goods such as liberty and self-respect).

In explaining and defending the capability approach, Sen typically demonstrates the flaws in these alternative approaches and then shows that such flaws are corrected in the capability approach. For example, economic theory has often interpreted welfare peculiarly in terms of psychological happiness or desire-fulfilment, yet the *magnitude* of change in mental utility states (for example) may not track in any predictable fashion the *value* of a change. Sen often gives the example of how the perennially deprived become reconciled with their circumstances and appreciative of small mercies, thus their desires are muted and their psychic pleasure at small improvements to their situation is disproportionate to the benefit judged from another perspective. Dadi Taja, for example, a terribly poor but devout widow, may often be serene and even happy.[16] In a different vein, Sen questions Rawls's proposal to require equality in the space of primary goods because the same *amount* of rice (or other goods) will be converted into radically different levels of physical vigour for a child, in the case of a disabled teenager, as against an agricultural worker, or an elderly woman. Sen argues that Rawls's reasoning can be broadened to take greater note of the contingency of

---

[14] 1999a: 75.

[15] Sen traces the roots of this approach to human flourishing to Aristotle's writings in both *The Nicomachean Ethics* and *Politics* (1992a: 39, 1999a: 73). Nussbaum's work investigates this heritage: see especially (1988, 1990a, 1992, 1993, 1995a). For an inspection of both authors' conceptions of functionings see Crocker (1995).

[16] Biswas-Diener and Diener (2000) likewise document the satisfaction in slums of Calcutta to be higher than expected, given the objective circumstances of life for pavement-dwellers, sex workers, and slum dwellers.

circumstances. For we are really interested in what persons are actually able to do or be—that is, in their functionings—not in the pounds of rice they consume.

Sen acknowledges that mental states and command over commodities are both relevant to well-being. For example, his entitlement analysis of famine directs attention at an individual's ability to command food supplies. Furthermore he acknowledges that the work of others who have tried to correct the shortcomings of utilitarian or commodity-focused approaches has ongoing relevance even if these approaches themselves are not fully adopted.[17] And both utility and commodities can be used as proxies of individual advantage when further information is unavailable. But Sen's claim is that both approaches fail to provide an adequate conceptual basis for comparisons of well-being, and that neither is *sufficient* as a basis of social evaluation.

2.2. Freedom

A person's *achieved functionings* at any given time are the particular functionings he or she has successfully pursued and realized. But in assessing human development, a focus on achieved functionings alone, like a focus on utility, is incomplete. It does not necessarily incorporate what Sen terms 'agency'[18] or freedom.[19] In order to attend to the foundational importance of freedom Sen introduces the concept of capability. Capability refers to a person's or group's *freedom to* promote or achieve valuable functionings. 'It represents the various combinations of functionings (beings and doings) that the person can achieve. Capability is, thus, a set of vectors of functionings, reflecting the person's freedom to lead one type of life or another . . . to choose from possible livings.'[20] It is the presence of this term 'freedom to'—Sen's assertion of the inherence of free choice in development activities—that led Sen to name this distinctive approach the 'capability' approach.

In the capability approach, freedom is concerned with 'the *real opportunity* that we have to accomplish what we value'[21] (emphasis in original), and like Aristotle and Marx among others, Sen argues that freedom has intrinsic as well as instrumental value. 'The "good life" is partly a life of genuine choice, and not one in which the person is forced into a particular life—however rich it might be in other respects.'[22]

What it might be easy to overlook in his account is the phrase, 'to accomplish *what we value*' (emphasis added). Without qualification the prominence of choice in Sen's

---

[17] 1985b: 24, and the references there listed.
[18] Agency refers to the freedom to bring about achievements one considers to be valuable, whether or not these achievements are connected to one's own well-being or not. See (1992a: 56–7, 1999a: 191), and Sen's third Dewey lecture (1985a: 203–21). Those who are most familiar with the principal–agent terminology in economics might notice that Sen's use is the opposite: 'I am using the term "agent" not in this [principal–agent] sense, but in its older—and "grander"—sense as someone who acts and brings about change, and whose achievements can be judged in terms of her own values and objectives, whether or not we assess them in terms of some external criteria as well' (1999a: 19).
[19] See (1987a: 45 n. 15, and 1982a,c, 1988b, 1992a, 1999a).
[20] 1992a: 40.   [21] 1992a: 31, see 1999a: 74.   [22] 1996a: 59.

account would be open to the (empirically testable)[23] comment that choice is of more importance in some societies than others. But the prominence *is* qualified: Sen argues that increases in choices *per se* do not necessarily lead to an increase in freedom, in part because the options added may not be ones we value anyway, and in part because (however valuable or not options may be) we may lose the option to live 'a peaceful and unbothered life'.[24] 'Indeed sometimes more freedom of choice can bemuse and befuddle, and make one's life more wretched.'[25]

So it is becoming apparent, as intimated earlier, that a number of kinds of evaluation are inescapable in the specification of capabilities and freedoms. At minimum, an evaluation must consider: which achieved functionings people value rather than regard as trivial or evil or undesirable; how valuable alternative people's or future generations' functionings are; how valuable it is to have further (valuable) options as opposed to enjoying the tranquillity of not having to choose; and how to evaluate different people's conflicting claims about what functionings are valuable at all.

Besides distinguishing valuable 'range of choice' and 'freedom', Sen also distinguishes freedom from 'control'.[26] Sen considers freedom to include 'a person's ability to get systematically what he *would choose* no matter who actually controls the levers of operation'.[27] For example, if, given the choice, we *would* choose to live in a malaria-free environment, then *ceteris paribus* a public programme to drain malaria ponds *does* indeed enhance our freedom, even if we were not in fact asked, because in the absence of this public programme we would not have the effective freedom to live in a malaria-free environment. This is the case even if the 'number of alternatives' we have to choose between does not increase (in fact we lose the freedom to choose to get malaria). Clearly often what is important actually *is* who has the levers of control (oneself/one's group or another). But Sen points out that direct control is not the *only* expression of freedom, though it has often been mistaken as such.

The 'revealed preference' approach also places importance on people's choices. Recall that Samuelson (1938) proposed that consumers' actual choices in two sets of circumstances reveal their preferences between two or more goals. But Sen is perhaps most thorough in his rejection of the form of utilitarianism that is manifested by this approach. He regards the term 'preference' as 'an elaborate pun'.[28] For in the revealed preference approach, there is no way of identifying preferences except by observing people's choices. Preference is an inference from choice. Sen points out many flaws in this way of inferring preference from choice (and, separately, details the 'bizarreness' of Samuelson's assumption of the internal consistency of choice).[29] For instance, you may not in all cases choose what furthers your own well-being. You may buy 'fair trade' coffee not because you prefer the taste—in fact it may be quite bitter and dried out—but because you believe in better wages for coffee pickers. Or you may be indifferent between brands of milk on the shelf but need a pint, so pick one up

---

[23] Veenhoven *et al.* (1994), Smith and Bond (1993), Hofstede (1980), Inglehart (1997, 2000), Kahneman *et al.* (1999).   [24] 1992*a*: 63.
[25] (1992*a*: 59). See Sen (1985*b*, 1991*d*, 1997) and the references therein.   [26] 1982*c*.
[27] 1992*a*: 65.   [28] 1986*a*: 62.   [29] 1970, 1993*f*, 1995*d*.

quite randomly. In both cases the 'revealed preference theorist' would interpret the action as expressly 'preferring' the chosen option (brand of milk) to the alternatives. Sen never argues that actual choices and preferences are not important; in fact he argues *for* choice-salience.[30] But he argues that the importance of actual choices and the importance of desires and happiness arise in so far as they reflect the states of affairs and processes that we value, and because choosing may pertain to our well-being.[31] Yet a complete reliance on choice behaviour to the exclusion of information about the valued 'beings and doings' people understand themselves to be pursuing is inadequate. This is the case even though there are well-known difficulties in acquiring information about values accurately and directly.

In the rose project, Oxfam chose to work in income generation, and to focus this work on the poor. But the small group, not Oxfam, collectively decided to cultivate *roses*. Bananas, they decided, were too heavy and physically demanding for the women; okra and onions had only seasonal harvests, so would not provide a steady income; sunflowers did not fetch a good price. The rose group managed the project, deciding how to divide up the weeding and how much to pay garland-sellers. This 'control' proved to be empowering—participants gained confidence in their ability to make decisions and undertake new responsibilities. Also, one of the strongest impacts was their inner peace from an activity that was meaningful *as well as lucrative*. The freedom to choose was valuable in itself and generated an economic activity that was valued on multiple levels. It is these sorts of 'valued freedoms' with which we will be continuously concerned.

2.3. *Pluralism*

At this point the capability approach may well seem unwieldy. It is not exactly clear how far we are to understand and apply the ample phrase 'valuable beings and doings' but it seems to cover a generous terrain—from friendships to fragrance to job satisfaction. Clearly, in order to construct even individual capability sets much less compare capabilities we need a great deal of information which will not be straightforward to obtain. Some operational concerns will be addressed eventually, but it may be valuable first to pause and appreciate the very breadth of the capability term.

Sen emphatically defends the breadth of the capability approach and the pluralism of its information base (his defences are normally motivated by a prior discussion of the paucity of information that routinely enters utilitarian calculus in economics). Capabilities may relate to things near to survival (the capability to drink clean water) or those which are rather less central (the capability to visit one's aunt, the capability to eat rich sweets). The *definition* of capability does not delimit a certain subset of capabilities as of peculiar importance; rather the selection of capabilities on which to focus is a *value judgement* (that also depends partly on the purpose of the

---

[30] e.g. in 1997*d*.   [31] See 1985*b*: 32; 1999*a*, ch. 3.

evaluation), as is the weighting of capabilities relative to each other.[32] For instance, in an article called 'The Living Standard',[33] Sen had suggested that one 'separate "material" functionings and capabilities (e.g., to be well-nourished) from others (e.g., being wise and contented)' and evaluate standards of living with reference to material capabilities. But later Sen reflected that he was less sure of this separation. He suggested instead that considerations of living standard encompass *all valued functionings*. 'It is possible that this way of drawing the line is a little too permissive, but the alternatives that have been proposed seem clearly too narrow.'[34] So the capability approach appreciates *all* changes in Dadi Taja's quality of life, from knowledge to relationships to job and inner peace, to fragrant clothes and the various valued activities made possible by the rose income. None of these changes is ruled out as irrelevant at all times and places. One can thus analyse the capabilities of a rich as well as a poor person or country, and analyse basic as well as complex capabilities.

Sen also notes that individual advantage can be assessed in at least four different spaces: *well-being achievement*, *well-being freedom*, *agency achievement*, or *agency freedom*. Individual advantage can be assessed in relation to one's well-being whether defined in an elementary fashion (nutritional status) or in a more complex manner (self-esteem). Or it can relate to agency—one's ability to pursue goals that one values (getting funding for a new school, serving the poor). In either case advantage can refer to the well-being or agency *achievements*, or to well-being and agency *freedom*. Sen argues that we cannot simply choose to focus on one or another of these four possible spaces; there are good arguments for keeping all in mind. He argues this while accepting that these objectives may conflict: your well-being achievement may increase, but your freedom to promote things you value may decrease.

This means two things. First, when Sen advocates that social arrangements should be evaluated with respect to 'freedom',[35] he is advocating equality in a 'space' that has quite a substantial degree of internal plurality and requires further specification. It includes the medley of things like the social organizer's freedom to be an agent of social change in Arabsolangi, and the group members' capability to be nourished.

Secondly, and taking a step back, Sen argues that equality in the space of capabilities is only one principle of several which might be of relevance: 'the capability perspective, central as it is for a theory of justice, cannot be entirely adequate for it'.[36] One may wish to consider efficiency, and liberty or negative freedom for example (Ch. 3 Sect. 5.2). These principles might even pertain to capability equality, if viewed in the long term. But they may each support radically different courses of action.

---

[32] 1992a: 42–6; 1999a: 76–85.   [33] 1984a.
[34] Sen (1987b: 27). See the exchange between Williams and Sen on pp. 98–101 and 108–9. In (1993a: 37) Sen writes that assessments of the standard of living focus on 'those influences on well-being that come from the nature of [the person's] life, rather than from "other-regarding" objectives or impersonal concerns'.
[35] (1992a: 129); see (1993: 49), where Sen clarifies that the capability approach can be used for evaluation in all four spaces 'though not with equal reach'.   [36] (1992a: 87), see (1999a: 76–7).

The capability approach enriches the considerations that inform the analysis of social choices and social welfare by widening the informational basis of such analyses to include a greater range and kind of welfare than simply happiness or revealed preference, and by expanding the moral principles that coordinate this information to include considerations besides welfare. In this way it supports pluralism, the view that valid well-being and valid social welfare come in diverse forms.

2.4. *Incompleteness*

The capability approach is deliberately incomplete. Sen is far less concerned with taking and defending a substantive but contentious position than he is with showing how the capability approach can be shared by persons of diverging, even contradictory, philosophical systems.[37] The intention behind this foundational plurality is to allow economists and development practitioners to work on pressing issues for which consensus on fundamentals is not necessary. Also Sen is more concerned with ruling out 'patently unjust', inefficient, or otherwise unacceptable possibilities than he is with identifying a complete ordering of options. He concentrates on drawing attention to the serious oversights of certain utilitarian approaches to problems rather than clarifying exactly how one employing the capability approach might arrive at a judgement.

This incompleteness can seem evasive and willowy, but it is in fact one of the most important advantages of the capability approach and one to which we will return again and again. In *Inequality Reexamined* Sen identifies two grounds for allowing incompleteness: fundamental and pragmatic. The 'fundamental reason for incompleteness' (which Sen also refers to as 'assertive incompleteness') is that

> the ideas of well-being and inequality may have enough ambiguity and fuzziness to make it a mistake to look for a complete ordering of either ... The 'pragmatic reason for incompleteness' is to use whatever parts of the ranking we manage to sort out unambiguously, rather than maintaining complete silence until everything has been sorted out and the world shines in dazzling clarity ... 'Waiting for toto' may not be a cunning strategy in a practical exercise.[38]

In either case, Sen argues that the residual incompleteness is honest rather than disappointing: 'Babbling is not, in general, superior to being silent on matters that are genuinely unclear or undecided'.[39] Furthermore, it may be possible to rule out clearly unsuitable practical options before there is agreement on metaphysical or theoretical doctrines, or complete data, or a consensus between all relevant parties.

---

[37] For example, Sen and Anand (1994*a*) show how sustainability can be defended either as an issue of distributional equity or as a deontological principle.

[38] Sen (1992*a*: 49), also see Sen (1999*a*: 253–4, 1989*b*). Elsewhere he calls this 'assertive' incompleteness, which means that even the provision of additional information would not identify one unique optimum. [39] 1992*a*: 134.

The framework for specifying valuable capabilities advanced in the following chapters certainly preserves the 'fundamental' incompleteness of Sen's capability approach, and retains a good deal of pragmatic incompleteness. Still, there are good reasons for welcoming other alternatives, and certainly for not setting forward this framework as the *only* way in which capabilities can be specified.

3. CRITICISMS[40]

But how are capabilities to be measured? How are value conflicts to be resolved? As Sugden noted, 'Given the rich array of functionings that Sen takes to be relevant, given the extent of disagreement among reasonable people about the nature of the good life, and given the unresolved problem of how to value sets, it is natural to ask how far Sen's framework is operational'.[41] At one level it obviously is: Sen and others have conducted empirical work that is consonant with the capability approach, and produces results that challenge those generated by alternative theories.[42] Yet this does not actually answer our question, does the capability approach provide adequate direction regarding (i) how to identify *valuable* capabilities; (ii) how to make strategic economic decisions that weight and prioritize capabilities; (iii) what to do when value judgements conflict; and (iv) how capability sets may be measured, such that one can evaluate changes brought about by economic initiatives?

In a way, Sugden's question is rhetorical, for Sen has never made the claim that the capability approach *is* fully operational and he has explicitly acknowledged that it is not a complete 'theory of justice'.[43] The reason for asking this question is that some criticisms highlight issues that must be considered as the capability approach is further developed.

Frances Stewart gives two practical examples in which Sen's approach, theoretically considered, seems more able to rationalize than to resolve value conflicts. In the first case, the task is to rank two situations, one in which all people's basic needs are fulfilled at a low level of equally distributed income, and secondly, where many persons enjoy a wide range of functionings; others have unmet basic needs. The capability approach, she writes, could not rank them, because it has not specified which capabilities are basic, nor has it addressed the problem of how to assign relative weights to the goals of 'poverty alleviation' and 'capability equality'. Likewise if there were two possible consumption sets for a person, one in which all basic needs were fulfilled, and the other in which some basic needs were not fulfilled and more drink and tobacco were consumed, the capability approach, she argues, could not decide which was preferable. In each case, the 'strong element of valuation' that the basic needs approach incorporates makes it 'more robust about ranking

---

[40] See Beitz (1986), Basu (1987), Daniels (1990), Cohen in Nussbaum and Sen (1993), Crocker (1992, 1995), *Giornale degli economisti et Annali di economia*, 53 (1994), *Journal of International Development*, 9 (1997), and 12 (2000), Nussbaum (1993, 2000a), *Politeia*, 12: 43–4 (1996), Qizilbash (1996a,b, 1998b), Sen (1987b), Stewart (1996), Sugden (1993). [41] Sugden (1993: 1953).
[42] Drèze and Sen (1989, 1995, 1997); UNDP (1998).   [43] (1995c: 268). See also Sen (1994b).

alternatives'. Thus Stewart advocates the capability approach be strengthened by including 'the valuation that priority should be given to achieving basic capabilities (and implicitly that these capabilities be identified)'.[44] Such changes would bring it closer to the basic needs approach's ability and Sen's explicit intention[45] to be 'robust about ranking alternatives'.[46]

Stewart's suggestion that 'basic' capabilities be explicitly identified at a general level was put forward theoretically by Bernard Williams in his comments on Sen's Tanner Lecture on *The Standard of Living*:

The questions that I have raised about capabilities and their identification all suggest that one has to put some constraints on the kinds of capability that are going to count in thinking about the relation between capability on the one hand and well being or the standard of living on the other. In fact, I have slipped into that, by starting to talk about *basic* capabilities, and I think that it is difficult to avoid taking into account the notion of something like a basic capability, or . . . a basic set of [co-realizable] capabilities.[47]

Williams is not merely calling for a list of basic capabilities so that the operational phase may be entered, but rather for an extension of the theoretical conception of human flourishing, by reference to which a decision to select certain capabilities as basic could be defended. 'There are many pressing questions about the identification of what a capability is, and they cannot be answered without a good deal of further theory. We are forced to ask what kinds of facts are presented by human nature in these respects, and also how we should interpret local convention.'[48]

Williams's recommendation that the capability approach requires 'a good deal of further theory' has been actively advanced by Martha Nussbaum, who criticizes the generality of Sen's capability approach: 'It seems to me . . . that Sen needs to be more radical than he has been so far in his criticism of the utilitarian accounts of well-being, by introducing an objective normative account of human functioning and by describing a procedure of objective evaluation by which functionings can be assessed for their contribution to the good human life'.[49] Her work, which is discussed in Chapter 2, Section 2, develops just such an account.

On a subject related to the tobacco problem raised by Stewart, David Crocker argues that Sen's capability approach is not able to categorize any capabilities as *not* being valuable. He attributes this specifically to Sen's assumption that capabilities are opportunities rather than latent powers of a person, and suggests that this definition compromises the extent to which Sen's work is able to discriminate valuable from evil capabilities.[50] Qizilbash formulates additional criticisms: (i) that Sen fails to give sufficient consideration to the *means* of freedom and (ii) that negative freedom does

---

[44] Stewart (1996) in all three quotes. [45] Sen (1981: 209). [46] Stewart (1996).
[47] Sen *et al.* (1987: 100).
[48] Sen *et al.* (1987: 102). Beitz (1986) likewise raised the difficulty of identifying the relative significance of different capabilities.
[49] Nussbaum (1988: 176) quoted and discussed by Sen (1993a: 47).
[50] (1995: 167–9). See also Qizilbash (1996b: 1211–12, 1998b: 54).

not come into Sen's account of advantage.[51] Their criticisms (not all of which are necessarily accurate) highlight the need to explore not only which capabilities are basic for well-being, but also how to distinguish capabilities which are broadly 'ethical' or at least not evil, and pursue them in a similarly ethical manner.

Let us try to put this need for specification in context. Poverty reduction initiatives, development economics, and welfare economics all address the problem of how to generate and allocate productive resources to achieve the best social state. Reflections on this problem can be broken into three sub-components: (i) what kinds of information are necessary in order to define social states? (ii) how are more valuable social states to be distinguished from less valuable? (iii) what rules or principles guide (or constrain) the procedures of attaining/sustaining social states? The Bergson–Samuelson Welfare Theorem on which the greater part of welfare economics depends provided, for example, the answer that social states are to be measured as sum-rankings of individual ordinal utility, with greater aggregate sums defining better social states, and the necessary and sufficient principle being to maximize aggregate utility. The capability approach argues (i) that social states should be defined, for welfare purposes, primarily in the space of human capabilities, (ii) that more valuable states are those that have 'expanded' valuable human capabilities, (iii) the determination of which and whose capabilities are valuable and their relative weights should be subject to explicit scrutiny and public discussion over time, (iva) that the single rule of social utility maximization is insufficient, and (ivb) that plural rules, based on principles of practical reason, apply.

The implications for welfare economics of assessing social states in terms of 'capabilities' rather than utility are substantial. In particular, the role of the market is subordinated to an enlarged framework of decision-making, that employs an extended informational basis, and a substantive rationality.[52]

In the case of functionings and capabilities, since there are no markets directly involved, the weighting exercise has to be done in terms of explicit valuations, drawing on the prevailing values in a given society . . . This explicitness is not, in itself, a bad thing, since it gives the public a clear opportunity to question the values and to debate the decisions.[53]

The problem is that, although Sen regularly refers to the need for explicit scrutiny of individual and social goals, for reflectiveness, value judgement, practical reason, and democratic social choice, he chooses not to specify the possible range of procedures by which valuational issues are to be resolved or by which information on valuations is to be obtained. Jonathan Glover argued that an appropriate further 'research programme' must include a 'more precise account of values and principles to guide action'.[54]

These comments point to the need for a framework for 'valuing freedoms' in order to put the capability approach into practice.

[51] (1996a: 147), but see Sen (1992a: 87, 1999a).
[52] e.g. Sen (1986c, 1987a, 1989b, 1993c, 1994a, 1995b, 1996a, 1997b,c, 1999a).
[53] (1996a: 58). See (1999a: 30, 80, 125–6).
[54] Glover in Nussbaum and Glover (1995).

4. THE NEED FOR A FRAMEWORK

Systematic and operational treatment of value questions in both welfare economics and development have regularly been side-stepped since the 1930s (Robbins's 1932 essay is often cited as a watershed) by using an implicit utilitarian ethic that frames social choices as maximization exercises that yield an optimal solution(s) mechanically—that is, without explicit consideration of value judgements that the solution does (or does not) imply.

In development economics, values questions have been kept alive on several fronts. For example, many have argued that while some development aimed at economic growth has been successful, it has also contributed with disturbing regularity to increases in inequality, conflict, unemployment, corruption, dependence, unmanageable urbanization, environmental degradation, and loss of cultural identity. By reflection on these problems they have identified values for which GNP growth is an insufficient proxy—for example, human capital, health, gender disparity, concern for the interests of future generations, participation in institutions, empowerment, inclusion, absence of violent conflict, and a sustainable natural environment. Some critics reject development outright as necessarily antagonistic to cultural pluralism.[55] Others argue that additional values *also* pertain to development and should be taken into account. They have developed a set of effective goals, including for example the poverty-focused basic needs approach, and its successor, 'human development'. Authors and institutions in this trajectory wish to construct an alternative paradigm—comprising theory, policy instruments, methodologies, movements, and institutions—that will provide a basis for more ethical and participatory development.[56]

An overriding problem that has faced those attempting to develop alternatives is addressing values issues adequately. For example, in the 1970s, a number of writers in the basic human needs tradition called for development goals to be oriented towards human beings and 'full lives' as the ends of development.[57] This approach did not confine its interests merely to the commodity requirements of a minimally decent life, but recognized commodities as instrumental to a full life.[58] Yet in practice it was never made clear *how*, methodologically, 'practitioners' were to define human ends and specify requisite commodities, nor what the role of participation was in this process.[59]

---

[55] Apffel-Marglin and Marglin (1990, 1996), Escobar (1984–5, 1995), Illich (1978), Nandy (1994), Sachs (1992), and others.

[56] Blackburn and Holland (1998), Chambers (1993, 1997), Cornia *et al.* (1987), Forester (1999), Ghai (1988), Goulet (1995), K. Griffin (1989), Griffin and McKinley (1994), Haq (1995), Holland and Blackburn (1998), Max-Neef (1993), North (1990), Sen (1990*a*), Stewart (1985, 1996), Streeten (1994), Streeten *et al.* (1981), UNDP (1990–2000), among others. It goes without saying that these views unfold along a spectrum.

[57] Stewart (1985, chs. 1, 2); Streeten *et al.* (1981: 33–4), Van der Hoeven (1988: 11–12), Sandbrook (1982: 1); Crosswell (1981: 3).

[58] See Stewart's 'full life' goal of the metaproduction function (1985: 11). Sen's criticism that basic needs has a commodity fetish is discussed in Ch. 5.   [59] Streeten (1984), Lederer (1980).

Introduction: Capability and Valuation 15

In 1984 Paul Streeten published a short article in *World Development* that tried to identify the 'unsettled questions' of the basic needs approach (with which he grouped Sen's capability approach). He asked, who defines needs? Is the goal of development full human flourishing, or meeting basic needs? Where does participation fit in? Which needs can institutions legitimately plan to meet? How should international funding be coordinated for the meeting of basic needs?

Over fifteen years later these goals *still* require systematic responses, or else a strong argument for why systematic responses are impossible and how to generate appropriate responses in each context. For example, on the one hand, a chorus of actors advocate participation; on the other hand, many of the same actors advocate the energetic implementation of programmes that will realize the international development goals. This is true for the capability approach as well as for basic needs-based poverty alleviation efforts lest these be subverted by harmful simplifications. For this reason a more systematic link between theory and methodology in the issue of specifying values seems necessary.

Given the important lesson from basic needs of the importance of procedures for addressing values questions, this book will do two things. Part I will draw Sen's work into discussion with a number of authors and critics, especially John Finnis, in order to suggest one possible way in which the values issues may be addressed coherently, and the methodological implications worked out, in a participatory manner. Part II will critically discuss one narrow set of methodologies—namely, those of micro-project evaluation—and suggest a tool for improving the evaluation of participatory projects that is consistent with the tenets of practical reason advanced in Part I. Before outlining these further, an overview and some terminological housework is in order.

5. FINNIS'S APPROACH

The next three chapters will refer repeatedly to the writings of John Finnis, an Australian professor of jurisprudence in Oxford, UK and Notre Dame, Indiana who writes on matters of Catholic Christian moral theology.[60]

Although Finnis's writing is in a different discipline than Sen's, there are parallels between them. In particular, both urge their colleagues not to seek a value-free discipline, but rather to put human flourishing squarely as the 'end' of their professional endeavours. Twenty years ago when Finnis published the text *Natural Law and Natural Rights* which I use extensively (and which he wrote whilst at the University of Malawi), it was the equivalent of a treatise on human development that challenged the regnant legal philosophy, which tried to make law 'value-free' (much in the same way Sen has challenged the revealed preference theories in economics). Finnis elucidated, in particular, an alternative way of raising and rationally considering what is good for people—again much as Sen has proposed 'capability' as an alternative to

---

[60] Finnis (1980, 1983, 1992a, 1994), Grisez *et al.* (1987).

ordinal 'utility' in economics. The opening two paragraphs of *Natural Law and Natural Rights* give some sense of this:

> There are human goods that can be secured only through the institutions of human law, and requirements of practical reasonableness that only those institutions can satisfy. It is the object of this book to identify those goods, and those requirements of practical reasonableness, and thus to show how and on what conditions such institutions are justified and the ways in which they can be (and often are) defective.
>
> It is often supposed that an evaluation of law as a type of social institution, if it is to be undertaken at all, must be preceded by a value-free description and analysis of that institution as it exists in fact. But the development of modern jurisprudence suggests, and reflection on the methodology of any social science confirms, that a theorist cannot give a theoretical description and analysis of social facts unless he also participates in the work of evaluation, of understanding what is really good for human persons, and what is really required by practical reasonableness [or ethics].[61]

I use Finnis's work because it has a clear, explicit, structured treatment of some of the values issues that Sen raises (how to identify and enable people to identify what is valued, how to make value judgements between actions that produce very different kinds of benefits, how to identify who decides or by what process), and at the same time shares the fundamental attitude of Sen's capability approach: that of judging institutions according to whether or not they enable human beings—in all of their complexity and diversity—to flourish.

In particular, Finnis' work has these attributes:

- *Structure yet flexibility* The primary reason for considering Finnis's work is that he provides a clear, full structure for individuals and communities to make the value judgements that must be made in order to use Sen's capability approach, and to make these judgements in a participatory manner that can be adapted to different institutional settings, and to communities with different existing cultures and commitments.
- *Pluralism* Finnis's ethical theory is founded on practical reason alone. It does not derive epistemologically from a particular set of metaphysical beliefs or 'comprehensive doctrine of the good'.[62] As such it can be useful to persons and communities of different cultures and belief systems.
- *Informational pluralism* Finnis, like Sen, argues that there are two categories of relevant information: one regarding (plural) human ends (which is the subject of Chapter 2); the other regarding (plural) principles (Chapter 3).
- *Central role for freedom* Finnis's account of the central value of *authentic self-direction* mirrors the centrality of freedom in Sen's work. Like Sen, Finnis recognizes that cultural and personal expressions of, and preferences for such freedom

---

[61] 1980: 3.
[62] Lisska (1996) notes Finnis is distinctive among natural law theories because of his theory's foundation in practical reason.

vary, hence the appropriate forms of self-direction will likewise vary. Also Finnis, like Sen, writes much of partial orderings, incompleteness, and the need for (and human value of) underdetermined free choice.

- *Intellectual roots* Finnis develops the theory of natural law in the Aristotelian tradition (informed by later developments of it, and by Aquinas's in particular). Sen likewise traces key ideas back to Aristotle's discussions of functionings (the term in particular comes from his work), practical reason, and the instrumental nature of wealth. Both also consider other authors, and diverge from Aristotle.
- *Analytical clarity* Finnis is a careful and clear philosopher. This may not seem much of a 'selling point' in a book that is to focus on practical matters. Yet the particular practical matters under discussion (the basis of social choices and value judgements in the course of development) are deeply contested. They greatly exercise welfare economists, activists, feminists, defenders of cultures, defenders of human rights, activists, political elite, and the politically repressed—often in opposite directions.[63] A clear account of how an objective human development theory can combine normative elements and participatory procedures simply has not been established. Finnis provides such an account.

Finnis's writings are superbly well-structured and compact, but also dense and philosophical. Luckily there are not too many of them—Finnis introduces all of the topics I mention in a slim text for undergraduate philosophy students called *Fundamentals of Ethics* and fully explains them in chapters 3 to 6 of *Natural Law and Natural Rights*. The fifty-two-page journal article Finnis co-authored with Joseph Boyle and Germain Grisez, 'Practical Truths, Principles, and Ultimate Ends' has a thorough treatment of these concepts and engages with some of the criticisms.[64] However, despite this accessibility, Finnis's theory has been misread and misunderstood in the secondary literature with surprising regularity. An alternative valuable introduction to Finnis's theory, Rufus Black,[65] was written in part to clarify and emphasize the most often misunderstood aspects of Finnis's theory.

Finnis has also written on more applied issues, and discussion of these lies beyond the scope of this book, although Chapter 2 will (i) identify exactly how Nussbaum, among others, has misrepresented Finnis's work, and (ii) clarify that Finnis's controversial writings on concrete issues (such as contraception) are *not* entailed by the fundamentals of his theory—as is evidenced by the fact that liberal Christians have also found the theory tremendously useful in articulating alternative concrete positions.[66] Finnis's applied writings in, for example, sexual ethics, use not only the theory I will introduce, but in addition, a particular form of act analysis that is not defended in the central writings and that I do not propose or endorse.

Finnis's account of rationality can be introduced in three parts. First, he gives an account of human value; how one recognizes human 'ends' (Ch. 2, below). Secondly, he articulates an overarching principle for pursuing these ends (Ch. 3, below).

---

[63] e.g. Okin *et al.* (1999), Nussbaum and Sen (1993).   [64] Grisez *et al.* (1987).
[65] Biggar and Black (2001).   [66] ibid.

This principle is not *sufficient* for resolving value conflicts and disputes.[67] Yet this principle, and the plural principles that specify it, *can* be used to exclude some options, and to analyse the moral qualities of other options. Thirdly, free choice is crucially necessary in order to effect closure between competing options. But this role for free choice is not a regrettable necessity. Rather, free choice both for individuals and groups can be valuable of itself, as an exercise of human agency, of creativity and of self-direction (Ch. 4, Sect. 2).

The following three chapters comprise a sustained effort to explore the relevance of Finnis's practical reasoning theory to the capability approach.

6. TERMS AND STRUCTURE

6.1. *Terms*

Most terms will be introduced in the following chapters; yet some attention needs to be given to the key concepts: functionings, capability, human development, and operationalization.

Sen's definition of functionings was given above. The word comes from Aristotle's discussion in book I of *Nicomachean Ethics*.[68] Yet the English word 'functioning' is somewhat at odds with Sen's definition of it, for it seems to connote mechanical action, perhaps more deterministic than free (e.g. 'my furnace is not functioning'). This makes the term functioning appear rather odd at first to readers unfamiliar with the capability approach (hence my use of the phrase 'valuable functionings'). I continue to use the word 'functionings' as Sen defines it in order to relate this discussion as fully as possible to the capability approach; yet at times I introduce and employ other words, such as flourishing, that seem to relate to 'human ends'—that for the sake of which something is done—more comfortably than the word functioning.

Also, since the initial exposition in his first Tanner Lectures, Sen has referred to his approach as 'the capability approach' (or, sometimes, the capabilities approach).[69] But he began a later clarification of the approach with the remark that 'Capability is not an awfully attractive word . . . Perhaps a nicer word could have been chosen . . .'.[70] And by the publication of *Development as Freedom* Sen used the word freedom rather

---

[67] '. . . there are many ways of going wrong and doing wrong; but in very many, perhaps most situations of personal and social life there are a number of incompatible *right* (i.e. not-wrong) options. Prior personal choice(s) or authoritative social decision-making can greatly reduce this variety of options for the person who has made that commitment or the community which accepts that authority. Still, those choices and decisions, while rational and reasonable, were in most cases not required by reason. They were not preceded by any rational judgement that *this* option is *the* right answer, or the best solution' (Finnis 1992a: 152).

[68] In I.vii Aristotle discusses sculptors, artists, joiners, shoemakers, players of reed flutes, and considers that the 'goodness' of each lies in how well he performs his given functioning. Then he asks, 'Just as we can see that eye and hand and foot and every one of our members has some function, should we not assume that in like manner a human being has a function over and above these particular functions?'

[69] (1980a). There does not seem to be a substantive distinction between them in Sen's usage. I have used 'capability approach' in this book. [70] 1993a: 30.

Introduction: Capability and Valuation 19

than capability in many instances. The problem with the word 'capability' is that it does not immediately conjure the image of intrinsically valuable human ends; it *seems* to be engaged in *observing possibilities* rather than *looking forward to valuable actualizations* of functionings, to actual realizations of freedoms. And yet, as is already clear, the capability approach is distinctive as an approach to justice or economic development in that it attaches intrinsic importance only to *human* processes, acts, and states (rather than to utility or real income or primary goods, for example). What is fundamentally important is that people can enjoy valuable beings and doings that they have, or would have, chosen. Again although the word seems to focus attention on one's opportunity set, the fundamental objective of the capability approach is not to produce opportunities, but to create meaningful and fulfilled lives. I have retained the use of the term capability in most discussions partly because the word 'freedom' has several uses (as a synonym for capability, but also to distinguish achieved agency from agency freedom) and partly because for many persons still the word freedom has different connotations so the use of 'capability' may be clearer. In discussions where the context is clear, and as well in the title of the book, I prefer the word 'freedom'.

In using the term 'poverty reduction' I intend the fullest description of poverty, a description which shifts the objective of economic activity from economic growth to human development. This shift towards a 'multidimensional' view of poverty emerged gradually in reaction to and as a criticism of mainstream economic development that focused on growth in gross national product per capita.[71] Growth, though a component of economic progress, is insufficient as an objective, since aggregate growth can go along with wrenching deprivation among the poor, with political oppression, or with any number of other less desirable states of affairs, at least in the medium term.[72] For this reason Hollis Chenery *et al.* emphasized the need for redistribution with growth, or growth with equity, accomplished by increasing the productivity of the poor. The basic needs approach enlarged this objective to the provision of 'a minimally decent life, defined in terms of levels of health, nutrition and literacy' and other things instrumental to a full life.[73] Sen worked constructively to articulate a theory that situated the basic needs approach within a more 'general' account of the development process. Sen wrote, 'What is needed is to take the basic needs approach out of the arbitrarily narrow box into which it seems to have got confined. To see it as just one part of the capabilities approach—to which it is motivationally linked—would do just that.'[74] The *Human Development Reports* (HDRs) of the United Nations focus on people as the ends of development. Sen's influence on these reports is ongoing: 'Human development is a process of enlarging people's choices. Enlarging people's choices is achieved by expanding human capabilities and functionings.'[75] The World Bank's recent *Voices of the Poor* studies[76] and *World Development Report 2000/2001* on the

---

[71] This is obtained by dividing the gross national product by the population, so only indicates an average portion of income per person but says nothing about distribution—if A earns £1 million a year, and B earns £10,000 a year, then the average per capita income of A and B is £505,000 each.
[72] Ranis *et al.* (2000). Also Streeten (1994). [73] Stewart (1996), see Ch. 5, Sect. 2.
[74] 1984b: 515. [75] UNDP (1998: 14). [76] Narayan *et al.* (2000a, 2000b).

theme of Poverty refer to the goal of 'poverty reduction' as do, of course, the international efforts to support 'poverty reduction strategies'. This terminologically focuses the discussion on the deprived, whose concerns should be explicitly prioritized (to whom we have an 'imperfect obligation'). But it imbues this term (hopefully) with the multidimensional and participatory tones of recent discussions.

To render Sen's 'freedom' or capability approach ready to put into practice in the assessment of poverty reduction activities entails basting (i) Sen's proposition that individual advantage be judged in the space of capabilities rather than economic growth or primary goods with (ii) an account of how non-utilitarian assessments of valuable beings or doings that respect pluralism may be founded; (iii) an account of the role of actual individual and social choices in identifying value and resolving conflict; (iv) an account of how basic capabilities relevant for the pursuit of human development may be defined in general (or by institutions) and of the further permanent need to specify and weight basic capabilities according to participants' reflectively held values; and (v) current best practice methodologies of micro-project assessment. These are diverse fabrics but operationalization would be incomplete without each. The following two sections explain how the book proceeds.

6.2. *Structure: Part I*

Sen himself conceives of the foundations of welfare economics in terms of utility, capability, and practical reason, and overtly owns the Aristotelian and Marxist roots of his approach.[77] Thus it seems constructive to consider whether and in what ways a fully developed account of practical reason might be useful if the goal of economic development is conceived not as the maximization of utility but as the expansion of valuable capabilities. Finnis has developed and refined an approach to the pursuit of integral human fulfilment based on an account of practical reason. The structure of practical reason is analytically well-defined, having plural dimensions of functioning and plural principles that enable it to contain the ethical ambiguity of choices. It is also 'operational' in that it has been taught and used to analyse actual 'dilemmas' (such as nuclear deterrence policies)[78] in order to illustrate what the different considerations of the decision might be. Furthermore, it holds that many choices are *underdetermined free choices*. This term means that not only are persons free to choose inefficient as well as efficient options, or beneficent as well as harmful options, but also that there may be no option which is most efficient and most beneficent, for example, or 'best' overall. This parallels Sen's idea of fundamental incompleteness. Finnis's conception of choice brings an interesting angle to issues of pluralism and participation, because when there is not necessarily an overall best alternative he argues that choice may still be made on intelligible rather than random grounds, by taking into account persons' and communities' culture, commitments, and current institutions. While these institutions might be observable by an outside observer, the decision of which to respect is a value judgement, often best made from within.

[77] 1992: 39, 1997*a*,*b*,*d*, 1999*a*.   [78] Finnis *et al.* (1987).

Each of the next four chapters synthesizes one aspect that must be specified in the operationalization of the capability approach, then proposes a framework for doing so. The issue of the second chapter is how one 'specifies' the dimensions of valuable functioning or capability. Nussbaum's work on central human capabilities, and Finnis's work on basic human reasons for action are both presented, and then alternative accounts of universal human needs and values are briefly considered. The third chapter considers (i) the kind of ethical rationality that accompanies the capability approach, in which free choice between plural ends is given central place, and (ii) the information required to complete rational comparisons of diverse human development initiatives. The fourth chapter considers the relationship between choice, self-direction, and the construction of cultural values and identities. It analyses the different possible values of community participation in poverty reduction initiatives. It also draws out considerations regarding the responsibilities that outside actors may have in generating and providing to decision-makers the information necessary to make informed choices. The fifth chapter returns to the issues of (i) whether, none the less, basic capabilities pertaining to absolute poverty may be identified from without, and (ii) whether in poverty reduction activities it is necessary to focus on 'achieving functionings' rather than 'expanding capabilities'. It asks what, in practice, it means to address absolute poverty within the capability approach, and proposes a schematic four-part 'operational' definition of the capability approach in this regard.

While each chapter addresses an issue on which a great number of authors have written, it has been necessary to restrict reference to all but two or three discussions in order to treat these adequately. A full analysis is distinct from an operational account, and this study has the latter more modest aim. The fact that the main authors considered have articulated their own ideas with a great deal of precision and consistency elsewhere enables what could otherwise be a tortuous conversation to be conducted quite simply.

6.3. *Structure: Part II*

The sixth and seventh chapters consist of one practical and much narrower application of the capability approach as specified here, namely, a discussion of how economic analysis (cost-benefit analysis) and systematic qualitative information on human impacts can be combined in order to assess the relative effectiveness of particular development activities in expanding human capabilities. The sixth chapter defends the necessity of efficiency considerations, such as are incorporated in cost-benefit analysis, in project evaluation. It then reviews two prominent participatory methodologies that have been developed to supplement economic considerations with social data—one by the World Bank, the other as a result of US legislation governing public expenditure (in the first instance). Both lack a systematic method for identifying changes valued by participants themselves and for devolving real control over a decision to the lowest level capable of making it. This lack increases the chance of significant bias in gathering and interpreting value judgements. In response I describe a novel method of impact assessment which would complement and improve available assessment tools.

The method of impact assessment represents one way in which the framework of the preceding chapters could be used.

The seventh chapter comprises case studies of three small Oxfam activities in Pakistan on which both cost-benefit analysis and the further assessment of impacts were applied. The methodology described in Chapter 6 was developed, and these case studies were conducted, over nine months of field research in Pakistan with non-governmental organizations (NGOs) that undertake income generation activities among poor communities using participatory methods.[79] The aim was to develop a participatory method for evaluating development activities (at different stages of implementation) which field staff could implement themselves, and which would facilitate the kind of self-direction and scrutiny of values issues advocated by Sen's capability approach.

7. CONCLUSION

This book explores in depth the possibilities of Sen's capability approach. Prominent in Sen's exposition of *Development as Freedom* is the suggestion that economics as an academic undertaking and as a practical activity requires explicit consideration of valuational issues. Valuational issues, he argues, are part of the proper domain of economic decision-making, and cannot be relegated and confined to philosophy or political science. Certain sections of the book therefore necessarily address foundational issues of rationality, choice, and values. The aim of such discussions is, however, practical. They aim to clarify how and by what process the value judgements that underlie Oxfam's assessment of activities such as those in the three case studies *can* be made without serious oversight, and thereby to offer one way of operationalizing the capability approach.

---

[79] This was followed by over three further months in Pakistan in which a team of twenty-two persons used the method to evaluate a country-wide 'NGO initiative' for social sector development.

PART I

2

Poverty and Human Development

The relevant features of the situation may not all jump to the eye.[1]

If economic policies designed by economists affect, which they do, the *whole* of society, economists can no longer claim that they are solely concerned with the economic field. Such a stance would be unethical since it would mean avoiding the moral responsibility for the consequences of an action.[2]

There can be substantial debates on the particular functionings that should be included in the list of important achievements and the corresponding capabilities. This valuational issue is inescapable in an evaluative exercise of this kind, and one of the main merits of the approach is the need to address these judgmental questions in an explicit way, rather than hiding them in some implicit framework.[3]

1. IDENTIFYING VALUABLE CAPABILITIES

Dadi Taja appreciated the income from rose cultivation activity, and also spoke of her aesthetic pleasure from working with roses, her enjoyment of working with the others in the group, her inner peace because the garlands were used for religious practices, and so on. We have seen by the capability approach thus far that none of these can be deemed 'irrelevant' (Ch. 1, Sect. 2.3). But how does one know whether Dadi Taja's comments reflect the *complete set* of functionings or fulfilments of capabilities that have been affected by the rose project? How does one know whether if one returns in a week or a month, the reported benefits will have changed altogether, or new significant capabilities will be cited that were overlooked before? As Wiggins remarked, the relevant capabilities may not naturally rise to the eye.

Quite often, when one reads a text on economic, social, or human development, one stumbles across a 'list' or array or set of items that the author has written down as ingredients of the quality of life or as basic human needs, elements of the utility vector, aspects of well-being, or universal human values. The list may have been jotted (swiftly) or it may have grown reflectively, in long silent evenings or penetrating empirical analysis. It may trail off with 'etcetera'[4] or it may try to be complete.[5] It may be offered as 'one person's opinion' of what may be 'universally' true,[6] or it may be

---

[1] Wiggins (1998: 230).   [2] Max-Neef (1992: 15–16).   [3] Sen (1999a: 75).
[4] Galtung: 'Longer lists could be imagined' (1994: 20).
[5] Max-Neef: 'Fundamental human needs are finite, few, and classifiable' (1992: 20).
[6] Griffin: 'It does not matter if you disagree with my list' (1996: 30).

used, revised, and offered as a best (to date) attempt at a general account.[7] Its elements may be extremely vague[8] or quite specific.[9] It will have economic[10] and political implications.[11] It may be supported by appeal to philosophical argument, literary example, qualitative or quantitative evidence, broad consensus, or common sense.

Why do persons engaged in development regularly do this? Perhaps they have a hunch that certain professional problems could be addressed more efficiently by use of a 'list'—a simple set of items that jog the memory. For example,

- In developing a methodology for community exercises in rural and urban areas, Chilean academic and activist Manfred Max-Neef[12] constructed a matrix of ten human needs. Consideration of these needs in a participatory manner enables a community to interpret its own situation holistically.
- After an extensive survey of the Quality of Life literature, Robert Cummins[13] identified seven domains of well-being which, he argues, together indicate the quality of life of an individual. He developed a Comprehensive Quality of Life Survey instrument, that collects subjective and objective indicators in these seven domains.
- Based on her interpretation of Aristotle, and in an endeavour to extend Sen's capability approach, Martha Nussbaum has widely circulated and defended a list of ten central human capabilities, with the express intention that these should provide the basis for 'constitutional principles that should be respected and implemented by the governments of all nations'.[14]
- In analysing a large study of *Voices of the Poor* from twenty-three developing countries, Deepa Narayan and others noticed that six dimensions of well-being emerged as important, in very different ways, to poor people all over the world.[15]
- In gathering consensus among development assistance institutions as to international development targets for their coordinated efforts, the OECD has chosen to identify seven goals that, if jointly realized, would significantly reduce poverty in its multiple dimensions.[16]
- In developing his account of *Development as Freedom* economist Amartya Sen instrumentally investigates five categories of capabilities. He argues: 'Each of these

---

[7] Finnis: 'I suggest that other objectives ... will be found, on analysis, to be ways or combinations of ways of pursuing ... one of [these] basic forms of good, or some combination of them' (1980: 90).

[8] Doyal and Gough's principle of 'autonomy' (1993: 59 ff.).

[9] Nussbaum (2000a): 'Being able to hold property (both land and movable goods), not just formally but in terms of real opportunity; and having property rights on an equal basis with others; having the right to seek employment on an equal basis with others; having the freedom from unwarranted search and seizure. In work, being able to work as a human being, exercising practical reason and entering into mutual relationships of mutual recognition with other workers.'

[10] Doyal and Gough (1993): 'We contend therefore that universal objective basic needs exist, can be identified and their satisfaction monitored'.

[11] Nussbaum: 'I shall now specify certain basic functional capabilities at which societies should aim for their citizens.' (2000a: 82–3). [12] Max-Neef (1993).

[13] Cummins (1996).

[14] (2000a: 5). Nussbaum's theory has been presented in (1988, 1990a,b, 1992, 1995a,b, 1998b, 2000a,b). The most complete articulation of this approach to date is in (2000a).

[15] Narayan et al. (2000a,b).

[16] OECD (1996).

distinct types of rights and opportunities helps to advance the general capability of a person. They may also serve to complement each other.'[17]
- In developing the work of the Basic Needs School, Frances Stewart identified ten features of the 'full life'.[18] Doyal and Gough[19] identified eleven 'intermediate needs' that governments' social policies should address.

As these examples suggest, in many practical undertakings, be they participatory monitoring or data collection, constitution-building, policy-making, or needs assessment, leaders in development have found it useful to construct a list of the different dimensions of poverty or well-being.

The problem is focused by the fact that institutions tend to prioritize certain capability changes. In 1990 the World Bank renewed its commitment to poverty alleviation as the overarching objective of its work. But critical scrutiny of the operational directives, strategy papers, *World Development Reports*, and similar documents used from 1990 until 1993 showed that the intrinsically worthwhile 'dimensions' of development at which this poverty alleviation work aimed were *education, health, nutrition, consumption, and amenity (including the environment)*. Any changes, whether positive or negative, in relationships, aesthetic arrangements, religion, participation, culture, meaningful work or play were not registered as intrinsically important. These dimensions were missing from the Bank's field of vision. Were these changes not valuable?

This question surfaces when one tries to apply the capability approach, because in order to see whether the capability set, taken as a whole, has expanded or contracted, one needs to identify the valuable impacts a development initiative has—positive and negative, tangible and intangible, quantifiable and qualitative. Only *after* these have been identified (if not the comprehensive set at least the salient subset) and *after* they have been weighted and ranked, can at least a partial assessment possibly be made about capability expansion.

Moreover, if we are not able to propose how information on valuable capabilities *might* be obtained that is relatively complete and also sensitive to diversity, then the capability approach is operationally stymied. What is needed is a procedure to overcome the informational constraints that typically oblige organizations such as the World Bank and Oxfam to concentrate only on certain dimensions of poverty.

This chapter will propose the theoretical conception of basic human values that has been developed by John Finnis, as being a conception that (i) enables and requires participatory dialogue in application, but also (ii) has objective foundations and (iii) can coherently engage with and be refined by the large and growing empirical literatures on happiness, subjective well-being, quality of life indicators, and views of the poor—which have not been well-integrated with poverty reduction approaches. The conception can also mesh well with methodological literatures on participation, and be used by persons with diverse philosophical approaches and opinions.

---

[17] 1999a: 10, 38–40. [18] Stewart (1985). [19] Doyal and Gough (1991).

1.1. *The difficulty of identifying all valuable capabilities*

This chapter will argue that in order to go forward, some *process* for identifying capabilities (while retaining Sen's deliberate incompleteness) is required (Ch. 2, Sect. 1). A useful list is not a bad idea to explore—as lists, for better or worse, often elicit value-based responses (if only the accusation that the people who tend to use lists are either dominant by personality, or merely forgetful). The following section (Ch. 2, Sect. 2) argues that while the list of central human functional capabilities proposed by Nussbaum has been very constructive in widening the domain of capabilities under discussion for national constitutions and Bills of Rights, its relevance for small NGO activities is constrained by the prescriptive character of the list, by its orientation to national institutions and policies, and by the uncertain authority of participatory processes. I will introduce, as an alternative, Finnis's practical reason-based identification of 'dimensions' of human development (Ch. 2, Sect. 3). These dimensions, I argue, are useful for promoting a process of public discussion and scrutiny of the capabilities that are to be valued and pursued in diverse societies. In particular, they are useful for small activities in poor communities.

The fourth and final section of this chapter connects this discussion with similar discussions across the disciplines. I introduce similar 'lists' and the projects from which they ensue, whether these be 'barefoot economics' or social indicators research, whether psychological studies of happiness or philosophical studies of universal values. The reason for this is twofold: first, to look at similarities and differences between alternative proposals of dimensions of well-being, and secondly, to point out that some of these data issues that deeply concern economists already have well-developed literatures of their own. In particular, I consider the work of Martha Nussbaum, Manfred Max-Neef, Deepa Narayan, Shalom Schwartz, Robert Cummins, Maureen Ramsay, Len Doyal and Ian Gough, Ronald Inglehart, and Mozaffar Qizilbash (see Table 2.9). After surveying these lists and mentioning over thirty others, I revisit Finnis's criteria by which a contestable synthesis of such sets might coherently occur. I argue that the inexact and inherently contentious process of synthesizing lists into one favoured set is far less important than using a roughly decent set in the field and modifying it as necessary.

1.2. *Sen's arguments against specifying capabilities*

It would be well before continuing to review the way in which Sen has both acknowledged the class of critiques such as Stewart's, Nussbaum's, and Williams's (introduced in Ch. 1, Sect. 3) and defended his own position (which neither specifies nor prioritizes capabilities).[20]

Sen recognizes that capabilities must be identified, and can be ranked from the more central to the trivial, that both of these tasks involve an evaluative exercise and even that 'it is valuation with which we are ultimately concerned in the functionings

---

[20] In 1980*a*, 1987*b*, 1993*a*, 1994*b*, 1996*e*, 1997*c*, 1999*a*.

approach'.[21] He also recognizes that the identification of multiple basic capabilities is practically required for poverty measurement and analysis.[22] In *Inequality Reexamined* and later writings Sen traces the philosophical basis of the capability approach 'to Aristotle's writings, which include a penetrating investigation of "the good of man" in terms of "life in the sense of activity" (see particularly *The Nicomachean Ethics*, 1.7)'.[23] He wrote that Nussbaum's Neo-Aristotelianism 'would not be inconsistent with the capability approach presented here, but *not*, by any means, *required* by it'. And he recognizes that introduction of such an account of human functioning would be 'a systematic way of eliminating the incompleteness of the capability approach'.[24]

Sen has not himself further specified the capability approach because of five reservations:

- 'this view of human nature (with a unique list of functionings for a good human life) may be tremendously overspecified . . . ';
- 'the use of the capability approach as such does not require taking that route';
- the introduction of such a list would require 'a great deal of extension as a theory for practical evaluation';
- such a list may not have wide relevance, and thus the capability approach should permit 'other routes [presumably to the specification of human fulfilment] to be taken';
- there is a positive value in an incomplete theory which is 'consistent and combinable with several different substantive theories' and which may be filled in by reasoned public debate, itself a valuable process.[25]

Sen may not think it possible to specify the capability approach any further without effecting closure, without undertaking a universal 'valuational exercise', deciding on the mechanism by which valuable functionings are to be identified, and subsequently choosing relative weighting and aggregating. Further specification at a theoretical level would involve, in Sen's account, the choice of 'exactly one interpretation of the metaphysics of value' (the idea of a comprehensive doctrine of the good)[26] and, as he argues, 'it is not obvious that for substantive political and social

---

[21] 1985b: 32, see 1987b: 108 f., 1992a: 44 f., 1999a and 'Description as Choice' in 1982b.
[22] (1980a, 1983d, 1993a, 1997a, 1999a); Drèze and Sen (1989, 1995); UNDP (1997).
[23] 1992a: 39. [24] 1993a: 47, both quotes.
[25] (1993a: 47), all quotes. For other similar critiques of Nussbaum's work, see Qizilbash (1996a,b); Gasper (1997).
[26] See the discussion in Sen (1992a: 79–84, 1990b: 117–21, 1999a: 63–5). Also Rawls (1993: 178–86). John Rawls describes reasonable comprehensive doctrines as having three main features: 'One is that a reasonable doctrine is an exercise of theoretical reason: it covers the major religious, philosophical, and moral aspects of human life in a more or less consistent and coherent manner. It organizes and characterizes recognized values so that they are compatible with one another and express an intelligible view of the world. Each doctrine will do this in ways that distinguish it from other doctrines, for example, by giving certain values a particular primacy and weight. In singling out which values to count as especially significant and how to balance them when they conflict, a reasonable comprehensive doctrine is also an exercise of practical reason. Both theoretical and practical reason (including as appropriate the rational) are used

philosophy it is sensible to insist that all these general issues be resolved *before* an agreement is reached on the choice of an evaluative space'.[27]

None the less Sen does argue that in comparison with the utilitarian basis of welfare economics the capability approach has considerable 'cutting power'[28] even before capabilities are identified. Much of this is due to the comparative advantage of capabilities as the space in which justice is to be evaluated, rather than utilities or 'primary goods' (the defects and ongoing value of which Sen has exhaustively outlined), and also the capability approach's insistence that *some* functionings and capabilities have intrinsic value.

Furthermore, Sen identifies two procedures for identifying capabilities sets *without* undertaking value judgements directly but rather making the maximal use of consensus: the *dominance partial ordering approach*, and what I call *the general functionings approach*.

1.2.1. Dominance partial ordering approach

Sen suggests that if certain functionings/capabilities are identified as valuable, then it is evident that, even if there is substantial disagreement as to the relative weights of the various capabilities, having more of *each* of them would be an improvement.[29] Sen terms this 'dominance partial ordering', and refers to it as one way in which perhaps quite substantial agreement might be reached on issues without requiring any agreement on relative weights. Dominance partial ordering may be extended by the intersection method to order a particular pair of valuable objects, even without full agreement on relative values of the objects. Sen gives the following clear example: 'if there are four conflicting views claiming respectively that the relative weight to be attached to x vis-à-vis y should be 1/2, 1/3, 1/4, and 1/5, there is, then, an implicit agreement that the relative weight on x should not exceed 1/2, nor fall below 1/5'.[30] This *intersection approach* permits pair-wise ordering: an $x:y$ ratio of 1 : 2 is clearly better than a 2 : 1 ratio, if y is always more highly valued. Similarly, dominance partial ordering may be extended to order ratios of value objects by considering not relative weights, but indifference curves or surfaces (which need not be complete), and by evaluating the relative merit of value-object-combinations by their placement *vis-à-vis* the indifference surfaces. The dominance partial ordering may be particularly suitable for judging vector bundles in which the valuation differences are significant, for example, judging the relative functioning vectors of a very deprived person and a typical person.[31]

---

together in its formulation. Finally, a third feature is that while a reasonable comprehensive view is not necessarily fixed and unchanging, it normally belongs to, or draws upon, a tradition of thought and doctrine. Although stable over time, and not subject to sudden and unexplained changes, it tends to evolve slowly in the light of what, from its point of view, it sees as good and sufficient reasons' (1993: 59).

[27] 1993a: 49. [28] 1993a: 48, see 1995c: 266 f., 1999a, ch. 3.
[29] 1992a: 46, see 1985b: 35–7, 1999a: 78–9. [30] 1992a: 46.
[31] On this see Chakraborty (1995, 1996).

1.2.2. General concrete functionings

In different discussions, Sen suggests that the space for consensus might be widened if the capabilities and functionings are conceived at a sufficient level of generality: 'there may be more agreement on the need to be entertained, or to have the capability to take part in the life of the community, than on the form that entertainment must take or on the particular way the life of the community may be shared'.[32] While Sen never elaborates the 'general functionings' approach directly or at length, he refers approvingly to Cass Sunstein's treatment of incompletely theorized agreements.[33] Sunstein argues that

> well-functioning legal systems tend to adopt a special strategy for producing stability and agreement in the midst of social disagreement and pluralism: Arbiters of legal controversies try to produce *incompletely theorized agreements*. Sometimes these agreements do involve abstractions, accepted amid severe disagreements on particular cases; thus . . . those who argue about homosexuality and disability can accept an abstract anti-discrimination principle. But sometimes incompletely theorized agreements involve concrete outcomes . . .
> When people disagree on an abstraction—Is equality more important than liberty? Does free will exist?—they often move to a level of greater particularity. This practice has an especially notable feature: It enlists silence, on certain basic questions, as a device for producing convergence despite disagreement, uncertainty, limits of time and capacity, and heterogeneity. Incompletely theorized agreements . . . are an important source of social stability and an important way for people to demonstrate mutual respect.[34]

Sunstein's articulation of incompletely theorized agreements—that balance both the general and the 'concrete'—seems implicit in Sen's own work. For example, in *Development as Freedom* Sen investigates instrumentally five kinds of general yet concrete freedoms: political freedom, economic facilities, social opportunities, transparency guarantees, and protective security.[35] He does not seek consensus on abstract principles such as liberty, nor on particularities of situations such as debating the capability to eat caviar; rather he focuses his discussion on general concrete issues such as life expectancy, hunger, and poverty.

The dominance partial ordering approach, and the 'general functionings' approach both work by making the best, yet mechanical, use of consensus. Neither provides an overt mechanism for dealing with deep conflict (if a person thought that the relative weight be attached to x vis-à-vis y should be 25 : 1, for example, then the area of intersection in the above example would not exceed 25 : 1 nor fall below 1 : 5, and the dominance partial ordering does not get one very far because the range is too great).

While Sen has not discussed the resolution of deep value conflicts, in several places he does describe a process by which the area of consensus may be enlarged through a process of dialectical discussion or of information sharing. Chapter 4 develops this in

---

[32] 1992a: 109, see pp. 133 f. Clearly there are parallels between this and the emic and etic distinction, but these lie beyond the scope of this discussion.   [33] 2000c: 935.
[34] 1996: 4–5. Emphasis in original.   [35] 1999a: 10, 38–40.

more detail.[36] We turn now to Martha Nussbaum's work, which has treated these issues somewhat differently.

2. CENTRAL HUMAN CAPABILITIES: NUSSBAUM'S APPROACH

Based on her interpretation of Aristotle, and in an endeavour to extend the capability approach, Martha Nussbaum has set forth a specification of central human capabilities, with the express intention that these should provide the basis for 'constitutional principles that should be respected and implemented by the governments of all nations'.[37] While Sen and Nussbaum did collaborate on several initiatives,[38] their capability approaches are not the same. Nussbaum's capabilities approach is more determinate than Sen's; her emphasis is on legal and political rather than socio-economic applications; and her definitions of capability and functioning are somewhat distinct from Sen's.[39]

I will suggest that while Nussbaum's approach is valuable at a political level, it is overdetermined for use in development at a microeconomic level. A more rudimentary, more open-ended account—with a sound epistemological foundation—to be filled in procedurally, is required in the latter context. This being said, her approach has provided rich insights for all to bear in mind as they develop the capability approach at other levels. To quote another, 'My comments . . . critical as they are inevitably apt to sound are offered in the spirit of one wanting to join in a common enterprise'.[40]

2.1. *Method, functionings, characteristics*

Nussbaum's defence of a 'universal normative approach' powerfully rebuts the subjectivist attack on universal values from philosophers as well as feminists (an attack that Finnis also counters). She defines human capabilities as 'what people are actually able to do and to be' and develops an Aristotelian account of the central human capabilities that should form the basis of constitutional guarantees and international comparisons of quality of life. In her account Nussbaum engages internal reflection, imagination, and expressions of human dignity or its absence (such as tragic artwork), and identifies 'areas of informed agreement' between groups that differ otherwise in culture and comprehensive doctrines of the good.[41] In *Women and Human*

---

[36] 1967, 1983*b*, 1993*e*, 1997*f*, 1999*a*.   [37] 2000*a*: 5.   [38] Nussbaum and Sen (1989, 1993).

[39] See Crocker (1995) for a discussion of these differences, and also (1992: 599), and Arneson (2000) and Nussbaum (2000*a*: 11–15). This chapter does not further discuss the differences.

[40] Susan Wolf, commenting on Nussbaum (Nussbaum and Glover 1995: 104).

[41] Aspects of this methodology are presented in Nussbaum (1988: 174–6, 1990*a*: 218, 1992: 214–16, 1995*b*: 123–4 and 98–102). 2000*a* does not refer to internal essentialism as foundational, leaving the reader uncertain as to whether there has been a change of view. Rather, it endorses Rawls's procedure as a method of political justification, without otherwise addressing foundational issues. On problems with the epistemological foundation in earlier works issues see Alkire and Black (1997). Subsequently Nussbaum

Development Nussbaum adopts a procedure akin to Rawls's reflective equilibrium to justify the list politically (in the Rawlsian sense of politically): 'we lay out the arguments for a given theoretical position, holding it up against the "fixed points" in our moral intuitions; we see how those intuitions both test and are tested by the conceptions we examine'.[42] Subsequently, 'we ... lay out other competing conceptions, compare them in detail to this one, and see on what grounds ours might emerge as more worthy of choice. And we would have to consider the judgements of our fellow citizens, as well as our own'.[43] The goal, in the long run, is that this reflective process might support a fully universal program: 'that the community of nations should reach a transnational overlapping consensus on the capabilities list, as a set of goals for cooperative international action and a set of commitments that each nation holds itself to for its own people'.[44]

Nussbaum distinguishes three kinds of capabilities: basic, internal, and combined. *Basic capabilities* are 'the innate equipment of individuals that is the necessary basis for developing the more advanced capabilities and a ground of moral concern'—for example, seeing and hearing, and the capability for speech, language, love, gratitude, practical reason, work.[45] *Internal capabilities* are 'developed states of the person herself that are, so far as the person herself is concerned, sufficient conditions for the exercise of requisite functions ... mature conditions of readiness'—that is, bodily maturity, capability for sexual functioning, religious freedom, freedom of speech.[46] *Combined capabilities* are 'internal capabilities *combined with* suitable external conditions for the exercise of the function'.[47] If one is able to form one's point of view and is also able, within the political and cultural systems, to express it, then one enjoys a combined capability of expression (if one is capable of expressing a view but not able to for fear of repercussions, one has the internal capability for freedom of speech but lacks the combined capability).

Nussbaum's 'list' of central human capabilities is a list of *combined* capabilities. To provide these capabilities, governments must attend to the development of persons' internal capabilities or powers, as well as to an appropriate enabling environment for their exercise—that is, to both material and social aspects. The central capabilities 'have value in themselves' (rather than being merely instrumental), and are specific yet open to plural specification.[48] Her list is *incomplete*—it identifies only the subset of human capabilities that are necessary for a dignified human existence anywhere. It is

---

has omitted the references to empirical support for the list (1995*b*: 74), but the relationship between political and ethical justifications of her list remains unclear—see similar concerns expressed by Antony (2000) and Nussbaum's response (2000*b*: 16–24). Nussbaum's longer and more philosophical 'marathon' treatise promised in 2000*a* will surely clarify her position.

[42] 2000*a*: 101, 151; Deneulin (forthcoming) observes that only slight modifications of the 'list' occurred when Nussbaum changed her political positions, which does call into question which form of reasoning actually established the list (Deneulin argues that it was internalist essentialism).

[43] 2000*a*: 102.   [44] 2000*a*: 104.   [45] 2000*a*: 84, see 1988.   [46] 2000*a*: 84.

[47] 2000*a*: 84–5. Emphasis in original.

[48] Nussbaum (2000*a*: 74) Nussbaum's account of the capability approach is developed in Nussbaum (1988, 1990*a*, 1992, 1993, 1995*a,b*, 1997), and most comprehensively in (2000*a*).

also *flexible*: her proposed list has already been revised a number of times and is still proposed 'in a Socratic fashion, to be tested against the most secure of our intuitions'. Also, the list is open to *multiple realizability* (what Nussbaum earlier called plural specification): 'its members can be more concretely specified in accordance with local beliefs and circumstances. It is thus designed to leave room for a reasonable pluralism in specification.'[49] She claims such a list 'can command a broad cross-cultural consensus'[50] and that indeed the current list already represents an overlapping consensus. By overlapping consensus she intends the same definition as John Rawls: 'that people may sign on to this conception as the free-standing moral core of a political conception, without accepting any particular metaphysical view of the world, any particular comprehensive ethical or religious view, or even any particular view of the person or of human nature'.[51]

Like Sen, Nussbaum does not claim that she puts forward a complete theory of justice. Unlike Sen she does not frame the objective in terms of expanding valuable capabilities, or pursuing equality in capability space. Rather, she argues that the objective of governments should be to provide each and every person with the social basis of those capabilities that are essential for a 'truly human' and worthy life. Her list of combined capabilities describes that *threshold*—that dividing line between human and truly human lives—with which governments should be concerned.[52]

In the course of developing her account of capabilities, Nussbaum came to endorse Rawlsian political liberalism rather than social democracy.[53] This reoriented her account of how capabilities are to inform public action. Now Nussbaum provides her neo-Aristotelian account of universal values 'as a basis for basic political principles that should underwrite constitutional guarantees'.[54] Nussbaum describes the outcome of her inquiry as a set of central human capabilities which 'can always be contested and re-made' but which, like Rawls's primary goods, 'can be endorsed for political purposes, as the moral basis of central constitutional guarantees, by people who otherwise have very different views of what a complete good life for a human being would be'.[55]

Her list has been revised several times; the following refers to the 2000 version found in Table 2.1.

The characterizing features of Nussbaum's approach—its need for local and plural specification, its hope that humans internationally will recognize in the capability approach something relevant to their lives, its support for informed choices, its project of making political and economic development decisions respect a great range

---

[49] Nussbaum (2000a: 77), both quotes.   [50] Nussbaum (2000a: 74).

[51] Nussbaum (2000a: 76). See Nussbaum discussing Metaphysical-Realist Essentialism in (1992: 206–7, 212 f.). Her claim that her concept is free of any particular metaphysical view of a person has been contested.

[52] (2000a: 6, 73) see (1988, 1993, 1995b). The emphasis on threshold has increased over time; see (2000b: 102).

[53] This shift is mentioned in (1998a); in real rather than published time, she took up this position in 1994, as mentioned in (2000b: 102).   [54] Nussbaum (2000a: 5, 70–1).

[55] Nussbaum (2000a: 77 and 74, respectively).

Poverty and Human Development

Table 2.1. *Nussbaum: central human functional capabilities*

Life. Being able to live to the end of a human life of normal length; not dying prematurely, or before one's life is so reduced as to be not worth living.

Bodily health. Being able to have good health, including reproductive health; to be adequately nourished; to have adequate shelter.

Bodily integrity. Being able to move freely from place to place; having one's bodily boundaries treated as sovereign, i.e. being able to be secure against assault, including sexual assault, child sexual abuse, and domestic violence; having opportunities for sexual satisfaction and for choice in matters of reproduction.

Senses, imagination, thought. Being able to use the senses, to imagine, think, and reason—and to do these things in a 'truly human' way, a way informed and cultivated by an adequate education, including, but by no means limited to, literacy and basic mathematical and scientific training. Being able to use imagination and thought in connection with experiencing and producing self-expressive works and events of one's own choice, religious, literary, musical, and so forth. Being able to use one's mind in ways protected by guarantees of freedom of expression with respect to both political and artistic speech, and freedom of religious exercise. Being able to search for the ultimate meaning of life in one's own way. Being able to have pleasurable experiences, and to avoid non-necessary pain.

Emotions. Being able to have attachments to things and persons outside ourselves; to love those who love and care for us, to grieve at their absence; in general, to love, to grieve, to experience longing, gratitude, and justified anger. Not having one's emotional development blighted by overwhelming fear and anxiety, or by traumatic events of abuse or neglect. (Supporting this capability means supporting forms of human association that can be shown to be crucial in their development.)

Practical reason. Being able to form a conception of the good and to engage in critical reflection about the planning of one's own life. (This entails protection for the liberty of conscience.)

Affiliation. (i) Being able to live for and towards others, to recognize and show concern for other human beings, to engage in various forms of social interaction; to be able to imagine the situation of another and to have compassion for that situation; to have the capability for both justice and friendship. (Protecting this capability means protecting institutions that constitute and nourish such forms of affiliation, and also protecting the freedoms of assembly and political speech.) (ii) Having the social bases of self-respect and non-humiliation; being able to be treated as a dignified being whose worth is equal to that of others. This entails, at a minimum, protections against discrimination on the basis of race, sex, religion, caste, ethnicity, or national origin.

Other species. Being able to live with concern for and in relation to animals, plants, and the world of nature.

Play. Being able to laugh, to play, to enjoy recreational activities.

Control over one's environment. (i) Political. Being able to participate effectively in political choices that govern one's life; having the right of political participation, protections of free speech and association. (ii) Material. Being able to hold property (both land and movable goods), not just formally but in terms of real opportunity; and having property rights on an equal basis with others; having the right to seek employment on an equal basis with others; having the freedom from unwarranted search and seizure. In work, being able to work as a human being, exercising practical reason and entering into mutual relationships of mutual recognition with other workers.

Source: Nussbaum (2000a: 78–80).

of kinds of human flourishing—are widely acclaimed contributions, on which this approach endeavours to build.

Yet there are three overlapping difficulties in her approach, which raise questions about both its coherence and local operationalizability, that is, for the assessment of the rose cultivation activity:

- *Prescriptivity issue* Nussbaum's listed capabilities are all prescriptive, in that she argues that there are political obligations to protect each of these capabilities. It might also be valuable to offer a theory of human beings that was able to (i) identify and describe beings and doings that realized something of value (be these debatably worthwhile or wicked or unrealistic or quintessential), and (ii) deal separately with the process of setting priorities and deciding what to do, informed by the local institutional fabric.
- *Epistemological issue* The description of her method as it has evolved seems to be based on different kinds of reasoning (practical—from own experience and also vicarious association with literature or imagined communities—and overlapping consensus). There is a serious problem in giving distinct accounts of the reasoning process which generates the lists, because one is making the (unverified) assumption that all processes will lead to the same list.
- *Power issue* It is never clear who the 'we' is; who decision-makers are or are to be. It is unclear who specifies her approach. It could be valuable to have a clearer view of how this specification is to take place, especially at the microeconomic level, given that it is key to avoid paternalism and to allow groups to exercise practical reason. Furthermore it is unclear from her method how a constructive defence of or disagreement with an item or sub-item on her list is to proceed, whether this be based on practical reason, consensus, or experience.

2.2. Prescriptivity

The first problem is the (increasing)[56] specificity of the capabilities list and Nussbaum's suggestion that these specifications should be prescribed universally.[57] In constructing her own approach Nussbaum develops Aristotle's approach in two stages.[58] The first is to notice the different incommensurable 'spheres' in which humans *must* make choices and act somehow: 'if not properly, then improperly'.[59] She refers to this stage as 'the initial demarcation of the sphere of choice'—for instance, the ten general categories of functionings.[60] At the second stage, one inquires 'into what the appropriate choice, in that sphere, *is*'—in other words, what choices in that sphere bring one across the threshold of a truly human life.[61] People will, of course, 'disagree about what the appropriate ways of acting . . . are'.[62] This is because humans and cultures are 'advancing competing specifications of the same virtue'.[63] Still, Nussbaum saw and continues to see one role of development ethics to be that of evaluating different *specifications* and selecting the optimal ones for an international consensus.[64] Furthermore,

---

[56] (2000b: 102). Nussbaum mentions that she has made a conscious shift towards 'the increasing specificity of the capabilities list itself'.

[57] (1993: 251). On the issue of prescriptivity see also Hurley and O'Neill in Nussbaum and Glover (1995), Qizilbash (1996a,b), Arneson (2000), Gasper (1997).

[58] (1993: 246), in which she describes Aristotle's general approach in the course of explaining her own. See Qizilbash (1996b: 150), where he refers to Nussbaum (1990a: 209–11).

[59] 1993: 247.   [60] 1993: 249.   [61] 1993: 250. Emphasis in original.
[62] 1993: 247.   [63] 1993: 247, see 251.   [64] 1993: 247, 2000a: 104.

Nussbaum argues that the central human capabilities, thus specified, 'are legitimately used in making comparisons across nations, asking how well they are doing relative to one another in promoting human quality of life'.[65]

This project raises obvious concerns regarding paternalism and imposition. Hence in developing her approach, Nussbaum has directed considerable attention to such criticisms. Substantively, Nussbaum builds 'respect for pluralism' into her conception in five ways.[66] The first is *multiple realizability*: 'we specify the list at a rather high level of generality, leaving a lot of room for nations to specify the items in accordance with their history and their current problems'. Multiple realizability corresponds to Sen's general functionings approach. The second allowance for pluralism is Nussbaum's description of the political objective of *providing capabilities rather than functionings* in many instances. The third is the prominence that she gives to *practical reason*. Practical reason—specified as various liberties as well as choice itself—together with affiliation are, she argues, architectonic capabilities that 'both organize and suffuse all others, making their pursuit truly human'.[67] The fourth is the *political liberalism* in which her advocacy of capabilities is embedded: 'we interpret the whole list as a list of capabilities to be promoted for political purposes, a core that can be the object of an overlapping consensus of many distinct conceptions, not as a fully comprehensive conception of the good'. Fifthly and finally, she argues that for the most part, these capabilities are *advised, not required*: 'the implementation of such principles must be left, for the most part, to the internal policies of the nation in question, although international agencies and other governments are justified in using persuasion—and in especially grave cases economic or political sanctions—to promote such developments'.[68]

The 'prescriptivity' issue concerns how in practice a normative list can be implemented in such a pluralist way. Concern for a procedural account was identified in different ways by nearly every contributor to *Women, Culture, and Development*. For example, Benhabib writes, 'What I find lacking in the Aristotelian account of human capabilities is the space, both in theory and in practice, which allows one's understanding of the "human condition" in Aristotelian terms to be translated into actively generated moral insight on the part of human actors'.[69]

A critical weakness in Nussbaum's approach is that it cannot fulfil both the 'respect for pluralism' and the other characteristics at the same point in time and it does not give a procedural account of how these processes of local specification and cross-national comparison are to unfold over time. To take just one example, at one point in time how can the list be both deeply flexible *and* useful for cross-national comparisons (recall from above that Nussbaum explicitly argued that the central human capabilities 'are

---

[65] 2000a: 35.
[66] In 1993: 256–7 she identified three of these—a plurality of acceptable accounts, optional alternative specifications, and context sensitivity. [67] 2000a: 82.
[68] (2000b: 132, all quotes); see parallel discussion in (2000a: 105).
[69] Nussbaum and Glover (1995: 255); see remaining contributions in the book and Alkire and Black (1997); see also Nussbaum's discussion of this in the introduction as the 'most urgent' issue arising from that book (1995: 9).

legitimately used in making comparisons across nations, asking how well they are doing relative to one another in promoting human quality of life')?[70] Directly comparable aspects of the list such as 'protections against discrimination on the basis of race, sex, religion, caste, ethnicity, or national origin' leave little room for pluralism. Deeply flexible aspects of the list—for example, expressions of senses, imagination, and thought—are notoriously difficult to compare meaningfully between countries.

The importance of the specification process heightens when one tries to imagine how Nussbaum's capabilities approach might guide not constitutional and legal arrangements but concrete microeconomic investments. A water-buffalo veterinarian who trains women in good milking practice might be legitimately baffled were she told to protect affiliation in her practice area by 'protecting institutions that constitute and nourish such forms of affiliation, and also protecting the freedoms of assembly and political speech'. Microeconomic activities of their nature will be temporal, limited in their focus to only a few 'central capabilities' for a limited community; and limited in their pursuit of those capabilities to very particular aspects of them. Also, microdevelopment initiatives have to work in practice not in theory; they are utterly constrained by what is possible. In order for these investments to have as their objective 'capability expansion' rather than economic growth, it seems a process would be needed to identify the contingently vital, valuable, and possible ways to expand capabilities in one context—but this process is very unclear.

The specificity of Nussbaum's project considerably restricts the domain of flexibility which is available to give 'priority' to the particular. It is also difficult to reconcile with a dynamic understanding of community and value. If indeed the 'local' and 'particular' are to be given ongoing priority, then the capability approach would seem to require a sketch of the *process* by which the national 'normative conception of the human' is to be developed in local forms, rather than *a* sketch of *the* normative human conception (and its associated political institutions), such as she gives. If there were a procedural account, then what might be most useful as a companion to it would not be a fully *normative* account of the human being but rather a set of dimensions of human being that could usefully spark conversation. The account Finnis develops moves in this direction.

2.3. *Epistemology*

The second issue in Nussbaum's method is epistemological, meaning how do we know what we claim to know about what 'people' and 'society' prefer and should choose. This subject (the epistemological basis of social choice) is one of the more vexed in the history of welfare economics. In Sen's Nobel lecture on 'The Possibility of Social Choice', for example, he mentioned that Robbins's rejection of interpersonal comparisons of utility took hold (leading to the rise of revealed preference theories) because Robbins was able to portray 'the epistemic foundations of utilitarian welfare economics' as 'incurably defective'.[71]

[70] 2000*a*: 35.   [71] 1999*c*: 352.

Nussbaum's methodology of developing her set of capabilities includes (i) internal reflection using practical reason, (ii) discussion to the point of reaching informed agreement with persons from different cultures, and (iii) empirical observations of institutional priorities such as property rights.[72] The problem is that it is not clear how these different foundations relate to one another. Such an eclectic *foundational* account of capabilities thus creates practical problems: how are abiding disagreements about her 'central human capabilities'—this universally normative account—to be resolved? What is the role for research on institutions, and for ongoing public debate, for reflection on the deeper matters of life?

The original foundation of the Nussbaum approach was practical reason—meaning the internal reflection of each person upon her own thoughts, reading, imagination, and experiences.[73] This is likewise the foundation of Finnis's approach which I support. However, it is not without its difficulties. Of particular note is the tension between a basis in practical reason and the capability approach's recognition of false or socially conditioned consciousness.[74] This tension is quite a significant difficulty (of which Nussbaum is aware), and will recur as an issue for Finnis's approach, but in a different way. Put simply, if Natasha has consulted her own experiences and employed internalist essentialist reasoning and generated thereby a 'shape of a human being', and these disagree with Nussbaum's, how would Nussbaum determine whether Natasha's findings were compelling or whether Nussbaum should employ a method of structured questioning[75] to help Natasha overcome her false consciousness and understand Nussbaum's list? As John Watson stated the danger in describing the esoteric methods of psychology prevalent at the beginning of the twentieth century, '[i]f you fail to reproduce my findings, it is not due to some fault in your apparatus or in the control of your stimulus [or, we might add, to some genuine moral insight on Natasha's part], but it is due to the fact that your introspection is untrained'.[76] This seems to leave the Keepers of the Findings in the suspiciously powerful position of being able to train others' introspection to agree with theirs (I query this accusation below). Lewin signals why this question is so pertinent if one contemplates reintroducing an introspective-based concept of well-being in economics:

[John Neville] Keynes, like many social scientists of his time, emphasized the distinction between mechanical behavior and human action. The 'facts of human nature' on which economics was based were to be derived, not from direct observation of human behavior, but

---

[72] Nussbaum and Glover (1995: 424), Nussbaum (2000a).
[73] This foundation was clearly expressed in earlier work (1988, 1990a, 1992, 1993, 1995c: 360–95). See also 'The Discernment of Perception' (in 1990b) and 'Non-scientific Deliberation' (in 1986). However *Women and Human Development* does not reiterate this foundation, and so it is not terribly clear if Nussbaum still endorses it or has replaced it entirely with Rawlsian 'overlapping consensus'. See Deneulin (forthcoming).
[74] Li in Nussbaum and Glover (1995: 425). See Nussbaum (1990a: 230; 1988: 175).
[75] Nussbaum and Sen (1989) describe such a procedure. See also Nussbaum (1994a).
[76] Quoted in Lewin (1996: 1305). For Robbins's critique of introspection see (1935: 140). See also Sen (1982b, ch. 12).

from 'an *introspective* survey of the operation of those motives by which men are mainly influenced in their economic activities'.[77]

Lewin has argued that it was this introspection, called 'verstehen' by Weber, against which Watson and the behaviourists reacted to found a revealed choice economics which utterly shunned introspection. The behaviourists' point must therefore be addressed if, as Nussbaum's (and Finnis's) theory would entail, the basis of welfare judgements is again to include a significant element of introspection.[78]

In addition to practical reason (or perhaps replacing it—and it is this unclarity that is at issue), Nussbaum indicates that some kind of consensus is necessary for epistemological and also political reasons:

it seems to me very important that people from a wide variety of cultures, coming together in conditions conducive to reflective criticism of tradition, and free from intimidation and hierarchy, should agree that this list is a good one, one that they would choose. Finding such areas of informed agreement is epistemically valuable, in two ways: first, it points us to areas of human expression that we might have neglected or underestimated. Second, it tells us that our intuitions about what would make a political consensus possible are on the right track. The methodology that has been used to modify the list shows this: for I have drawn both on the results of cross-cultural academic discussion and on discussions in women's groups themselves designed to exemplify certain values of equal dignity, non-hierarchy, and nonintimidation. In other words, I have proceeded as if it is important that there should be a substantial convergence between the substantive account and a proceduralist account, where the procedure itself is structured in accordance with certain substantive values.[79]

The two reasons for seeking informed agreement—pointing out areas we might have missed, and testing out political consensus—are well put and we will come back to these again both in discussing Finnis's work later this chapter and in discussing participatory mechanisms in Chapter 4.

The problem is that deep disagreements remain—among feminists and among different philosophical approaches—on these issues. If Nussbaum intends to support 'an international feminism' that has 'bite'[80] then she cannot rely on foundational consensus to build up an objective account of what is not vicious (because if we all agree, where exactly is the bite?).

Finnis argues that consensus can be a 'mark of truth' only under ideal conditions, in which parties are knowledgeable, of good will, and disposed to be frank (and only in regard to matters for which consensus is appropriate). And even in these conditions consensus is not a criterion of truth, but a mark of truth—that is, a

---

[77] (1996: 1298), referring to J. N. Keynes (1890), *The Scope and Method of Political Economy* (emphasis Lewin's). Note that J. N. Keynes proceeded then to *deduce* laws from 'a few simple and indisputable facts of human nature' (Lewin 1996: 1298); this kind of deduction has no role in Nussbaum's capability approach; J. N. Keynes is of interest to the current discussion because of his place in the history of economic thought rather than because of particularities in his philosophical approach.

[78] These problems, are, of course, familiar as the 'informed desire account' of utilitarianism. See Sen (1985b: 24), Sen and Williams (1982), Griffin (1986), and the references therein. See Nussbaum and Sen (1989), and Nussbaum (1994a). [79] 2000a: 151.

[80] 2000a: 34, opening sentence of ch. 1.

welcome consequence of discussants' willingness to engage in practical reflection.[81] Some such account of the relationship between Rawlsian overlapping consensus and Nussbaum's earlier work on practical reason would be useful operationally because when disagreements arise, one could then determine whether the appropriate response was further negotiation to reach consensus or further scrutiny and consideration of the issues, such as Nussbaum attributes to the law student Nikidion.

In addition to practical reason and consensus, it seems that Nussbaum's capability approach has evolved because of new knowledge regarding institutional values. For example, Nussbaum explains that an experience led to her decision to increase the prominence of property rights in her approach and overcome her suspicions that these were associated with libertarianism:

> My experience in India showed me that women attach intense importance to the right to hold property—demanding, at the very least, equal inheritance and property rights with men, but also attaching considerable importance to the possibility that they will be able to acquire some land in their own names. Listening to these voices (in a context shaped by the marks of a norm-infused proceduralism), I came to the conclusion that my own thinking had simply been muddled in this area; the evidence of desire led me to see something that I had refused to see before.[82]

This responsiveness to new insights is illuminating and provides an example of how access to others' experience can be constructive in value formation. But Nussbaum's insights are from case studies, rather than from large-scale empirical studies, or even from a set of case studies in different countries and across time. If understanding what *institutional arrangements* lead to deeply *valued capability outcomes* actually is key to accurate specification of central capabilities (in addition to practical reason and consensus), then it would seem that the further development of the capabilities approach should consult these literatures, or undertake a large sample international research programme, to study this inferred empirical relationship (between property rights for women and subjectively valued capabilities). Yet such research has not been called for, nor is it clear how studies of this nature (and 'theoretical reason'), could constructively engage Nussbaum's approach.

A final concern is that, by not addressing these concerns, Nussbaum tacitly suggests that practical reason/internal essentialism, consensus, and empirical relationships between institutions and capability outcomes will coincide in their support of a list of 'central human capabilities'—which would be a hypothesis worth testing, but does not resolve the foundational issues.

2.4. *Power and voice*

The third issue is related to that above, but the focus is not on epistemological agreement but on political voice. Nussbaum does not actively identify who is to develop a set of capabilities for national use but it is clear that *some people* are expected to do so. Throughout the book *Women and Human Development* the

[81] Finnis (1998*b*: 54, 1999: 355). [82] 2000*a*: 156.

pronoun 'we' is employed without explanation. Sometimes the 'we' seems to be the unspecified community that is developing the capability approach; sometimes it seems to be an intellectual or legal or political elite who are currently in authoritative offices. For example, when she explains the centrality of practical reason and affiliation, she points out that a recognition of their centrality 'sets constraints on where *we set* the threshold, for each of the separate capabilities, and also constraints on which specifications of it *we will accept*'.[83] When explaining the value of capability over functioning she explains, '*We set the stage* and, as fellow citizens, present whatever arguments *we* have in favour of a given choice; then the choice is up to them'.[84] Who might this 'we' be?

The problem would not be resolved by a phrase of terminological clarification. Rather, the observation is that Nussbaum does not develop a proactive account of *who* these 'reflective equilibrium' discussions should involve. But will the suitable 'we' emerge passively—for example, in the village of Arabsolangi?

As Nussbaum herself points out, the voices of the poor, of women, of the marginalized do not automatically sing out; these groups may not articulate their views unless specific effort is made to involve them. This is well-known, and efforts ranging from participatory poverty reduction strategies to national conservation plans to constitution-building exercises regularly and deliberately engage a wide cross-section of communities and subgroups in hopes that the resultant general strategies will include their views and concerns. So Nussbaum's omission surely is not an oversight. Rather, either Nussbaum deems the 'we' fixed externally—for example, by appointment to the Supreme Court or by elections—or she assesses that proactive involvement of poor women in this exercise is not essential.

Yet, if indeed Nussbaum regarded it as 'very important' that persons from different *cultures* agreed on the list (see the quote in the previous section), would it not be equally important that persons from lower *economic classes* took equal part in the dialogue—given that their perspectives may differ deeply from those of the educated and privileged?[85]

Setting aside the issue of whether there might be additional value to procedures that involved Vasanti and Jayamma directly and so empowered them personally, Nussbaum's lack of elaboration of the 'we' that is invested with the power of specifying capabilities and constituting an overlapping consensus—especially given her acknowledgement of the fragility of democracies in developing countries[86]—leaves her approach vulnerable to self-selected elites who might legitimize their own views in eloquent capability language. At the microeconomic level, where the 'governance'

---

[83] 2000*a*: 83; emphasis added.   [84] 2000*a*: 88; emphasis added.   [85] Narayan *et al.* 2000*a,b*).
[86] 2000*a*: 103–4.

structures of community organizations are yet more flexible, and the probability of local elite capture is high, a direct account of 'who should participate' is essential.

In considering how one might structure the identification of valuable capabilities in such a way as to address the identified above more satisfactorily, it may be helpful to consider a similar neo-Aristotelian approach set forward by Finnis *et al.*

3. THE PRACTICAL REASONING APPROACH

Let's go back to the lists mentioned near the beginning of the chapter, and to the rose cultivation project and Dadi Taja. This will be a slightly inside-out presentation, where I will first give a concrete example of a 'list in action' and then step back into the rationale for it.

Oxfam wanted to do a participatory 'impact assessment' of the rose cultivation project, to see what the cultivators considered the most valuable and significant changes (in their capability sets) to be, and what negative impacts the activity had had. There is a common method for ascertaining an activity's impacts, which is for the cultivators to explain to visiting NGO staff, both verbally and diagramatically, the different kinds of changes that occurred, and to identify which were more important (this has been teasingly called 'Phir kya hua'—'And then what'—because this phrase is repeated over and over again by the visitors). But rather than asking utterly open-ended questions (which have risks of bias associated with them, however fond many people are of them), Safia, the women's income generation officer, asked, 'what changes did the project have on your life, or your health or your security? You see I don't know how the project went for you—whether carrying all those roses made you so tired that your legs ached, or whether when you were learning to make rose-water you poisoned your desserts and your guests have never come back again, or whether the roses flowered only in some months and were silent in others, or whether you used some roses for your own wedding and haven't told me yet! But let's hear from each one of you whether there was any change that you trace back to your life/health/security as you define them. It can be a good thing or a bad thing. If there was, will you share it with us?' After going around the circle, and noting that participants were animated by this discussion, she went on next to relationships. 'This word relationship, it has many different levels—it can mean friends we feel affection for and give presents to, or it can mean people you just meet once. How do you define it? Were there any changes—good or bad—in your relationships through the rose project?' So she went on, taking eight or nine different dimensions altogether. In each case she tried to spark the imagination of the listeners so that the dimension 'came alive' in people's own lives and focused their attention and they knew exactly what they wanted to say.

Safia was trying, after a fashion, to identify the 'valuable' freedoms that had changed (expanded or contracted) as a result of the rose project, in eight or nine dimensions. This is at root a simple idea—although it raises many questions which will be addressed in due time (Ch. 6). Finnis's theory, described below, explains what the dimensions are philosophically, and how they relate to actual values that people have.

Finnis's theory has a carefully articulated account of valuable, but in themselves non-moral (in a sense to be explained) 'basic human goods'. It is based on an exercise of practical reason that yields substantive, objective descriptions of dimensions of human flourishing while preserving a space for historical, cultural, and personal specification. The theory has a different structure from Nussbaum's in that it separates the identification of these dimensions from normative and ethical judgements, which come later. This separation enables the dimensions to represent the perceived value of *any* free choices or comprehensive doctrines of the good, be these moral or immoral. They are, so to speak, the primary colours of 'value' *per se*.

Finnis's theory has a well-articulated epistemological basis for 'basic goods' but requires a process of specification in order to develop proposals with normative or moral content. Nussbaum's normative model of the human person specifies a conception of the good life but does not explain its procedural use at the local level; I will argue that the open-ended identification of dimensions of functioning combined with procedures for specification provides an apt structure for combining 'thickness' with 'vagueness' for small participatory activities.[87] Furthermore, the relationship between theoretical and practical reasoning, and between these and consensus, is not developed in Nussbaum's account. This raised questions as to how empirical studies might coherently inform her account, and how to engage with competent adults who disagree with her set of central human capabilities. Finnis's account of basic reasons for action is epistemologically based on practical reason alone. Finnis clearly specifies how empirical data can inform the dimensions, and how dissenters can proceed to challenge a suggested set of basic dimensions, or a prescriptive proposition (Ch. 2, Sect. 4.3). As regards the question of 'who decides', Finnis's approach supports subsidiarity—the principle that the most local agent(s) capable of making a decision should make it.

It may be important to re-emphasize that in the following discussion what is *not* at issue is the integrity of the authors' interpretation of Aristotle or the soundness of positive judgements they have published on the basis of their theory (regarding liberalism or homosexuality, for example), but rather their potential constructive

---

[87] Nussbaum defended her 'thick and vague' conception of human good *vis-à-vis* Rawls's 'thin' conception. Thick means 'dealing with human ends across all areas of human life'. Vague means 'admits of many concrete specifications' (1990*a*: 217). 'By this name [thick vague conception of the good being] I mean to suggest that [Aristotle's conception] provides a (partially) comprehensive conception of good human functioning (in contrast to Rawls's "thin" theory) but at a high level of generality, admitting of multiple specifications'. Nussbaum claims her conception 'can be expected to be broadly shared across cultures, providing focus for an intercultural ethical-political inquiry' (1990*a*: 206).

contribution to the capability approach as a theory guiding microeconomic decision making.[88]

3.1. *Identification of dimensions*

Finnis introduces the two chapters of *Natural Law and Natural Rights* in which he explains the basic human values by writing, 'Neither this chapter nor the next makes or presupposes any moral judgments. Rather, these two chapters concern the evaluative substratum of all moral judgments. That is to say, they concern the acts of practical understanding in which we grasp the basic values of human existence and thus, too, the basic principles of practical reasoning.'[89] He begins his inquiry into 'the basic values of human existence' by observing that 'a study of the nature of a being is . . . a study of the potentialities or capacities of that being'.[90] This requires an understanding of 'the principal *objects* [objectives] of human life'. Our practical reasoning, he argues, proceeds by considering (consciously or not) one or more of these principal objects.[91]

We use practical reason all the time, just not by that strange name. You have probably used it today. Practical reasoning, very simply, is reasoning about what to do (whether making a plan or making an arrangement). So when Oxfam's income generation officer and a group of 'poorest' persons began to discuss how they wished to generate income, they were engaged in 'practical reasoning'. Remember that they thought bananas were too heavy and okra was too seasonal. Besides, the idea of roses had delighted them from the start. Oxfam had initially suggested only female participants, but the poorest widows themselves objected that men were necessary for some of the harder work such as digging out the irrigation ditches to water the roses. Also, they explained that in their village, because they were of one caste, the women and the men did not keep purdah from one another so could work together without scandal. These considerations—of physical constraints, of culture, of inclination, of income flow—all come into practical reasoning.

The point of practical reason 'is the intelligent direction toward human fulfilment'.[92] People and communities use practical reasoning to make intelligent choices as to how to establish and use capabilities. For example, a mature person who does not suffer from significant mental or physical disabilities could recapture, report previous instances of, and so reflect on her previous chain of 'practical reasoning' in the following way. She could ask 'why do I do what I do?' and 'why do others do what they do?'

---

[88] This focus has an additional cost: there are further areas in which the writings of Nussbaum and Finnis or Grisez have strong parallels which would benefit from constructive comparison, for example, of the relationship between the emotions and morality, and the conception of political authority and obligation.
[89] (1980: 60). See Murphy (2001). [90] 1983: 1.
[91] It is necessary to establish a few verbal equivalencies. Finnis refers to these as 'basic values of human existence' or 'basic practical principles of practical reasoning', 'basic human goods' and 'basic reasons for action' (1980: 59 f.). They are all substantially synonymous, but stress the relatedness of a basic good to different things. I refer to them together as a 'list' or a 'set', meaning by this term all of the basic reasons for action taken together. [92] Grisez *et al.* (1987: 120).

Finnis suggests that this question, when asked repeatedly by any individual as a reflection on, or recovery of, her previous experiences of practical reasoning, leads to the recognition of a *discrete heterogeneous set of most basic and simple reasons for acting which reflect the complete range of kinds of valuable human states and actions* (the complete range of functionings).

It is easiest to clarify this process by considering an example. I may ask, 'Why did you come to this Prisoners' Dilemma lecture?' To which you might reply vaguely, 'because it seemed interesting'. I would ask again (utterly baffled), 'Why did it seem interesting?' To which you might reply—giving me a further inkling of your reasons—'I was curious as to what the issues were, although it is not at all related to my own work'. I would persist, as only a 2 year old or philosopher can, to ask, 'Why?' To which you might explain, with your boundless patience, 'it is simply good to know these curious things'. In other words, the simplest reason you give to explain your action refers to something you recognize as associated with the word 'knowledge-for-its-own-sake'. Of course it may be that there were several reasons for your coming—that you were going to a dinner afterwards and wanted a topic of conversation (i.e. to participate in sociability), or that you wanted to *avoid* meeting someone who was sure to come by and annoy you (i.e. evading them allowed you to participate in self-integration!), or that you were in fact an economist, and wished to advance your ability to footnote accurately in this area (skilful performance of work).

This set of basic goods is based in practical reason. In reflecting on 'why do I/others do what we do?' a person observes the most general reasons for action that she has implicitly 'recognized' to be valuable on the basis of her life experiences, her historical situation, relationships, projects, tastes, beliefs, and the lives of others she knows or has read or heard about. She is not examining the human from an Archimedean standpoint, or engaging in a theoretical study of human nature. Rather she is observantly following the thread of her own thought processes to their roots. Furthermore, in contrast to Nussbaum's list, which includes within each category a description of certain expressions of a valuable capability, and certain political rights she associates with it, Finnis's category of *reasons* for action is not tied to any one particular cultural or political expression of a reason. The reasons he points to are more general, and a list such as Nussbaum's would represent one way—but not the only possible way—in which concern for these reasons might be expressed in a political constitution.

Still, the set of reasons seem robust cross-culturally: Finnis brings in cross-cultural anthropological and psychological studies 'not, indeed, by way of any "inference" from universality or "human nature" to values (an inference that would be merely fallacious), but by way of an assemblage of reminders of the range of possibly worthwhile activities and orientations open to one'.[93] The objects of human life are

---

[93] (1980: 81, see 81–5, 97). The inference would be 'merely fallacious' because you cannot derive an ought from an is. Finnis discusses this inference at length, both in relation to Aquinas, and in relation to

not established by theoretical knowledge;[94] they are open to verification using theoretical knowledge, but not to direct deductive proof (Ch. 2, Sect. 3.2). Knowledge of the general dimensions of human flourishing remains, epistemologically, a recognition of the reasons that actually engage practical reason.

One final point of clarification may be noted. Finnis, like many others (including for that matter Rawls), does not claim that no real metaphysical truths exist. He merely points out that whether or not there are such (and this is a separate question), the moral framework does not derive from them epistemologically.[95] Further metaphysical exploration may be possible but is not necessary unless one requires a complete explanation.[96]

Finnis (who has revised his list more than once) wrote even at the outset that there is 'no magic number' of basic reasons, and there is 'no need for the reader to accept the present list, just as it stands, still less its nomenclature (which simply gestures towards categories of human purpose that are each, though unified, nevertheless multi-faceted)'. He claims the list is analytically useful[97] and contains 'all the basic purposes of human action'.[98] The applied ethical deliberations of Finnis and his colleagues demonstrate the powerful analytical value of specifying basic reasons for action.[99] Turning now to the content of the lists, Finnis has, over many years, suggested and refined a substantive set of these dimensions. Table 2.2 sets out the three major versions.

The text below uses the 1987 version of Finnis's list because the separation between practical reasonableness or authentic self-direction and self-integration seemed reasonable, and the dimension 'marriage', less convincing.[100]

Hume—who is not likely to be the author of the insight but is often credited with that honour—as well as to Samuel Clark, Hugo Grotius, and their sources (1980: 33–48).

[94] Finnis (1987: 113). See Sen (1967).

[95] The fact that a theory based in practical reason 'can be understood, assented to, applied, and reflectively analysed without adverting to the question of the existence of God [or any other transcendental truths] does not of itself entail either (i) that no further explanation is required for the fact that there are objective standards of good and bad and principles of reasonableness (right and wrong), or (ii) that no such further explanation is available, or (iii) that the existence and nature of God [or . . .] is not that explanation' (Finnis 1980: 49).

[96] Finnis holds that the framework derives from metaphysical truth 'ontologically'—because what basic values (and thus good actions and valuable capabilities) are depends on what sort of creatures humans are. Nussbaum similarly argues that central human capabilities are related to the distinctive 'being' of human persons (in comparison with beasts or the gods), although she claims, disputably, that this does not involve metaphysical realism (Nussbaum 1995b: 68 f.).

[97] 'In this way we can analytically unravel even very "peculiar" conventions, norms, institutions, and orders of preference, such as the aristocratic code of honour that demanded direct attacks on life in duelling' (1980: 91). [98] 1980: 92.

[99] e.g. see Grisez (1997). Such ethical deliberations obviously require the principles introduced in the previous chapter, but also an act-analysis that is not here presented or implied. For an introduction to these see Alkire and Black (1997), George (1993, introd.), Finnis (1980, ch. V), Finnis et al. (1987, part II).

[100] See Alkire (2001).

Table 2.2. *Finnis: basic reasons for action*

Finnis (1980) Natural Law and Natural Rights	Grisez, Boyle, and Finnis (1987) Practical Principles, Moral Truth and Ultimate Ends	Finnis (1994) Liberalism and Natural Law[1]
Life Knowledge Play Aesthetic experience Sociability (friendship) Practical reasonableness[2] 'Religion'	'*Life* itself—its maintenance and transmission—health, and safety' *Knowledge and aesthetic experience*: 'Human persons can know reality and appreciate beauty and whatever intensely engages their capacities to know and to feel.' Some degree of excellence in *work and play*: 'human persons can transform the natural world by using realities, beginning with their own bodily selves, to express meanings and serve purposes. Such meaning-giving and value-creation can be realized in diverse degrees.' *Friendship*: 'various forms of harmony between and among individuals and groups of persons—living at peace with others, neighbourliness, friendship'. *Self-integration*: 'within individuals and their personal lives, similar goods can be realized. For feelings can conflict among themselves and be at odds with one's judgements and choices. The harmony opposed to such inner disturbance is inner peace.' *Self-expression*, or *practical reasonableness*: 'one's choices can conflict with one's inner self. The corresponding good is harmony among one's judgments, choices, and performances—peace of conscience and consistency between one's self and its expression.' *Transcendence*: 'most persons experience tension with the wider reaches of reality. Attempts to gain or improve harmony with some more-than-human source of meaning and value take many forms, depending on people's world views. Thus, another category . . . is peace with God, or the gods, or some nontheistic but more-than-human source of meaning and value.'	*Bodily life*—and the component aspects of its fullness: health, vigour, and safety *Knowledge* of reality (including aesthetic appreciation) *Skilful performance in work and play* for its own sake *Friendship*—harmony and association between persons in its various forms/strengths The sexual association of a man and a woman which, though it essentially involves both friendship between the partners and the procreation and education of children by them, seems to have a point and shared benefit that is irreducible either to friendship or to life-in-its-transmission and therefore (as comparative anthropology confirms and Aristotle and the 'third founder' of Stoicism, Musonius Rufus, came particularly close to articulating) should be acknowledged to be a distinct basic human good, call it *Marriage*. The good of harmony between one's feelings and one's judgements (inner integrity) and between one's judgements and one's behaviour (authenticity), which we can call *practical reasonableness*. *Harmony* with the widest reaches and most *ultimate source of all reality, including meaning and value*

Notes: [1]1994: 691–2. [2]'the basic good of being able to bring one's own intelligence to bear effectively (in practical reasoning that issues in action) on the problems of choosing one's actions and life-style and shaping one's own character. Negatively, this involves a measure of effective freedom; positively, it involves that one seeks to bring an intelligent and reasonable order into one's own actions and habits and practical attitudes' (1980: 88). See the parallels with Sen's correspondence and reflection irrationality in Sen (1985c, 1999a).

3.2. *Characteristics of dimensions*

In recognizing most basic reasons for acting of individuals and communities, one is recognizing reasons which are, in James Griffin's words, 'worth wanting',[101] that is, *good*. But they are good in a particular not-yet-virtuous way, and because *so much* rests on this distinction I will quote in full the passage where Finnis explains this relationship between a dimension (*knowledge* in this example) and its *goodness* or *value*:[102]

> A number of common misunderstandings threaten to short-circuit our understanding of practical reason and its relationship to morality, just at this point. So we should bracket out these misunderstandings one by one ... (i) To think of knowledge as a value is not to think that every true proposition is equally worth knowing, that every form of learning is equally valuable, that every subject-matter is equally worth investigating. Except for some exceptional purpose, it is more worth while to know whether the contentions in this book are true or false than to know how many milligrams of printer's ink are used in a copy of it. (ii) To think of knowledge as a basic form of good is not to think that knowledge, for example, of the truth about these contentions, would be equally valuable for every person. (iii) Nor is it to think that such knowledge, or indeed any particular item of knowledge, has any priority of value even for the reader or writer at the moment; perhaps the reader would be better off busying himself [or herself] with something else, even for the rest of his life ... (iv) Just as 'knowledge is good' does not mean that knowledge is to be pursued by everybody, at all times, in all circumstances, so too it does not mean that knowledge is the only general form of good or the supreme form of good. (v) *To think of knowledge as a value is not, as such, to think of it as a 'moral value'; 'truth is a good' is not, here, to be understood as a moral proposition, and 'knowledge is to be pursued' is not to be understood, here, as stating a moral obligation, requirement, prescription ... In our reflective analysis of practical reasonableness, morality comes later.* (vi) At the same time, finally, it is to be recalled that the knowledge we here have in mind as a value is the knowledge that one can call an *intrinsic* good, i.e. that is considered to be desirable for its own sake and not merely as something sought after under some such description as 'what will enable me to impress my audience' or 'what will confirm my instinctive beliefs' or 'what will contribute to my survival'. In sum (vii) to say that such knowledge is a value is simply to say that reference to the pursuit of knowledge makes intelligible (though not necessarily reasonable-all-things-considered [nor moral]) any particular instance of human activity and commitment involved in such pursuit.[103]

Finnis suggests that these dimensions are *pre-moral*, which means that one can analytically identify the intelligible 'ends' of most immoral actions with reference to these same dimensions. A robber may obtain money by mugging as a means to buy paintings so he can enjoy aesthetic appreciation, or as a means to lots of entertaining so he can enjoy food and friendship; a terrorist may plant a bomb in order to express solidarity with the home community.

The dimensions are common both for individuals and for society. This is a crucially important point. For example, one of the dimensions is friendship—in which

---

[101] 1996: 28.   [102] See also Finnis *et al.* (1987: 126 f.), Finnis (1998*a*: 103–31).
[103] 1980: 61; emphasis added.

Miriam sees Thomas's well-being as somehow fulfilling to her, as his friend. Thomas's flourishing although different from her own *can be expressed in the same dimensions of value*. Furthermore part of her good can only be realized socially; so this approach systematically allows for common goods. In this way the dimensions of value become not just 'various ends' that people may or may not value, but the starting-points for collective action. Finnis points out that this account corrects for an error in social theories (including economic ones) that envisage a chasm between what Sidgwick called 'Universal Reason and Egoistic Reason, or Conscience and Self-Love'—or benevolence and self-interest, or morality and prudence.[104]

Finnis also claims the dimensions are *per se nota* or self-evident (anyone who has the necessary experience and openness could understand the value just by knowing the meaning of its terms).[105] This is, importantly, the approach Sen likewise adopts to universal values. For example, Sen writes that no value, to be considered universal, 'must . . . have the consent of everyone'—because not even motherhood is so universally regarded. 'Rather, the claim of a universal value is that people anywhere may have reason to see it as valuable . . . any claim that something is a universal value involves some counterfactual analysis—in particular, whether people might see some value in a claim that they have not yet considered adequately. All claims to universal value . . . have this implicit presumption'.[106] Finnis further characterizes these as *incommensurable*, by which he means that all of the desirable qualities of one are not present in the other, and there is no common measuring scale between them.[107] Thus the set of dimensions is *irreducible* (the list cannot be made any shorter).

It seems important to signal that these dimensions are understood by Finnis as never permanently 'achieved' once-and-for-all. Therefore it is more appropriate to speak of 'pursuing' well-being, or 'participating' in a dimension, than 'achieving' it. Likewise, while one may have an 'objective' of human development, this objective *can never correctly be said to have been achieved*. Other objectives, such as the provision of clean water to a village for five years, or literacy for person X, can be achieved. Nutrition can be said to have been achieved for a certain population group over a

---

[104] 1998a: 111 f., esp. n. 34.

[105] Self-evidence is used in a very particular philosophical sense which 'entails neither (a) that [the dimension] is formulated reflectively or at all explicitly by those who are guided by it, nor (b) that when it is so formulated by somebody his formulation will invariably be found to be accurate or acceptably refined and sufficiently qualified, nor (c) that it is arrived at, even only implicitly, without experience of the field to which it relates' (1980: 68). See the instructive exchange between George and Perry (George 1989, 1993; Perry 1989).

[106] 1999c: 12.

[107] In addition, Finnis recognizes a second kind of incommensurability. This is the incommensurability between different instantiations of the same basic reason(s) for action. For example, one may need to decide whether to take a vacation in the mountains or at the seashore. Even if one could validly assume that the value of a vacation in both instances related to the same basic reason(s) for action—perhaps rest, friendship, and/or aesthetic appreciation—one can still notice that the value will not be instantiated *in the same way* in each option. 'When one has a choice, no option includes in the instantiation of the good it promises everything promised by its alternative—even when the alternative would instantiate the very same basic good'. Grisez *et al.* (1987: 110). For alternative approaches to incommensurability and practical reason by James Griffin, David Wiggins, John Broome, Elizabeth Anderson, Joseph Raz, Stephen Lukes, Charles Taylor, Cass Sunstein *et al.* see Chang (1997).

certain period of the past, but it must continue to be pursued in the future. I will continue to use the word 'achieve' for functionings, but with the understanding that achieving is an ongoing pursuit.

Another key characteristic of the dimensions is that they are *non-hierarchical,* which means that at one time *any* of these dimensions can be the most important for a person or group, and others may be legitimately sidelined. They cannot be arranged in any permanent *hierarchy* either for an individual or for a community (although, as mentioned before, there is some structure, i.e. from practical reason and sociability).[108] On the day of a significant performance a singer may not eat very much, nor see friends, nor read the newspapers, nor go to the market, because he is preparing himself to sing with all the resonance and beauty he can.

In the longer term, people and communities make commitments which affect the mix of values they will participate in. A teenager is well aware that if she goes to medical school she cannot also go to the art academy, nor perhaps live in her parent's home, so she would not participate in art, nor in the particular relationships of her family, to the same extent. Similar 'commitments' also characterize families, businesses, villages, towns, unions, and nations.

The only feature the dimensions hold in common is that the pursuit of each, or the actualization of human potentialities that partially express a dimension, could contribute in its own unique way to the well-being or flourishing of a human life. Whether or not the pursuit actually does contribute to flourishing either of the actor or of others in society depends on how these are pursued, and this is discussed in the next chapter.

Finally, happiness or enjoyment or psychic utility is not a separate dimension. Rather participation in dimensions of values is anticipated to bring enduring happiness. Finnis writes,

> By participating in [the dimensions] in the way one chooses to, one hopes not only for the pleasure of successfully consummated physical performance and the satisfaction of successfully completed projects, but also for 'happiness' in the deeper, less usual sense of that word in which it signifies, roughly, a fullness of life, a certain development as a person, a meaningfulness of one's existence.[109]

Thus we come full circle from the scant definition of utility in welfare economics through Sen's wide-ranging capabilities that better represent well-being (and add agency), to dimensions in which 'valuable' beings and doings may regularly fall, to anticipation that the pursuit of valuable freedoms will bring forth the flourishing that was sought at the start.

3.3. *Dimensions of human development: a proposition*

I have referred to these basic reasons for action as 'dimensions' in order to continue Sen's metaphor of 'space' in discussing capabilities. They might be called dimensions of human functioning in that they express the complete irreducible dimensions of

---

[108] Grisez et al. (1987: 137–40).   [109] Finnis (1980: 96).

value, with reference to which the value of 'valuable' human functionings could be expressed. But 'functioning' is somewhat mechanistic, hence I prefer the term 'flourishing'—which also communicates the sense that people pursue and participate in but never realize these dimensions once-and-for-all. However, 'flourishing' also imports the idea of goodness and indeed when Finnis does introduce morality, as we shall see in the next chapter (Sect. 5.1), he uses the term 'integral human flourishing'. I propose—and the implications of this proposal will become clearer in the next chapter—that if (and only if) poverty is seen to be multidimensional, then Finnis's basic reasons for action also might be dimensions of poverty reduction, broadly conceived. Taken together the dimensions of human flourishing comprise a complete set of the most basic reasons for which people act in seeking 'wholeness' or 'well-being', in pursuing normative 'human development'. If poverty reduction is increasingly recognized as possibly encompassing any aspects of well-being (see Ch. 5, Sect. 1.3), it may be more helpful to construe Finnis's basic reasons for action as *the dimensions of poverty reduction*.

In other words, if well-being is to be evaluated in the space of functionings/capabilities, then it can be expressed by a vector—as Sen described in *Commodities and Capabilities* (see Appendix). Assessment of these capabilities, then, requires a valuational function.[110]

It is possible to imagine that the set of all possible human values could comprise the permutations of all possible values pertaining to spatio-temporal circumstances, possibly further expanded by personal, or at least cultural, features. It need not be finite. Yet it is also possible to conceive of the elements of the valuational function at a substantially higher level of generality, as the minimum number of *different* kinds of things people value—things like friendship and health and knowledge. I call these elements of valuations, *dimensions*. It is worth emphasizing that they are a way of structuring the space in which humans flourish rather than, as Nussbaum does, identifying the 'best' forms within it. Any particular value should be representable as a coordinate in n-dimensional space, where the dimensions (axes) are the n countable elements of d_i.

Put differently, the dimensions of development are like the 'primary colours' of values. An infinite range of shades can be made from our three primary colours, and not every painting (or life or community or income generation project) uses all or even most shades, but if, for example, all red hues were entirely missing, then my understanding of colour would be consistently skewed. Likewise if the value of each capability is represented by a colour, then if we were to have a complete set of tubes of primary colours, we could describe anything that is valued in any culture be it moral or otherwise as a mixture of several of these primary colours.

I suggest that Finnis's basic reasons for action (as conceived in principle, even if the actual list evolves) represent the dimensions of functioning and capability (recall that functionings and capabilities share the same evaluative space). That is, his account of basic reasons for action attempts to specify neither only basic or non-basic dimensions,

---

[110] For an application of this approach to environmental goods see Casini and Bernetti (1996: 58 ff.).

nor thresholds of capabilities, nor capabilities which should be publicly supplied nor only immoral or virtuous capabilities. Rather, it is a general model of the possible dimensions of humanly valued beings and doings, which leaves the functionings and capabilities within each dimension open-ended. *I suggest that this model may be seen as building upon what I earlier called Sen's general functionings method of resolving disputes regarding valuable capabilities*: 'there may be more agreement on the need to be entertained, or to have the capability to take part in the life of the community, than on the form that entertainment must take or on the particular way the life of the community may be shared'.[111] Chapter 4 will discuss how the simplicity of the dimensions allows for significant flexibility in the interpretation of each dimension either within a community or a value system, or by an individual.

Poverty reduction, then, is a function of these dimensions (whether or not it is a function only of a subset of them we will consider in Ch. 5). That is, all valuable capabilities can be represented in terms of these dimensions of poverty reduction (d_i), these primary colours among values. This is *not* to imply that individual or group flourishing requires a positive level of participation in *each* dimension. This property (that it is not necessary to participate in every dimension in order to pursue fulfilment, nor is it necessary to participate in each to a certain level) significantly increases the flexibility and accessibility of this approach to persons of varying value systems and abilities (Ch. 5, Sect. 3).

It is this kind of identification of dimensions which, I suggest, Clifford Geertz is describing when he describes the discipline of cultural anthropology as 'mostly engaged in trying to determine what this people or that take to be the point of what they are doing'.[112]

[They] tack between the two sorts of descriptions—between increasingly fine-comb observations (of how Javanese distinguish feelings, Balinese name children, Moroccans refer to acquaintances) and increasingly synoptic characterizations ... in such a way that, held in the mind together, they present a credible, fleshed-out picture of a human form of life. 'Translation', here, is ... rather closer to what a critic does to illumine a poem than what an astronomer does to account for a star.[113]

The purpose of identifying such dimensions is not to argue that abstract reflection on a palette containing three (or nine) colours led Monet to see waterlilies (that people or communities actually make decisions by abstract reflection about 'values'), nothing so absurd. Rather it is to offer a framework within which different values that communities have may be understood (within which, therefore, our informational base of social welfare may be expanded)—as a basis for discussions such as the one between Safia and the rose cultivators.

To take up for a moment the concern with flexibility, the question will immediately arise whether according to this approach it is essential that one accept the

---

[111] 1992a: 109.
[112] (1993: 4). I am conscious of the implications of using Geertz, but it seems that even an anthropologist who argues for cultural relativism, such as Geertz, can see the need for 'synoptic characterizations' of different practices. [113] 1993: 10.

existence of cross-culturally valid dimensions of human flourishing. Finnis defends this view as do I, but it might be worth mentioning that it *would* be possible to accept the practical *method* of identifying dimensions of development outlined here and yet actually *identify* not merely the specifications but also the very 'dimensions of development' *locally* by a process of iterative questioning.[114] The resulting dimensions might be incomplete or biased but would still be useful as tools for reflection on common commitments, and the grounds for their critique.

To take up a second immediate question, it may be pointedly observed that the basic reasons for human action are not, in fact, recognized even by persons who seem to have the knowledge and openness to do so—here again we return to Lewin's critique. The foundations of this (as any) theory are contentious. If one disagrees, or wishes to defer judgement, about these foundations, is it worth reading on? I argue it is, for the following reasons. The primary use to which I have put the set of dimensions, both conceptually and in the case studies, is to obtain more complete information from agents about the full range of valuable changes they have experienced relative to the alternative methods of asking open-ended questions (Ch. 6, Sect. 3.2.2). One could recognize the need for and value of this information without subscribing to a fuller account of the values. One could even see the set of dimensions as a theoretical 'hypothesis' about the categories of universal values, and submit this hypothesis to further empirical testing (as Schwartz and others have done). This would be an incomplete hypothesis, since it would avoid the foundational questions altogether. But it would support the same methodological application of the dimensions that I propose.

Rawls has argued that there is something to be said for a 'method of avoidance'— for skirting around as many foundational issues as possible in the interests of forming a consensus about, in this case, the dimensions of human value. Although it may be useful in many practical circumstances,[115] this 'method of avoidance' does not dissolve the questions it avoids, and is left speechless if there is an 'evil' consensus. Still, when this approach seems necessary—for instance because a goodly proportion of the population are quite convinced that their sole source of moral or political guidance is some other theory or scripture—the same practical methodology may still be employed.

3.4. *Contrast with Nussbaum I: dimensions not normative accounts*

It is necessary to signal the central ways in which these dimensions differ from Nussbaum's list. These arise from the character of Finnis's dimensions as both valuable and pre-moral. Most centrally, this list is precisely not a list of normative things-to-be-done (normative issues will be discussed, but in Ch. 3). In fact, an action may intend

---

[114] This might be a far more constructive way of empirically 'testing' the proposition that there are universal values than the tests constructed by Rokeach, or similar surveys of global values (Bond 1988; Schwartz 1992). It should be noted that this approach is still incompatible with an extreme relativism.

[115] See Sunstein's work on incompletely theorized argreements, discussed also in Sen 2000c, and Ch. 2, Sect. 1.2.2, and Ch. 3, Sect. 2.2.

and realize some basic good or another and yet be itself a cruel or inhuman act. Finnis describes the dimensions as principles 'which indicate the basic forms of human flourishing as goods to be pursued and realized, and which are in one way or another used by everyone who considers what to do, however unsound his conclusions'.[116]

This has a number of key consequences. First, it differentiates Finnis's account from Nussbaum's, because her functionings are normative and 'rule out vicious capabilities'.[117] Notwithstanding the controversial character of judgements of 'evil', it is clearly a good thing to rule out vicious capabilities, and one criticism of Sen's capability approach is that it does not necessarily do this. But conceptions differ between agents of development as to what is 'evil'. With Finnis's account, the process of discussion and thought as to what is considered 'evil' is transparent—as Finnis's own writing has shown—and however controversial his own judgements have been, those who disagree with him are able to articulate precisely where and how they do so. Critics of Nussbaum's approach do not have this option, because her account of evil is not publicly available. Secondly, the basic reasons for action are able to explain the intelligibility and rational attraction of some immoral, even Crocker's 'evil', actions, because even some immoral acts intend one or more of the dimensions of human flourishing.[118] This has practical applications—for example, it is quite relevant to consider the 'good' that is pursued by local elite capture of poverty reduction interventions, for example, to explore whether some synergies might be achieved. Thirdly, the list itself must necessarily remain utterly simple; *the dimensions cannot be further specified*. Finnis endeavoured to show that such a list could be generated by the iterative questioning of experiences, and distilling of reasons for action until a set of most basic reasons for acting remained, which people recognize as representing the irreducibly distinct valuable dimensions of their actions. As this process could not coherently reverse and build in less basic attributes, this set of dimensions is *not* susceptible to the danger of progressive overspecification, which is one danger that led Sen not to specify a list.[119]

For example, consider how the category of 'life' is constructed or construed in both accounts. Finnis's description of this as of other dimensions tries to point the reader to the intrinsic value of the dimension that he or she has already grasped in experience:

A first basic value, corresponding to the drive for self-preservation, is the value of life. The term 'life' here signifies every aspect of the vitality (*vita*, life) which puts a human being in good shape for self-determination. Hence, life here includes bodily (including cerebral) health and freedom from pain that betokens organic malfunctioning or injury. And the recognition, pursuit, and realization of this basic human purpose (or internally related group of purposes) are as various as the crafty struggle and prayer of a man overboard seeking to stay afloat until his ship turns back for him; the teamwork of surgeons and the whole network of supporting

---

[116] 1980: 23.

[117] For a discussion of vicious capabilities in Nussbaum, and Sen see Qizilbash (1996a: 149, 1996b: 1214–15, and 1211–12, respectively), and Crocker (1995).

[118] See Grisez *et al.* (1987: Sect. VII.C 'How to make immoral choices'). The only immoral actions which do not participate in one or more dimensions are actions motivated exclusively by feelings.

[119] Sen (1992a: 47).

staff, ancillary services, medical schools, etc.; road safety laws and programmes; famine relief expeditions; farming and rearing and fishing; food marketing; the resuscitation of suicides; watching out as one steps off the kerb . . .[120]

As this example shows, the 'values' are not defined. Rather, they are described in a general way, and various instantiations of this value (among others) which might be familiar to the reader, are recalled, to remind the reader of the breadth of possible concerns. Safia's discussions with the rose cultivators followed this pattern of wide-ranging suggestive examples also. Throughout, the reader is encouraged to reflect on his or her past chains of practical reason as a method of grasping and evaluating their own experience or awareness of this dimension.

In contrast, Nussbaum's parallel categories of life, health, and bodily integrity, are specified quite differently (Table 2.1). For example Nussbaum's category of life is: 'Being able to live to the end of a human life of normal length; not dying prematurely, or before one's life is so reduced as to be not worth living'.[121] As Nussbaum's descriptions show, her lists identify certain general functionings (life expectancy, nutrition, shelter, healthcare, rights of movement, safety, sexual expression, and reproductive choice) which are to be further specified, then pursued politically, it seems, in all countries (regardless of their institutional framework).

Finnis's list of basic reasons for action could never include a determinate set of capabilities or political obligations, because his list has a different *character* than Nussbaum's. If his approach were used by a community as a tool with which to generate a set of recommendations such as Nussbaum has, (*a*) the choice of particular capabilities that instantiate the relevant basic goods, (*b*) their further specification, and (*c*) the discussion of whether the government was the appropriate agent to provide them (as opposed to a community-based organization, as in the rose cultivation case), would each be distinct exercises. Given not only the cultural diversity and pluralism among nations, but also the different institutional configurations, the flexibility inherent in Finnis's approach would seem to confer a distinct strength.

3.5. *Contrast with Nussbaum II: dialogue and empirical support*

The second and third difficulties with Nussbaum's approach were that she did not specify a process for deliberating about disagreements about central human capabilities, nor did she clarify how the consideration of empirical data is to complement, support, or challenge her dimensions.

Finnis *et al.* have clarified the ways in which empirical data and theoretical reflections may substantiate the set of dimensions they propose. First, they make the familiar argument that the very intelligibility of other cultures requires a universally recognizable set of the most basic reasons for human actions. If this commonality did not exist, the behaviour of peoples in different cultures would be unintelligible to outside observers, even on their own terms, because those terms could not be understood.[122]

---

[120] Finnis (1980: 86).   [121] 2000*a*: 78.
[122] Grisez *et al.* (1987: 113). See Nussbaum's similar point in (1995*b*: 69); also Geertz (1993).

Secondly, they argue that theoretical studies of natural human inclinations—from psychology, sociology, physiology, anthropology, and philosophy—can and should be considered. In so far as the data 'support' the proposed set of dimensions of human action, the hypothesis (that x represents a simplest reason for action which is incommensurable with other such reasons) stands; in so far as the data challenge the proposed set, it must be reassessed (see Ch. 2, Sect. 4.2). While there might be no particular difficulty in Nussbaum's accepting this approach, it is the case that she does not distinguish as clearly the respective epistemological roles of practical and theoretical reason, nor does she identify the shift in level from non-moral understanding to morally structured normativity of the dimensions, and hence she does not have a clear procedure for treating conflict regarding the constituent elements of her list.

Furthermore they argue that theoretical reflection on a proposed category may usefully identify whether it is a combination of several different reasons for action or is itself basic. Consider the example of reputation. Thomás may diligently pursue an academic career because he hopes to get a good reputation. Is the simplest reason that explains his diligence, then, the value of 'a good reputation'? Why might he value it? In Thomás's home a good reputation may enable one to enjoy the respect of, and meaningful relationships with, one's colleagues, and so to enjoy friendships; it may be valuable in part because one can learn from others' estimation of oneself. And it may be valuable because it evinces that Thomás has carried through his early hope of becoming an academic; he has realized the capacities he chose to pursue, and so a good reputation represents a successful exercise of self-determination. But what if the surrounding culture were different? For example, if good reputations were awarded randomly, or on political grounds, then having a good reputation might *not* realize the value of self-determination and certainly would not truly reflect one's true ability and character. In fact if people responded to academics that had a good reputation with jealousy or competition then a reputation might be a barrier to friendships and other valuable relationships. So the value of reputation seems not to be 'basic'; rather its value is contingent upon a cultural framework. Reputation is valuable, when it is, for a complex of other reasons.

Finnis *et al.* also specify a process for evaluating whether a proposed addition to the set of dimensions is in fact an additional dimension, by identifying four common ways in which proposed additions seem like new dimensions but are not. These will be considered shortly (Ch. 2, Sect. 4.3).

Taken together, these procedures show that Finnis's approach is not as susceptible to Lewin's critique of introspective methods (Ch. 2, Sect. 2.3), because it identifies the kinds of questioning which might arise (given that, as Sen said, we may not know what our basic values are (Ch. 4, Sect. 2.3)). Furthermore an appeal to others to consider a proposed value as true is just that: an appeal. This explicit identification of procedure means that their list is also open to debate; Nussbaum's or John Neville Keynes's neglect to specify a procedure precludes a debate where the criteria of evaluation are publicly available. Despite these significant differences, obviously the explication of an intellectual process cannot dissolve the practical problems that may arise due to the power imbalances between Lewin's questioner and the questioned.[123] Yet what is at issue in that case would not be the truth or otherwise of the dimensions, but rather the relationship between power and knowledge.

3.6. *Nussbaum's criticisms of Finnis*

Over the past twenty years Finnis *et al.* have also applied their theory to issues of law, war, government, and social concerns.[124] Finnis *et al.* also defend particular and highly contested positions on public issues such as abortion, contraception, homosexuality, and euthanasia. But it is important to reiterate that the particular positions they defend *are not entailed* by Finnis's theory as described here.[125] In fact these concrete positions can be challenged using the same theory. I clearly, then, differ from Martha Nussbaum's appraisal of Finnis's approach, which is described below.

In 'Good as Discipline, Good as Freedom'[126] Nussbaum contrasts her liberal Aristotelianism with two other forms, one of which she ascribes to Finnis *et al.* She refers to this theory as tyrannical, and claims that they view 'the state as a protector and producer of virtue', hence their Aristotelianism could sanction laws against contraception, political speech, flag-burning, and artistic expression.

Nussbaum's point is persuasive; but her attribution of this to the position Finnis sets forth in *Natural Law and Natural Rights* or other works that relate to the fundamentals of his theory[127] or its political application is misguided. In chapter VII of *Aquinas* (1998*a*) Finnis presents (both as Aquinas's and, it seems, his own) an account of the state's jurisdiction that is radically dissociated from Aristotle's, and limited to the protection of justice and peace, that is, to interpersonal harmony. In this account children are treated as having the right to a morally sound upbringing, and in this respect the state is concerned with moral issues beyond certain versions of liberalism, but it is still very far from the unrefined paternalism Nussbaum has in her sights. *Natural Law and Natural Rights* likewise defends paternalism only with respect to children (a paternalism Nussbaum herself defends in *Women and Human Development*).[128] In particular, given Finnis's account of the good of self-direction and authenticity on the one hand (see Ch. 3), and his nuanced theory of the state's limited authority on the other, Finnis *et al.* would clearly not 'legislate a highly specific idea of the correct forms of sexual and familial functioning'[129] or other functionings, as Nussbaum claims they would.[130] We will return to these discussions in Chapter 4.

---

[123] Chambers (1994*d*).

[124] The theory which John Finnis articulates is the product of a collaborative effort between himself, the theory's originator, theologian Germain Grisez, Joseph Boyle, and others. In the present context Finnis's work is the most helpful to focus upon, because it philosophically addresses legal, political, and social policy issues.

[125] It is *only* when his theory is combined with a particular form of act-analysis (in which the full intention of the action determines the rightness or wrongness of the action) and with a particular interpretation of the basic goods, that Finnis *et al.* can apply their theory concretely. See Finnis (1991, 1995*a*), for example. [126] 1998*a*.

[127] Finnis (1980, 1983, 1992*a*, 1994, 1998*a*).

[128] 2000*a*: 89 f. [129] 1998*a*: 326.

[130] Grisez and Boyle, Finnis's co-authors, are yet more hostile to any form of state paternalism or enforcement of virtue. See Grisez and Boyle (1979), which argues for example that the objective good of

So where are we? The first part of this chapter has argued that, as poverty reduction is 'inherently multidimensional', there is a need to establish dimensions so that important cultural terms and values are not obliterated from discussion before it begins. Poverty reduction activities should not be colour-blind to dimensions of the human.

4. OTHER ACCOUNTS OF DIMENSIONS[131]

Thus far I have proposed that Sen's capability approach could be extended by building in Finnis's description of the method of generating dimensions of human fulfilment, his characterization of these dimensions, and his description of how they can be dialectically altered. I have not proposed that Finnis's list necessarily should be adopted, nor have I proposed the generation and publication by some person or group of exactly one list. This section will consider whether there are grounds for identifying a list for use in any context, and if so what dimensions of poverty reduction might be included.

4.1. *Partners in dialogue*

In order to undertake this, it is necessary briefly to become more ecumenical in terms of the relevant authors and schools of thought and disciplines. This section will consider what the content of dimensions of development might be, by reference to a pool of candidate dimensions/elements drawn from lists in economic development and philosophy. We shall consider the lists of: Martha Nussbaum (2000*a*), Manfred Max-Neef (1992), Deepa Narayan *et al.* (2000*b*), Shalom Schwartz (1997), Robert Cummins (1996), Maureen Ramsay (1992), Len Doyal and Ian Gough (1991), Ronald Inglehart (1997), and Mozaffar Qizilbash (1996*a*). Afterwards, we shall briefly consider a spreadsheet of other sets.

Although there is no dearth of 'lists' of well-being, universal values, and human needs, the sets of values authors propose often represent different philosophical kinds of things (more or less clearly). Furthermore, authors' lists have been shaped to a great extent by the intended operational purpose for which their list has been developed. Hence it would not be appropriate simply to sort the 7, or 20, or 40 lexical items into categories, because such an exercise would fail to take into account the underlying project of each author. I begin by introducing briefly each author whose list is to be considered, and sketching, with unfortunate brevity, how the set of needs, values, or domains they specify has arisen in their own work, gesturing to the problem for which the set forms a part of the solution, and presenting its components.

4.1.1. *Martha Nussbaum: central human capabilities*
As we have seen, Martha Nussbaum, the Ernst Freund Professor of Law and Ethics at the University of Chicago, is developing a neo-Aristotelian account of universal values 'as a basis for basic political principles that should underwrite constitutional

---

human life, and the objective moral wickedness of murder and suicide, are not sufficient grounds for state prohibition of euthanasia.

[131] Please refer to Table 2.11 at the end of this chapter, where all lists are reprinted.

guarantees'.[132] Nussbaum describes her central human functional capabilities in considerable detail (see Table 2.1). For Finnis et al., a one-word or one-phrase description of the elements, accompanied by a range of examples, is actually sufficient—persons supply the rest by recognizing the value from their own experience and discussion. In contrast, Nussbaum's categories specify institutional or legal means that facilitate the concerned capabilities. This marks her approach as significantly different from Finnis et al.'s, because whereas theirs represents generic dimensions of human value, hers is further downstream the operational process, and has already specified the threshold of combined capabilities that should be politically provided.

Her list of central capabilities was explained under the following headlines: *life, bodily health, bodily integrity, senses, imagination, thought, and emotions, practical reason, affiliation, other species, play,* and *control over one's environment*.[133] In comparison with Finnis's set of reasons for actions, Nussbaum does not include excellence at work (she does, play), or harmony with greater than human source of meaning and value.[134] She separates life from bodily health and bodily integrity, and practical reasonableness from 'control over one's environment'. Her categories 'senses, imagination and, thought' (which include some knowledge), and 'emotions' are related to conditions of self-expression such as inner integration, and inner and outer harmony. Her category of affiliation seems roughly parallel to Finnis's friendship. The category 'other species' is a new proposition.

4.1.2. *Manfred Max-Neef: axiological categories*

Manfred Max-Neef, activist and Rector of a Chilean University, has, together with his associates, developed a matrix of human needs. He uses this matrix practically to conduct community exercises in rural and urban areas. The matrix has been used in Argentina, Bolivia, Chile, Colombia, Sweden, and the UK at least. The exercise divides participants into groups of ten individuals, who gather for two days. In 'an intense process of introspective analysis',[135] the groups analyse the needs and 'satisfiers' that have constructive or destructive effects in their society. They describe four kinds of expressions of these needs: being (attributes), having (tools, norms), doing (agency), and interacting (social expressions in time and space). Their analysis is provoked by ten classes of need that Max-Neef has proposed.

For example, one community's interpretation of the human need for 'understanding' might have the expressions found in Table 2.3.[136]

Max-Neef's classification is generic, like Finnis's. He proposes that 'needs can be satisfied at different levels and with different intensities'. Also, needs can be satisfied at the level of the individual, of the social group, or of the environment.[137] Needs which are not adequately satisfied reveal an aspect of human poverty. In his own

[132] Nussbaum (2000a: 70–1).
[133] Nussbaum's list, like the lists of Finnis et al., has evolved over time. See Nussbaum (1993, 1995b, 1997, 1998b, 2000a).
[134] She refers to religion under both senses, imagination, and thought, and affiliation but does not consider it a separate dimension (see 2000a, ch. 3).
[135] 1993: 42.   [136] From Max-Neef (1993: 32–3, table 1).   [137] 1993: 18.

Poverty and Human Development 61

Table 2.3. *Max-Neef: four expressions of the human need for understanding*

Need	Being	Having	Doing	Interacting
Understanding	Critical conscience, receptiveness, curiosity, astonishment, discipline, intuition, rationality	Literature, teachers, method, educational policies, communication policies	Investigate, study, experiment, educate, analyse, meditate	Settings of formative interaction, schools, universities, academies, groups, communities, family

work with groups, Max-Neef devotes considerable attention to the thesis that poverty generates social pathology.

Max-Neef describes several criteria he has used in constructing his classification of ten human needs such that it would be of use to a community wishing to interpret its own situation holistically (see Table 2.4). The criteria indicate that this set of needs *is* intended to be exhaustive: to indicate all dimensions of human need that are universal, even though they may not all be observable in all communities (because there may be unmet needs, or poverties). Max-Neef's list remains 'provisional' and open to modification. Also, the fact that each need must be 'readily recognizable and identifiable as one's own' seems similar to a practical reasoning-based approach.

The ten elements of Max-Neef's matrix are: *subsistence, protection, affection, understanding, participation, leisure, creation, identity*, and *freedom*. Interestingly, they form the closest parallel to Finnis's set: subsistence and protection together parallel life; understanding parallels knowledge; creation and leisure parallel work and play. Participation and identity parallel practical reason. Participation does so in so far as it refers to the valuable process of choice-making which practical reason concerns. Identity does so in so far as it refers to the goodness of choices which in shaping (as every choice does) the identity of the chooser, do so in a way that promotes inner integrity and outer authenticity, or what Finnis calls practical reason/self-direction and self-expression or self-integration.[138] And affection parallels friendship. Max-Neef has no distinct category for religion/transcendence. He writes that he does not think transcendence is a universal need yet, but it may become so as the human race evolves.[139]

4.1.3. *Deepa Narayan et al.: dimensions of well-being*

Deepa Narayan, the Principal Social Development Specialist in the World Bank's Poverty Reduction Group, led a pioneering study of the values of poor persons, which is

---

[138] In Grisez *et al.*'s (1987) formulation, identity might parallel self-expression. See Ch. 4, Sect. 2.4.

[139] Max-Neef (1993: 27). See likewise Schwartz (1992). Max-Neef does not give a complete account of the evolution of human needs nor of processes for recognizing the emergence of new needs. Therefore his conceptual account of needs is incomplete, because it is not clear, for example, how he would judge whether or not 'transcendence' had become a universal need.

Table 2.4. *Max-Neef: criteria for generating a classification of human needs*

The classification must be understandable; the needs listed must be readily recognizable and identifiable as one's own.

The classification must combine scope with specificity; it must arrive at a limited number of needs which can be clearly yet simply labelled but, at the same time, be comprehensive enough to incorporate any fundamental felt need.

The classification must be operational; for every existing or conceivable satisfier[1] one or more of the needs stated must appear as a target-need of the satisfier (in other words, any action or organization must be intelligible by reference to the needs as 'reasons for action').

The classification must be critical; it is not sufficient for the categorization to relate satisfiers to needs. It is essential to detect needs for which no desirable satisfier exists. Also, it is crucial to identify and restrain those satisfiers which inhibit the actualization of needs.

The classification must be propositional; to the extent that it is critical and capable of detecting inadequacies in the relation between the existing satisfiers and the fulfilment of needs, this classification should serve as a trigger mechanism to work out an alternative order capable of generating and encouraging satisfiers for the needs of every man and woman as integral beings.[2]

Note: [1] For Max-Neef, 'It is the satisfiers which define the prevailing mode that a culture of society ascribes to needs. Satisfiers are not only the available economic goods ... Satisfiers may include, among other things, forms of organization, political structures, social practices, subjective conditions, values and norms, spaces, contexts, modes, types of behaviour and attitudes, all of which are in a permanent state of tension between consolidation and change' (1993: 26–7). [2] Ibid. 31.

entitled *Voices of the Poor*. First, in a study subtitled *Can Anyone Hear Us?* Narayan et al. synthesized 81 poverty assessments conducted by the World Bank in 50 countries. Secondly, Narayan, together with Chambers, a pioneer of participatory methodologies at the Institute of Development Studies in Sussex, UK, Shah, and Petesch led a new study subtitled *Crying Out for Change* in 23 countries, all of which followed a standardized participatory methodology. Both studies gathered and analysed data, including subjective data and quotations of the poor, regarding what poor people—people who were identified as poor by other members of the community and by themselves—considered to be dimensions of poverty and dimensions of well-being. Together, both studies represent over 60,000 persons.[140] It is pioneering because it is the only cross-cultural study of this magnitude to date which includes primarily poor, illiterate, and in some cases remote, respondents. As such it is of central interest.

A major finding of the study was that the poor view and experience poverty as multidimensional.[141] In *Crying Out for Change*, 'the starting question was "How do people define well-being or a good quality of life, and ill-being or a bad quality of

---

[140] Roughly 40,000 in the first study; 20,000 in the second.

[141] That statement appears to be a contradiction in terms (if you ask a poor person to define poverty, then implicit in your selection of persons to approach is a definition of poverty already). However, the procedure followed was to inquire in each location who was poor in the village or neighbourhood, and to gather a group of those whom the community considered poor, and discuss with such groups the concepts of well-being and ill-being. Chapter one of *Can Anyone Hear Us?* (2000a) illustrates the dimensions; chapter two of *Crying Out for Change* (2000b) relates how the poor define well-being and ill-being.

life?" Facilitators elicited and used local terms so that participants would feel free to express whatever they felt about a good life and a bad life'.[142] The reports contained both direct quotations and summaries of responses. The qualitative data (translated into English) was then analysed to see what components of 'well-being' and (separately) 'ill-being' emerged in common across climates and cultures, countries and conditions.[143] Substantial areas of commonality were noted by the research team, and described in Table 2.5.

There is remarkable similarity between Finnis's 1987 categories and the *Voices of the Poor* account. However, in *Voices of the Poor,* life was subdivided into material well-being, physical well-being (health), and security—which parallel Finnis's description of the category (bodily health, vigour, and security). Knowledge was not considered a good-in-itself (although human capital in the instrumental sense of being an asset, was). Work was mentioned; play was not. Relationships were clearly valued, and the subcategory of familial relationships was distinguished from wider community relationships. Self-integration, in the sense of psychological well-being—having peace of mind and happiness—was present, as was practical reasonableness/self-direction, in the sense of freedom of choice and action. Harmony with the sacred is present in both accounts but is classified as a subcategory of psychological well-being in *Voices*.

4.1.4. *Shalom Schwartz: universal human values*

Shalom Schwartz holds the Clara and Leon Sznajdermain Chair as Professor of Psychology at the Hebrew University of Jerusalem. He has proposed and revised a 'theory of the universal content and structure of human values' based on empirical cross-cultural research. In developing a framework for the empirical research, Schwartz *et al.* have tried to formulate (i) 'the substantive content' of values, (ii) the 'comprehensiveness' of the values identified, (iii) whether the values have some equivalence of meaning across groups of people, and (iv) whether there is a meaningful and identifiable structure of relations among different values. As Schwartz's work has the most substantive empirical grounding of current values research, it seems productive to consider it in detail.

Schwartz defines values as

desirable transsituational goals, varying in importance, that serve as guiding principles in the life of a person or other social entity. Implicit in this definition of values as goals is that (i) they serve the interests of some social entity, (ii) they can motivate action, giving it direction and emotional intensity, (iii) they function as standards for judging and justifying action, and (iv) they are acquired both through socialization to dominant group values and through the unique learning experiences of individuals.[144]

---

[142] Narayan *et al.* (2000*b*, ch. 2).

[143] The dimensions of ill-being were not mirror images of well-being, although some direct comparisons were, of course, noted (e.g. food). I consider the dimensions of well-being that emerged, because these are the closest thing to a practical reason-based definition of human flourishing by the poor.

[144] (1994: 21). See also Schwartz and Bilsky (1987, 1990), and Schwartz (1992).

64 Poverty and Human Development

Table 2.5. *Narayan et al.: well-being according to the voices of the poor*

Material well-being: having enough
    Food
    Assets
    Work
Bodily well-being: being and appearing well
    Health
    Appearances
    Physical environment
Social well-being:
    Being able to care for, bring up, marry, and settle children
    Self-respect and dignity
    Peace, harmony, good relations in the family/community
Security:
    Civil peace
    A physically safe and secure environment
    Personal physical security
    Lawfulness and access to justice
    Security in old age
    Confidence in the future
Psychological well-being:
    Peace of mind,
    Happiness,
    Harmony (including a spiritual life and religious observance)
Freedom of choice and action

Source: Narayan *et al.* (2000*b*: 25–30, 37–8); see Narayan *et al.* (2000*a*: 32–65) for a similar but not identically categorized discussion on the dimensions of well-being that emerged in the first study. I have chosen to use the 2000*b* set as it is explicitly described as a synthesis of the dimensions of well-being valued by the poor.

In contrast to Rokeach and others, Schwartz argues 'there is a values space that can be carved into (arbitrary) categories that relate to one another on a motivational continuum. The latter is why they form a coherent structure'.[145]

Schwartz has progressively tested his theory in different countries (in all inhabited continents), regions, religions, and language groups, and made adjustments to the list of values along the way. The respondents initially were generally university students and school teachers; more recent data includes thirteen near-representative[146]

---

[145] Personal communication, 18 July 1998.
[146] Near-representative samples represent subgroups in proportions similar to their population proportions, and cover the full range of ages, gender, occupations, and educational levels. But near-representative samples do *not* employ rigorous sampling techniques. The thirteen countries include 'Australia—a near representative sample of Adelaide adults (n = 199); Chile—a representative national

national samples, and eight samples using adolescents. Respondents were presented with a list of about thirty terminal values and about twenty-six instrumental values, identified by two or three brief phrases. Respondents 'set their scale' by choosing and rating the most important value as seven ('of supreme importance'), the least important value as zero. They then rated how each value fared 'as a guiding principle in my life' on a scale from negative one to seven.[147]

Schwartz selected the fifty-six values by drawing on values literature[148] and modified his substantive list of value dimensions in response to evidence from about 200 surveys in sixty-four countries involving well over 60,000 respondents.[149] His current set of comprehensive[150] value dimensions are listed in Table 2.6.

Schwartz asserts, in defence of this list, that '[i]t is possible to classify virtually all the items found in lists of specific values from different cultures ... into one of these ten motivational types of values'.[151] Schwartz also tested an eleventh value, 'the goal of finding meaning in life' or spirituality, but found that, as it is not derivable from universal human requirements[152] it may not be recognized across cultures.

Schwartz's dimensions do not identify life (in the sense of health and reproduction—security is mentioned). Achievement appears again as a value that may parallel accomplishment or 'excellence in work and play'. Pleasure and stimulation appear again, and there are new suggestions—power, conformity, tradition, and universalism—that have not been encountered in previous lists.

---

sample (n = 304); China—a near representative sample of Shanghai factory workers (n = 208); East Germany—a near representative sample of Chemnitz adults (n = 295); Finland—two representative national samples averaged (n = 3,120); France—a representative national sample (n = 2,339); Israel—a near representative sample of Jerusalem adults (n = 170); Italy—a representative national sample (n = 210); Japan—a representative sample of Osaka adults (n = 207), the Netherlands—a representative national sample of employed males (n = 240); Russia—a representative sample of Moscow adults (n = 189); South Africa—a representative sample of employed Whites in Midrand (n = 249); West Germany—a near representative sample of adults from several states (n = 213)'. Quoted from Schwartz, personal communication, 19 May 1999.

[147] 7: of supreme importance; 6: very important; 5, 4: unlabelled; 3: important; 2, 1: unlabelled; 0: not important; −1: opposed to my values. Subsequently Schwartz designed an instrument specifically for less educated populations. This new instrument, called the Portraits Questionnaire (PQ), presents brief descriptions of 29 different people. Each portrait consists of two sentences that characterize the person's goals, aspirations, and wishes, all expressive of a single value type. The PQ has thus far been used only in Uganda; see Munene and Schwartz (2001).

[148] Schwartz cites Rokeach (1973), Braithwaite and Law (1985), Chinese Culture Connection (1987), Hofstede (1980), Levy and Guttman (1974), Munro (1985), and the 'examination of texts on comparative religion and from consultations with Muslim and Druze Scholars' (1992: 17).

[149] Schwartz (1994) summarizes progress until that date. His work also cross-references other values theories and research. The 64 countries include two African, two North American, four Latin American, eight Asian, two South Asian, eight East European, one Middle Eastern, fourteen European, two Mediterranean, Australia, and New Zealand.

[150] For an explanation of the test of comprehensiveness see (1992: 37).

[151] 1994: 23.

[152] Schwartz identifies three universal requirements: needs of individuals as biological organisms, requisites of coordinated social interaction, and requirements for the smooth functioning and survival of groups. Discussion of the empirical findings of spirituality is in Schwartz (1992).

66   *Poverty and Human Development*

Table 2.6. *Shalom Schwartz: universal human values*

Power	social status and prestige, control or dominance over people and resources
Achievement	personal success through demonstrating competence according to social standards
Hedonism	pleasure and sensuous gratification for oneself
Stimulation	excitement, novelty, and challenge in life
Self-direction	independent thought and action—choosing, creating, exploring
Universalism	understanding, appreciation, tolerance, and protection for the welfare of all people and for nature
Benevolence	preservation and enhancement of the welfare of people with whom one is in frequent personal contact
Tradition	respect, commitment, and acceptance of the customs and ideas that traditional culture or religion provide
Conformity	restraint of actions, inclinations, and impulses likely to upset or harm others and violate social expectations or norms
Security	safety, harmony, and stability of society, of relationships, and of self

As these dimensions suggest, Schwartz has tested and rejected Rokeach's separation of terminal and instrumental (mode of conduct) values.[153] This might make his work more difficult to compare with Finnis's than previous writers, because the dimensions named above conflate principles of practical reasonableness and basic human goods.[154] Yet Schwartz claims that *each* of these value areas contains both terminal and instrumental aspects. If that is the case then one could try to imagine and consider the claimed 'terminal' aspect of each dimension (for example, universalism and benevolence must relate somehow to goods of affiliation/relationship with people and other species).[155]

4.1.5. *Robert Cummins: quality of life domains*

Robert Cummins, Professor of Psychology at Deakin University, Australia, has surveyed theoretical and empirical literature regarding the 'quality of life' and classified the terminology within them into 'domains of subjective well-being'.[156] Domains of subjective well-being are generally used on a questionnaire that would ask 'how satisfied are you with *domain*?' Initially, Cummins reviewed 27 different accounts of 'quality of life' domains—distinct accounts from those Schwartz considered[157]—and found that a clear majority supported five of Cummins's seven domains; 22 per cent and 30 per cent supported the remaining domains of safety and community, respectively.

---

[153] See (1992: 15–6, 36–7). The validity of his hypothesis to test the terminal–instrumental distinction might be challenged, but discussion of these procedures lies well outside the boundaries of this chapter.
[154] See especially Finnis's account of the principles in Chang (1997 at sect. IV).
[155] Alternatively, one could consider the 30 terminal values tested—see Schwartz (1992: 60–1).
[156] Cummins (1996).
[157] The seminal work in social indicators research was Andrews and Withey (1976), who identified 29 'concern clusters' for social indicators research (1976: 38–9); this literature develops their work.

Subsequently, Cummins 'tested' his seven domains in the following way. Over 1,500 articles relating to quality of life were identified. Cummins constructed five criteria for allowing data on the quality of life to be included in his study (i.e. a minimum of three domains, broad range, happiness criteria were excluded, etc.), and thirty-two studies of the 1,500 fulfilled these criteria. Together these thirty-two studies—overwhelmingly Western—proposed 173 names of 'domains' for quality of life indicators (the aggregate number of domains was 351, but there were some repetitions). Cummins classified each named domain into one of the seven categories or left it unclassified as a residual.[158] His work was checked by two colleagues, and differences of opinion were resolved by discussion. Cummins found that 68 per cent of the 173 values domains (83 per cent of the 351 domains mentioned) could be sorted into seven headings.[159] He subsequently developed a Comprehensive Quality of Life survey instrument, consisting of subjective and objective measures of quality of life in each of the seven domains. This instrument, which can be downloaded from http://acqol.deakin.edu.au/instruments/ComQol_A5.rtf, is based on the following propositions: (i) quality of life (QOL) can be described in both objective (O) and subjective (S) terms; (ii) each objective (OQOL) and subjective (SQOL) axis is composed of seven domains: material well-being, health, productivity, intimacy, safety, place in community, emotional well-being; (iii) the measurement of each OQOL domain is achieved by obtaining an aggregate score based on the measurement of three objective indices relevant to that domain. For example, 'material well-being' is measured by an aggregate score of income, type of accommodation, and personal possessions; (iv) the measurement of each SQOL domain is achieved by obtaining a satisfaction score of that domain which is weighted by the perceived importance of the domain for the individual. Thus, SQOL $= \Sigma$ (Domain satisfaction $\times$ domain importance).

The seven headings are *material well-being, health, productivity, intimacy/friendship, safety, community, and emotional well-being*. Material well-being, health, and safety clearly parallel Finnis's 'life' dimension; productivity may be a partial outcome of 'excellence in work and play'; intimacy/friendship parallels Finnis's friendship; emotional well-being is a sub-component, perhaps, of practical reasonableness (harmony of thoughts and feelings); the category community parallels friendship or sociability. Missing from Cummins's synthesis (not from his sources, nor from Andrews and Withey) is knowledge, practical reasonableness in the sense of meaningful choice, and harmony with a greater than human source of meaning and value.

Cummins aggregates and consolidates empirical work entirely on the basis of consensus rather than reasoned argument, hence provides a taxonomy of some quality of life literature. He then uses his taxonomy to construct a comprehensive Quality of Life survey instrument, for use across cultures, and has different forms for children aged 11 to 18, and for the mentally impaired. Also, as the form of the subjective question 'How satisfied are you with X?' suggests, elements on Cummins's list have to be readily intelligible domains that are appropriate for public discussion.

---

[158] A table of these terms and the residual appears in Cummins (1996: 309).   [159] 1996: 309.

4.1.6. Maureen Ramsay: universal psychological needs

A similar exercise in list consolidation was done by Maureen Ramsay. Ramsay was interested in identifying 'objective and essential' physical and mental health needs prior to developing empirical indicators for these needs and identifying means to satisfy needs or restore natural mental functioning. She studied the psychological needs identified by nine authors (these are again different from Rokeach and Andrews's streams): Brentano (1908), Maslow (1943), Fromm (1956), Nielsen (1977), Lane (1969), Davies (1963), Packard (1960), Galtung (1980), and Krech et al. (1969). Ramsay classified their lists into six categories of needs: *physical survival; sexual needs; security; love and relatedness; esteem and identity; and self-realization* based entirely on convergence, rather than reasoned argument.[160] She draws mainly on clinical studies to substantiate that each category is a 'need'.[161]

Ramsay's work is included because it draws on a literature that was known to, and has informed, the basic needs tradition in economic development.[162] Her approach, like Cummins's, classifies lists of need according to the author's taxonomy—which is a distinct exercise from the synthesis project to be discussed shortly (Sect. 4.3), but is useful to study.

4.1.7. Doyal and Gough: basic human needs

Doyal and Gough, in *A Theory of Need* proposed to develop a concept of need that is grounded—both philosophically[163] and practically—with respect to the indicator debates and other debates in the social sciences. Their theory describes universal needs as 'preconditions for human action and interaction'[164] and concludes that needs 'can be shown to exist, that individuals have a right to the optimal satisfaction of these needs and that all human liberation should be measured by assessing the degree to which such satisfaction has occurred'.[165] In particular, they propose exactly two universal 'basic needs'—physical health and autonomy. Physical health is conceived 'transculturally in a negative way. If you wish to lead an active and successful life in your own terms, it is in your objective interest to satisfy your basic need to optimise your life expectancy and to avoid serious physical disease and illness conceptualised in biomedical terms. This applies to everyone, everywhere.'[166] Autonomy of agency is expressed 'with reference to [individuals'] capacity to formulate consistent aims and strategies which they believe to be in their interest and their attempts to put them into practice in the activities which they engage'.[167] Each sub-component of the needs is further defined. Doyal and Gough specify eleven 'intermediate needs', involving culturally invariant characteristics of commodities which usually generate desirable capabilities.

---

[160] Ramsay (1992: 149–78).

[161] For example, 'Spitz (1949) made a comparative study of infants raised in nurseries by their own mothers and those raised in a foundling home. 100 per cent of the first group survived and developed into normal healthy adults. In the second group there was a 37 per cent mortality rate by the end of the second year, and those who did survive were more apathetic or hyperexcitable' (Ramsay 1992: 154).

[162] A similar exercise was done by Carol Ryff (1989).

[163] They draw on David Braybrooke, Raymond Plant, Alan Gewirth, David Wiggins, and Amartya Sen.

[164] 1991.   [165] 1991: 3–4.   [166] 1991: 59.   [167] 1991: 59–60.

Table 2.7. *Doyal and Gough 1993: intermediate needs*

1. Nutritional food/water
2. Protective housing
3. Work
4. Physical environment
5. Health care
6. Security in childhood
7. Significant primary relationships
8. Physical security
9. Economic security
10. Safe birth control/childbearing
11. Basic education

These needs are distinct from the definitions of 'dimensions' in two interesting ways. First, Doyal and Gough are deliberately limiting their scope to *preconditions* of well-being, not well-being itself. Their project, then, is fundamentally different from the current one, for it did not intend to identify the full range of relevant areas of well-being. Their approach is none the less included as a representative of the kinds of 'basic needs' which many others have also put forward.[168]

A second difference of this approach is that basic needs are defined such that their fulfilment is normative. While Doyal and Gough would say that the 'satisfiers' of these needs may vary widely, they argue that needs themselves can be specified (at varying levels of specificity—a need to be without cholera; a need for 'adequate' housing) *without* consultation of the related population. Furthermore, because these needs are understood to be the 'preconditions' of a fulfilled life, there is always a normative duty, they argue, to fulfil them.

4.1.8. *Ronald Inglehart: world values survey findings*

Ronald Inglehart is one of a number of writers who have studied value priorities in societies that are undergoing modernization. That is, he looks not at the values that societies hold overall, but the relative weights that they ascribe to different values. His central thesis is that 'economic, cultural, and political change go together in coherent patterns that are changing the world in predictable ways'.[169] 'Traditional', 'modern', and 'postmodern' societies have different value patterns—different value priorities. This is not to say that cultures will become identical—

we see no reason to expect that the Chinese will stop using chopsticks in the foreseeable future, or that Brazilians will learn to polka. But certain cultural, value and political changes do seem to be logically linked with the dynamics of a core syndrome of modernization, involving

---

[168] See the complete discussion of basic needs in Ch. 5.   [169] 1997: 7.

urbanization, industrialization, economic development, occupational specialization, and the spread of mass literacy.[170]

His book *Modernization and Postmodernization* uses the World Values Surveys that provide data (roughly 60,000 respondents) from 43 societies representing, he claims, 70 per cent of the world's population[171] to test the relationship between cultural norms and economic and political processes.

In particular, he tracks a shift in emphasis on certain values as countries modernize. For example the World Values Survey measures value priorities for materialism versus postmaterialism using the following question.

There is a lot of talk these days about what the aims of this country should be for the next ten years. On this card are listed some of the goals which different people would give top priority. Would you please say which one of these you, yourself, consider the most important? And which one would be the next most important?[172]

The respondent is then shown three cards, each having four items on them, two of which correspond to the hypothesized 'materialist' values, the other two to 'postmaterialist' priorities. If both of their selections are from the 'materialist' column, they are labelled materialist; if one from each, they are considered 'mixed'; if both are postmaterialist they are considered postmaterialists.

Inglehart also tries to predict value changes across time in domains such as attitudes towards sexuality, towards faith, towards the family, and towards governmental authorities. The World Values Survey Data 1981–90 accurately showed a change towards more sexual permissiveness (attitudes towards homosexuality, abortion, and divorce are more permissive), less religiosity (fewer said that God was very important in their lives), but more spirituality (more said that they often think about the meaning and purpose of life), and less emphasis on governmental authority. However, in contrast to Inglehart's prediction, the importance of a nuclear family (agreement that child needs a two-parent home to be raised happily) seems to have increased rather than decreased, perhaps because of the problems that are now evident with children from one-parent families.

There are significant difficulties with Inglehart's claim that postmaterialist values are more evident in developed countries, and with his claim that the sample represents 70 per cent of the world's population. The first claim has been disputed, for example, by Trump (1991) and Duch and Taylor (1993). The LDCs included in the 43 countries are China ($n=1,000$), India ($n=2,500$), and Nigeria ($n=939$), Brazil ($n=1,782$), Mexico ($n=1,531$), Chile ($n=1,500$), South Africa ($n=2,736$), and Argentina ($n=1,001$) and the sampling frames in *all* these countries are strongly

---

[170] 1997: 69.
[171] Argentina, Austria, Belarus, Belgium, Brazil, Bulgaria, Canada, Chile, China, the Czech Republic, Denmark, Estonia, Finland, France, Germany (with separate samples in the East and West regions), Great Britain, Hungary, Iceland, India, Ireland, Northern Ireland, Italy, Japan, Slovakia, South Korea, Latvia, Lithuania, Mexico, greater Moscow, the Netherlands, Nigeria, Norway, Poland, Portugal, Russia, Romania, Slovenia, South Africa, Spain, Sweden, Switzerland, Turkey, and the United States.
[172] Inglehart (1997: 108).

Table 2.8. *Inglehart values*

Materialist	Postmaterialist
Economic security	*Self-expression, aesthetics*
Rising prices	More say on the job
Economic growth	More humane society
Stable economy	More say in government
Physical security	Ideas count
Maintain order	Freedom of speech
Fight crime	Beautify cities and countryside
Strong defence forces	

biased to urban (90 per cent) and literate respondents. The survey instrument (a face to face questionnaire) also seemed to have difficulties in bluntness. For example, the 'trust question' is: 'Generally speaking, would you say that most people can be trusted or that you can't be too careful in dealing with people?' (1) Most people can be trusted. (2) Can't be too careful . . . More than one respondent might find these choices unsatisfactory—for example, because it does not allow respondents to distinguish from trusting members of their family/clan/network from others. Furthermore Inglehart argues that (i) 'traditional' and (ii) 'modernizing' societies *don't* attach priority to friends, leisure, women, tolerance, ecology—rather they prioritize religion that maintains the status quo, or economic growth. According to Inglehart only *after* a society attains economic security through modernization and moves to the post-materialist, postmodern phase, can it worry about wider aspects of 'well-being'. This assertion is in tension with, for example, the data from these case studies or from Narayan *et al.* (2000*a*), which found relationships to be a key dimension of well-being among the very poor.

Inglehart's materialist categories of economic and physical security have direct parallels to Finnis's categories of life/health/security. His post-materialist categories directly parallel Finnis's on self-expression, practical reason, and meaningful work. The other categories of value priorities he studies—family and faith—directly parallel Finnis's basic values of sociability and harmony with the divine. The category of deference to authority seems to be heterogeneous and contains both what the next chapter will refer to as principles of practical reasonableness, and aspects of Finnis's basic values such as relationship, or security.

4.1.9. *Mozaffar Qizilbash: prudential values*

Qizilbash has incorporated the recent work of James Griffin on prudential values into development ethics, to propose a list of prudential values, comprising 'everything that makes a person's life go better'.[173] There are two kinds of prudential values: 'core' values which are recognized by everyone, and non-core values which 'may play a part in some people's lives but not in others' but which are 'generally recognized as

---

[173] (1996*a*: 155). This account is developed in (1996*a*,*b*, 1997*a*, 1998*b*).

72   *Poverty and Human Development*

Table 2.9. *Qizilbash: prudential values for development*

1. Health/nutrition/sanitation/rest/shelter/security
2. Literacy/basic intellectual and physical capacities
3. Self-respect and aspiration
4. Positive freedom, autonomy or self-determination
5. Negative freedom or liberty
6. Enjoyment
7. Understanding or knowledge
8. Significant relations with others and some participation in social life
9. Accomplishment (of the sort that gives life point/weight)

prudentially valuable'.[174] Qizilbash argues that this approach nets a 'consensual' 'culturally non-relative' account of human development that is open to different cultural specifications. It is consensual because each value 'is a candidate for prudential value ... for any human being, in any culture, with any personal conception of the good or any plan of life'.[175] It is culturally non-relative, being applicable to rich as well as poor countries, and applicable to countries with different *moral* values. Qizilbash's particular list of nine values (see Table 2.9) contains instrumental and intrinsically valuable goods, and development involves 'having more of the elements of prudential value'.

In comparison with Finnis's values, Qizilbash's blend the instrumental and the intrinsically valued, and are, as Nussbaum's, more concrete. Still, Qizilbash has parallels for health, for knowledge, for practical reason, for friendship. His categories of liberty and enjoyment are, in Finnis's view, not dimensions of well-being *per se*. His category of 'self-respect and aspiration' and of 'accomplishment' are new propositions.

4.2. *Method of analysis*

As may be apparent, the description and consideration of even as few as nine different lists raises more issues than can be adequately addressed, and there would be a number of ways of organizing a discussion about points raised.

One might, at this point, try to establish a synthetic list of basic dimensions of human development based on the evidence so far. I do not do so here, for the following reasons.[176] First, the lists here are partly biased to Western sources; a synthesis exercise should ideally take into account a much wider literature. This is not because Western sources are *necessarily* biased (many use cross-cultural data); it is because until one compares their accounts with those *analysed in* other cultures, one will not know whether or not they are. Secondly, as the authors have shown, the lists may vary slightly depending upon the project to which they are applied. Thirdly and most importantly, even if one did propose a synthesis it would need recurrent (i) empirical testing, and (ii) participatory processes of discussion and deliberation. As Sen's capability approach gives a central role to others' agency, it would seem appropriate to leave

[174] (1996*a*: 155). This account is developed in (1996*a,b*, 1997*a*, 1998*b*).   [175] 1996*a*: 156.
[176] See Alkire (2001), where I have worked through to a rough synthesis using a similar set of lists.

that rounding out to others—especially because there will always be some residual arbitrariness in any working set of dimensions, even if it proves useful, which is what authors have gestured to when they point out that their categories are 'provisional', and that there is no 'magic number' of elements. Finally, lists are useful not if they are universally acclaimed but if they are effectively deployed.

What I do hope to show is that such a set of dimensions *could be* suggested and would be of operational value. For example, the impact assessment of Chapter 6 used a modification of Finnis's list, comprising life, knowledge, meaningful work/play, relationships, religion, self-integration or inner peace, participation or practical reason, art and aesthetic appreciation, and the environment.

4.3. *How to add or remove a dimension*

It would be well to be clear on the grounds on which a set of dimensions might be distilled from, and/or supported by, the very different kinds of research and investigation represented by these studies. In seeking to distil a set of dimensions we seek to assess the adequacy of Finnis's *actual set* of basic reasons for action against his *definition* of basic reasons for action that I have called dimensions of human development. His definition of basic reasons, recall, is substantively different from the definitions different authors used in their lists. For this distillation, some procedures for inquiry may be established. First, evidently this approach will differ considerably from the taxonomy/consolidation exercises of Cummins and Ramsay, because the *kind* of category of interest—the level of generality if you will—has been chosen; categories that were not basic reasons for action would need to be articulated as reasons for action in order to engage this discussion. Secondly, while the overlapping consensus of a number of writers and/or empirical studies about the validity of a certain dimension may indicate quite strongly that a proposed new dimension be carefully considered (the hypothesis being that consensus reflects convergence on basic goods after a process of practical reasoning), consensus is not a *sufficient* basis for any proposition to modify or append the current list because consensus might eventuate for other reasons than the one hypothesized above. Still, empirical (and theoretical) studies of the dimensions is a constructive avenue for research, and Table 2.12 presents thirty-nine sets of human needs drawn from various sources that may be worth considering in this regard. Thirdly, it must be stated clearly that there will be a different kind of validity to the different formulations needs/values/capabilities—such as the formulations of the nine authors sketched here—and a judgement that a particular category is or is not a basic reason for action in Finnis's sense *does not entail any judgement as to this category's appropriateness or otherwise in the author's own practical undertaking*. Fourthly, a critical assessment of the empirical studies which are claimed to support particular lists is outside the scope of this discussion.

In 'Practical Principles, Moral Truth and Ultimate Ends' Grisez, Boyle, and Finnis outline criteria for dialectically evaluating candidates to be added or deleted from their set of basic reasons for action. Summaries of these criteria are found in Table 2.10 (I have substituted the word 'dimension' for basic reason for action or basic good).

Table 2.10. *Finnis et al.: criteria for dimensions of human flourishing*

The dimension must be such that it could count as a reason for action (not e.g. a fact about what I am thinking). Food is not precisely a reason for action so could not be a dimension. The food-related reason for action might be 'friendship' (if you are cooking for me or giving me sweets) or simply nutrition, sustenance, and therefore 'life'.

The dimension must be irreducible—dimensions are reasons for action which need no further reason. The dimensions must not include items which are a subset of some other valuable and basic reason for acting. For example, Julia may do good deeds because she wants 'a good reputation'. But if Julia were asked again, she may figure out one or two 'more basic' reasons she did good deeds (e.g. to feel good about herself—to be 'self-integrated'—and also to be thought well of, so that she had good 'relationships' with other people). I cannot know what Julia would come up with, but if she could find simpler reasons for wanting a good reputation, then 'a good reputation' is not a dimension of human development.

The dimension must represent complete reasons for acting—i.e. it cannot be a basic motive (pleasure, pain) which is valuable only when its pursuit coheres with the pursuit of a valuable reason. Also, the dimension must be intrinsically rather than only instrumentally valuable ('only' is an important qualification because some basic items—like life or knowledge—will also have an instrumental dimension).

The dimensions are not virtues: dimensions of human flourishing represent the basic values people are seeking when they 'be and do and have and interact'—morally or immorally. They are neither virtues nor personal qualities (gentleness, self-respect).

Note: This simple method of evaluation is proposed and defended in Grisez *et al.* (1987: 111–13).

The criteria above suggest a few of the *kinds* of categories proposed by some other authors that *could not enter*. I will sketch a few of these.

1. Doyal and Gough, Qizilbash, and at times Nussbaum include items in their sets that are argued (by them) to be instrumentally 'rather than' intrinsically valuable. This approach would propose that *all* dimensions of capability be intrinsically valuable—be understandable as 'human ends' (although they may clearly also be intelligibly instrumentalities to other ends).
2. The elements of the set would be values that provide general *reasons* people give for doing what they do. The description of some elements is quite particular (Nussbaum, Qizilbash). The proposed approach would argue for a simple, short explanation of each dimension that referred the reader or participant to the 'reason for acting', and allowed them to recognize, define, and choose examples or instances of it themselves (see Schwartz, Finnis, Max-Neef). For example, we value affection, but the *reason* we do so may be related to the goodness of deep personal friendships. Also, a dimension would be a reason for action rather than a heterogeneous cluster of instantiations; Qizilbash's health, nutrition, sanitation, rest, shelter, security category might be valued because these things conduce to life taken as an end in itself (as well as being instrumental to further ends).

Table 2.11. *Dimensions of human development*

Grisez et al. (1987) Basic human values	Nussbaum (2000) Central human capabilities	Max-Neef (1993) Axiological categories	Narayan et al. (2000a) Dimensions of well-being	Schwartz (1994) Human values
Bodily life—health vigour and safety Knowledge Skilful performance in work and play Friendship Practical reasonableness Self-integration Harmony with ultimate source of reality	Life Bodily health Bodily integrity Senses, thought, imagination Emotions Practical reason Affiliation Other species Play Control over one's environment	Subsistence Protection Affection Understanding Participation Leisure Creation Identity Freedom	Material well-being Bodily well-being Social well-being Security Psychological well-being Freedom of choice and action	Power Achievement Hedonism Stimulation Self-direction Universalism Benevolence Tradition Conformity Security

Cummins (1996) Domains of life satisfaction	Ramsay (1992) Human needs	Doyal and Gough (1993) Intermediate needs	Qizilbash (1996a) Prudential values for development
Material well-being Health Productivity Intimacy/friendship Safety Community Emotional well-being	Physical survival Sexual needs Security Love and relatedness Esteem and identity Self-realization	Nutritional food/water Protective housing Work Physical environment Health care Security in childhood Significant primary relationships Physical security Economic security Safe birth control/childbearing Basic education	Health/nutrition/sanitation/rest/shelter/security Literacy/basic intellectual and physical capacities Self-respect and aspiration Positive freedom, autonomy or self-determination Negative freedom or liberty Enjoyment Understanding or knowledge Significant relations with others and some participation in social life Accomplishment (the sort that gives life point/weight)

3. The focus on reasons would be carried through the synthesis itself. Rather than imitating the *taxonomic* exercise conducted by Cummins and Ramsay (valuable as this may be in their context) the full elements from all of the different candidate lists would need to be consolidated with respect to the *reasons for action* they exemplified.
4. The separation between the dimensions of value and ethics or moral obligations is such that the dimensions are not themselves *automatically* human rights or needs which have a one-to-one relation to political obligation, or virtues we should strive to live out or write into constitutions. Rather, they are the *ingredients* from which (together with procedural principles such as equity, and attention to commitments and identity—see Ch. 3, Sect. 5) normative commitments can be generated. This distinguishes dimensions from Nussbaum's or Qizilbash's which do all of this in one step.
5. Any elements that were parts of each other or of one/several other dimensions could be expressed in terms of a combination of other dimensions, making the final list irreducible. So, one might suggest that Cummins's 'productivity' is a subset of Max-Neef's 'creation' and Finnis's 'work and play'. There will be an element of arbitrariness in this process, but it may be less than appears at first sight.

The actual 'name' of the dimension is less important than the *reason* it gestures to. In fact several names might be employed, because different people may have different resonances with them and also several words might better indicate the range of reasons indicated by the dimension (e.g. friendship and sociability).

I have tried to show the outlines of a satisfactory account of dimensions of human development around which operational consensus could form. Some preliminary objections—for example, that the project is impossible—can be rejected. Some features of the dimensions—their generality, their basis in practical reason, and their relationship to morality and obligation—can be articulated. The actual task of coming up with a definitive list is not undertaken, although a particular list is employed in the case studies (see Ch. 6, Sect. 3.2.2).

4.4. *Conclusion*

Earlier we noted that Sen's reservations against the specification of basic capabilities were that such a list might be (i) overspecified, (ii) irrelevant, (iii) overly normative, or (iv) pertaining to only one metaphysical outlook. The dimensions proposed here avoid these charges. In simple terms, this account addresses the problem of overspecification by proposing generic dimensions, rather than needs or virtues or capabilities, that represent the *most basic* reasons for action which are incommensurable in kind (recognizing also that there will be incommensurabilities within expressions of a single dimension). This account addresses the problem of irrelevance by establishing those dimensions on the basis of practical reason—dimensions which persons can come to recognize they or others *already are using* as reasons for action (the evidence in Chapter 7 also suggests these may not be irrelevant). This account addresses the normativity question by suggesting that these dimensions are reasons for action which pertain to moral and immoral actions alike; hence their description *alone* does not allow *any* moral conclusions regarding trade-offs.[177] The 'metaphysical' response is straightforward because of the epistemological basis of the dimensions in (anyone's) practical reason, not in deductive or empirical proof: the identification of basic reasons for action which are valid cross-culturally commits one to a broadly realist ethic (in line with the capability approach), although not, on the face of it, to a *single* metaphysics.

The above discussion, and the identification of dimensions of poverty reduction, most exemplifications of which are not the direct objectives of economic investent, are valuable in throwing light on all of the *possible* angles of discussion on poverty reduction, and on the respective roles of the market and political and institutional systems in promoting it.[178] But it is evident that (i) different instantiations of different dimensions are resource-dependent to different degrees; (ii) the data available on aspects of the dimensions, and their comparability, varies dramatically, and (iii) individuals and cultures pursue these dimensions in radically different ways, and (iv) that in order for poverty reduction to become an operational *objective* in the sense of a feasible goal for which planning, monitoring, and evaluation frameworks can be designed, heroic specification is required. In the spirit of the capability approach, the assumptions on the basis of which this specification takes place should be collaborative, visible, defensible, and revisable. If the process of public discussion and the emergence of consensus is important, then a given fixed list cannot have some irresistible or definitive status.

---

[177] As these are 'basic reasons for action' which are recognized by practical reason as being 'valuable' (not necessarily moral), then one might suspect an action which pursues one of them to be 'better than' an action which pursues none. But this judgement of 'better' cannot meaningfully be made: consider Thomás who, instead of sitting in the fog of depression and gloom, goes out in search of fresh bread, and steals it from an urchin to whom the baker had just given a warm loaf. In order to assess the 'goodness' or 'badness' of this action *even for Thomás* (who may sink further into gloom because of his action later), additional principles are required.

[178] Kenneth Arrow (1997) again stresses the need for co-ordination of such systems to protect 'invaluable goods'.

Table 2.12. *Thirty-nine lists of dimensions of human development from different disciplines*

Agenda 21 Dimensions of development	Allardt (1993) Comparative Scandanavian welfare study	Andrews and Withey (1976) Concern clusters	Argyle (1991) Causes of 'joy'	Braybrooke (1987) Needs
Peace as the foundation	*Having*	Media	Social contacts with friends, or others in close relationship	Life-supporting relation to environment
The economy as the engine of progress	Economic resources	Societal standards	Sexual activity	Food and water
The environment as the basis of sustainability	Housing	Weather	Success, achievement	Excretion
Justice as a pillar of society	Employment	Government	Physical activity, exercise, sport	Exercise
Democracy as good governance	Working conditions	Safety	Nature, reading, music	Periodic rest, including sleep
	Health	Community	Food and drink	Whatever (else) is indispensible to preserving the body intact
	Education	House	Alcohol	Companionship
	Loving	Money		Education
	Attachments/contacts with local community, family and kin, friends	Job		Social acceptance and recognition
	Associations work-mates	Services		Sexual activity
	Being	Recreation facilities		Freedom from harrassment
	Self-determination	Traditions		Recreation
	Political activities	Marriage		
	Leisure-time activities	Children		
	Meaningful work	Family relations		
	Opportunities to enjoy nature	Treatment		
		Imagination		
		Acceptance		
		Self-adjustment		
		Virtues		
		Accomplishment		
		Friends		
		Religion		
		Health		
		Own education		
		Beneficence		
		Independence		
		Mobility		
		Beauty		

Brentano (1973) Needs	Chambers (1995) Dimensions of deprivation	Cummins (1996) Domains of life satisfaction	Davitt (1968) Value areas	Diener and Biswas (2000) Twelve life domains	Doyal and Gough (1993) Intermediate needs	Grisez, Finnis, Boyle (1987) Basic Human Values
Maintenance of life—food, clothes, rest, or recreation	Poverty	Material well-being	Life and reproduction	Morality	Nutritional food/water	Bodily life—health vigour and safety
Sexual needs	Social inferiority	Health	Protection and security	Food	Protective housing	Knowledge
Recognition by others	Isolation	Productivity	Title (Property)	Family	Work	Skilful performance in work and play
Provision for well-being after death	Physical weakness	Intimacy/friendship	Sexual union	Friendship	Physical environment	Friendship
Amusement	Vulnerability	Safety	Decision-making	Material resources	Health care	Practical reasonableness
Provision for future	Seasonality	Community	Responsibility	Intelligence	Security in childhood	Self-integration
Healing	Powerlessness	Emotional well-being	Knowledge	Romantic relationship	Significant primary relationships	Harmony with ultimate source of reality
Cleanliness	Humiliation		Art	Physical appearance	Physical security	
Education in Science and Art			Communication	Self	Economic security	
Need to create			Meaning	Income	Safe birth control/ childbearing	
				Housing	Basic education	
				Social life		

Table 2.12. (cont.)

Fromm (1956) Human needs	Galtung (1980)	Galtung (1994) Human needs	Goulet (1995) Values sought by all	Griffin (1996) Prudential values
Relatedness Transcendence-creativity Rootedness Sense of identity and individuality The need for a frame of orientation and devotion	Input-output (nutrition, water, air) Climate balance with nature (clothing, shelter) Health Community Symbolic interaction and reflection (education)	**Survival needs:** *to avoid violence* individual and collective **Well-being needs:** *to avoid misery* nutrition, water, air movement, excretion, sleep, sex, protection against climate, against diseases, against heavy, degrading, boring work, self-expression, dialogue, education **Identity needs:** *to avoid alienation* creativity, praxis, work, self-actuation, realizing potentials, well-being, happiness, joy, being active subject, not passive client/object, challenge and new experiences, affection, love, sex, friends, offspring, spouse, roots, belongingness, networks, support, esteem, understanding social forces, social transparency, partnership with nature, sense of purpose, of meaning, closeness to the transcendental, transpersonal **Freedom needs:** *choice* in receiving/expressing information and opinion of people/places to visit and be visited, in consciousness formation, in mobilization, confrontation, occupation, job, spouse, goods/services, way of life	Life sustenance Esteem Freedom	Accomplishment Components of human existence Deciding for oneself/agency Minimum material goods Limbs and senses that work Freedom from pain and anxiety Liberty Understanding Enjoyment Deep personal relations

Krech, Crutchfield, and Livson (1969) Human motives	Lane (1969) Needs which inform political behaviour	Lasswell (1969) Human values	Maslow (1943) Instinctive and universal needs	Max-Neef (1993) Axiological categories	Murray (1938) Needs	Myers and Diener (1995) Correlates of high subjective well-being
Survival and security and satisfaction and stimulation needs: • pertaining to the body • pertaining to relations with the environment • pertaining to relations with other people • pertaining to self	Cognitive needs—curiosity, learning, understanding Consistency needs—emotional, logical, veridical Social needs (affiliation, being linked) Moral needs Esteem needs Personality integration and identity needs Agression expression needs Autonomy needs Self-actualization needs Need for instrumental guides to reality, object appraisal	Skill Affection Respect Rectitude Power Enlightenment Wealth Well-being	Physical needs Safety needs Affective needs Esteem Self-actualization	Subsistence Protection Affection Understanding Participation Leisure Creation Identity Freedom	Achievement Sentience Sex Aggression Dominance Succourance	Certain traits: (a) self-esteem (b) personal control (c) optimism (d) extraversion Strong supportive relationships Challenging work Religious faith

Table 2.12. (cont.)

Narayan (2000) Dimensions of well-being	Nielsen (1977) Central elements of human need	Nussbaum (2000) Central human functional capabilities	Packard (1960) Eight hidden needs towards which marketing theory is orientated	Qizilbash (1996) Prudential values for development	Ramsay (1992) Human needs	Rawls (1971) Primary goods
Material well-being	Love	Life	Emotional security	Health/nutrition/sanitation/rest/shelter/security	Physical survival	Rights
Bodily well-being	Companionship	Bodily health	Self-esteem	Literacy/basic intellectual and physical capacities	Sexual needs	Liberties
Social well-being	Security	Bodily integrity	Ego gratification	Self-respect and aspiration	Security	Opportunities
Security	Protection	Senses, imagination, thought	Recognition and status	Positive freedom, autonomy or self-determination	Love and relatedness	Income and wealth
Psychological well-being	A sense of community	Emotions	Creativity	Negative freedom or liberty	Esteem and identity	Freedom of movement and choice of occupation
Freedom of choice and action	Meaningful work	Practical reason	Love	Enjoyment	Self-realization	Social bases of self-respect
	Adequate sustenance	Affiliation	Sense of belonging	Understanding or knowledge		Powers and prerogatives of offices and positions of responsibility
	Shelter	Other species	Power	Significant relations with others and some participation in social life		
	Sexual gratification	Play	A sense of immortality	Accomplishment (sort that gives life point/weight)		
	Amusement	Control over one's environment				
	Rest					
	Recreation					
	Recognition					
	Respect of person					

Rawls (1993) Primary goods	Rokeach (1973) Terminal values	Ryff (1989) Dimensions of wellness	Schwartz (1994) Diener (1995, 1997)[1] Value-based quality of life index
The basic liberties Freedom of movement, freedom of association and freedom of occupational choice against a background of diverse opportunities Powers and prerogatives of office and positions of responsibility in political and economic institutions Income and wealth The social bases of self-respect	A comfortable life (a prosperous life) An exciting life (a stimulating, active life) A sense of accomplishment (lasting contribution) A world at peace (free of war and conflict) A world of beauty (beauty of nature and the arts) Equality (brotherhood, opportunity for all) Family security (taking care of loved ones) Freedom (independence, free choice) Happiness (contentedness) Inner harmony (freedom from inner conflict) Mature love (sexual and spiritual intimacy) National security (protection from attack) Pleasure (an enjoyable, leisurely life) Salvation (saved, eternal life) Self-respect (self-esteem) Social recognition (respect, admiration) True friendship (close companionship) Wisdom (a mature understanding of life)	Having a positive attitude towards oneself and one's past life (*self-acceptance*) Having goals and objectives that give life meaning (*purpose in life*) Being able to manage complex demands of daily life (*environmental mastery*) Having a sense of continued development and self-realization (*personal growth*) Possessing caring and trusting ties with others (*positive relations with others*) Being able to follow one's own convictions (*autonomy*)	Affective autonomy Intellectual autonomy Mastery Harmony Hierarchy, conservatism Egalitarian commitment

Note: [1]Diener grounded his 'value-based quality of life index' in Schwartz's work (somewhat simplified; Schwartz had 45 etic values in these seven categories), and used it in 55 countries.

Table 2.12. (cont.)

Schwartz (1994) Human values	Sen and Anand (1994) Basic features of well-being	Sen (1999) Five types of freedom	Wilson (1967) Correlates of avowed happiness
Power	Longevity	Political freedom	Young
Achievement	Infant/child mortality	Economic facilities	Healthy
Hedonism	Preventable morbidity	Social opportunities	Well-educated
Stimulation	Literacy	Transparency guarantees	Well-paid
Self-direction	Nourishment	Protective security	Extroverted
Universalism	Personal liberty and freedom		Optimistic
Benevolence			Worry-free
Tradition			Religious
Conformity			Married
Security			Person with high self-esteem,
			Job morale,
			Modest aspirations,
			Of either sex, and
			Of a wide range of intelligence

3

Range, Information, and Process

Economics brings the solvent of knowledge. It enables us to conceive the far-reaching implications of alternative possibilities of policy. It does not, and it cannot, enable us to evade the necessity of choosing between alternatives. But it does make it possible for us to bring our different choices into harmony. It cannot remove the ultimate limitations on human action. But it does make it possible within these limitations to act consistently. It serves for the inhabitant of the modern world with its endless interconnections and relationships as an extension of his perceptive apparatus. It provides a technique of rational action.[1]

I entertain the unfriendly suspicion that those who feel they must seek more than all this provides want a scientific theory of rationality not so much from a passion for science, even where there can be no real science, but because they hope and desire, by some conceptual alchemy, to turn such a theory into a regulative or normative discipline, or into a system of rules by which to spare themselves some of the torment of thinking, feeling, and understanding that can actually be involved in reasoned deliberation.[2]

Disciplined economic thought is helpful. It brings to light the complexity of the impact which one's choices have, beyond their purpose or intention. It constantly reminds us that to spend on one thing is to use up what might have been spent . . . on other purposes. But it cannot capture the idea of justice or the sense of our purpose to be just and to do justice.[3]

1. MULTIDIMENSIONALITY AND EVALUATION

The capability approach conceives of poverty reduction as multidimensional.[4] That is, it recognizes that more than one human end (enjoyment, knowledge, health, work, participation) has intrinsic value in a society, and that the set of valued ends and their relative weights will vary with the diversity of individuals and cultures. But if human ends are diverse in kind and cannot be adequately represented by a common measure such as income or utility, this creates a problem. It becomes impossible to choose 'rationally' between options that pursue different sets of ends, *if* one means by rational what is meant by 'rational choice theory', namely, the identification and choice of a

---

[1] Robbins (1932: 140). [2] Wiggins (1998: 237). [3] Finnis (1992b: 189–90).
[4] Stewart (1985), Bay in FitzGerald (1977), Griffin and McKinley (1994: 2), Haq (1995), UNDP (1990–8), UNESCO (1995), UNRISD and UNESCO (1997), Norton and Stephens (1995), World Bank (2000), Narayan *et al.* (2000*a,b*).

maximally efficient or productive option, the one (or one of the set) in which the total benefits minus the total costs is the highest possible. The problem is compounded by the need not only to advance different kinds of capabilities, but to aggregate capabilities across individuals who are likely to value these differently, and to compare capabilities for different groups. And it is further compounded when one considers the other live concerns that development organizations have—for targeting the poor, building institutional capacity, supporting environmentally sustainable activities, investing in activities that will carry on when funding ceases, and being themselves accountable to their supporters and funders.

1.1. *Multidimensionality in small NGO activities*

Consider again the rose cultivation activity. How does Oxfam decide whether an alternative activity would expand capabilities more than this one did? If we consider the impact on income alone, surely an alternative could have been found that generated a higher rate of economic return or generated equivalent income for more people. This is possible even if we consider only alternatives that also involved the poorest. One way to consider capability expansion is to select a subset of 'basic' capabilities and look for changes only in this subset. For example, Drèze and Sen analyse Indian economic development in terms of the expansion of basic capabilities such as 'the ability to live long, to read and write, to escape preventable illnesses, to work outside the family irrespective of gender, and to participate in collaborative as well as adversarial politics'.[5] If Oxfam evaluated changes in this subset, their assessment of the rose cultivation activity would be quite negative. Dadi Taja's capability to be healthy changed a bit, in that if she or her son were sick, they might go to the social organizers and seek help, and use the money from the roses to purchase medicine (if there were enough)—and her son could drink goat milk. But she remains illiterate, her social security situation has not changed; her water supply is still a handpump, her ability to earn a living wage remains constrained by a lack of employment opportunities (although she finds the rose work deeply meaningful), there are no sanitation facilities available to her, and being unable to save 30 Rs every month, she is still not a member of the women's organization. Similarly positive changes affected her co-cultivators.

Yet the rose project had impacts that alternatives might not have had. The group chose the project themselves—after scrutinizing their options and assessing the risks inherent in each—and so developed and exercised skills of self-direction. Threading rose garlands was both more aesthetically appealing and 'meaningful' than agricultural labour—characteristics that Sen and Drèze's analyses overlook but the participants valued. And it raised the social status of the group, as visitors from Oxfam and other organizations came to meet not the landlord or the religious leader, but the 'rose cultivation group'.

---

[5] 1995, p. vii.

How, then, is Oxfam to compare very different income generation projects—having to do with roses or goat-rearing or lacquer-working or tile-making or date-packaging?

1.2. *Evaluative considerations*

Sen has written not only on capabilities and functionings but also, significantly, on social choice, rationality, justice, the market, public action, agency, economic methodology, consequentialism, human rights, public debate, commitments, interpersonal comparisons, cost-benefit analysis, and various other procedures and institutions by which capabilities are pursued and realized in human communities. When I discuss Sen's capability approach I include these writings in addition to the bare definitions of capability and functioning.

Many others have chosen to conceive of Sen's capability approach more narrowly, as being (only) the proposition that justice is to be evaluated in the space of capabilities rather than in the space of utility or primary goods or functionings or the satisfaction of some deontological principle(s). There are good reasons for focusing on this proposition, probing and evaluating it as distinctive of Sen's approach. But the proposition alone is quite abstract, and it would seem rather arbitrary to disregard Sen's accounts of the processes by which it can be put into action—*especially* if one is fundamentally interested in putting the capability approach into action. Furthermore a good number of commentators 'complain' that Sen's capability approach does not address questions they put to it—when Sen has actually developed very clear responses to their very questions elsewhere. It is worth keeping these in view.

Still others conceive of Sen's capability approach in terms of his applied writings—for the United Nations' *Human Development Reports*, or on India. And again these writings serve to illustrate in many ways the distinctiveness of the capability approach when it is applied to poverty analysis. But as Sen signals, these analyses are also influenced by other matters, such as the availability of data, and the policy appeal of results. It would seem unnecessarily limiting and error prone to extrapolate the capability approach from these exemplifications of it, especially when direct sources are available.

A further reason for considering Sen's wider writings is that these, taken together, characteristically address one of the common disagreements within development ethics. This is the disagreement between those who focus on 'processes' and those who focus on consequences or outcomes. An activist who is concerned *only* with 'letting the people decide' (no matter what they decide) is a proceduralist; a lobbyist who is concerned *only* with defending a particular human right, without concessions or consideration of economic costs or other human rights violations, is a proceduralist. On the other hand an economist who is interested only in generating a certain growth rate, or an activist who focuses only on meeting basic needs, is primarily focused on consequences and outcomes. In the introduction to *Women, Culture, and Development*, Jonathan Glover and Martha Nussbaum acknowledge this 'urgent' tension between the two approaches:

Among the issues on which consensus was not found in the present volume, this one appears the most urgent: should we give priority, in development ethics, to a procedural account and let that procedure generate our substantive moral conclusions? Or should we focus on the normative theory of human functioning and its defence . . . ? (Nussbaum and Glover 1995: 9)

Sen has, characteristically, affirmed the importance of both emphases, and argued for a combined approach that bridges both, as we shall discuss below.

The capability approach simply proposes that evaluations of social arrangements, especially in so far as these relate to well-being, freedom, or achievement, be largely undertaken in the space of capabilities. Yet the capability approach (CA) requires substantive and valuational judgements (SVJ) in order to assess actual social arrangements, or be operational. There are various ways of raising values questions and various procedures for making SVJ, which may confer decision-making authority upon participants or economists or political bodies. Some procedures will employ one or another account of rationality. Sen has gone some way towards developing an account of ethical rationality. This chapter will propose the ingredients for making SVJ in dialogue with Sen's writings and concerns on related subjects. But, acceptance of Sen's CA as a space in which equality is to be demanded or changes to be tracked does *not* entail acceptance of his account of ethical rationality; it might be perfectly possible to accept the capability approach (CA) and reject the features of ethical rationality identified by Sen, or those offered here, and raise or make SVJ in a different way or indeed vice versa. What will be argued is that the wider conceptions of rationality identified by Sen and Finnis offer systematic ways of approaching SVJ that retain the 'fundamental' incompleteness of the capability approach and do not impose a comprehensive doctrine of the good.

1.3. *Response in this chapter*

In Chapter 2, we talked about the dimensions of value and how they could help us to identify the full set of capabilities. However, we did not reach closure on them. So the current state of affairs is distinctly untidy—the reader now has a broad informational landscape before her and encounters deep questions of comparability and prioritization. These questions will persist, unaddressed, until Chapter 4, which discusses participatory processes, and Chapter 5, which considers how to select basic capabilities for direct action, and also considers the 'operational' distinction between capability and achieved functionings.

Chapter 3 is broader still. That is, it points out yet more information that may need to be taken into account in evaluating capability expansion. It introduces the information under the following topics: the role of ethical rationality in economics, informational pluralism, and principle pluralism.

How does this 'broadening' of vista contribute to the aim of the book, which is operationalizing the capability approach in concrete microeconomic activities? In an article on revolutions, John Hicks gives a graceful image about the necessity of brave simplifications: 'In order that we [economists] should be able to say useful things about what is happening, before it is too late, we must select, even select quite violently. We must concentrate our attention, and hope that we have concentrated it in the right place. We must work, if we are to work effectively, in some sort of blinkers'.[6] Hicks called economic theories 'blinkers in this sense', and as we have seen and will see, Sen has protested vehemently against the particularly blinding arrangement of blinkers with which welfare economics horses are commonly arrayed.

But Hicks concluded that economic revolutions necessarily come when the appropriate area of concentration shifts (as it will). And Sen clearly advocates a shift of concentration. For example, Drèze and Sen write, 'The limitations of the Indian experience in planning lie as much in omissional errors in the dark part of the stage as it does in the commissioning mistakes in the spotlit section. The first step is to bring the darker part of the stage more into consideration'.[7]

Hicks's essay on revolutions then describes two ways in which academic economists could be on the lookout watch for when to adjust their blinkers: (i) by stepping back to consider more general theories, or (ii) by leafing through economic history:[8]

> One is by generalisation, by constructing 'more general' theories, theories which put more things into their places, even if we can do less with them when we have put them there ... The same function can be performed by the history of economics in another way. If we seek to discover how it was, and why it was, that concentrations of attention have changed, and theories (effective theories) have changed with them, we find ourselves 'standing back' just as we do when we pursue the generalisation method; we get something of the same gain, and it may be that we run less risk of losing our appreciation of 'effectiveness' as we get it. But I have no need to champion one of these ways of broadening our minds against the other. There is plenty of room for both.

Sen's work on practical reason and ethical rationality represents a 'more general' approach to economics—in which Sen puts more things into their places (identifies more information that is pertinent), even if in doing so it becomes less apparent (initially) what we can do with them. This is summarized in Table 3.2, found in Section 7.1. The following chapters will argue for some brave simplifications, which will be articulated against the landscape set out in this chapter. If readers disagree with the simplifications I propose, then perhaps they might construct superior alternatives.

2. ETHICAL RATIONALITY IN POVERTY REDUCTION

Economics requires an account of rationality to explain how the economic solution is related to the human problem people are interested in solving. Consider the description of the problem set forth by Lionel Robbins:

> From the point of view of the economist, the conditions of human existence exhibit three fundamental characteristics. The ends are various. The time and the means for achieving these ends are at once limited and capable of alternative application. Here we are, sentient creatures with bundles of desires and aspirations, with masses of instinctive tendencies all urging us in different ways to action. But the time in which these tendencies can be expressed is limited. The external

[6] 1983: 4. [7] 1995: 8. [8] 1983: 6.

world does not offer full opportunities for their complete achievement. Life is short. Nature is niggardly. Our fellows have other objectives. Yet we can use our lives for doing different things, our materials and the services of others for achieving different objectives.[9]

Sen has suggested that the rationality even in its most general form, exemplified in much of economics—the rationality of Walras or Kautilya or Robbins for example—is only one of alternative rational approaches to economic problems.[10] This engineering rationality is technical. 'The ends are taken as fairly straightforwardly given, and the object of the exercise is to find the appropriate means to serve them'.[11] The other approach to economic problems deliberates the intrinsically valued goals, procedures, and side-effects of an activity. It employs a wider rationality, which is at its font an ethical rationality. Sen argues that the monopolization of economics by the engineering approach has been misplaced. Ethical rationality is required to generate appropriate responses to many problems economists regularly address.

To make his point, Sen has consistently whittled away the utilitarian basis of welfare economics (which is one of the locations of 'engineering rationality') by showing the ethical insufficiency, the logical flaws, and the empirical inaccuracy of the prevalent conception of economic 'rationality' for evaluating poverty reduction. He has sharply criticized internal consistency of choice, optimization, sum-ranking, pareto optimality, certain interpretations of Arrow's impossibility theorem, and other building blocks of economic decision-making. These are argued to be insufficient representations of human rationality for many economic decisions.[12]

Sen has often structured his criticism of utilitarianism around a clear analysis of its component parts. He writes,

Utilitarianism as a moral principle can be seen to be a combination of three more elementary requirements:

1 '*welfarism*', requiring that the goodness of a state of affairs be a function only of the utility information regarding that state;
2 '*sum-ranking*', requiring that utility information regarding any state be assessed by looking only at the sum-total of all the utilities in that state;
3 '*consequentialism*', requiring that every choice, whether of actions, institutions, motivations, rules, etc., be ultimately determined by the goodness of the consequent state of affairs.[13]

Sen has examined and roundly criticized each of these components of utilitarianism because of the information that they exclude (such as information on freedom or agency). By showing the insufficiency of the standard treatments of these ideas (and

---

[9] Robbins (1932: 12–13). Robbins retained and defended a much narrower conception of economics and rationality than Sen does, or than is here advocated. However, Robbins also presumed a far greater degree of collaboration between economics and other disciplines than is now common: 'by itself Economics affords no solution to any of the important problems of life. I agree that for this reason an education which consists of Economics alone is a very imperfect education' (1932, p. ix).
[10] Sen (1987a). [11] 1987a: 4.
[12] e.g. Sen (1970, 1993e, 1995d, 1999a). Arrow *et al.* (1997), Basu *et al.* (1995), Farina *et al.* (1996), Gerrard (1993). [13] 1987a: 39 and elsewhere.

in particular the paucity of the information that they use) Sen has worked to unseat the inappropriate uses of engineering rationality and made the case for an alternative.

Sen draws out the distinctions between ethical and engineering rationality in order to point out that the nature of the subject of economics requires both approaches to be deployed: '[t]here is no scope at all ... for dissociating the study of [technical] economics from that of ethics and political philosophy'.[14] The need for a wider rationality in economics can be argued independently from the capability approach to welfare or prescriptive economics. Indeed Sen argues that a more adequate account of rationality is necessary in descriptive and predictive economics as well.[15] But given the ethical origin and evident ongoing purpose of prescriptive economics, he regards it 'as somewhat of a mystery that so many notable economists have been involved in debating the prospects of finding value-free welfare economics'.[16] Such a debate risks reducing a welfare economist to an 'instrumental rationalist'—a figure Sen gaily described as 'a decision expert whose response to seeing a man engaged in slicing his toes with a blunt knife is to rush to advise him that he should use a sharper knife to better serve his evident objective'.[17]

Sen noted that his dissatisfaction with economic rationality can be divided at the highest level into two branches.[18] The first is that rationality is too narrowly specified. The second is that the assumptions regarding the motives of human behaviour are too narrow and not empirically verified. This chapter focuses on the first problem: how to give an account of the wider economic rationality. The literature on economics and rationality is substantial; this chapter is strictly confined to Sen's contributions on the topic. Similarly a great number of philosophers have written insightfully on these issues. This discussion confines consideration to the named authors.

The second, empirical question—how persons' actual behaviour relates to any account of what would or would not be rational for them to do—is not treated. Related issues, such as whether rational motivation is best characterized by the maximization of self-interest or by consistency or by more complex motivations including altruism, cooperation, and power, are also beyond the boundaries of this discussion.[19]

Sen does not give very specific recommendations for relating the engineering and ethical approaches that he argues should be applied; rather he simply suggests that 'it is a question of balance of the two approaches to economics'.[20] The practical difficulties raised by this 'question of balance' are significant. This is the case in general, and also with respect to the capability approach.

---

[14] Sen (1987a: 3) The distinction between the ethical and engineering forms of reasoning is itself in Aristotle, in the form of 'the basic distinction between *praxis* and *poiesis*, between doing and making, and correspondingly between the ethical and the technical as irreducibly distinct domains' (Finnis 1997: 211). See Sen (1987a: 7). See *Nic. Eth.* VI.4:1140a2–23, which also (like I.1:1094a4–6) assimilates *poiesis* with *techne*: VI.5:1140b3–4; also *Politics* I.4:1254a8.
[15] 1987a. [16] 1970: 56. [17] 1995b: 16. [18] 1987a: 10–12.
[19] See Oostendorp (1995), Sen (1970, 1977, 1982b, 1983a,e,f, 1986a,f, 1987a, 1989b, 1991g, 1994b, 1995b, 1997i, 1999a), Stewart (1995), Ellerman (forthcoming), Frey (1997), Stark (1995), Nussbaum (1996), Alkire and Deneulin (2000), and the references therein. [20] 1987a: 6.

2.1. *Setting the stage: ends, reflection, democratic discussion*

In his address as president of the American Economic Association in 1995 Sen pointed out some issues that an account of the rationality of social choices (of which welfare economic choices are a part) must address: whose desires; whose ends are to be pursued? Does a 'collective' rationality exist? How do group and individual identity relate? Should a procedure-based account replace consequentialism? What is the best model of individual rationality? How do social interactions develop values, and these in turn influence decisions?[21] He showed how the answers to these questions bear directly on economic issues. The need for a wider rationality in economics, addressing these issues, exists independently of whether or not social welfare comes to be judged in the space of capabilities.

How is that rationality to proceed? It seems that Sen suggests at least three elements.

First, it is to be framed with reference to plausible 'ends' of development rather than means or procedures. For example, Sen introduces the intent of Drèze and his work on India as being 'to link strategies of development to something more fundamental, in particular, the *ends* of economic and social development . . . It is only with an explicit recognition of the basic ends that debates on means and strategies can be adequately founded.'[22] These ends are not confined to basic capabilities (although it surely includes them as capabilities are 'ends' of development). Rather 'the overall ethical objectives of a society can include concerns *other than* the elimination of economic deprivation.'[23] Ethical rationality must evaluate competing ends—reforestation, national security, the preservation of cultural sites, drug control programmes, research—each of which may be valuable.

Secondly, the rational scrutiny is to be a kind of critical reflection on the kind of society or culture that people value.[24] 'Socrates might have overstated matters a bit when he proclaimed that "the unexamined life is not worth living," but an examination of what kind of life one should sensibly choose cannot really be completely irrelevant to rational choice.'[25] Critical reflection means the examination of existing customs and traditions and the value of continuing them, as well as examination of possible innovations that will change them.

Thirdly, ethical rationality is to engage public discussion and judgement (what he sometimes calls democratic social choice) as a means of generating appropriate weightings.

A capability framework points towards a space, but even when the functionings have been selected and some ranges of weights specified, there will be the possibility that a particular policy A would be better for equality, while policy B is better for aggregate achievement. These trade-offs are also part of public judgement, and what this exercise requires is . . . the

---

[21] Sen (1995*b*, 1999*a*).   [22] 1997*e*: 2.
[23] (1997*a*: 166). See Nussbaum and Sen (1989), and Sen (1986*c*, 1997).   [24] 1996*d*: 483.
[25] 1995*b*: 16.

identification of relevant considerations, suggesting particular proposals and encouraging public discussion on those considerations and proposals.[26]

We return to these issues in Chapter 4.

Sen has actively advocated that economic 'development' strategies be framed *vis-à-vis* valuable human ends, which are legitimately plural and diverse; that there be periodic explicit scrutiny of the value of the objectives, norms, and institutions that are in place; and that there is something intrinsically worthwhile in public participation in this process of debate and decision-making. When one compares this 'rationality' for economic strategies with that of utilitarianism, the force of Sen's suggestion begins to emerge.

2.2. *Focusing the stage: Which decisions? How explicit?*

In a paper on cost-benefit analysis, Sen favourably observes that one of the 'first general conditions' of cost-benefit analysis is that value judgements are identified and made explicitly: 'which demands full explication of the reasons for taking a decision, rather than relying on an unreasoned conviction or on an implicitly derived conclusion'.[27] Yet—and this is what is key at the moment—explicit valuation, and its associated full application of rational consideration, is not appropriate for every decision. It might take too much time, or make a person's life 'quite unbearably complicated'. Thus the entire content of this chapter is only of relevance in some decisions. Which might those be?

Sen points out that accountability demands are higher for public decisions—whether in programme selection or in implementation. Non-decision-makers may legitimately enquire into the grounds of a particular choice. 'There is, thus, a case for fuller articulation and more explicit valuation in public decisions than in private ones.'[28] Clearly within public decisions some will be more complex, and more important, thus more appropriate for the investments required for explicit valuation.

Yet—and we will return to this point again in Chapter 4—even some important and complex decisions may not bear too much explicit scrutiny. In some cases, 'a consensus on public decisions may flourish so long as the exact grounds for that accord are not very precisely articulated'.[29] Various stakeholders may have very different reasons and values that will be served by a concrete choice, and these may be mutually incompatible. In these instances what Cass Sunstein calls 'incompletely theorized agreements'—agreements that deliberately *refrain* from giving abstract reasons for themselves (that may be contentious)—may be the more appropriate.

Having expressed these caveats and qualifications, Sen still makes a case for explicitness 'if only to encourage the possibility of reasoned consent and to present some

---

[26] 1996e: 117.
[27] 2000c: 935. Sunstein (2000), in the same journal, justifies cost-benefit analysis on cognitive grounds, arguing that it produces a more systematic and accurate appraisal of a situation than alternative analyses.
[28] 2000c: 935.   [29] Sen (2000c: 935).

kind of a barrier against implicit railroading of unacceptable decisions that would be widely rejected if properly articulated'.[30]

3. SEN'S INFORMATIONAL PLURALISM

Underlying the argument that economists should employ a wider rationality is Sen's argument that the informational basis upon which economic evaluation rests needs to expand.

Sen has drawn attention to the fact that conditions widely used to obtain economic results—such as the Pareto principle(s) in welfare economics, Kenneth Arrow's social choice condition of the independence of irrelevant alternatives, or Kant's categorical imperative—function in part by *excluding* extra information from consideration. 'The basic form of an informational constraint is that of an invariance requirement: if two objects x and y belong to the same *isoinformation set I*, then they must be treated in the same way $\mathcal{J}$. For all $x, y: x, y \in I \Rightarrow \mathcal{J}(x, y)$.'[31] The exclusion of information is a necessity—any theory of justice, such as those proposed by Rawls, Dworkin, or Nozick, has a limited informational base.[32] However Sen has drawn attention to the informational basis of welfare economics because he objects that it excludes information *that should not be excluded*. Furthermore, Arrow's 'Impossibility' Theorem does not hold if further information is introduced.

This link between information and moral or economic principles is key to everything that follows in this chapter, and it is important to take it in. It is especially important because it may be counterintuitive. One example would be that each moral theory comes with a pre-programmed spreadsheet software such as TurboTax—which itself represents an operational moral theory of sorts, although this observation may not ameliorate the displeasure with which 'doing one's taxes' is associated. The executor of the moral/economic theory is only able to input data (information, indicators, processes) on those things for which data entry pages exist in the software wizard. Anything, however vitally relevant in her opinion, that does not have a data entry page, cannot come into the calculation. If there were several alternative software for generating taxes, *each of which calculated taxes using different sets of information*, then we would obviously examine the pre-programmed software *very carefully*, searching for the data or information that we consider important, but that would *not* be considered (deducted) in this software. It is with this same energetic attention to excluded information, Sen argues, that we should select our welfare economic theories.

After exposing the undesirably narrow effect of utilitarianism because of the information it excludes, Sen argues for an approach to welfare economics which takes into account more information of two kinds. 'One is in terms of plurality of

---

[30] 2000c: 935.
[31] (1985a: 170)—the subject of the first Dewey lecture is 'Moral Information' and is a particularly lucid account of our subject. See (1974b, 1979a, 1982b, 1983b, 1986b, 1992a, 1995c).
[32] Sen (1992a: 74).

Table 3.1. *Alternative evaluative spaces*

A Income	B **Externally chosen functionings**	C **All valuable capabilities**	D **Considerations of principle**
Some increase	Life expectancy	Self-direction	Activity engages the poorest
	Literacy	Meaningful work	Economic efficiency
	Health	Appreciation of fragrance	Sustainability
	Work	Social respect	Uncertainty of success
	Political participation	Friendship with others	Imperfect obligations
		Health	Is participatory

principles (I shall call this *principle pluralism*), and the other in terms of plurality of informational variables (to be called *information pluralism*).'[33]

Recall the discussion at the start of this chapter, summarized in Table 3.1. One way of assessing the activity was to consider its impact on income; another was to consider impacts on the particular capability set that Drèze and Sen mention. The last two columns include 'further information' that might or might not influence the assessment. Column C lists all the above-mentioned valuable functionings that the rose cultivation activity impacted, whether or not they were 'basic'. Column D lists 'procedural criteria' that were mentioned.

Columns B and C intuitively introduce 'information pluralism' as it relates to rose cultivators' human development. Column D mentions the plural principles that may (or may not) come into an assessment of the rose project. Our focus for the rest of this chapter and the next will be on how a rational framework may enable Oxfam to evaluate Columns C and D better.

3.1. *Information pluralism versus revealed preference*

In a paper delivered to the Aristotelian Society in 1981 Sen argued that there were substantial advantages in considering utility as a vector of incommensurable kinds of valuable goods. This view, which he traced variously to Aristotle, Mill, Ricardo, and Marx, acknowledges 'coexisting aspects' of utility—not coexisting *interpretations* of utility (desire, pleasure, pain avoidance)—but *kinds* of utility (intellectual, sensual). Sen argued that Mill chose to bring in the judgment of the 'experienced' to determine an ordering based on moral parity, not because Mill viewed this to be morally preferable to an objective utility aggregate, but because the objective

[33] 1985a: 176.

aggregate *does not exist*. Different kinds of pleasures are objectively incommensurable. Sen argued that the vector view provides a richer description of human well-being, and gives rise to 'a wider class of interesting moralities than utilitarianism and—more generally—welfarism permit'.[34]

This incommensurability (non-existence of an objective aggregate)[35] persists if one instead considers a desire interpretation of utility—or indeed any other. 'How do we *sum up*, on the basis of some objective measures of intensities, the respective desires for an ice cream, freedom from a headache, writing the most beautiful sonnet ever written, going to bed with one's favourite film star, and being morally impeccable?'[36] The article closes with a brief gesture to the then-nascent capability approach, and suggests this approach (utility-supported rather than utilitarian) merits exploration because it includes within it important information (objective states, opportunities) that even a vector view of utility or desire would exclude.

Because information pluralism is so central to his entire approach, it is worth visiting Sen's display of arguments against revealed preference theory. The counter-argument would be that there is no need for economics to have any further account of ethical rationality; a refined software of 'revealed preference theory' can incorporate sufficient information.

Revealed preference theory proposes to infer information on 'ends' (utility or well-being) by observing persons' choices. This information is assumed to reflect persons' values—the interests (conception of benefit; ends; happiness; even identity)[37] that have survived their own deliberation, by whatever method is appropriate. This information would be sufficient, it might be argued, to identify valuable capabilities and their relative weighting, and assess which of two options will expand valuable capabilities more.

Paul Samuelson's objective in writing his seminal article on the theory of revealed preference was 'to develop the theory of consumer's behaviour freed from any vestigial traces of the utility concept'.[38] In his revealed preference approach, it is not necessary to understand what introspective individuals conceive of as their utility or consult them about what they regard to be valuable. Rather, one may merely notice that the individual chose x when she could just as well have chosen y. One infers from this behaviour that y was not preferred to x. This procedure claims to solve the problem of how to gain empirical information on what individual preferences and values are (a problem of significant note in working across cultures). In order to link this procedure to theories of consumer behaviour Samuelson introduced a simple consistency condition, which is that if an individual has chosen x when y was available, then she must not at another time choose y when x is available. This condition, known as the 'Weak Axiom of Revealed Preference' forms the spine of economic decision theory. There are quite a few related axioms and conditions.

---

[34] 1980/1: 193.

[35] Some mechanisms such as pricing falsely appear to commensurate the incommensurable. See Sen (1995*a*), and also Sandel (1998), and also Sunstein in Chang (1997).

[36] 1980/1: 200.   [37] Akerlof and Kranton (2000).   [38] 1938.

While this particular axiom has tremendous pragmatic value, Sen alongside many others has criticized it on conceptual and empirical grounds.[39] The question is whether on the basis of these criticisms the approach may be modified satisfactorily, or whether it is fundamentally flawed. First, Samuelson developed this approach in order to avoid the need to look inside consumers' heads (because looking into their heads can be contentious). Yet it makes sense to refer to a consumer who reveals a preference for x over y on one occasion, and y over x on another, as a person exhibiting 'inconsistent' behaviour only if you do 'peep into the head of the consumer'.[40] Secondly, Samuelson's axiom does not rest on a strong empirical basis. 'Faith in the axioms of revealed preference arises . . . not from empirical verification, but from the intuitive reasonableness of these axioms interpreted precisely in terms of preference.'[41] The barriers to such verification are significant. For example, to assess whether people choose consistently one would require information on choices under infinite price–income configurations. The time span for observing choice behaviour would need to be long enough that the last purchase was not still 'in the larder' (in which case Miriam's stock of beans in the pantry would affect her food purchases) but short enough that tastes have not changed. Thirdly, in many common situations choices clearly would not reveal preferences directly, because of the interdependence of consumers' preferences and behaviour or because of indifference. For example, in a 'Prisoners' Dilemma' situation, in order to get the outcome that each prisoner prefers for himself or herself (minimal sentencing), the prisoners must *choose* against the strictly dominant strategy—that is '*as if* they are maximizing a different welfare function from the one they actually have'.[42] Another example is a situation of indifference, in which a person does not have a preference in either direction yet still must choose something (or else suffer the fate of Buridan's ass). In these examples an external observer who inferred the actors' preferences directly from their choices would have a flawed understanding.

A substantial set of arguments query further the relationship between revealed preferences and individual welfare.[43] For example, preferences reveal the preferred element from a fixed set. Even if one could infer that Donna's choice of n from the set (k, l, m, n) meant that she actually preferred element n, one has no information regarding the value of that element *vis-à-vis* a wider set. The situation in which k, l, m, n, refer respectively to winning the lottery, playing a Stradivarius, marrying an Olympic athlete, and finishing one's theatre script is very different from where they refer to a menu whose items differ trivially from one another—brands of washing

---

[39] Sen's first paper in this area was 'Choice Functions and Revealed Preference', *Review of Economic Studies*, 38 (1971), reprinted as Sen (1973). See North (1990, 1993), Alston *et al.* (1996), Cook and Levi (1990), Hausman and McPherson (1996), Bell *et al.* (1988), Farina *et al.* (1996).

[40] Sen (1973: 62). These arguments were all made in Sen's 1973 paper, although they are not unique to him. [41] 1973: 57.

[42] 1973: 66.

[43] Note that Sen gives a balanced evaluation of 'Individual Preference as the Basis of Social Choice' in Arrow *et al.* (1997:15 ff.). See Sen (1997*d*) for an axiomization of this and other ways of building choice into maximization exercises.

powder[44]—or to a menu of bad or evil choices—losing the lottery ticket, stealing the Strad, misleading the mate, or plagiarizing the play. Sen has argued for the significance of evaluating both freedom and capability with reference to the 'menus' from which one chooses rather than, as revealed preference theory does, valuing a set by its best element ('elementary evaluation') or, as some modifications do, valuing a set by counting the number of its elements (regardless of whether they are valuable, trivial, or evil).[45]

Revealed preferences, then, may not accurately reflect the ends people value. Furthermore, even a refined account of revealed preferences cannot exclude the possibility that controversial, inconsistent preferences might be held by different agents. Revealed preference theory does not arbitrate conflicting preferences, and is not *itself* an argument against the possibility of doing so. As Sen has shown, in order to make moral assessments, as utilitarianism claims to, information on revealed preferences must be complemented by a combining principle that is, aggregation, and a moral theory, that is, consequentialism.[46]

In this 1973 paper Sen concluded that '[t]he thrust of the revealed preference approach has been to undermine thinking as a method of self-knowledge and talking as a method of knowing about others'.[47] The next sections and also Chapters 4 and 5 will discuss how Sen reintroduces 'thinking and talking' into economic evaluations.

3.2. *Some informational bases of evaluation*

By now it should be clear from Sen's informational analysis of moral principles that systematic ethical oversights can often be traced to incomplete information. The provision of more adequate information has been a central focus of the succession of approaches to poverty reduction. For example, the human development index, which ranks all countries on the basis of achievements in life expectancy, education, and real per capita income, produces a very different ranking from the World Bank's ranking of the same countries on the basis of income per capita alone.[48] And participatory assessments complement household surveys, producing yet richer, more lively presentations. But *what* information is to be considered?

Having established that Sen clearly and unequivocally argues for a wider informational basis for 'ethical' rationality in economics, this section introduces some of the disparate 'kinds' of information that he defends *in addition to information on capability expansion* that was mentioned earlier.[49] Most of his discussion of these topics has arisen both in the course of criticizing welfare economics and in the course of discussing human rights, consequentialism,[50] and evaluator relativity. The following sections

---

[44] The example is Bernard Williams's. See his explanation in Sen *et al.* (1987: 98–101), and Sen's response (pp. 108–9).   [45] 1997*d*, 1999*a*: 75.
[46] Sen and Williams (1982), Sen (1992*a*, 1995*b*).   [47] 1973: 72.   [48] UNDP (1990–2001).
[49] This information is developed in Sen (1967, 1970, 1979*a,b*, 1980, 1980/1, 1982*a,c*, 1983*a,b*, 1985*a,d*, 1986*c*, 1992*a*, 1993*d*, 1996*b*, 1997*d*, 1998*c*, 1999*a*).
[50] Sen writes that his use of the term consequentialism is 'entirely compatible' with Philip Petit's definition of consequentialism: 'Roughly speaking ... consequentialism is the theory that the way to tell

identify three categories of information in addition to capabilities that, Sen argues, are to be considered: human rights, responsibility, and unintended consequences.

3.2.1. Human rights and obligations

Sen has consistently argued that moral rights in general can be considered within a broadly consequentialist framework.[51] Human rights in particular can be framed as capability rights:

> It is not unusual to think of rights as a relation between two parties *i* and *j*, for example, person *i* having the claim on *j* that he will do some particular thing for *i*. There is, however, some advantage in characterizing goal rights as a relation not primarily between two parties but between one person and some 'capability' to which he has a right, for example, the capability of person *i* to move about without harm.[52]

So framed, one of the goals of the moral system can be the realization of capability rights. In this way, Sen shows that consequentialism can incorporate concern for human rights. Furthermore, it can do so in such a way that is more nuanced than 'trade-off-barred deontology'—in which agents are equally bound to respect all 'rights'—regardless of the fact that some may be more important than others.

For example, if one menu option is to fish, but in order to fish a teenager has to skewer a worm on a fishing hook and he happens to be particularly appalled by this action and hold that worms have rights too, then all things equal he should seek a different way to catch a fish—a net, perhaps. But if on the other hand, his family is at risk of missing meals if he doesn't catch fish regularly, and nets don't work, then he may disregard his worm-hooking views and fish—because his family's right to food security will probably have a higher relative weight than his philosophical notions about the rights of worms (although he still may regret the necessity of making this choice—on 'regret' see Ch. 3, Sect. 7.7). The difference, Sen points out, is that the 'right' that is violated in hooking a worm (or for that matter eating fish) can be associated with a weight of moral importance relative to other rights and values.[53] This weight may be infinite for certain absolutely egregious actions, but for many more actions, even terrible actions, it may *not* be infinite.

This right can be attributed directly to an institution or individual who is obligated to fulfil that right (such as if the state rather than the boy were charged with providing food security for his family). This would be an example of a 'perfect obligation' which is quite familiar. And in that case, the description of a state of affairs would include a description of whether or not the institution had fulfilled its obligation.

---

whether a particular choice is the right choice for an agent to have made is to look at the relevant consequences of the decision; to look at the relevant effects of the decision on the world' (Petit 1993, p. xiii), quoted in Sen (2000*a*: 478).

[51] Sen defines a goal rights system as 'A moral system in which fulfilment and nonrealization of rights are included among the goals, incorporated in the evaluation of states of affairs, and then applied to the choice of actions through consequential links' (1982*a*: 15).

[52] (1982*a*: 16), see also (1980: 215–20).

[53] Sen's example was murdering someone—a rather more vexing case.

Yet Sen also argues for the cogency of what Immanuel Kant called 'imperfect obligations'—that is, obligations that are 'inexactly specified (telling us neither who must particularly take the initiative, nor how far he should go in doing this general duty)'.[54] The 'neglect or disregard of such general obligations may be plausibly seen as a bad thing to happen, and can be taken into account in evaluating states of affairs'.[55]

In sum, in addition to information on capability change, we must consider the human rights that are respected or abused in a given state of affairs.

3.2.2. *Situated evaluation: who does what*
Sen has used a sequence of terms to describe what he most recently calls 'situated evaluation'—the requirement 'that a person not ignore the particular position from which she is making the choice'.[56] Earlier he had referred to the practice, in describing the state of affairs, of ascribing responsibility for actions one would undertake in a given state of affairs to the actors involved, as, variously, describing 'evaluator relativity'[57] and 'positional objectivity'.[58] In both cases he argues that this information can and should be brought into a description of a state of affairs and its evaluation.

To illustrate the importance of situated evaluation Sen describes a conversation in the Indian religious epic the *Mahabharata*, between Arjuna, a warrior, and Krishna, just before a massive battle will occur between factions of Arjuna's family. 'Arjuna rebels against fighting (on the grounds that many people will be killed on both sides, that many of them are people for whom Arjuna has affection and respect and, furthermore, that he himself—as the leading warrior on his side—would have to do a lot of killing) . . .'[59] Sen argues, with Arjuna, that an adequate description of the choice and consequential state of affairs under consideration *must* include the fact (*a*) that Arjuna has affection for some of the people who will die and (*b*) that Arjuna himself will have to do some of the killing—and will have to take moral responsibility for doing so. It is only when the situation is thus fully described (and when the alternative situations would also be fully described—including the persons and causes that Arjuna would leave unprotected by not fighting) that, Sen argues, an adequate evaluation can be made. Thus in addition to capabilities, we must consider who does what.

3.2.3. *Unintended but predictable consequences*
The third type of information relates to unintended effects. Unintended consequences are a familiar artefact in economics—for example, Adam Smith's 'invisible hand' supposedly takes self-interested behaviour of the rich, and uses it 'to advance the interest of society' precisely without their 'intending it, without knowing it'.[60] Carl Menger and Friedrich Hayek took up this insight and gave great prominence to unintended consequences in economics.

---

[54] Sen (2000*a*: 495); see (1999*a*: 230). O'Neill (1996) discusses the Kantian notion of perfect/imperfect obligations extensively, but reaches somewhat different conclusions (that the term virtue should be used rather than imperfect obligation).
[55] 2000*a*: 495.   [56] 2000*a*: 484.   [57] 1983*b*; see 1982*a*.   [58] 1993*d*; see 1985*a*.
[59] 2000*c*: 937, see 2000*a*: 480–2.
[60] Quoted in Sen (1999*a*: 256)—from Adam Smith's *Theory of Moral Sentiments* (1759); rev. edn. 1790, repub. 1976, ed. D. D. Raphael and A. L. Macfie. Oxford: Clarendon Press, pp. 26–7.

Sen is more restrained than Hayek in his assessment of the centrality of unintended consequences in human development—because much that people work for (e.g. increasing literacy rates) they actually do achieve roughly as intended. The insight Sen fully endorses, however, is that economists must seek and consider information on predictable, foreseeable, but unintended, consequences of economic actions:[61]

> It is not so much that some consequences are unintended, but that causal analysis can make the unintended effects reasonably *predictable* . . . An *unintended* consequence need not be *unpredictable*, and much depends on this fact. Indeed, the confidence of each party in the continuation of such market relations rests specifically on such predictions being made or being implicitly presumed.

If this is the way the idea of unintended consequences is understood (in terms of *anticipation* of important but unintended consequences), it is in no way hostile to the possibility of rationalist reform. In fact, quite the contrary. Economic and social reasoning can take note of consequences that may not be intended, but which nevertheless result from institutional arrangements, and the case for particular institutional arrangements can be better evaluated by noting the likelihood of various unintended consequences.[62]

A case in point is the one-child family policy in China. Sen notes that the *intended* consequences of this policy was to reduce the birth rate. The government did not *intend* the resultant and tragic increase in female infanticide, in sex-specific abortions, or in a higher female infant mortality rate. Rather, these consequences came about because of the cultural preference for male children, which was prevalent in many communities. But—and this is the important point—the tendency that parents' existing cultural preference for male children could endanger female infants if parents were only allowed one child, could have been perceived and considered in advance—and should have been:

> The nature of economic and social reforms in China could have benefited from more predictive analysis of causes and effects, including unintended effects. The fact that the adverse effects were *not intended* did not imply that they could not be at all predicted. A clearer understanding of these consequences could have led to a better conception of what was involved in the proposed changes, and possibly could even have led to preventive or corrective policies.[63]

Another very common and vitally important set of unintended consequences that, Sen argues, should be considered, are cultural impacts of globalization—impacts that arise 'when it turns out that some parts of tradition cannot be maintained along with economic or social changes that may be needed for other reasons'.[64] We will return to this (Ch. 4, Sect. 2.4). Clearly the 'unintended' but foreseeable impoverishment of significant populations as a result of structural adjustment policies is also of this category.

Of course an unintended consequence could be 'information' of any of the types thus far discussed, such as a capability expansion (or contraction), or a rights violation, or a drop in income, or a process that did or did not occur. The point is that

---

[61] Dörner (1996) draws on the logical oversight in failed complex operations, which is often a lack of consideration of predictable but unintended impacts. [62] 1999a: 257. Emphasis in original.
[63] 1999a: 259.   [64] 1999a: 31.

we should not restrict our attention, in evaluating actions, only to those consequences that are consciously intended by the agents involved but consider other predictable effects as well.

3.3. *Further kinds of information*

Sen unequivocally holds that information on rights, on contextual situations of choice, and on foreseeable unintended consequences are to be taken into account in the evaluation of states of affairs. And these three are particularly important because consequentialism has been discarded by many on the presumption that it could not take such information into account. But these types of information do not exhaust the kinds of relevant information in addition to well-being and agency that could be considered. For example, both in his work on freedom and agency and his work on maximization, Sen has argued very strongly that freedom is important, and includes information on who chooses. But in addition the direct control of certain choices is sometimes less important than having choices that respect one's preferences (if Maria passes out and is taken to hospital and her friends demand homeopathic treatment on her behalf because they know this is what she would prefer).

Other kinds of information that Sen notes possibly impinge upon the evaluation of a choice include: information on the *menu* of choices (the alternatives one can feasibly consider), information on persons' *motivations* for their action (the sincerity of an apology), information on the *processes* involved in a state of affairs, *actions* taken to bring the state of affairs into being and continue it, information on the *psychic states* associated with a state of affairs, and so on. In fact, Sen calls for more articulation, within the discipline of consequential analyses, on what he terms 'non-exclusion of state components'. That is, if certain possibly relevant components of a description of a state of affairs are excluded, this exclusion must be justified. 'In terms of the discipline of consequential evaluation, it would be arbitrary to exclude a priori any particular component of the state as being beyond the pale of consideration.'[65]

Thus information on human rights, on responsibility, and on foreseeable unintended consequences is all relevant to evaluating a state of affairs. We will return to this proposition shortly with a strong eye for feasibility, but first consider the other type of pluralism Sen describes, which is principle pluralism.

4. SEN'S PRINCIPLE PLURALISM

Sen also argues that plural principles should be used in the making of prescriptive welfare economic choices. For example, in a paper on the foundations of welfare economics Sen argues that there is no 'royal road'; no one principle suffices for all normative economic problems.

Welfare economics is a major branch of 'practical reason'. There are no good grounds for expecting that the diverse considerations that are characteristic of practical reason, discussed,

---

[65] 2000a: 484.

among others, by Aristotle, Kant, Smith, Hume, Marx, or Mill, can, in any real sense, be avoided by taking refuge in some simple formula like the utilitarian maximization of utility sums, or a general reliance on optimality, or going by some mechanical criterion of technical efficiency or maximization of the gross national product.[66]

Principle pluralism, simply put, allows more than one procedural or ethical principle to come into play in (i) the evaluation of alternative possible actions or (ii) the evaluation of states of affairs.[67] While Sen does not enumerate these principles at length he illustrates what they are commonly recognized to be, for example, by acknowledging that economic policies and poverty evaluations are made in the light of such principles as equality, efficiency, and maximization of well-being.[68]

Principle pluralism sees the problem of economic decision-making not in terms of 'picking the best principle' but in coordinating the use of several. In *Inequality Reexamined* Sen writes,

[e]quality would typically be one consideration among many, and this could be combined with *aggregative* considerations including *efficiency* . . . The real question is not about the kind of equality to ask for *if* that were the *only* principle to be used, but [how] in a mixed framework in which aggregative considerations as well as equality are taken into account, the demands of equality as such are best represented . . .[69]

And again, 'the pursuit of equality can be properly evaluated only within a broader context in which other demands are not arbitrarily ignored'.[70] The reason for using several principles is to introduce different concerns; consideration of several principles also broadens the information base which is permitted to influence social judgements.[71]

The immediate practical objection to principle pluralism is easy to see: different principles will sometimes lead to irreconcilable judgements as to the preferred state of affairs or action. 'The issue is not the likely absence of rationally defendable procedures for social decisions, but the relative importance of disparate considerations that pull us in different directions in evaluating diverse procedures'.[72] Marx gave the example of the conflict between 'the German Workers Party's simultaneous loyalty to the principles of "equal distribution" and the worker's right to get "the undiminished proceeds of labor" '.[73] Mill argued that in order to resolve such conflicts one

---

[66] Sen (1996a: 61).   [67] See Sen (1979a: 129–31).

[68] In a paper on the 'Ethical Issues in Income Distribution' Sen identified eight principles on which 'a person's moral claim to income' is commonly said to rest: utilitarianism, leximin, Rawlsian difference, need-based axioms, libertarian principles, labour entitlement theories, Nozick's entitlement theories, and agent-relative action moralities. (1984b esp. 277–87). See also Sen (1970).

[69] 1992a: 92.   [70] 1992a: 138; see 131–5.

[71] For example, in (1979a) Sen demonstrates how principles which are narrow parts of 'outcome utilitarianism' (end-statism, independence of irrelevant alternatives, welfarism, anonymity, strong anonymity, separability, cardinal unit separability) each exclude a certain kind of information; together creating a paucity of information that is not satisfactory for social choice.   [72] 1995b: 11.

[73] Sen's description of Marx's critique (1985a: 177), referring to *Critique of the Gotha Programme*, 1875 (New York: International Publishers, 1966).

would have to introduce an 'umpire' principle, which (he argued, contentiously) usurps the value of having principle pluralism in the first place.

> There must be some standard by which to determine the goodness or badness, absolute and comparative, of ends or objects of desire. And whatever that standard is, there can be but one: for if there were several ultimate principles of conduct, the same conduct might be approved by one of those principles and condemned by another; and there would be need for some more general principle as umpire between them.[74]

Mill was presuming that principles must be sufficient to enable closure, or unique choice: for this a meta-principle *is* necessary. But as mentioned earlier, Sen suggests that it may not be either possible or necessary to have only one best option. Sen distinguishes open incompleteness, in which more information would be able to extend the partial ordering, from closed or assertive or fundamental incompleteness, in which it would not: '[t]hough the demands of practical choice may force us to choose one or the other, there is—on [the assertive incompleteness] view—no additional moral criterion that can be used to rank the unranked pairs *in terms of moral goodness*'.[75]

In the case of assertive incompleteness, rather than relying on Mill's experienced judges, Sen introduces the need for underdetermined choice. He concludes, provocatively, 'we must decide, we must act . . . But this does not require that the chosen alternative be seen to be "best" in that set of feasible alternatives, since there may be no best alternative at all, given the incompleteness of our moral ranking'.[76]

Does the fact that no best alternative may be identifiable mean that principle pluralism is unhelpful? On the contrary, even in cases in which several outcomes are taken to be morally non-comparable (and Sen admits it to be 'arguable that assertive incompleteness should never be "accepted" because that may discourage moral inquiry'),[77] *the principles have done some work in eliminating other alternatives* that were less just, less equitable, or less efficient, than the ones that remain. The elimination could be completed in part by combining consistent principles.[78] Furthermore the alternatives that remain could be ordered into some meta-ranking.[79] As the judgements of 'equity' and 'justice' are moral judgements, their function could be restated

---

[74] *A System of Logic*, book VI, ch. XII; cited in Sen (1985a: 177); see surrounding discussion and Richardson (1997: ch. VI). Sen argues against Rawls that principle pluralism does not necessarily require intuitionism. 'The suggestion that if there are many ultimate principles (and they are not in a hierarchy), then the balance among them *must be* struck by intuition is, of course, completely baseless' (1985a: 176).

[75] 1985a: 180. Emphasis in original. [76] 1985a: 181. [77] 1985a: 180.

[78] The possibility of combining is particularly important when some of the principles have a very narrow domain but are very persuasive over these domains. They may rank rather low in the context of ordering a much wider domain included in X, because of being silent on a great many comparisons. But since they are likely to be compatible with other principles with a narrow scope dealing with other types of comparisons, combining them may be both feasible as well as effective in generating highly valued rankings of X' (Sen 1979a: 126–7).

[79] (1970, 1979a, 1982b). For an explication of how there can be an *absence* of conflicts between consistent principles see (1979a: 121–3).

as addressing the problem of 'moral parity' which Mill recognized.[80] But the possibility of underdetermined choice will always remain.

Sen, then, clearly believes that plural principles should be considered. But much in the same way that he identifies basic capabilities in the course of his analysis, but does not prioritize a particular set of basic capabilities, so too he uses a number of principles in analytical work, but *does not identify a specific hierarchy of particular principles*, other than the general rule of maximization of an aggregated function.[81]

Therefore for a systematic set of plural principles I will turn again to the approach of John Finnis. Finnis's principles have significant affinities with Sen's idea of plural principles. Finnis itemizes a set of principles (sustainability, universalizability, working for the common good) that may be worthwhile to consider and that likewise have their roots in Plato, Aristotle, Kant, and Mill. Furthermore, Finnis's principles have an equivalent 'structure' to the one Sen describes. That is, Finnis's plural principles do not have an umpire or necessarily lead to closure. They can rule out some actions as worse than others that can be chosen instead, but they may not identify a 'best' alternative.

5. FINNIS'S PRINCIPLE PLURALISM

Finnis *et al.* argue that irrational or immoral choices, upon analysis (whatever else they may be), can be seen to be choices that do not take into account all the relevant information.[82] He, like Sen, argues that there are two categories of relevant information: one regarding (plural) human ends; the other regarding (plural) principles. Finnis recognizes that choices made in an attempt to apply utilitarianism, for example, may be technically rational, in that the option chosen produces the overall biggest increase in social utility, as defined by the particular form of exercise. These decisions may still be deeply unreasonable because they are made by more or less deflected or fettered rationality—because the utilitarian 'thinking through' process leaves out information that it should consider. Finnis's account is particularly helpful because it explicitly identifies the information which should be brought to bear upon alternatives, and the next three sections elaborate his account.

The next sections introduce the ethical content of Finnis's work, which arises, he argues, not from any one of the basic reasons for action taken alone, but from the

---

[80] See a diverting example in 'Choice, Orderings, and Morality' in (1982b, ch. 3), where Sen tests the Prisoners' dilemma situation out using principles of Kant's 'moral law', Sidgwick's 'principle of equity', Rawls's concepts of fairness and justice, Hare's two 'rules of moral reasoning', Suppes's 'grading principle', and Harsanyi's 'ethical principles' (by none of which the prisoners confess).

[81] 'Maximization does not . . . demand that all alternatives be comparable, and does not even require that a best alternative be identifiable. It only requires that we do not choose an alternative that is worse than another that can be chosen instead . . . for optimization to work, there should *exist* a best alternative to be chosen (not necessarily a *uniquely* best alternative, but a best alternative nevertheless). Maximization does not require that' (Sen 2000a: 486–7). See also especially (1997d).

[82] 'Immoral choice fetters reason by adopting a proposal to act without adequate regard for some of the principles of practical reason, and so without a fully rational determination of action' (Grisez *et al.* 1987: 125).

'integral directiveness' of all taken together—that is, *all* of the basic human values or general reasons for action, considered as relating to the fulfilment of *all* people.

5.1. *Integral directiveness: a principle for human development*

In order to move from a non-moral, descriptive account of people's values to a normative one, Finnis and his colleagues introduce two self-evident (not moral) practical principles. One is the *principle of non-contradiction*—which is a principle of all reasoning, including practical reasoning. This principle simply requires that incoherence or inconsistency, if it is discovered, be eliminated.[83] It demands that any incoherent pair of propositions that a person or group holds be re-evaluated.

The other self-evident principle, which they call the 'first principle of practical reason', is *the principle that good is to be done and pursued*. That is, actions are to be undertaken for the sake of some intelligible benefit, whether for one's own sake or for the sake of others (this is not terribly stringent or controversial; when chosen in preference to alternatives, sleeping, play, and joking are undertaken for some benefit; computer games are played for relaxation; even most morally bad actions 'have their point'[84]—for example, the Mafia do work for the well-being of their particular human community, but their pursuit of the human good is partial and disregards the good of other human persons and communities). The principle 'functions as a norm by directing that pointlessness *be eliminated* when it is discovered'.[85] Neither of these principles, taken alone, is original. And neither is moral.

Morality only enters if these principles are combined with each other and with the basic reasons for action. That is, if a person or institution undertakes to act *only* so that each action furthers human ends or the dimensions of development (whether for oneself or another or for the natural environment),[86] then there is still the problem of deciding which of the manifold avenues for action to undertake. The task of deciding which possible activities are to be pursued—and how they are to be pursued—is the task of practical reason, and the principle governing this can be understood to be ethical in the broadest sense.

The kernel of the argument is as follows. As we discussed in Chapter 2, many actions, moral or immoral, pursue one or more dimensions of human flourishing. They can therefore be explained as 'rational' or 'practically reasonable' in the limited sense that they pursue an intelligible good. (It is important to notice that this sense of 'rational' is *very* different than the 'technical' or 'engineering' concepts of rationality employed in economists' use of 'rational choice'.) But all reasoning which pursues these dimensions is not necessarily moral or ethical. The distinction between 'rational' and 'ethical' actions is *one of degree*. *Ethical* actions and practices make their way towards human flourishing coherently—*in such a way that is consonant with the*

---

[83] See Nussbaum and Sen (1989), where they propose that this principle be used by those who challenge objectionable cultural practices from within their own culture.
[84] Grisez *et al.* (1987: 121).   [85] ibid. 120.
[86] These ends need not be anthropocentric. Black and I argued (with Nussbaum but against Finnis) that harmony with the natural world was a basic reason for action (Alkire and Black 1997).

desire for all people across time to enjoy sustainable human development in any or all the dimensions. As Finnis puts it, 'Moral thought is simply rational thought at full stretch'.[87]

Finnis formulates the first principle of morality as follows: '*in voluntarily acting for human goods and avoiding what is opposed to them, one ought to choose and otherwise will those and only those possibilities whose willing is compatible with a will toward integral human fulfilment*'.[88] Integral human fulfilment refers to the fulfilment of all persons and their communities across time, in all dimensions of their well-being or flourishing—it refers to what others have meant by human development. 'The ideal of integral human fulfillment is that of the realization, so far as possible, of all the basic goods in all persons [past, present, and future], living together in complete harmony.'[89]

It is worth spending a moment considering how this 'moral principle' arises. The key basic goods in this regard are friendship and 'practical reason'. The second pre-moral principle states that 'good is to be done and pursued'. And the good is constituted not by a single idea but rather by the set of plural human ends discussed above. One of these is sociability, the relational good which people often pursue in friendship and social interactions even with strangers. Now if Adam is interested in pursuing his own good, then one way he may choose to do so is to cook a nice meal for himself, or learn to excel in hang-gliding. Another way to pursue his own good, perhaps, is to cultivate a friendship with Tarit.[90] However when he considers friendship, the understanding of possible human ends immediately becomes more complex. This is because friendship involves him in considerations not only of his own good, but also Tarit's. And Tarit's 'good' might also be understood with reference to any of the various reasons for action, including *Tarit's* friendship or sociability with yet more people.

Finnis argues that it is the pursuit of friendship, together with the pursuit of practical reasonableness, that knits together individual and social rationality.[91] 'For there can be no friendship or real harmony between persons where one fails to recognize, or to take as a reason for action, the good of other person(s) as worth pursuing and respecting as an end in itself, for the sake of the other(s) rather than merely for one's own sake'.[92] So, returning to the first principle of morality, we see that in order not to contradict oneself, and to pursue 'good' things, one's actions will (i) each take as their end any one or more of the basic reasons for action (because, as argued above, all of the incommensurable aspects of 'good' can be articulated with reference to these reasons), and (ii) consider not only one's own good, but those of others.

---

[87] Finnis in George (1992: 136).
[88] Grisez *et al.* (1987: 128; emphasis added). Finnis (1996) inserts 'and other persons, sofar as satisfying their needs is dependent on one's choosing and willing, have a *right* that one choose and will'.
[89] Grisez *et al.* (1987: 131).
[90] It is not necessary for him actually to pursue friendship in order to be flourishing—he may be a flourishing hermit instead of course. But ideally a hermit could, on Finnis's account, recognize the intelligibility of other people's value and pursuit of friendship.
[91] Nussbaum, too, states that 'Among the capabilities, two, *practical reason* and *affiliation*, stand out as of special importance, since they both organize and suffuse all the others, making their pursuit truly human'. (2000a: 52, 1990a: 226 f., and 1992).   [92] 1998a: 112.

The first principle of morality, they argue, is necessary but not sufficient for the purposes of making ethical decisions. It is not an umpire principle; it does not purport to 'solve' the problem of incommensurability; it still requires free choice. To consider how the principle none the less guides fully rational choices, it is necessary first to have an account of how it may itself be further specified.

5.2. *Plural principles of practical reasonableness*

Plato and Aristotle (and also Mill who, it is sometimes forgotten, did not believe an objective aggregate of constituents of utility could be constructed) relied on the human experience, intelligence, and practical wisdom of the 'phronimos' or virtuous person to determine when and how to pursue the basic goods.[93] This general approach is being revitalized in some forms of virtue ethics. But—and this is a key departure of Finnis's theory from these roots—*Finnis supplements (but does not replace) this reliance on scrutinized character with a handful of principles of practical reasonableness.*[94] Finnis introduces them as follows:

> In the two millennia since Plato and Aristotle initiated formal inquiry into the content of practical reasonableness, philosophical reflection has identified a considerable number of requirements of *method* in practical reasoning. Each of these requirements has, indeed, been treated by some philosopher with exaggerated respect, as if it were the exclusive controlling and shaping requirement. For, as with each of the basic forms of good, each of these requirements is fundamental, underived, irreducible, and hence is capable when focused upon of seeming the most important . . . Each of these requirements concerns what one must do, or think, or be if one is to participate in the basic value of practical reasonableness . . .[95]

Finnis argues that these other principles of practical reasonableness specify the first principle of morality, or justice, which is, again, *in voluntarily acting for human goods and avoiding what is opposed to them, one* [one being an individual, a group or an institution] *ought to choose and otherwise will* [and other persons, so far as satisfying their needs is dependent on one's choosing and willing, have a *right* that one choose and will][96] *those and only those possibilities whose willing is compatible with a will toward integral human fulfilment.*

The specifications arise by considering the constraints under which human beings, and institutions within the human community, operate—limited life span, need to coordinate multiple commitments, uncertainty—and the ways in which human feelings/motives are likely to 'fetter' the principle of morality. In other words, the principles may be thought of as reminders of common oversights in their practical reasoning or thinking about what to do (rather like overlooking foreseeable but unintended effects of actions). It is vital to note that only when all of the practical principles

---

[93] It is this conception—and the possibilities of error which accompany it—that fuelled Hilary Putnam's opposition to natural law. See Putnam (1995: 208). For Finnis's explanation of the *phronimos* and the mean in Aristotle, see (1980: 128).

[94] These principles or 'modes of responsibility' were first suggested by Grisez (1967).

[95] 1980: 102.   [96] This is added in Finnis (1996).

function together can an action be said to be rational; many, perhaps all, irrational or immoral actions will still satisfy some principles of practical reasonableness.

Finnis has specified the first principle at different times in different ways—for individuals[97] and for institutions.[98] The first specifications are summarized in Table 3.2.[99]

These principles might be thought of as the different modes of moral responsibility, but perhaps a better account of them is that they describe the anatomy of immorality. Finnis argues that if a proposal for action successfully runs the gauntlet of these principles (and it is worth trying this out on your own), it can be trusted as moral; that is, that these are sufficient principles for the selection of moral actions.

But they cannot effect closure as to what *should* be done. Often there may be no best or optimal alternative; but even if there is, closure requires a community or authority or individual's free choice. Finnis states this formally.

A basic human good always is a reason for action and always gives a reason *not* to choose to destroy, damage, or impede some instantiation of that good; but since the instantiations of human good at stake in any morally significant choice are not commensurable by *reason* prior to choice, there can never be a sufficient reason not to take that reason-not-to as decisive for choice.[100]

To return to Sen's observation: the principles contribute by ruling out options and this is helpful whether or not there is an 'umpire' principle that resolves intransitivities and supports rote choice.

5.3. *The principle of efficiency*

How does all of this relate to Sen's earlier discussion of the two rationalities—the engineering and the ethical? As mentioned earlier, Sen wrote that one cannot simply choose between ethical and 'engineering' or technical rationality, 'it is a question of

---

[97] In *Fundamentals of Ethics* (1983: 75) Finnis gives the following set: (1) have a harmonious set of orientations, purposes, and commitments; (2) do not leave out of account, or arbitrarily discount or exaggerate, any of the basic human goods; (3) do not leave out of account, or arbitrarily discount or exaggerate, the goodness of others' participation in human goods; (4) do not attribute to any particular project the overriding and unconditional significance which only a basic human good and a general commitment can claim; (5) pursue one's general commitments with creativity and do not abandon them lightly; (6) do not waste your opportunities by using needlessly inefficient methods, and do not overlook the foreseeable bad consequences of your choices; (7) do not choose directly against any basic human good; (8) foster the common good of your communities; (9) do not act contrary to your conscience.

[98] In 'Natural Law and Legal Reasoning' (1992*a*) Finnis describes three principles of particular relevance in law: (1) *do not meet injury with injury*, or respond to one's own weakness or setbacks with self-destructiveness. Do not make damage or destruction to another person one's end; (2) *fairness*: do to others as you would have them do to you; do not impose on others what you would not want to be obliged by them to accept. This has two component parts: *impartiality* between persons, and pre-rational commensuration accomplished by 'one's intuitive awareness, one's own differentiated feelings towards various goods and bads' (1992*a*: 149). In communities, preliminary commensuration is from previous decisions or choices (i.e. speed limits); (3) *do not choose to destroy or damage any basic good* in any of its instantiations in any human person—that is, do not choose to harm 'some basic aspect of someone's existence and well-being' as a means to some further end (1992*a*: 138). See also (1997).

[99] Finnis (1980: 100 ff.).   [100] 1992*a*: 138.

Table 3.2. *Finnis's principles of practical reasonableness*

1. *A coherent plan of life* for an individual or group—akin to Rawls's 'rational plan of life'[1] although it need not be explicit. If one practice—e.g. the introduction of a cinema—is anticipated to undermine many others that the group values, these interrelations should be considered so that groups pursue commitments that harmonize with each other.

2. *Do not leave out of account, or arbitrarily discount or exaggerate any of the dimensions* While individuals and communities will pursue certain dimensions more than others, they are to respect other persons' and groups' focus on other dimensions: 'It is one thing to have little capacity and even no "taste" for scholarship, or friendship, or physical heroism, or sanctity; it is quite another thing, and stupid or arbitrary, to think or speak or act as if these were not real forms of good'.[2]

3. *No arbitrary preferences amongst persons* This is the Kantian principle of universalizability—the so-called Golden Rule formulated not only in the Christian gospel but also in the sacred books of the Jews, and not only in didactic formulae but also in the moral appeal of sacred history and parable'. It prohibits arbitrary discrimination i.e. by race, gender, class, age, kinship, citizenship, 'group bias'.[3] But it could support non-arbitrary or reasoned preferences, such as targeting the poor.

4. *Detachment* This is an argument for flexibility, and recommends that one not attribute to any particular project the overriding and unconditional significance which only a dimension of human flourishing and a general commitment can claim. Some degree of detachment from projects is appropriate, as is an openness to novelty. The next principle counter-balances this one.

5. *Pursue general commitments with creativity and do not abandon them lightly* This principle calls for sustainability but also for creativity: 'One should be looking creatively for new and better ways of carrying out one's commitments, rather than restricting one's horizon or one's effort to the projects, methods, and routines with which one is familiar'.[4]

6. *The (limited) relevance of consequences; efficiency, within reason* 'This is the requirement that one bring about good in the world (in one's own life and the lives of others) by actions that are efficient for their (reasonable) purpose(s)'.[5] All of what Sen terms 'engineering' rationality would fit into this principle, for example, and Finnis describes it at greater length than any of the other principles. In the course of Finnis's discussion one specification emerges that parallels Sen's focus on unintended but predictable consequences: (6a) *Do not overlook the foreseeable bad consequences of your choices*.

7. *Respect for every basic value in every act* This principle prohibits every violation of basic human rights—every action which '*of itself does nothing but* damage or impede a realization or participation in any one or more of the basic forms of human good'.[6] Unlike Sen, Finnis restricts the term 'human rights' to a very few rights with relative weights of infinity.

8. *The requirements of the common good* This is one of the most pertinent principles for all of social choices and is extensively discussed by Finnis in the course of discussing justice, authority, promissory obligation, and unjust laws.
9. *Following one's conscience* 'The ninth requirement . . . is the requirement that one should not do what one judges or thinks or "feels" all-in-all should not be done.' This principle expresses 'the dignity of even the mistaken conscience' and 'flows from the fact that practical reasonableness is not simply a mechanism for producing correct judgements, but an aspect of personal full-being, to be respected (like all other aspects) in every act as well as "over-all"'—whatever the consequences.[7]

Notes: [1] Finnis (1980: 103) referring to Rawls (1971: 408–23). [2] Finnis (1980: 105). Nussbaum (2000a: 96) alleges that by this phrase Finnis restricts the liberty of others 'to say or think what they like about the goodness of the relevant functions' of others. This is not the case (for his position on free speech see Ch. 2, Sect. 3.6). Rather, Finnis and Nussbaum both urge a thicker conception than Rawls's thin theory of the good, and insist that persons respect others who wish to participate in dimensions of life that they do not wish to personally (a monk should respect persons who desire sexual fulfilment, as Nussbaum claims). Their positions are quite similar on this point. [3] Finnis (1980: 107), both quotes. [4] Finnis (1980: 110). [5] Finnis (1980: 111). [6] Finnis (1980: 118). Finnis and Sen do not, on the face of it, agree *at all* on the possibility of consequentialist 'weighting' of human rights. However, Finnis focuses *only* on certain basic human rights (Finnis 1991)—such as the 'direct killing of the innocent' or the 'manufacture of babies') which do not admit to exceptions—that is which would have a relative weight of infinity. Finnis's 'rights' do *not* include a right not to have one's room broken into, or a right to financial privacy. It is these lesser rights which Sen 'trades off' against more fundamental rights of bodily integrity and murder. [7] Finnis (1980: 125–6).

balance of the two approaches to economics'.[101] But Sen's image of balance—although it was just that, an image and not a serious proposal—is an image of complementarity between two equal halves, and this is not quite adequate.

It seems vital to explore the relationship between the two kinds of reasoning in greater depth, as overlooking the 'complexities and ambiguities' of their distinction is, Finnis argues, the source of a great deal of theoretical reductionism.[102] Furthermore, as Chapters 6 and 7 will demonstrate, the coordination of both kinds of analysis is practically necessary.

Finnis regards engineering rationality as pertaining to the principle 'employ efficient means to one's objectives' (Sect. 5.2). Thus it functions as only one of the plural principles that a full account of ethical rationality will contain.[103] In this proposition, the criterion of efficiency—what Sen called engineering rationality—will always be relevant. But it will only sometimes be decisive. In a paper on legal and moral reasoning, Finnis argues that technical (engineering) reasoning (i.e. cost-benefit analysis, 'rational choice theory') is *sufficient* for decision-making 'only when (*a*) goals are well-defined, (*b*) costs can be compared with some definite unit (e.g. money), (*c*) benefits can also be quantified in a way that renders them commensurable with one another, and differences among means, other than their efficiency, measurable costs, and measurable benefits, are not counted as significant'.[104] But even when the above conditions are *not* met, if option *A* is not efficient, then—all other comparisons apart—it is *irrational* not to try to make an inefficient option more efficient.[105]

5.4. *Free choice*

As the principles can only rule out options, how does decision-making enter? In a manner parallel to Robbins, Finnis and his colleagues regard the move from a concept of well-being to its active or operational pursuit as very important. It may be quite difficult to recognize the spectrum of elements that conduce to human development or well-being (this is the subject of the next chapter). But it is certainly difficult to know what to do if one has all of this information: 'the real problem of morality, and of the point or meaning of human existence, is not in discerning the basic aspects of human well-being, but in integrating those various aspects into the intelligent and reasonable commitments, projects, and actions that go to make up one or other of the many admirable forms of human life'.[106] Finnis refers to the mechanisms of this integration as free choice and commitments. Free choice may be described as, 'the adoption of one amongst two or more rationally appealing and incompatible, alternative options, such that nothing but the choosing itself settles

---

[101] 1987*a*: 6.   [102] Finnis (1992*a*: 140), see also Finnis (1997: 230–2).
[103] See Finnis (1992*a*: 143–5). Finnis challenges the metaphor of 'balance' Dworkin uses in *Law's Empire* (1986), which is an innovation on Dworkin's earlier suggestion that the hard legal cases be resolved by lexical ordering.
[104] Finnis (1992*a*: 146). See Finnis *et al.* (1987 at ix.5; see also ch. ix and sects. x.6, x.7, xiii.2). See also Finnis (1980: 36–8, 157 and 1997), and Grisez (1975: 230–40).
[105] See Finnis (1980: 111–18).   [106] Finnis (1980: 100) see Sen (1985*a*: 179).

which option is chosen and pursued'.[107] Rationally appealing options include both good and evil options, as was discussed in Chapter 2.

The framework of Finnis's approach to ethics is distinctive in the centrality it gives to free choice as defined above. The choice between a moral and an immoral alternative is a free choice; the choice between two moral alternatives is a free choice; the choice between two intelligible immoral alternatives is a free choice. In other words, all choices that engage ethical rather than technical reasoning are free choices. This is, it may be helpful to point out, one of Finnis *et al.*'s key departures from Aristotle, and one that makes their approach deeply committed to pluralism and incompleteness: 'the reality of free choice is incompatible with the supposition—for instance, of Aristotle—that there is a single natural end of human life'.[108]

One decides and in deciding creates. As Finnis writes,

There is real creativity in free choices . . . And this creativity is also self-creative, self-determining, more or less self-constitutive. One more or less transforms oneself by making the choice, and by carrying it out, and by following it up with other free choices in line with it. One's choice in fact *lasts* in, and as part of, one's character . . . Choices . . . can be reversed by subsequent [choices that are] inconsistent [with the earlier] choices . . . Still, until such a reversal, they last . . . To choose is not only to set out into a new world, it is already to become a person (or society) more or less different from the person (or society) that deliberated about the goods and bads in the alternative available options.[109]

The above quotation mentions some of the characteristics of self-determination (including group self-determination) that Finnis attributes to choice:[110] by choice the person or society create their character and determine their ongoing identity. Choices change the world—they have real effects. Choosing itself is open-ended and uncertain, but it does anticipate certain benefits to the option chosen. Choices can be reversed. And choices can be free. Even fully rational choices can still be free, because the 'reasons are not causally determinative'. Finnis writes, 'One's having these reasons is a necessary but (even when morally sound and obligatory) not a sufficient condition for making one or the other choice'.[111]

6. ETHICAL RATIONALITY RECONSIDERED

6.1. *Consonance with select ideas of economic science*

In *Inequality Reexamined*, at the close of a chapter on 'Welfare Economics and Inequality', Sen mentions the deep challenge of the capability approach for economic theory. 'If the fundamental fact of human diversity and its far-reaching implications come to be recognized more widely in welfare-economic analysis and in public-policy

---

[107] Finnis (1992a: 136).
[108] Grisez et al. (1987: 101, see also sections IV(B); X; XI(A)). See similarly Wiggins (1998: 215–38; Griffin (1996: 30–1). [109] 1997: 220.
[110] These characteristics of free choice are described in Ch. 4 Sect. 2.4.
[111] 1997: 220 both quotes.

assessment, then the approach[112] would certainly need some radical transformation'.[113] A legitimate question in many minds is whether, after such a transformation, the discipline remaining would be economics in any recognizable form.

Some light is shed on this issue by Lionel Robbins's essay on *The Nature and Significance of Economic Science*. Robbins has gone down in history partly as one who wished to slice the discipline of economics away from ethical assessments.[114] But it is worth looking at the place which Robbins would have had economics take up. Robbins argued strongly that the unity of economics was to be found in the problem it was able to solve, but that this problem was, emphatically, *not* the study of the causes of material welfare.[115] Nor was economics to confine its concern to affairs of the institutions of the exchange economy. Rather, Robbins defined economics as 'the science which studies human behavior as a relationship between ends and scarce means which have alternative uses'.[116] The crux of the economic input, by Robbins, is (i) to identify alternatives that are economical from those that are uneconomical, that is, that are wasteful of some scarce resources, (ii) to identify the alternative uses of means (to alternative ends) that a choice rejects, (iii) to show the full implications of the alternative that is selected. Robbins does not, note, recognize choice to be anything other than instrumental; his final role for economics is thus narrower than Sen's. But economic analysis does serve to forge peaceful agreement where this is possible and to provide information such that *ethical* or *political* decisions can be taken that pursue harmonious ends.

So, three pages after his infamous quote about the association of ethics and economics, Robbins writes,

> But what, then, is the significance of Economic Science? . . . Surely it consists in just this, that, when we are faced with a choice between ultimates, it enables us to choose with full awareness of the implications of what we are choosing . . . Faced with the problem of deciding between this and that, we are not entitled to look to Economics for the ultimate decision. There is nothing in Economics which relieves *us* of the obligation to choose. But, to be rational, we know what it is we prefer. We must be aware of the objective implications of the alternatives of choice. For rationality in choice is nothing more and nothing less than choice with complete awareness of the alternatives rejected. And it is just here that Economics acquires its practical significance. It can make clear to us the implications of the different ends we may choose. It makes it possible for us to will with knowledge of what it is we are willing. It makes it possible for us to select a system of ends which are mutually consistent with each other.[117]

The role of 'ethical' economic rationality, then, is not to find 'the' best answer; it is not to accept every answer as equally choice-worthy. Rather, it is to identify the characteristics of different options or proposals which make them more or less

---

[112] Sen is referring at this point to the Atkinson approach of inequality measurement but it could be generalized to similar measures. [113] 1992a: 101.
[114] Robbins is perhaps better known for rejecting interpersonal comparisons of utility.
[115] This element, which Robbins found to be common to Cannan, Marshall, Pareto, and J. B. Clark, represented the dominant definition of economics in Anglo-Saxon countries of his time.
[116] 1932: 15.   [117] 1932: 135–6.

choice-worthy. It is to aid economists and decision-makers in identifying and 'thinking through' the complete significance and possible drawbacks of different options. Rational deliberation is an intermediate process between the identification of a problem and alternatives for addressing it, and the practical choice itself.

Consider that the decision-makers have just purchased a house with a wild walled garden, and know nothing about plants, but Miriam, who is a friend of theirs, is a gardener and they ask for her advice. She will spend hours in the garden, separating and studying the plants, the sunlight and soil and bugs. Eventually she will report back. She will introduce the group to the different plants, and explain their characteristics. 'This is clematis—you cannot see it now but in the late spring it will bloom. This is bindweed, yes it has a white, quite pretty and fragrant flower, but it is also vicious and strangles other growth. The garden soil is like this, and this is what the garden might look like in ten years if you never weed it; this is what it might look like if you tend it an hour a day. These are the vegetables that would grow well if you decide to turn the plot into a vegetable garden. You could also get an extension to the house, but you would need to call someone else to get an estimate on this.'

Such a report might seem elementary, but think about how much effort it would require for a group of city-dwellers who could not tell a nettle from lemon balm to obtain such a clear understanding. Ethical rationality, and its richer informational requirements, is necessary even to obtain such a description. But technical problems remain.

Those working in human development have often had a marked ambivalence towards some exercises of formal economics, an ambivalence that will not stand it in good stead in complex analyses. It is hoped that a clear understanding of the possible ways in which the capability approach can address ethical issues directly will support the human development school to address 'the tragic necessities of choice which has become conscious'. But it is also hoped that a clear delineation of the need and validity of purely 'technical' rationality will reinstate these analyses in a helpful place.

If 'ethical rationality' did nothing but bring to the decision-makers' attention all of the costs and benefits relevant to a decision, whether or not these enter the utilitarian calculus, the improvement to welfare might well be momentous. The process of moving from the current paradigm to the capabilities alternative is a two-handed one. One task for ethical rationality is to build the *full and fully relevant description* of the proposals or policy options that present themselves for choice. The other is to generate appropriate procedures by which such a rich informational base can inform reasonable *choice*. While these processes will in practice be intermixed rather than sequential, and will influence each other rather than be independent, both pertain to the making of rational choices between incommensurable options.

7. OPERATIONAL CONSIDERATIONS

Standing back from all of the rich information and principles which have been introduced as relevant in this chapter, we return to consider, more narrowly, how this account of ethical rationality aids in the operationalization of the capability approach. On the face of it Sen's break from the Pareto-optimal arrangement of welfare economics seems a bit like the experience of catching a small tiger shark by accident—breathtakingly exciting at first (as you think about how much more flavour and character it has than grouper—not to mention that there is more of it), and then increasingly troubling as you think about landing it (will your line be strong enough; will the net hold; will you be able to tire it out sufficiently that it will not overpower you; if you do land it will it bite your foot or bite the boat?). What seemed so delicious now poses a threat to your and your boat's very survival and it is tempting to cut the line and comfort yourself with less ambitious undertakings.

The fear underlying many criticisms of the capability approach is that it is simply not feasible, because of a spray of practical considerations—such as the cost and time required to obtain the requisite information, or the willpower a development strategy breezily presupposes, or the depth of consensus and discipline of reflection it assumes. Furthermore, as one can anticipate that these deeper decisions will be contested by different persons and groups, the 'rational' approach may ignore the fact that contention may form into violent opposition. For example, some collective action models expect a committee to reach a best conclusion by sitting around discussing the problem, and dispersing amicably having agreed to abide by the final decision, but do not recognize that this mode of personal interaction and decision-making is only one possibility among several.

Other critics are concerned that even if specified in its fullest form, Sen's capability approach will be too vague and general to generate answers anyway, hence is a bad investment of time and consideration. A full account of capability expansion may give 'overcomplete' judgements because different principles apply to a circumstance, but give conflicting recommendations.[118] Or it might be underdetermined, because there is assertive incompleteness.

Sen, well aware of these reactions (especially to the measurement of capabilities in particular), admits that 'The informational problem is undoubtedly serious'.[119] But with persuasive nonchalance, he also writes:

The seriousness of the informational problems of the capability approach has to be assessed in the light of what the alternatives are. Maurice Chevalier had remarked, on his 72nd birthday, in reply to the question, 'How do you like being old?': 'Considering the alternative, it is not too bad at all'. We have to consider the 'alternatives' while scrutinizing the capability approach.[120]

This section will, however, stay with those who consider the feasibility concerns to be decisive, and who view the chance that this approach will be feasible as remote. Many issues are up in the air—and they are in vexed areas that could go very wrong indeed. The purpose of this chapter was to flush out of the trees Sen's wider ethical rationality, without which an understanding of his capability approach

---

[118] See Sen (1987a: 65–8).   [119] 1994b: 336.   [120] ibid. 337.

is incomplete indeed. This concluding section will show how these first two chapters address some of the fundamental 'feasibility' criticisms.

7.1. *The informational landscape: a birds' eye view*

To orient this final discussion, just for illustrative purposes consider Table 3.3, which summarizes the last two chapters.

The first column itemizes the different kinds of plural information and principles we have discussed in this chapter and the last. The second column reminds us that any person or group that is seeking to evaluate a change in welfare would need information on the unit of analysis; the third column reminds us of the need for value judgements as to the relative weights or importance of different aspects of well-being, or of any other kind of information, to the individual(s), or group, or culture. Because there is likely to be a diversity of valuations, different groups' views may be recorded. There are many processes for gathering and analysing this information—attention to the data-gathering 'process(es)' is a separate question upon which much lively debate is focused.[121] Resource constraints and information constraints affect how an assessment will proceed. Also, as people's well-being as well as their values are dynamic—they change and evolve over time—any evaluation and its associated value judgements must be attached to a particular time period.

The last column is the decision mechanism—which can be identified not only by a normal institutional description (market, law, voting, rank order, representative democracy), but also, more generically, by the kind of collective choice procedure it exhibits. For example, Sen writes, in chapter 11 of his 1970 textbook *Collective Choice and Social Welfare*, of institutions and frameworks. He there observes that, while the collective choice procedures may be somewhat wider than Arrovian social welfare functions, it is not infinite nor even very large. 'The existence of great varieties of collective choice procedures is . . . somewhat illusory.'[122] The institutional frameworks for making different types of social choices are actually quite limited. He identifies five:

1. *institutional mechanisms of social choice* (method of majority rule, free market system, provisions for individual freedom);
2. *planning decisions* (parliament, committee—that relate goals of planning to individual preferences, perhaps by the maximin rule, 'welfare of the worst-off group', or by the aggregation rule);
3. *making social criticism/arguing on social policy* (these 'typically take the form of postulating principles of collective choice which the existing mechanisms do not satisfy');
4. *committee decisions* (whether committees are 'large or small, formal or informal' these have systems of taking account of intensities of preference, or vote trading);
5. *public cooperation* ('The difference between success and failure in planning is often closely related to public enthusiasm and cooperation . . .'[123] especially if an action imposes a sacrifice).

---

[121] Carvalho and White (1998), Tashakkori and Teddlie (1999), Hentschel (1999), Bamberger (2000), Kanbur (2001). [122] 1970: 191.

[123] 1970: 192, this and two prior quotations.

Table 3.3. *Menu of informational categories relevant for choosing between actions*

Information and principles	For whom? Individual(s) group(s)	Relative weights (whose?)	Resources	Data	Time period	Decision mechanism
Achieved functionings[1]						
Life, health, security						
Work and play						
Relationships/friends						
Knowledge/understanding						
Self-direction/participation						
Inner peace/spirituality						
Environmental harmony						
Actions (who does what)						
Capabilities (ongoing)						
Life, health, security						
Work and play						
Relationships/friends						
Knowledge/understanding						
Self-direction/participation						
Inner peace/spirituality						
Environmental harmony						
Culmination outcomes						
Exact circumstances of choice						
(situated evaluation)						
Agency freedom						
Motives						
Imperfect obligations						
Perfect obligations						
Menus						
Goal rights						
Human rights, property rights						
Utility/happiness						
Principles						
Coherent strategic plan?						
All dimensions considered?						
Universalizability/golden rule?						
Detachment from projects?						
Commitment to projects?						
Efficiency/cost-benefit ratio?						
Respect for human rights?						
Contribute to common good?						
Follow one's conscience?						

[1] As will be discussed in Chapter 5, Sen writes 'We can judge the capability set in one of three different ways':

1. by the *entire set* of options open to the person (weighing all the different alternatives in some responsive way);
2. by the *option actually used* (concentrating just on that as the focal point of the set);
3. by a *maximally valued option* from the capability set (again concentrating only on that) (1994b: 339–40).

Achieved functionings refers to the second way of assessing capabilities; ongoing capabilities (below) to the first or, in some cases, the third.

Table 3.3 might be thought to function, as Hicks suggested, as a 'general' set of all possibly relevant information for capabilities evaluation. It is not a comprehensive matrix which 'is to be applied'; rather, it is a set of possible considerations. And recall that while the categories themselves are Sen's, the specifications of dimensions of capability in Table 3.3, and of principles, are Finnis's.

On the basis of this explication of the capability approach I return now to consider some of the criticisms of it mentioned at the outset. The effect will be to demonstrate that Sen's general framework allows a great deal of what in other circles is called 'contextualization' to occur. Further, I will observe that this approach, by being so open-ended, *inherently* respects the agency of those who will operationalize it, far more than a more directive, decisive, and *apparently* 'operational' approach to poverty reduction might.

7.2. *'Too open-ended' criticism*

Recall Sugden's criticism from Chapter 1 that the capability approach is too open-ended: 'Given the rich array of functionings that Sen takes to be relevant, given the extent of disagreement among reasonable people about the nature of the good life, and given the unresolved problem of how to value sets, it is natural to ask how far Sen's framework is operational'.[124]

In the abstract the above statement is utterly true. But our problems are not abstract. Sen's approach has many degrees of freedom; concrete situations have far fewer. In view of the chart above, the feasibility considerations can usually be jotted in, and these at once limit the degrees of freedom. Consider the rose project. Here, the 'Time Period' was set at three years—the duration of the loan repayment period. The 'For Whom' was clear: this project involved Oxfam, the Marvi Women's Organization, the men's Village Organization (to a lesser extent), and the group of 'extreme poor' who had been invited for the first loan project. The 'Whose Values' had relative weights which had been agreed early on between groups: Oxfam's income officer would not give weighted opinions on the substance of the project but she could legitimately exert her 'values' to ensure as much as possible that the project would succeed technically (e.g. make sure the soil supported roses). Furthermore Oxfam and the WO had mutually agreed that loan recipients would be the poorer rather than richer community members. The Women's Organization (WO) could enforce repayments, and select (poor) recipients for the central revolving loan, and demand a share in the profits (the male Village Organization also vied for a share but was denied—and this triumph was much remembered). The participants could decide the loan project (provided that it would generate sufficient returns to repay the loan), their division of labour, their schedule of meetings, their division of profits. The relative weights of individuals were not specified; in practice the loan participants tended to function by a consensual process, the WO tended to rely on the leadership of the president and her committee. Financial resources were restricted to the loan;

[124] Sugden (1993: 1953).

information was limited to the knowledge of all persons involved, and of the income generation officer's research. Finally, the 'Decision Mechanism' for participants was an informal committee (of everybody); for the WO it was both a committee and the setting of procedural rules.

Going through this exercise verbally is dreadfully tedious of course (more on this—and the critique that this example is overly rationalistic and Cartesian—shortly) and I've surely abbreviated the full exercise here. However, it does demonstrate two things. First, in many concrete instances the information-gathering and analysis requires discussion and joint deliberation rather than private calculation. Sen defends this process with its attendant loose ends:

> A choice procedure that relies on a democratic search for agreement or a consensus can be extremely messy, and many technocrats are sufficiently disgusted by its messiness to pine for some wonderful formula that would simply give us ready-made weights that are 'just right.' However, no such magic formula does, of course, exist, since the issue of weighting is one of valuation and judgment, and not one of some impersonal technology.[125]

Secondly, Sen has provided an analytical map of important variables which can be useful to practitioners who are deeply sensitive to the context, and which can be adapted, shaped, and fitted to many different institutional levels, time periods, groups, and so on. Sen's refusal to 'fill in all of the blanks', his decision to leave the prioritization of basic capabilities to others who are engaged directly with a problem, demonstrates his respect for the agency of those who will use this approach. The approach depends upon the thoughtful participation of many users—it is an example of what Banuri calls 'epistemological decentralization'.[126] For that reason it is very conducive to participatory undertakings, as Chapter 4 will discuss.

Furthermore this informational map does have a number of kinds of 'cutting power'. When one focuses on concrete instances and available information, then, 'it can also be shown that there may be no general need for terribly refined interpersonal comparisons for arriving at definite social decisions. Quite often, rather limited levels of partial comparability will be adequate for making social decisions.'[127]

Obviously using this framework seems awkward, complex, and strange—much in the same way that trying to release the clutch and depress the accelerator to edge a car forward seems quite a capricious and unreliable procedure at first, and in the way that learning to take data from entry through cleaning and preparing to running analyses to selecting and writing them up seems unbearably complicated, far-fetched, and arbitrary at first. Initial discomfort is most predictable. However, there are other good arguments to consider, and we turn to those.

7.3. *'Too expensive' criticism*

A further concern is that it costs too much to focus on capability expansion. The *informational requirements* necessary to determine the right course of action may be too

---

[125] 1999a: 79.   [126] 1990b.   [127] Sen (1999c: 356).

high: some information is unobtainable; some information is highly uncertain; much information that can be gathered relatively robustly none the less cannot be gathered in time, or would require significant expenditures (and the merit of allocating resources to this task rather than to others bears debating) or be simply too expensive.[128]

Here there are two answers. First, obviously the capability approach views more information to be relevant to poverty reduction decisions than alternative approaches have, as Sen's light comment about Maurice Chevalier's 72nd birthday suggested.

Secondly, the capability approach, by considering wider informational sources, can come up with distinct analyses having the same research budget. What would you do, for example, if you were in a radio competition, and you had to prepare two topics. In your morning competition, you had three hours to produce a five minute programme on 'the economic poverty of Uganda', and in the evening, you had three hours to produce a five minute programme on 'the capabilities of the poor in Uganda', and you had access to published and grey literature on Uganda. For the first radio programme probably you would look up the national poverty line, the international agencies' poverty lines, the trends, and prices of basic commodities in Uganda over some time period. And you would look at this poverty line disaggregated by gender and age, by urban and rural, by region and race and occupation. But what would you look at for the second talk? You would have to make do. First, you might look at the social indicators—the UNDP Human Development Indicators, the World Bank Poverty Profiles, and so on. From these you might pick focal variables where Ugandans (male and female, child and adult) were particularly underprivileged. Then you might leaf through publications by Transparency International, or Amnesty International, and jot some notes on press freedom, voting participation in poorer states in recent elections, and human rights. You might find a study on social capital among the poor, and a labour study on the occupations of poor women aged 15 to 24. You might run across a participatory poverty assessment that included three case studies of poor Ugandans describing their lives and families and work and spirit in their own words. And of course you would skim the Government's Poverty Reduction Strategy, and various local and international NGO criticisms of it. Your afternoon presentation on capability poverty would be more patchy than the morning's. There would be less time series data; the social capital case might have a poor sampling frame; the case studies might be lumped in the northwest; the labour study might say nothing about whether or not workers found their work to be meaningful. But you would have enough to say something, in five minutes, about how free Ugandan poor people were to pursue lives they valued (and that programme might be far richer and more informative to the listeners than the first, *even though* the technical quality of data and analysis would be substantially weaker). You'd probably also have a hefty list of 'unfound information' to hand to the librarian if he ever plans to use the question again!

---

[128] Sen (1985e).

Like the plucky radio competitor, Sen has made the best of the available information on health, education, life expectancy, and income, and has restricted his empirical work to areas for which data is available while also arguing for better data and sound empirical analysis on other variables. It also might be the case that, as unsatisfactory as it is from a research standpoint, some roughness of analysis is sufficient to its purposes. Sen has amply demonstrated that countries with 'a relatively free press' have never had a famine. The term 'a relatively free press' is not a terribly precise or technically grounded concept. But the use Sen has made of this observation could hardly have been more pointed.

7.4. *'Too hard to use' criticism*

Some critics' frustration with Sen's capability approach seems to stem in part from uncertainty as to whether or not they have 'done it right'. They would prefer not to take the responsibility for making the necessary decisions. It doesn't feel satisfying—it is unsettling to do. This group of criticisms may seem trite, but is actually vitally important.

For example, the popularity of cost-benefit analysis was constrained in part because of the emotional discomfort economists had in setting the various shadow prices, and wondering whether or not they had done distributional weighting right.[129] Similarly as mentioned before, some of the narrow implementation of basic needs approach in the field seemed to stem from certain needs for clarity and a sense of accomplishment. And tedious, overly information-hungry matrices—and even those as lean as the logical framework—have a less than sterling record.[130]

Yet once again the responsibility for a response lies with those who are charged with using the approach—to find simplifications and assumptions that are contextually appropriate (and may need to change over time), but that make the application of the approach user-friendly and satisfying, as well as effective (one is concerned, after all, with the well-being and 'meaningful work' of those who engage in Sen's approach, whether they are poor or not!). The force of this need for contextualization might become apparent if one considered the unthinkability of the alternative—namely, of the setting exactly one operational method, for rich and poor countries, for local and national governments. Sen may be criticized for leaving much up in the air. But that is a far preferable criticism to those that might arise had he claimed to solve everything. In fact it may even be a compliment.

7.5. **Dominating rationality**

Although each of the dimensions of human development is non-hierarchical and none has absolute priority, still the account of ethical rationality developed by

---

[129] Layard and Glaister (1994). [130] See Gasper (2000c).

Finnis, Sen, and Nussbaum is structured by practical reason and sociability.[131] The 'natural priority' of these dimensions has been criticized by some as pertaining to the way Western cultures (or particular subgroups and personalities within them) or the 'male psyche' or particular brain lobes go about decision-making.[132] The analytical approach to rationality in particular seems to sideline the 'intuitive' and the 'emotional', the 'organic' and the 'personal'. Others will reflect that the priority of practical reasonableness and/or of sociability (as they picture these taking priority) would not be appropriate in their own situation. When morality is so closely bound to rationality, can people be generous, or impulsive, or intuitive, or traditional? And what about people who are not patient enough or interested enough to reason systematically through complex considerations—what if it's just not their style?

Clearly, the proposal as developed here belongs to a particular discourse, style of communication, and community of authors. It is unlikely to be terribly interesting to others unless communicated in a different form. But this does not concede that it would be found inappropriate if it were communicated in a different form. In fact the case studies will suggest that rapport and sensitivity were essential to that particular method of identifying capability change. Finnis's proposal has been sketched briefly, without giving his account of how emotions, habits, and authority fit in. A fuller account would clarify that, while the structure of the theory rests on practical reasoning, its application entails a much wider range of practices. Still, the onus is on those who attribute rational discourse to Western sources to demonstrate practical alternatives that are indeed not rational but are none the less equal or superior to reasoning.[133]

7.6. *Regret*

Finally, the 'indeterminacy', and incompleteness and underdetermination of the capability approach do not provide any guarantee that there will be 'optimal' option(s). This was discussed previously. But nor—and this is new—do they provide any guarantee that even one of the alternatives that presents itself for scrutiny, that is feasible and possible, will be adequate. Not only may it be agonizingly difficult to decide which option to pursue, but the choice of *any* of the options may be tragic, by virtue of what it does not contain.[134] A choice may be the very most ethical response (or one of a set of equivalently ethical responses) to a situation, given the constraints, and still be tragic. There is, then, a need to retain alongside the choice an awareness of the ethical shortcomings of even the chosen option. As Sen wrote,

---

[131] Nussbaum and Sen discuss these features in the joint paper (1989: 317–21). See Grisez *et al.* (1987: 137–40). Nussbaum considers practical reason and affiliation to be 'architectonic functionings' that 'organise and arrange' all others. See Nussbaum (1990*a*: 226; 1995*b*, 2000*a*).

[132] See e.g. Apffel-Marglin and Marglin (1990, 1996); Nandy (1994).

[133] Against which see Sen (1997); Nussbaum and Sen (1989).

[134] This point is brought out singularly well in David Wiggins's account of incommensurability (1998: 377–9).

'the non-availability of public resources to help eliminate severe deprivations should not make us redefine poverty itself'.[135]

One of the best available responses to these feasibility concerns may be simply to agree wholeheartedly: they actually are decisive. The goal is not to consider the best of all possible worlds, but expand freedoms effectively in this world. And to do so various groups will have to tailor Sen's capability approach to their specific undertakings, making the necessary assumptions or simplifications or specifications required. The past two chapters have endeavoured to clarify the capability approach and the value judgements that inhere in its use; the next two chapters will articulate one particular approach to 'valuing freedoms', which the final two chapters demonstrate.

---

[135] (1992a: 108); see also 'Description as Choice' (in 1982b).

4

Participation and Culture

Social structures, types, and attitudes are coins that do not readily melt. Once they are formed they persist, possibly for centuries, and since different structures and types display different degrees of this ability to survive, we almost always find that actual group and national behavior more or less departs from what we should expect it to be if we tried to infer it from the dominant forms of the productive process.[1]

Historically growth has expanded choice only in some dimensions while constricting choice in others. . . . Not only can't you go home again, but you can't figure out whether or not you want to until it's too late to change your mind.[2]

To see ourselves as others see us can be eye-opening. To see others as sharing a nature with ourselves is the merest decency. But it is from the far more difficult achievement of seeing ourselves amongst others, as a local example of the forms human life has locally taken, a case among cases, a world among worlds, that the largeness of mind, without which objectivity is self-congratulation and tolerance a sham, comes.[3]

1. INTRODUCTION

Participation has clambered to the forefront of popularity among development institutions of all colours—as the World Bank exclaimed in its participatory manual, 'Participation Works!'[4] Dharam Ghai writes that the procedure of participation is important because any development activity should be 'regarded as a process for the expansion of [people's moral, intellectual, technical, and manual capabilities]' and participation facilitates this expansion. Again, the 'central purpose is the awakening of people's dormant energies and unleashing of their creative powers'.[5]

The rose cultivation project is an example of 'participatory' development.[6] Although Oxfam provided technical assistance and the seed capital that the community

---

[1] Schumpeter (1952: 14).
[2] Apffel-Marglin and Marglin (1990: 4 and 5 respectively). Empirical examples of times when new products displaced old, led to taste formation, and have negative consequences for poor sectors are drawn together in James and Stewart (1981). [3] Geertz (1993: 16).
[4] World Bank (1996d). Methodologically, 'participation' refers to the practice of involving local communities at all stages of planning and implementation and of development activities—as in the rose cultivation activity. [5] Ghai (1994: 14).
[6] See Stewart (1985), Streeten et al. (1981), Klugman (1994), Rahman (1988), Riddell (1990), Stiefel and Wolfe (1994), Blackburn and Holland (1998), Chambers (1992, 1993, 1994a–d, 1995, 1997), Holland and Blackburn (1998), World Bank (1996d, 1998a,b), Narayan and Ebbe (1997), Cernea and Kudat (1997), Wignaraja (1993), Salmen (1992, 1995, 1999), Paul (1989), ODA (1995), Oakley and Marsden (1984),

organization on-lent to the rose growers, Oxfam did not drive up in a jeep one day and offer to fund a rose garden. Rather, the women's organization (WO) contacted a third party NGO that had provided training earlier (NGO Resource Center—a sort of 'matching agency' between community organizations and donors) indicating that it wished donor funding for income generation activities. In a conference later that year, NGORC arranged a meeting between the president of the WO and Oxfam's income generation officer Safia, and they discussed mutual interests. Safia then visited Arabsolangi, spending several days there at a time, getting to know people, having long discussions with the women about their goals, explaining the central revolving fund, identifying the participants for the first loan (including a treasurer), sitting with the WO and participants to consider their first income generation activity—how the profits would be split and the loan repaid, locating technical help (agronomists to test the soil and discuss levelling, field visits for the men to another rose cultivating area some distance away), and, eventually, suggesting suppliers (to which the men went to purchase the rose plants). Safia's interaction with the community was designed to offer technical support and resources, while maximizing the choices and resources that the local organizations controlled. How does Oxfam Pakistan's investment in facilitating 'participatory processes'—in order to 'help people to help themselves'[7]—relate to Sen's capability approach?

This chapter draws Sen's well-articulated capability approach into discussion with the participatory processes which have been common in microeconomic development initiatives, and which are becoming increasingly popular in macroeconomic approaches as well. In particular, the chapter focuses on community participation in development activities that are partly supported by resources external to the community, whether these be from regional or national government, from NGOs, or from other sources.

However, participatory approaches are not monolithic; the methodologies vary, as do the way in which they are carried out. As their popularity and use spreads, a useful critical and self-critical literature has emerged.[8] Sen's capability approach does not intersect directly with this literature. Yet his analyses of democracy and of culture

---

Narayan (1995, 1993), Narayan-Parker and Pritchett (1997), Max-Neef (1992), Lisk (1985), Khan (1995), Kaufmann (1991), Jain (1994), Inshem *et al.* (1995), Ghai (1988), Gezelius and Millwood (1988), Finsterbusch *et al.* (1990), Edwards and Hulme (1992), Bamberger (1988), Bhatnagar and Williams (1992), Cernea (1982, 1991), Gould (1997), Davis and Soeftestad (1995), Blair (2000), Malan (1999), Bond and Hulme (1999), Esman and Uphoff (1984), Uphoff (1998), Michener (1998), Pitt and Khandker (1998), Korten (1980), Esman and Uphoff (1984), Wade (1988), Cooke and Kothari (2001).

[7] Oxfam's web page has this introduction to its development work: 'Oxfam is about people in over 70 countries joining together to fight poverty. Poor people know best what their problems are and often how to sort them out. Oxfam helps by giving money and advice: helping people to help themselves. In this way they grow more food, dig wells for clean water, train health workers, learn to read and write, plant trees—and gain confidence and build mutual trust' (http://www.oxfam.org.uk/development.htm). See Pratt and Boyden (1985: 14).

[8] See e.g. Nelson and Wright (1995), Mosse (1994), Cooke and Kothari (2001), Bell (1994), Michener (1998), Uphoff (1998), Bond and Hulme (1999), Malan (1999), Blair (2000), Gould (1997), Gezelius and Millwood (1988), Ghai (1988), Stiefel and Wolfe (1994), Vivian and Maseko (1994).

identify various rationales for using participation—he relates the use of participation, public debate, democratic practice, and other forms of 'group agency' to three or four goals. This chapter discusses participation as a procedure for making many of the various 'value judgements' that poverty-reducing activities embody, rather than relegating these judgements to a market mechanism, formal democracy, leadership by committee or by dictator, or a hybrid of decision processes. It draws on Sen's capability approach, and in particular his analyses of agency, democracy, and culture, to address the following kinds of issues: why does it matter who chooses? What wider significance do participatory choice processes have in the well-being of the individuals involved? How do cultural considerations supplement the 'rational' grounds for preferring one alternative over another? What value judgements do participatory processes make—if not explicitly then implicitly? What are they leaving out? What model of external assistance is appropriate for external NGOs?

I will develop the position that certain participatory approaches and Sen's capability approach have much in common. For example:

- the purpose of participation is both (1) to obtain outcomes that people value and choose, and (2) to support a choice process that may be intrinsically valuable or 'empowering'. Sen has identified and affirmed both of these types of freedom.[9]
- Participatory approaches see well-being and participation as inherently connected. 'Who decides' is important, and 'what is decided' is also important. This parallels Sen's conception of capability, in which the 'freedom to' pursue valuable beings and doings inheres in *each* capability, and does not relate only to formal political processes, for example.
- Participatory approaches presume underdetermination—that there may be no best choice, but that discussion and consideration can work out grounds for separating the 'better' from 'worse' choices. Sen recognizes many forms of the same, such as incompleteness, partial orderings, and the need for maximization not optimization.
- Participatory approaches support reasoned deliberation both for consideration of advantage and for interpersonal comparisons. This avoids Arrow's impossibility theorem as a mechanism for social choice. Also, 'reasoned' and explicit decisions can later be scrutinized and confronted.

The comparison between the capability approach and participation, however rich, is rather ungainly for several reasons. First, academic approaches to the topics of participation (or decision by discussion) properly reside in the field of political science, not economics, and have progressed since ancient times. This chapter does not engage with the very large current literature on public deliberation and democratic practice (both theoretical and empirical) which is directly concerned with these very same issues—not because this is not an important interface to work, but, to the

---

[9] e.g. 1982c, 1983c, 1985a, 1999c.

contrary, because it is too important to be done improperly. I respectfully leave that task to others who are already engaged in it.[10]

Secondly, the 'emphasis' on and practice of popular participation and self-determination in microeconomic development has to some extent grown up, come of age, and made its name in different regions with minimal—or if not minimal then certainly eclectic—theoretical guidance. Participation focuses on 'methodology' and not on 'theory' (this may or may not be its saving virtue)[11] but there is hardly a canonical methodology. Hence this chapter does not elect one authoritative 'writer' of participatory approaches, nor does it present any systematic descriptions of participatory practices (from 'handing over the stick' to chapati diagrams to humility and self-criticism).[12]

Thirdly, there is not a literature in social choice theory that formalizes and explores popular participation. Social choice theory has focused on deeply institutionalized and predictable forms of decision-making such as voting and committees. Given the variety of institutional forms of participation, and their inherent flexibility, it is difficult to know how they could be accurately formalized. Hence this conversation is 'informal'. That fact should not be taken as scepticism about the possible value of formal explorations of the topic. I simply leave these for others.

Fourthly, the major 'dialogue' between development economists and those involved in participatory approaches to development is about how the 'qualitative data'—such as assessment of poverty that arises from participatory discussions rather than survey work—can complement and enrich poverty studies.[13] But there is a puzzling paucity of professional interest in further obvious overlaps.[14]

As if the above complications were not sufficient, Sen has not written directly on participatory methods as they are carried out by CBOs (community-based organizations) and NGOs in small development activities—although he clearly is aware of and sets the conceptual stage for them. In *Development as Freedom* he writes that if there is a conflict between a traditional way of life and an activity that would reduce poverty 'then it is the people directly involved who must have the opportunity to participate in deciding what should be chosen'.[15] Elsewhere he writes a passionate endorsement of freedom that coincides with an underlying impetus of participation, 'The people have to be seen, in this [development as freedom] perspective, as being actively involved—given the opportunity—in shaping their own destiny, and not just as passive recipients of the fruits of cunning development programs'.[16] When he

---

[10] See especially Richardson (forthcoming) and Bohman (2000), both of whom carry forward Sen's work directly.

[11] Bell (1994) refers to the 'tyranny of methodology' in many participatory approaches. See also Cooke and Kothari (2001). [12] Chambers (1993, 1997).

[13] See especially Bamberger (2000), Kanbur (2001).

[14] These might focus on the nature of participatory data (how robust the data is—how much it is influenced by the 'mood' of the group or by the facilitator or by the time of the meeting, which yields 'best' data, how/whether this data should be made publicly available); or on the methodologies of information provision, the profile of facilitators, and the methodology of facilitated participation, that lead to the best performance in dimensions such as empowerment, economic performance, social cohesion, and institutional capacity-building. [15] 1999a: 31.

[16] ibid. 53.

discusses mechanisms of making decisions, though, he does not refer to the informal agglomerate of participatory practices used by community-based organizations and NGOs, but instead mentions institutional forms such as 'democratic systems, legal mechanisms, market structures, educational and health provisions, media and other communication facilities and so on'.[17]

The lack of discussion on this interface is worth remedying. Participation pervades economic development initiatives. Initially the province of NGOs and activists, the rhetoric and to a much lesser yet not insignificant extent the practice of participation has been taken up by large donor organizations, by governments, and by international and regional development banks. Yet the linkages between deeply participatory processes in microeconomic development and Sen's approach have not been well appreciated. Raff Carmen's insightful article 'Prima Mangiare, Poi Filosofare' draws attention to some of the latent connections between Sen's capability approach and deeply participatory, or 'from the inside-out' initiatives. But Carmen interprets the capability approach as being 'philosophically circumscribed'[18] thus far. It is time to make the connections between Sen's capability approach and participatory or community-driven development explicit.

2. PARTICIPATION: MEANS, ENDS, DEBATE, AND IDENTITY

'Participation' refers to the process of discussion, information gathering, conflict, and eventual decision-making, implementation, and evaluation by the group(s) directly affected by an activity.[19] In the best case, participatory processes attend to and correct for power imbalances within the group, so that the voices of shyer members are heard and conflicts are resolved without domination by one member.[20] How might participation be analysed by the capability approach?

As mentioned in Chapter 1, Sen locates four spaces in which human life can be evaluated: well-being achievement, well-being freedom, agency achievement, and agency freedom. *Well-being achievement* refers to the achievement of those things that are constitutive of one's well-being, and *well-being freedom* is 'one's freedom to achieve those things that are constitutive of one's well-being'.[21] *Agency achievement* 'refers to the person's success in the pursuit of the totality of her considered goals and objectives' and *agency freedom* is 'one's freedom to bring about the achievements

---

[17] ibid. 53.   [18] 2000: 1027.
[19] There are many definitions of participation, which fall along an axis between 'light' interaction in which participants supply information, to 'deep' participation in which the control of the decision-making and resources are in the hands of the participants. This definition, and the Oxfam rose project's, tend towards the 'deep' pole—that is, not only the decision-making authority, but also the control of financial resources, was local (Oxfam funded a one-time 'central revolving fund' to the village, and agreed with the Men's and Women's Organizations on principles for its use. The rose cultivation was funded by the first 'loan' from that fund, which was duly repaid so another project could begin).
[20] Chambers (1997).   [21] 1993a: 35, 1992a: 56–62.

one values and which one attempts to produce'. Examples of agency goals are 'the independence of her country or the prosperity of her community'. Participation concerns agency freedom and achievement.

Sen distinguishes well-being from agency because the two perspectives are irreducibly different, and each important for the evaluation of social arrangements. 'In one perspective, the person is seen as a doer and a judge, whereas in the other the same person is seen as a beneficiary whose interests and advantages have to be considered. This plural-information base cannot be reduced to a monist one without losing something of importance.'[22] Still, evaluations made from these separate perspectives may move in opposite directions. For example, a drowning man in the river beside which one is having a picnic causes one's agency freedom to expand by giving one the occasion to save the man's life. But that same occasion may *reduce* one's well-being (by making one cold and wet and worried if one fetches him) and one's well-being freedom (as one is not free to finish one's lunch in peace).[23] Sen argues that the relevance of well-being or agency may be stronger in some situations than in others but neither can be mechanically dismissed. Also, certain kinds of freedom may conflict with each other (e.g. the freedom to make lots of relatively trivial choices may conflict with the freedom to live a tranquil life). This discussion gestures again to 'the inescapable requirement of valuation involved in the assessment of freedom'.[24]

How does this tie into participation? Participation is a method of decision-making in which the participants who are directly affected by an action make the choice. As a method of choice, participation is distinguished from decision-making by committee, or by voting, or by representative democracy. It takes time, and is not appropriate or efficient for all choices. Yet participation can be related to Sen's account by focusing on the agency of poor groups that participatory processes claim to support.

In Sen's account, choices—and systems that support choices such as democracy (and, I will argue, participation)—have three possible kinds of effects.[25] One is that they may be personally valuable or of intrinsic importance to the chooser(s); another is that they have instrumental or transitive effects that improve outcomes for example on well-being; a third is that they have constructive importance in dynamic value formation. In addition to these Finnis adds a fourth, which Sen addresses somewhat differently but compatibly: that choices have reflexive or intransitive effects on identity and culture.

2.1. *Intrinsic value: self-direction and empowerment*

Sen defines agency freedom as 'what a person is free to do and achieve in pursuit of whatever goals or values he or she regards as important'.[26] He argues that the exercise of agency may be of intrinsic value to the chooser as doer and as judge: 'Acting freely and being able to choose are, in this view, directly conducive to well-being, not just because more freedom makes more alternatives available'.[27] Participatory initiatives support one

[22] 1985a: 208. [23] ibid. 207–8. [24] 1992a: 64. [25] 1999c: 10. [26] 1985a: 203.
[27] 1992a: 51.

specific form of agency freedom—the freedom of participants to express their views and, if consensus is reached, to act on them. And it seems clear that this freedom was valued, for example, by Dadi Taja. The various discussions of dimensions of capability in the last chapter suggest that distinct theoretical and empirical exercises likewise recognize its value. References to agency occurred under titles such as practical reason (Nussbaum, Finnis), participation (Max-Neef), self-direction (Finnis, Schwartz), self-expression (Inglehart), autonomy and self-determination (Doyal and Gough, Qizilbash).

Sen and Drèze's applied work directly suggests that participation, as an expression of agency, can have intrinsic value:

Participation also has intrinsic value for the quality of life. Indeed being able to do something not only for oneself but also for other members of the society is one of the elementary freedoms which people have reason to value. The popular appeal of many social movements in India confirms that this basic capability is highly valued even among people who lead very deprived lives in material terms.[28]

When a valuable exercise of self-direction or practical reason has occurred then, in Sen's terms, one can speak of 'agency achievement'. Oxfam used the term 'empowerment'.[29]

To see agency as a dimension of human development, or as a functioning, or even as an 'outcome' gives a framework for analysing the value of agency relative to other considerations in any particular commitment or choice.[30]

Acts of choice are, however, not necessarily valuable, and the value of agency achievement with respect to the value of participating in other domains of development is qualified, as was sketched in Chapter 2. Furthermore, just as all kinds of knowledge are not equally important, so too all choices are not valuable; in fact some may be bothersome distractions or too burdensome to bear. Agency achievement may be realized whether one is a unique decision-maker or a participant in a group decision, as in the case of participation. Where more than one decision-maker is engaged, the process and act of choosing may (not necessarily will) also have intrinsic value in instantiating friendship, exercising sociability, or consolidating a sense of community, purpose, and cooperation among the decision-making group. We shall return to this point.[31]

---

[28] Drèze and Sen (1995: 106) see also Drèze and Sen (1989).
[29] Unfortunately present usage of the word 'empowerment' is complicated by many alternative definitions that have nothing whatever to do with intrinsic value and are merely glosses for descriptive terms such as 'access to credit'. When I use the term empowerment (e.g. in the three case studies in Ch. 7), it carries the definition of agency achievement alone.
[30] It does not diminish the importance of a focus on capability rather than functioning, as the next chapter shall argue.
[31] Finnis argues that although a community admittedly presumes some unity in nature or the ability of communication, in shared knowledge and understanding, in language and culture and technology, 'no degree of unity in those ... three orders can substitute for ... co-operation and common commitment' (1980: 138).

Table 4.1. *Agency as an intrinsically valued dimension*

Sample dimensions
    Life/health/security
    Understanding
    Excellence in work and play
Self-direction or practical reasons (Agency)
    Friendship and affiliation
    Inner peace/self-integration
    Creative expression
    Spirituality/harmony with sources of meaning and value
    Harmony with the natural world

2.2. *Transitive effects: consequences*

Choices and their resulting actions have both transitive and intransitive effects. The transitive effects, 'are the states of affairs constituted by my [our] chosen behaviour and its further results in the world'.[32] As a result of the rose group's decision, rose plants were brought in by a truck and roses were produced. In the absence of their decision, roses would not have been around at all. All of the other Table 4.1 changes—from fragrant clothes to friendships to the capabilities provided by the rose income—are also transitive effects.

Transitive effects may be significantly wider than the intended or direct effects of a particular activity. They also include the unintended effects, the side-effects, the externalities, and the indirect effects.

Applying the concept of agency to choice, not only might the ability to make decisions be personally empowering (whether one is a poor widow or a dictator), but the 'transitive' effects of choices may be more or less valuable to the decision-makers themselves, and to other groups in society.

Political freedom may have an instrumental role in development, as Sen has demonstrated. The transitive effects of choices that are made with public scrutiny and/or participation may be more equitable than choices made privately. For example, famines have never occurred in a country that has regular elections and a free press (although undernourishment and many other kinds of absolute poverty persist in democratic systems).[33] In a similar manner, participation may have an instrumental role in improving effectiveness because the analysis of needs is more accurate, or because the local information is more accurate, or because participation motivates local contributions of resources and attention. Likewise decisions made by participatory processes may be more equitable because (if) they include the interests of the poor. This may be the case even when the poor persons do not actually speak (just like famines may be prevented even if the free press does not always actually write); the possibility that they

---

[32] Finnis (1983: 139).   [33] 1981a, Drèze and Sen (1989, 1990).

could speak is sufficiently real that decision-makers take active note of their interests. However, the converse of all these is also true: in hierarchical societies, or in societies with mafias, or in certain technical decisions, a participatory decision-making process may generate suboptimal transitive effects.

2.3. *Constructive effects: value formation*

Sen also argues that 'the practice of democracy gives citizens an opportunity to learn from one another, and helps society to form its values and priorities . . . In this sense, democracy has *constructive* importance.'[34] He cites the example of declining fertility rates, which have been 'much influenced by public discussion of the bad effects of high fertility rates on the community at large and especially on the lives of young women'.[35] In this example it was participation as much as formal democracy that created the change. Public discussions of family planning (fuelled by new information) gradually led to a reshaping of the values around family and child-bearing. There were two aspects to this change, which the quote above intimates: new information (learning from one another about family planning, declining infant mortality rates, overpopulation, economic analysis of alternative family structures) and a critical reflection on values (the value of many children for reasons of status and labor force, in relation to the value of maternal health, and the value of enabling higher aspirations for one's children). These are discussed individually below.

2.3.1. *Information and value formation*
The first insight—into the relationship between information and value change—is one of Sen's earliest. In a 1967 paper entitled 'The nature and classes of Prescriptive Judgements',[36] Sen considered the statement that sheared Anglo-American economics from ethics, since which they have not comfortably reunited. Robbins wrote, famously and in his time controversially, ' . . . it does not seem logically possible to associate the two studies [ethics and economics] in any form but mere juxtaposition. Economics deals with ascertainable facts; ethics with valuation and obligations.'[37] Robbins's statement, Sen wrote, 'would hold if ethics dealt only with basic judgments'. Basic judgements are ones in which 'no conceivable revision of factual assumptions can make [the decision-maker] revise the judgment'.[38] But the assumption that all of ethical decision-making deals with basic judgements, Sen argued, is not realistic. Many decisions are non-basic, in that they depend on particular factual assumptions, and will require revision if the particular underlying assumption proves false or changes.[39] And even if certain moral

---

[34] 1999c: 10.   [35] ibid. 11.   [36] See also Sen (1966a and 1970: 59–64).
[37] (1932). Cited in Sen (1967: 53).   [38] 1967: 54.

[39] Sen regards Mill's utilitarian ethics as non-basic and compulsive, although they derive from a basic non-compulsive utilitarian value plus factual assumptions (i.e. that 'all cases of justice are also cases of expediency') (1967: 58).

rules or principles *are* basic, he continued, they may be 'non-compulsive'[40] meaning (i) that they do not imply an imperative unconditionally although they do imply a hypothetical imperative ('in the absence of any other judgments one should do x rather than y'), (ii) that they may conflict with other 'non-compulsive' judgements, and (implicitly) (iii) that they should be taken into consideration in every case to which they apply, whether or not in the end the decision taken accords with them. Thus in cases where judgements are non-basic, or basic but non-compulsive, Robbins's position—that 'if we disagree about the morality of the taking of interest [Robbins's example] (and we understand what we are talking about), then there is no room for argument'[41]—does not hold: there *is* room for either further consideration of factual evidence, or for moral argument. Again, within a particular person's or community's system, conflicts in values are resolved either by relaxing compulsiveness or by relaxing basicness.

It will prove worthwhile to consider the concept of basic judgement further for a moment. Sen introduces the idea of basic judgements with this example, which shows that the distinctive quality of basic judgements is that they cannot be disputed by factual information:

[A] person may express the judgment, 'A rise in national income measured at base year prices indicates a better economic situation.' We may ask him whether he will stick to this judgment under all factual circumstances, and go on inquiring, 'Would you say the same if the circumstances were such and such (e.g., the poor were poorer and the rich a lot richer)?' If it turns out that he will revise the judgment under certain factual circumstances, then the judgment can be taken to be non-basic in his value system. If, on the other hand, there is no factual situation when a certain person will regard killing a human being to be justifiable, then not killing a human being is a basic value judgment in his system.[42]

Not only does this passage describe basic judgements; it also hints at an answer to the next question, which is how we find out what these judgements might be. While Sen thinks it possible, although unlikely, that a person has no basic value judgements, he thinks it far more likely that a person may not actually know whether her given judgement is basic or not. Therefore, as we have just seen, Sen offers a procedure for arriving at basic judgements by progressively removing factual assumptions:

Consider, for example, the value judgment, 'The government should not raise the money supply more than in proportion to the national output', based, let us assume, on a factual theory relating money supply and output to inflation. If this theory of inflation is disputed, which is a legitimate reason against the value judgment in question, the person may move on to a more fundamental value judgment, 'The government should not do anything that leads to inflation'. If that too is based on some factual assumption, making it non-basic, the process of moving backwards, as it were, may be repeated. From judgment J_0 based on factual

---

[40] *Non-compulsive judgements (NJ)*: imply an imperative, but are not unqualified: (x is nicer than y): 'if [it] is not to lead to an invariable assent to the command "Let me do x", there is need for explaining why not' (1967: 49)—i.e. a reason in favour of choosing y over x.

[41] (1932: 134). An interesting empirical exploration of the distinction between basic and non-basic judgements is Wainryb (1993).   [42] 1967: 50.

assumptions F_1 one moves to a judgment (or a set of judgments) J_1 independent of F_1; if that is dependent on factual assumptions F_2, one moves to judgments J_2 independent of both F_1 and F_2. In this way one might hope to reach ultimately, in this person's value system, some basic value judgments, J_n.[43]

This procedure, he notes, can never positively *establish* basicness, but 'it can establish that the judgment is not non-basic in any obviously relevant way'.[44] In fact, it seems that Sen does not consider it particularly necessary to establish basicness (and that is not a focus of this chapter in the least). To be precise, he does not dwell on the difficulty of establishing basicness so much as he appreciates the positive role of the reflective process:

It may be true that 'in the end there must come a point where one gets no further answer, but only a repetition of the injunction: "Value this because it is valuable" ' [quoting Ayer 1959: 244] but there is no sure-fire test which tells us whether such an ultimate point has in fact arrived. From this we do not, unfortunately, get a rule to decide when rational disputation is potentially fruitful and when it is not.[45]

The notion that learning can enable value formation recurs in Sen's writing on positional objectivity and evaluator relativity.[46] This work develops the observation that a statement may be *objective*, in the sense that any person who shared the position of the evaluator 'can understandably take much the same view for much the same reasons', but is not necessarily *true*, because the 'position' of the person (from which their statement was objective) may include ignorance, inexperience, or a particular mental tendency. For example, persons on earth might understandably think that the sun and the moon were the same size. Conversely, the discrepancy between self-reported health status of widows versus widowers in post-famine Bengal in 1944, or between women in Kerala and women in Bihar[47] can be explained, Sen suggests, by specifying 'in great detail a person's background and other positional features in that society', such as the systematic deprivation of women, or the relative levels of female education.[48] 'The positional objectivity of these views . . . command attention, and social scientists can hardly dismiss them as simply subjective and capricious. But neither can these self-perceptions be taken to be accurate . . . in any trans-positional understanding.'[49]

Sen sets out this analysis in order to develop his earlier observation that access to additional knowledge, knowledge from science, knowledge about the world, knowledge about predicted effects of actions, may affect cultural value systems. Sen actively sketches how dissenters and sceptics can access not only technical information, but

---

[43] ibid. 52.   [44] ibid. 53.
[45] (1970: 64). Sen does not give a 'list' of basic judgements but he does provide examples of what they might be. One candidate was the statement, 'a rise of national income means a better economic situation'. Other possibilities Sen considers are the ten commandments of the Judaeo-Christian tradition, and the principles 'non-violence', 'faithfulness', 'honesty', 'freedom of speech', and 'utilitarianism' (1967: 55).
[46] Sen (1982a, 1983b, 1995i); see also Nussbaum and Sen (1989).
[47] Sen (1985b, appendix B). Kynch and Sen (1983). Murray and Chen (1992).
[48] Sen (1993d: 13).   [49] ibid. 10.

also the observations and beliefs of other societies, and use these constructively to challenge a majority view.[50]

2.3.2. Value clarification

The second constructive role of participation is in clarifying values and value priorities. Recall from Chapter 3 that one function Sen attributes to ethical rationality is critical reflection on what people value. As quoted there, 'Socrates might have overstated matters a bit when he proclaimed that "the unexamined life is not worth living," but an examination of what kind of life one should sensibly choose cannot really be completely irrelevant to rational choice'.[51] Similarly, Sen describes in approving terms Tibor Scitovsky's work: '... the real departure from orthodox economic theory is Scitovsky's emphasis on critical reflection about what one wants, rather than on making cunning choices in line with given preferences'.[52] Hence a second constitutive function of participation can be to clarify what a group actually really wants. This entails the possibility of a partially explicit (as discussed earlier in Ch. 3, Sect. 2.2) discussion of the value issues involved in a decision:

> If informed scrutiny by the public is central to any such social evaluation (as I believe is the case), the implicit values have to be made more explicit, rather than being shielded from scrutiny on the spurious ground that they are part of an 'already available' metric that the society can immediately use without further ado.[53]

Sen discussed these issues in an earlier joint paper which addresses the rather thorny issue of internal debate about contentious traditions. They introduce the criterion of consistency.[54] That is, the paper offers 'a method for the evaluation and criticism of tradition that responds both (*a*) to the need for criticism and (*b*) to the worries about external imposition'.[55] The method comprises three criteria of appropriateness: (i) it must be internal, conducted by a member of the community, or one who will be accepted as such; (ii) the evaluator must be immersed in the values and hopes of the community, not detached from them; and (iii) the evaluator must be genuinely critical of what she encounters.

This method of evaluation is attributed to Aristotle, and it is worth quoting their presentation of the relevant passage in full:

> Aristotle insists that these two goals—individual clarification and communal attunement—can be achieved together by a cooperative critical discourse that insists upon the philosophical virtues of orderliness, deliberateness, and precision.
> 'Concerning all these things we must try to seek conviction through arguments, using the traditional beliefs as our witnesses and standards. For it would be best of all if all human beings could come into an evident communal agreement with what we shall say, but, if not, that all

---

[50] ibid., sect. vii.   [51] 1995*b*: 16.
[52] 1996*d*: 485. This element was developed as 'correspondence-rationality' in Sen (1986*c*). It was admitted in that paper that 'careful reflection is not, of course, a spectacularly precise concept' (p. 345).
[53] Sen (1999*a*: 80).
[54] Nussbaum and Sen (1989); see also Finnis (1999: 363–4), Robbins (1935), Sen (1997f), Wiggins (1998).   [55] Nussbaum and Sen (1989: 308).

Participation and Culture

should agree in some way. And this they will do if they are led carefully until they shift their position. For everyone has something of his own to contribute to the truth, and it is from these that we go on to give some sort of demonstration about these things. For from what is said truly but not clearly, as we advance we will also get clarity, always moving from what is usually said in a jumbled fashion to a more perspicuous view. There is a difference in every inquiry between arguments that are said in a philosophical way and those that are not. Hence we must not think that it is superfluous for the political person to engage in the sort of reflection that makes perspicuous not only the 'that' but also the 'why': for this is the contribution of the philosopher in each area' (Aristotle, *Eudemian Ethics*, 1216a 26–39).

Here again Aristotle insists, against the Platonist approach, on the fundamental internality of the reflective process that assesses values: the 'witnesses' and 'standards' of the process are the 'appearances' or the shared beliefs, and each participant has something to contribute to the truth. And yet the process does not give us back a simple repetition of what each person thought at the start. This is so because when we scrutinize what we think, we will notice inconsistencies and unclarities that we do not notice when we simply talk and act without reflecting. When the deliberative process confronts the reflecting participant with all of the alternative views on a topic, leads him or her through a thorough imaginative exploration of each, and shows how each choice bears on many others that this person wishes to make in a consistent way—then many unconsidered positions may be modified. And yet this modification, if it takes place, will take place, not as imposition from without, but as a discovery about that person's own values that are the deepest and the most central. This is self-discovery and discovery of one's own traditions.[56]

Sen did not further develop this particular 'method' directly. I cite it, however, because this gives an image of (and is reminiscent of) the kind of discourse and debate which may surround 'value clarification' in the presence of an activist or community mobilizer.

As was mentioned in the last chapter, Sen has become more explicit in his support for public debate and democratic practice as a procedure of making social choices and the value judgements they entail. For example, in his article 'Democracy as a Universal Value' Sen argues that the most important thing that had happened in the twentieth century was 'the rise of democracy . . . as a universal commitment'.[57] *Development as Freedom* clearly takes this line, arguing that 'The reach and effectiveness of open dialogue are often underestimated in assessing social and political problems'. The importance of public discussion in a participatory context stretches beyond value formation, but this is one aspect of it.

2.4. *Intransitive effects: identity*[58]

But free choices and their transitive effects constitute not only what a person or group or community effectively does, but also, to a degree, who they are—their identity and culture. The rose cultivation group, by virtue of their decision and subsequent

---

[56] ibid. 313–14. [57] 1999*b*: 3.
[58] The use of this term is awkward because of the large philosophical literature that surrounds it; the discussion that follows is strictly confined to Sen's and Finnis's contributions on the topic.

occupation, gained a distinctive identity (identities) in the village. Dadi Taja sold garlands in the village which were used for decorating the Qur'an Sharif and saints' shrines, and occasionally for weddings, so her identity as a rose-seller had overtones of facilitating worship and celebration. Of course she had other identities too—as a mother, or a member of the Solangi caste—that were not affected. Still, the intransitive effect of choices is that they simply *are* self-determining and self-creating.[59] Choices, whether deliberated or undebated, whether made in haste or by default, *simply do* shape identities. If the decision is made by someone else, it still shapes the identities of those who are affected (as well as the identity of the decision-maker).

Finnis points out that choices shape group identities: '[c]hoices have constitutive implications not only for individuals but for communities'.[60] One paradigmatic case of this is how the choice of political constitution may—*if* that constitution is enacted *and followed*—frame social interactions. Another example of how commitments create national character, or better, culture, is that they create different sets of moral norms. Finnis, when arguing against Mackie's 'argument from relativity', notes that moral variation in societies derives not necessarily (and certainly not only) from deficiencies in reasonableness—immoral choices—but also, desirable moral diversity derives from the freely chosen moral commitments. These in turn generate (and are sustained by) norms and duties, or, in North's terms, institutions.[61] Finnis argues that not only is self-constitution 'a foreseeable, intrinsic and necessary effect of one's free choices';[62] maintaining one's identity, or the identity of a community, is also a good.[63]

When Sen called for 'explicit scrutiny' about the ends in a development strategy, it seems he was largely advocating this exercise because of the intransitive effect of development strategies—because such strategies incrementally build up social habits and identities.[64] We consider this in the section on respecting culture below, but first deepen, a bit, the identity-constituting aspects of development choices.

2.4.1. Practices

One cannot 'enjoy' a dimension of human development or a general functioning without ever undertaking a particular action which pursues it. Actualized functionings will always have a particular form. One cannot drink 'nutrition' through a straw. One must drink a mango milkshake, or eat a plate of biscuits. Whether or not functionings need be accurately described at anything more than a general concrete level, their presence will always imply cultural and historical embodiment. What significance if any

---

[59] Or, to take a quite different example, when Socrates chose to 'leave and go home' rather than accompany the other four associates in bringing Leon of Salamis to be executed unjustly, his choice 'constituted (or reconstituted), established (or re-established) himself as a certain kind of person'. Plato's *Apology*, 32b–d, quoted and discussed in Finnis (1999: 363–4); cf. Finnis (1983: 139).

[60] Finnis (1983: 57).   [61] Finnis (1983: 76 f.).   [62] ibid. 141; see also 136 f.

[63] Finnis (1983: 39) argues the point and cites Aristotle: 'No-one chooses to possess the whole world if he has first to become someone else' (*Nicomachean Ethics*, 4:1166a19–22).

[64] See especially (1996d), where Sen appreciatively follows through Scitovsky's social analysis and advocacy of cultural change away from over-indulging in comfort.

does it have that these embodiments differ—that communities specify nutrition, or shelter, or leisure, differently?

In the course of explaining a 'core concept' of virtue, Alasdair MacIntyre introduces helpfully the term 'cultural practice' and sketches how practices build into cultural systems.[65] His definition could be simplified using terms already defined to the following: a *practice* is a kind of activity which is a socially established path for pursuing excellence in, or more simply, for enjoying, functioning(s) that instantiate one or more dimensions of human flourishing.[66]

This definition serves to flag certain characteristics of practices. First, a practice may be held uniquely by one community or society; diversity would be expected. Whereas the dimensions of human development are arguably relevant cross-culturally, the same does not hold for practices. Also, practices that appear the same may have different points and value. A string of convincing bird calls may be a musical performance in one setting, and a method of communication among hunters in another. Clifford Geertz describes the knowledge of practices as 'ineluctably local, indivisible from their instruments and their encasements'.[67] So sets of practices represent inherently particular patterns of realizing human development. Secondly, practices are not necessarily ethical. For instance, a culturally established practice of underfeeding female children may promote 'life' of the male children, and 'practical reasonableness' of the food allocator who depends on her sons for care later in life. It is intelligible but not necessarily ethical. Thirdly, and of particular relevance, practices have *histories*, and they entail *interactions among persons*. That is, a practice, such as copper-beating, involves relationships—both with the master who teaches the apprentice, and also with past masters who set the standards and designs.[68] Furthermore practices have histories: they change and evolve dynamically—the master copper worker can tell you the history of his particular patterns. Finally, the practices to which one person has access (as a member of different social groups) build on each other in the aggregate to form a loosely interlocked cultural system. And in this cultural system people learn experientially to pursue valuable functionings. The corollary to this is that when practices are destroyed, people's paths to enjoying human development are destroyed.

---

[65] For a fuller discussion see Alkire and Black (1997).

[66] MacIntyre's definition is: a practice is 'any coherent and complex form of socially established co-operative human activity through which goods internal to that form of activity are realised in the course of trying to achieve those standards of excellence which are appropriate to, and partially definitive of, that form of activity, with the result that human powers to achieve excellence, and human conceptions of the ends and goods involved, are systematically extended' (1981: 175 f.) This definition is narrower than MacIntyre's in that practices need not be complex, and that it is not a property of a practice *itself* that the 'human conceptions of ends and goods . . . are systematically extended'.

[67] Geertz (1993: 34).

[68] '[A practice's] goods can only be achieved by subordinating ourselves to the best standard so far achieved, and that entails subordinating ourselves within the practice in our relationship to other practitioners'. Put differently, 'Every practice requires a certain kind of relationship between those who participate in it' (MacIntyre 1981: 177).

And so, quickly and sharply, the implications of participation become abundantly clear. For it must be clear that *development has as one of its primary objectives the introduction of novel practices*—that is, of the practical possibility of realizing a common good which had never been feasible previously: different agricultural practices, different sanitation practices, different housing, nutritional or educational practices. Development exerts its force on existing practices (and on the commitments that organize and sustain them) *minimally* by offering an alternative practice. The very existence of a novel possibility for action demands a re-evaluation of the status quo.

Yet—and here MacIntyre's assessment becomes valuable—novel practices, recall, do not only change the direct paths by which people enjoy human development, they also affect practices with which they interlock. Novel practices, innovations which become socially established and integrated into the cultural fabric, also (intentionally or unintentionally) change the identity and character of the community. So it would seem that part of the evaluation of the novel practices that development proposes should rest not on their transitive effects, but also on their intransitive effects.

The issue that gives us pause and demands deeper exploration, of course, is the vexed issue of cultural and ethical disagreements that eventuate during development. As the *Oxfam Handbook* put it,

> The most difficult of all the issues in culture-sensitive development and relief work, and one which is therefore often overlooked, is dealing with cultural values very different from those of the donor agency and its supporters. One of the most common accusations against Northern based donor agencies is that they exceed their role of supporting development or relief programmes when they question certain cultural practices among the people they support.[69]

On the one hand 'it is difficult not to feel that some of these changes are beneficial to the societies that undergo them'.[70] On the other hand there is 'the sticking point; to have economic growth, must we buy a whole package that changes the society, the polity, and the culture along with the economy?' The package of changes allegedly includes 'environmental destruction, meaningless work, spiritual desolation, neglect of the aged . . .'.[71] A third issue is that participation, being fundamentally a process of consensus, seems unable to challenge any reasons or decisions around which consensus emerges. Are there 'reasons' we (whether 'we' are Oxfam or the Marvi Women's Organization or the rose growers) should reject?

2.4.2. *Sen's account of culture and identities*

In his writings on culture, Sen's main focus of discussion is no longer his disagreement with economists but rather with communitarians and guardians of tradition or of critics of certain value sets—be they development sceptics, religious fundamentalists, political elite, or cultural experts.[72] The writings are richly textured, hardly amenable

---

[69] Eade and Williams (1995: 257).   [70] Nussbaum and Sen (1989: 307).
[71] Apffel-Marglin and Marglin (1990: 2), both quotes.
[72] These categories are explicitly mentioned (1999a: 32). For Sen's writings on culture and identity see especially (1993i,j, 1996d,f, 1997f, 1998b,c,g, 1999a, 2000d,e,g).

to summary. But the heart of the analysis is germane to this chapter's consideration of agency. In an article on 'Indian Traditions and the Western Imagination' Sen explores with some depth the historical characterizations of India in the West, which settled on an India that was comfortably mystical and religious. Sen points out that this assigned identity discounts the well-developed atheistic, scientific, and rationalist traditions of India.[73] 'Indian traditions are often taken to be intimately associated with religion, and indeed in many ways they are, and yet Sanskrit and Pali have larger literatures on systematic atheism and agnosticism than perhaps in any other classical language—Greek, Roman, Hebrew, or Arabic'.[74] Ascriptions of 'Asian Values' and the other large-scale generalizations of cultural modes may be challenged on similar grounds—that they inevitably leave aside the breadth and internal diversity of cultural viewpoints.[75]

Furthermore, although an individual's identity is constrained by factors such as race or religion, yet each individual has plural alternative identities which he or she may stress more on some occasions than others: 'A person can simultaneously have the identity of being, say, an Italian, a woman, a feminist, a vegetarian, a novelist, a fiscal conservative, a jazz fan, and a Londoner'.[76] Thus Sen opposes Sandel's view that 'a person's identity is something he or she detects, rather than determines'.[77] Sen argues rather that within the constrained possibilities of identity open to any person, he or she can choose to emphasize and express certain aspects of identity, including cultural identity, more than others. His argument hinges on the observation that people actually do doubt, question, change, examine, and reaffirm their cultural values and practices. 'An adult and competent person has the ability to question what has been taught to her—even day in and day out.'[78] So not only do persons have plural identities, they are able to reason and to choose how to live these out.

Sen's observations are not distinctive except, perhaps, in their manner of expression. In fact he writes, that they 'are so elementary that they would be embarrassing to assert had the opposite not been frequently presumed, either explicitly or by implication'.[79]

2.4.3. Deciding cultural trade-offs

As one might suspect from the above quotation, the opposite views—namely, that 'culture' must be either preserved or discarded—have been forcefully pressed—as much by anti-development activists who wish to call a halt to globalization, as by political leaders who oppose human rights conventions, by anthropologists who wish to protect endangered cultures, and by religious leaders who wish to protect ancient traditions.

---

[73] (1997f). See Nussbaum and Sen (1989), which sketched the same broad argument. See also (1993j) where he describes three approaches to the investigation of India by outsiders, which he calls the 'exoticist' (focusing on what is strange), the 'magisterial' (from the point of view of those charged with governing the colony), and the 'investigative' (merely trying to understand it all from the outside).

[74] 1998c: 24.

[75] See Sen (1999a: ch. 10, 1996f, 1997k, 1998b, 2000g,e), Huntington (1996), Harrison and Huntington (2000).

[76] 1998c: 14.

[77] Sen (1998c: 16), summarizing Sandel's position. [78] ibid. 24. [79] ibid. 24–5.

Sen's decomposition of culture into different, evolving elements, and his further argument that persons have multiple different identities (cultural and otherwise) and can choose, within constraints, how to live out these identities, is a minor extension of his work on agency that we reviewed earlier this chapter. Yet it sets the stage for an understated but incisive analysis of power, which may not have been appreciated as fully as it deserves. To those who would block development on cultural grounds, Sen points out (to mix traditions with amusing accuracy) 'the indignity of speaking on another's behalf.'[80] That is, he points out that those who try to protect certain cultural traditions may be effectively short-circuiting the process of active deliberation which can and should be undertaken by those whose traditions these are. The same criticism could apply to those who try instead to change certain cultural traditions in the name of development or growth.[81] In *Development as Freedom* Sen writes that the real conflict is between:

the basic value that the people must be allowed to decide freely what traditions they wish or do not wish to follow; and the insistence that established traditions be followed (no matter what), or, alternatively, people must obey the decisions by religious or secular authorities who enforce traditions real or imagined.[82]

That is, Sen lumps together and criticizes quite different constituencies who protect (or criticize) some facet of a culture *if* they do so without ongoing public debate as to whether or not people value this cultural facet, and value it enough to bear the 'opportunity cost' of the alternative.[83] In resolving trade-offs between economic development and culture Sen calls for a participatory resolution at the lowest level, and thus for a procedural rather than a normative response:

There is an inescapable valuational problem involved in deciding what to choose if and when it turns out that some parts of tradition cannot be maintained along with economic or social changes that may be needed for other reasons. It is a choice that the people involved have to face and assess. The choice is neither closed (as many development apologists seem to suggest), nor is it one for the elite 'guardians' of tradition to settle (as many development sceptics seem to presume). If a traditional way of life has to be sacrificed to escape grinding poverty or minuscule longevity (as many traditional societies have had for thousands of years), then it is the people directly involved who must have the opportunity to participate in deciding what should be chosen.[84]

This account is quite interesting (although it has not touched upon some of the other hard questions, such as the observation that even to offer persons the

---

[80] Banuri 'recounts what one post-modernist, Deleuze, said of another, Foucault: "You have taught us something absolutely fundamental: The indignity of speaking on someone's behalf" ' (1990b: 96).

[81] For example Huntington (1996), Harrison (1983), Harrison and Huntington (2000). Sen addresses them in particular in (2000g). [82] 1999a: 31–2.

[83] To use an example Sen does not use but might have, Kuper noted that the intellectual architect of the apartheid system in South Africa, W. W. M. Eiselen, 'had been a professor of ethnology'. His studies led him to predict that 'if the integrity of traditional cultures were undermined, social disintegration would follow. [Hence] Eiselen recommended that government policy should be aimed at fostering "higher Bantu culture and not at producing black Europeans." . . . Segregation was the proper course for South Africa, because only segregation would preserve cultural differences' (1999, p. xiii). [84] 1999a: 31.

possibility of a coherent cultural identity may require a form of seclusion). In particular, it seems that Sen is protecting the freedom of persons to consider the intransitive or identity effects of their choice.

This section has identified four ways in which participation can interface with different agency roles. The next sections turn to the question of a model for the interaction of external actors with local groups.

3. SUBSIDIARITY

Only now, after a complete analysis of the role of agency, are we able to return to the question of who should make decisions—the 'power' question raised in Chapter 2. Given the radical underdetermination of Sen's and Finnis's approaches—in which the possible set of capabilities is very large, in which one can rule out less effective options but not necessarily single out a 'best' alternative, in which the relative weightings of capabilities vary by person, by time period, by commitment and resources and identity, a top-down decision-making procedure is not feasible. At the same time, what we have presumed but not elaborated much at all are the efficiency relationships which have traditionally been dominant in development economics (hence are elaborated at length elsewhere), and which point out that effective poverty reduction is a function of natural and financial resources and human capital and institutions and authority—that technical expertise and authority matter. One crucial aspect of the rose cultivation was the contribution by the agronomist confirming that roses would grow and identifying the appropriate breed for that environment. As a result the roses grew; had they not, however animated and widespread the participation, the project would have not realized as many impacts. The principle that pulls together these two considerations is subsidiarity.

The principle of subsidiarity[85] holds that the most local agent(s) capable of making a choice should make it. Its relevance in the light of the above discussion is twofold.

First, the principle of subsidiarity argues that the most local agents whose identity and well-being will be affected by a choice and who are capable of making it, should do so.[86] Intransitive changes may be inadvertently engineered by some agent. For example, Oxfam may have chosen to introduce goats into Arabsolangi because these had had high returns in nearby villages. But had they done so, Oxfam's choice would have been between one income generating practice and another, arguably more lucrative practice—not between one lifestyle (cutting goat fodder, marketing goats) and another (picking roses, threading garlands), or between one identity (goat-owner) or another (rose cultivator). The important decision of identity would have been made by default.

Secondly, for more fundamental or lasting choices, the deliberation of incommensurable options involves or requires a knowledge of the character or other

---

[85] The principle was formulated earlier this century by German Jesuit priests to insist 'that people should not be absorbed into giant enterprises in which they are mere cogs without opportunity to act on their own initiative' (Finnis 1983: 38–9).   [86] Khwaja (2001).

commitments of the person or group who will have to carry out the choices. As mentioned earlier, Finnis notes that the rational commitment will take account of 'one's assessment of one's capacities, circumstances, and even of one's tastes'.[87] This coheres with Sen's view that freedom can produce instrumentally better outcomes. For example, the rose group felt that bananas were too heavy, as many of the group were older women. Also, they had heard stories about handicraft income generation projects that had failed, and so they were not motivated to do handicrafts. Had Oxfam made a decision on technical grounds and ignored local knowledge, they might easily have chosen either bananas or handicrafts, in which case the women simply may not have cooperated.

Thus the principle of subsidiarity respresents the value of choice-making to the agent(s); it highlights the importance of the positional location of decision-making. At the same time it keeps in view crucial considerations of efficiency and effectiveness.

4. EXTERNAL ASSISTANCE

The question of who determines or selects the capabilities to be pursued is related to knowledge and decision-making power. We started this chapter by focusing on participatory processes, but by focusing in particular on those that are undertaken in cooperation with some 'external' agent—whether it be Oxfam, or a government ministry or a veterinarian. This section deliberately 'lowers the level of optical resolution'[88] quite a bit and studies the broad models of external development assistance that coordinate agency and well-being objectives, and expand the information base on which decisions are made.

The sharp end of the question, to which this section will be directed, is not only *whether* or not information regarding plural values and principles is to be used in an analysis of how capabilities have expanded, but *who* will conduct the analysis and *by what process* the information will enter. The model has two actors: the development agency, which has assymetric technical information and resources, and the community, which has asymmetric values information[89] and includes poor participants.

There are at least three possible ways development agencies can respond to the asymmetry in information on values: (i) adjust to be successful in reaching their original goal, (ii) adjust their goal, (iii) provide their information and resources while deferring to decisions made by the community. There are advantages and disadvantages of each of these approaches and they are complementary rather than competing ways of pursuing human development. The first two are rather familiar, so will only be presented in quick caricature.

Development agencies may, as mentioned earlier, seek to acquire local knowledge in order to be more effective or realize transitive effects. For example, imagine that the

---

[87] Finnis (1980: 105); Grisez (1993: 292, see pp. 291–4).

[88] The optical metaphor is from Wiggins (1998: 113).

[89] Bearing in mind that the values are not static but constantly in the process of formation and destruction.

original goal of an NGO called BAAB which has expanded into Aadvardia is economic growth, or profit maximization. In Aadvardia, though, people do not work over a week-long traditional semi-annual holiday because they value religious observance and/or social celebrations. The development agency BAAB installs a chicken farm which needs labour-intensive attention on a daily basis (but which also provides employment, raises productivity and income, increases human capital, and generates a profit). The holiday time comes; rather than changing their values, suppose that the employees do not work over the period. The chickens fall ill. BAAB will not be able to make a profit in Aadvardia if the illness recurs semi-annually. Therefore, rather than abandon the activity or relocate it, BAAB develops a chicken farm which can do with week-long periods of low-level maintenance. *In the interests of efficiency* vis-à-vis *the original goal, the development agency responds to local values.* This response does not require a departure from the original goal(s) of the development agency (profit maximization, possibly combined with employment, increased productivity, and human capital formation) and is inherent in both participatory and service-provision endeavours (note that BAAB could use either approach).[90] The 'success' or 'failure' of the initiative is determinable by the leadership of BAAB. Furthermore, this response is predicated on the supposition that the people did not change the practice which expressed a certain value (holiday, expressing the value of harmony with the transcendent and/or of sociability in the family gatherings and gift-giving and celebration) even when confronted with an employment activity which may have assumed these would change.

Alternatively, an NGO or other agent of development might adjust their goals to incorporate additional desired transitive effects. For example, structural adjustment policies were implemented in many countries in order to address balance of payments crises. But during the 1980s politicians, activists, policy-analysts, academics and economists—both from within countries undergoing structural adjustment and from outside—protested. One line of argument was to bring forward research on how the structural adjustment programmes were, in many but not all countries, exacerbating the effects of the world recession on the incomes and health of the poor. To simplify greatly, these economists challenged the international development agencies and argued that (i) the overarching goal of the development agencies should be human development, and structural adjustment was justified as an operational goal in so far as there were structural barriers to obtaining the growth required for this development, but (ii) another component of human development is poverty alleviation, and this aspect was not adequately captured in the current model and was being negatively affected, so (iii) the international development agencies should restructure their operational 'goal' of structural adjustment to include a concern for the poor as well as for economic growth, and develop criteria of evaluating their success or failure *vis-à-vis* this goal. In their own words, 'Our concern is . . . how the broader human issues of compelling and urgent importance can be *brought into* this

---

[90] If BAAB were participatory or even were fully self-managed, its leaders would have been aware of the holiday from the start, and made the adjustments before the activity began, but this change would have still been necessary in the interests of efficiency and productivity.

priority exercise of economic policymaking'.[91] Similarly, variables such as meeting basic needs and empowering participants have become direct objectives of microeconomic development activities.

Both of these broad kinds of responses are familiar and have been very valuable. The following chapter will take up the second response and discuss what the status of basic needs are with respect to local values. The third model actively devolves decision-making authority, while continuing to support value formation and choice by participants.

4.1. *Elements of freedom-expanding assistance*

Given the conceptually and practically validated importance of participation and informed choice in Sen's own writings, and the increasing professionalization of economic development initiatives, it might be interesting to consider more fully the model of informed choice.[92]

Beauchamp and Childress describe informed choice in such a way that it has a conceptual parallel with externally assisted poverty reduction. They point out that medicine, like poverty reduction, is an undertaking in which two norms for doctors (NGO staff)—the norm of beneficence/justice and particular expert knowledge or resources, and the norm of respect for the (patient's, community's) autonomy—operate and at times collide:

- economic development, like medicine, is supposed to be a '*beneficent*' activity; as the doctor's expertise and action 'serves' the patient's health, so the expertise and resources of development institutions are intended to improve people's well-being;
- the '*autonomous* authorization' of development initiatives by local groups is necessary in development, as well as in medicine, on the grounds of subsidiarity;[93]

---

[91] Cornia et al. (1987: 5). I am picking out one of a number of responses—others included protests, media reports, lobbying, and radical critiques. The authors of *Adjustment with a Human Face* explained why they chose this 'depth' of critique: 'For the authors as for many others, it is not difficult to imagine international economic policies and approaches which would provide a more positive and expansive environment within which developing countries could develop more dynamically . . . For the most part, we have spent little time exploring such policies and approaches in this document, on the grounds that many such analyses are available elsewhere and that progress towards them is, for the most part, stymied politically for the present. We have accordingly concentrated on what we believe could readily be done within the present international economic order' (1987: 7).

[92] There are also applications of informed consent in political science, in particular the contractarian tradition, to which I will not refer.

[93] Beauchamp and Childress write, 'Being autonomous is not the same as being respected as an autonomous agent. To respect an autonomous agent is, at a minimum, to acknowledge that person's right to hold views, to make choices, and to take actions based on personal values and beliefs. Such respect involves respectful *action*, not merely a respectful *attitude*. It also requires more than obligations of non-intervention in the affairs of persons, because it includes obligations to maintain capacities for autonomous choice in others while allaying fears and other conditions that destroy or disrupt their autonomous actions' (1994: 125).

- the nature of medicine as *necessary* to human *survival* at times precludes physicians from obtaining informed consent, for example—in cases of emergency or incompetence. Similarly, in cases of emergency or incompetence (which will need to be defined in a socio-political context—see below) there may be justification in an economic agency acting without 'autonomous authorization'. However, this is the exception rather than the norm.

Let us take, as an analogy, the example of a doctor and patient relationship.[94] Many will find the suggested analogy immediately offensive because it seems to portray an active expert and a passive victim. But I believe it will become clear quite soon that one purpose of the informed consent model is to remind medical professionals that an 'expert' attitude is inappropriate: the *patient* is not a victim but a person with many activities, needs, and values, of which health is only one. And the *medical professional* is not an expert in all things, but has a delimited area of knowledge and resources in relation to human health.

For example, consider the case of Helen, a 22 year old with painful juvenile arthritis in the hip joint. There are a number of different hip replacements from which she could choose, each of which has slightly different grounds of appeal but none of which, at present, lasts for more than twenty years. If she chose to have a hip replacement at this time she would have to have a second surgery (with its attendant risks) in twenty years. She could also wait ten years by which time, hopefully, a longer wearing hip would have been perfected. If she chooses to wait this could be in the current condition, which is painful but not damaging. Alternatively, she could have her hip 'fused' surgically such that she could walk but only with a limp and not for long distances.

In the procedure of informed consent, the health professional would explain to Helen the various alternatives and Helen would have time to make up her mind. She would return with a decision to go ahead, to stop treatment, or to seek further counsel and explore options about which the health professional knows less.

There are a number of prima facie practical appeals in this procedure, which suggest it may be salient in development:

- Helen has a chance to 'tailor' her health care to her wider values and commitments relating to her career, relationships, aesthetics, personal idiosyncrasies, and so on.
- Medical professionals research and share information on unintended but predictable side-effects then let the patient decide on her preferred course of action.
- The medical professional can be beneficent and communicate knowledge without threatening Helen's autonomy because Helen understands the value, kind, and limitations of medical knowledge and action.
- The physician is held accountable (in this case legally) for providing accurate and full information, communicating it effectively, and completing her work well. Beauchamp and Childress identify five elements of core information which

---

[94] While I refer to the patient in the singular in the text, this is a shorthand for the patient and their family and friends, in whose company most such choices would be discussed and made.

professionals are obligated to disclose: '(1) those facts or descriptions that patients or subjects usually consider material in deciding whether to refuse or consent to the proposed intervention or research, (2) information the professional believes to be material, (3) the professional's recommendation, (4) the purpose of seeking consent, and (5) the nature and limits of consent as an act of authorization'.[95]

- There may be some intrinsic value in Helen's informed reflection process and decision.
- The treatment chosen *will* have intransitive effects on Helen's identity and transitive effects on her capacities; her participation in making this decision allows these to cohere with her other commitments.

In the informed consent model the development agency refrains from acting unless the local community *chooses* the partnership and activities with full awareness of what it is choosing.[96] In a best-case scenario, the development agency recognizes that it has (presuming it does) a certain kind of expertise or resource base *vis-à-vis* a problem that is mutually recognized by the development agency and the community. It identifies and communicates the range of alternatives, the likelihood of success of each, the different side-effects (short-term and long-term; related to the problem and to other dimensions of human and social life) and their associated probabilities. It raises further issues such as the costs of the alternatives, the time range until each might take effect, and whether they, as an agency, would be in a position to implement these jointly with the community or who to contact if they could not. Finally, and most crucially, the development agency (which may or may not be participatory) also recognizes that the problem at issue is just one component in the life of this community, that the community will need to deliberate its present 'value', and the value or disvalue of different side-effects, in view of their wider values and institutions. The development agency recognizes that whether or not it can understand the values which are at stake in the choice, it is the community which must assume responsibility for deciding prospectively which path to follow.

The model also draws attention to the need for a way of recognizing 'valid' consent when the party concerned is a group rather than an individual. Attention to best-practice participatory methods could be maintained and sharpened in this model.

4.2. *Ellerman's autonomy-compatible models*

While the informed consent model focuses on the information interface between development agency and community, David Ellerman focuses on the behaviours and attitudes of development institutions that conduce to agency freedom of communities in the long term, when the communities internalize the knowledge that is now externally provided. He has helpfully synthesized what he terms 'autonomy-compatible' or

---

[95] 1994: 147.

[96] Obviously communities are overlapping, dynamic, internally plural, often conflictual historical entities with probably more than one set of competing values each with its peculiar claim to representativeness and authority, and probably only some of which are recognized by the leading/powerful group(s).

helper-doer models of knowledge-sharing and resource-provision from different disciplines (education, organizational theory, psychology, development). He uses Kant's term autonomy but writes that it has clear links to Sen's capability approach. Ellerman begins with the recognition that 'The notion of an autonomy-compatible intervention has a whiff of paradox since it is an external intervention that somehow does not override the internal locus of causality. If the helper has a significant impact, to what extent are the doers really "helping themselves," or if they are really helping themselves, what is the role of the would-be "helpers"?'[97]

He then turns to identify a coherent approach to autonomy-compatible interventions in development, and argues that it would be akin to the relationship Paolo Freire and John Dewey sketched between teachers and learners, the relationship Hirschman and Schumacher describe between development agencies and governments, the relationship Carl Rogers sketched between therapist and client, or Kierkegaard's account of the dynamic between spiritual teachers and spiritual learners. Drawing on these authors as well as McGregor and Saul Alinsky, Ellerman draws out five 'themes' of what he calls an autonomy-compatible 'helper-doer' relationship.

Theme 1: Helper Has to Start Where the Doers Are. A utopian social engineering approach tries to impose a clean model solution, wiping away the old solution if need be to make room for the new. Using an architectural metaphor, an old building is torn down to create a cleared space, a *tabula rasa*, for constructing the new building. The alternative, non-utopian incremental approach would be to repair one part of the building at a time, ending eventually with a completely rebuilt building. Rebuilding the old, rather than destroying it to engineer a new model on the cleaned slate, is one way of introducing the theme of starting where the doers are. To help the doers help themselves, helpers have to design their assistance based on the current starting point of the doers, not an imaginary clean slate.

Theme 2: Helper Has to See Through the Doers' Eyes. Since the goal is for doers to help themselves, helpers providing assistance need to see the situation through the doers' eyes. The doers' actions will be guided by their own knowledge, conceptual framework, values, and worldview, not those of the helpers.

Theme 3: Helper Cannot Impose Change on Doers. Transformative change comes from the internally motivated activities of the doers. Carrots and sticks used by the helpers will stifle the self-motivation of the doers and produce only superficially conforming behaviour, not transformation.

Theme 4: Help as Benevolence is Ineffective. Autonomy-compatible assistance is neither an imposition (theme 3) nor a gift (theme 4). Benevolent charity helps people, but it does not help people help themselves. It promotes dependency, putting the doers in the humiliating position of not being able to help themselves and leading to resentment and thwarted self-reliance.

Theme 5: Doers Must Be in the Driver's Seat. 'Being in the driver's seat' is a metaphor for autonomous self-activity and can be extended to the other four themes: (1) the car must start its journey from where the doer-driver is; (2) the vision of the road ahead is from the driver's vantage point; (3) it would be folly for guides (or 'backseat drivers') to grab the steering wheel and

---

[97] Ellerman (2001: 3).

try to drive; and (4) being driven by someone else weakens the driver's ability to get there alone.[98]

Both the informed consent model and Ellerman's helper-doer model are useful because they draw attention to key aspects of 'participatory development', which are described below.

4.3. *Autonomy-compatible poverty reduction*

The informed consent approach draws attention to the fact that, while health is certainly an important value to most people, and while health care is certainly a prerequisite to many other activities, and often to survival itself, health is not the *only* variable of interest, and it is not arranged in a *permanent* hierarchy above other values. For example, a terminally ill playwright may willingly accept an earlier and more painful death rather than take medication which would mean he would certainly not be able to concentrate and finish his script. Similarly, a person with a bad liver condition may continue to drink because she values the aesthetic image of elegant dinners (with which orange juice clashes) and the friendships which she enjoys only in the pub over a pint. Patients' decisions to allow other valuable functionings to dominate health do not reflect (in these examples) a failure on the part of the health professional, although they will be reflected in poor health functionings. Ellerman goes one step further in pointing out that in the case of development, unlike that of medicine, the agency has a further aim of making itself irrelevant by making a local doctor, so to speak. In order to achieve that the doer must be in the driver's seat.

These analyses might seem rather obvious were it not the case that development agents have rarely recognized that poverty-related variables are not the *only* things of value to poor people. For example, Apffel-Marglin criticized the programme of small-pox inoculation in India. Not only did the inoculation programme involve coercion and at times violence, but the British also outlawed the practice of variolation. Variolation was a more traditional method of small-pox vaccine which had a higher morbidity[99] but also was integrated into worship of the goddess Sitala, and was available in the countryside at low cost. This criticism highlights the failure of the colonial administration to recognize non-health values: the colonial government initially outlawed the practice on morbidity grounds, and simply 'dismissed' the value of the integration with worship practices. They acted as if health were the only relevant value to human flourishing. The informed consent model systematically guards against this possibility.

Furthermore, the informed consent model highlights, as Sen also does, the need for research on the unintended but predictable consequences of an intervention. In the medical profession laws prescribe what research on side-effects a pharmaceutical company, for example, must undertake before marketing a drug. While this research

---

[98] ibid. 3–4.
[99] Apffel-Marglin reports that 'the risk of death from variolation varied between 1 to 3 per 100', Apffel-Marglin and Marglin (1990: 109).

may not identify all side-effects, note that those which are described are also relevant to persons' ability to participate in other things they value, such as social relationships, excellence in work, self-integration, and so on (your hair will turn cyan; you may be irritable or excitable or listless or thirsty; you may have permanent difficulty conceiving). Hence, on the basis of the information provided plus reflection on their own case, a person can imagine the range of ways in which the particular treatment or medicine is likely to affect the other things they value doing, and make a rationally deliberated (free) choice that fits in with their other commitments.

In development the assumption that sufficient information is readily available on side-effects to enable a community to make rationally deliberated (free) choices is not valid, as Sen has stressed (Ch. 3, Sect. 3). While in part this is perceived to be due to the impossibility of accurate predictions, the feature of unpredictability is shared in the case of health care where it is impossible to predict with certainty how a medicine will interact with a particular body; instead probabilities are stated. The health professional's terrain is the human body which, while magnificent in its complexity, may be a slightly more manageable terrain. Yet these models require in no uncertain terms that procedures be developed for identifying predictable and relevant side-effects and for finding apt mechanisms of communicating this information.

In both informed consent and autonomy-compatible models, significant attention has been given to the different ways, however subtle, that the physician or helper infringes on the autonomy of the participants. Chambers's work on participation and power clearly articulates the extent to which the interface between development workers and communities has not been conducive to 'voluntariness' (similar examples occur at macro and meso levels).[100] The informed consent model would require and enforce attention to this issue.

The deepest problem in applying the informed consent model in particular with anything like the degree of precision with which it enters the medical-legal field, is that it is much more difficult to establish 'understanding' and 'competence' and 'valid consent' when the party concerned is a group (with internal disagreements) rather than an individual—and the question of who would do so is liable to affect adversely the average blood pressure in the development community as a whole. If, however, informed consent is understood as a broad model of engagement rather than as an enforceable legal framework, the 'problems' become focal points for discussion. The value of the informed consent framework is to focus attention on two areas: (i) on the responsibility which development agencies have to communicate direct and indirect impacts to local communities, and (ii) on the internal process of participation that would confer valid consent—which avoids elite capture for example. Attention to these and many other issues would help to catalyse the 'explicit public discussions' about development frameworks and objectives that Sen advocates.[101]

---

[100] Chambers (1994d, 1997). See Forester (1999), Dore (1994).
[101] See Marglin's chapter in the UNIDO (1972); Sen (1999a), Richardson (forthcoming).

5. CONCLUSION

The benefits widely attributed to participatory methods fall into several categories: (i) lower implementation costs because the community provides some labour, land, or materials; (ii) greater technical success because of access to accurate, ground-level information on local conditions; (iii) sustainability because the community continues the initiative after the cessation of external funding; (iv) 'empowerment' or 'self-determination' because the activity requires participants to set their own mixtures of objectives; and (v) sensitivity to local cultural values because persons who hold those values influence the initiative at all stages.

The first three benefits refer to 'transitive' effects: the argument is that participation can increase the efficiency and cost-effectiveness of development interventions. The reason it may do this is that participation is a means of transferring local knowledge of a theoretical nature. This is knowledge about what is the case in the particular village or region: what its history is; who its leaders, both official and unofficial, are; when the rains come; what formal and informal institutional structures are in place; which days are festivals; what ethical codes people aspire to; how many children go to school, and so on. These are questions to which there are answers of some sort, even if they require a fair bit of interpretation for an outsider (e.g. identifying unofficial power-holders or informal institutions) and even if it is difficult to access.[102] And this information is instrumental to activity success—either in technical terms (so that the water channel is not built *above* the water level in the dry season, for example) or in social terms (so that the project does not require labour that is unavailable, or unwilling).

The last two benefits refer to intrinsically valued and intransitive effects. Participation has been heralded as one methodology by which development comes to 'carry the flesh and colour of their people and their societies'.[103] It is claimed to enable communities to consider diverse dimensions of development and choose which to pursue (or protect) actively. At best this allows such communities to avoid the 'dysfunctioning of societies undergoing rapid modernization',[104] and creates 'a space in which traditional cultures can change on their own terms . . .'.[105]

Development entails prospective decisions about the introduction of new practices, and these kinds of decisions will change a community's identity and institutions. In some participatory approaches these decisions are made by the people who participate in the existing network of practices and institutions, by the communities they constitute. Participants decide what to do with the past they have (in this way a development choice is more like a mid-life crisis than an adolescent capering about wondering who to be), and which new capabilities to pursue.

This chapter has used both Sen's account of agency and Finnis's account of free choice to analyse the value of choice-making to the agents, and the need for local knowledge in order to make choices well. Taken together, these strongly support the principle of subsidiarity: the most local group capable of making adequate decisions

---

[102] See Leach and Fairhead (1994), Dore (1994), Chambers (1994d).   [103] Haq (1995: 6).
[104] Banuri (1990a: 59).   [105] Apffel-Marglin and Marglin (1990: 16).

makes them (and the capabilities of the most local group are to be strengthened). The final section sketched the process of informed consent as an approach that systematically characterizes the complex relationship between a 'beneficent' expert who has some necessary information or resources, and an autonomous agent. The autonomy-compatible assistance model likewise focuses attention on the motives, behaviours, and attitudes of helpers and doers. The intention of the last section has been to raise both models because they usefully highlight key issues in operationalizing Sen's concepts of public debate.

5

Basic Needs and Basic Capabilities

> Cultural freedom . . . refers to the right of a group of people to follow a way of life of its choice . . . [it] leaves us free to meet one of the most basic needs, the need to define our own basic needs.[1]
>
> Culture does not exist independently of material concerns, nor does it stand patiently waiting its turn behind them.[2]
>
> We have considerable freedom in making individual judgments (subject to our own reasoning and scrutiny), but when it comes to the need for agreed social priorities and acceptable public policies, we have to combine considerations of science with politics, to wit, effective opportunity for public discussion and scrutiny, along with reasonable guesses on representation and causal relations. The capability perspective is not a set of mechanical formulae, but a framework for informational analysis, critical scrutiny and reflected judgments.[3]

The fundamental importance of local decision-making in the face of underdetermined alternatives qualifies but does not *rule out* the possibility that some capabilities may be so basic to human welfare that they can be identified without any prior knowledge of the particular commitments that are held and expressed by an individual or group. When Oxfam staff came into Arabsolangi without any prior knowledge of this community, their goal was to collaborate with the Women's Organization in designing an income generation initiative that targeted the poorest. The project adapted itself in many ways but retained this focus. Oxfam may not have funded the Women's Organization had they refused to work with the poor, or had the poor group requested an elaborate statue for the village hall. Is Oxfam's position—of choosing to advocate certain capabilities without prior knowledge of, nor open-ended deference to, the community—consistent with the capability approach? In the last chapter we saw that one way economic institutions have responded to values issues is by incorporating shared variables into their own paradigm of success, as the basic human needs approach did and as structural adjustment eventually did. This chapter asks whether there are any variables related to human poverty that can be so incorporated, and how. That is, it addresses Paul Streeten's question, 'who is to determine the basic needs? Is it the people themselves, who may prefer circuses to bread, television to education, or soft drinks, beer and cigarettes to clean water and carrots? Would it not be very arrogant to lay down what people should regard as basic?'[4]

---

[1] UNESCO (1995: 15).   [2] Sen (1998b).   [3] 1996e: 117.   [4] 1984: 973.

The previous three chapters built up an account of values and of decision-making processes. This chapter will apply this account to the issue of poverty with which economic development is concerned. The chapter will consider first whether and if so how 'basic capabilities' can be specified. Secondly, it will discuss the relativity of these basic capabilities. Thirdly, it will discuss the operational implications of focusing on capability rather than functionings, and finally propose an operational definition for pursuing capabilities. The definition and conceptualization of poverty has a large literature; the focus here is on Sen's work.

The reasons why such an account is relevant are, briefly, the following: however generous a role one may wish for consensus and discussion (and as earlier chapters clarified, one may want a great deal),[5] if the fact of consensus (or consent) is not *sufficient* to identify claims that have a certain kind of priority over others, then one needs a further account to establish such priority.[6] Also, if institutions wish to develop expertise that may be valuable to the poor, then the identification of poverties for which data can be collected and tracked is necessary—as the Development Assistance Committee has argued. Even global networks of poor people's organizations[7] face the problem: how do international groups develop institutional capacities to fight poverty if they must hold their breath in suspense and allow definitions of poverty to emerge locally? Is it not possible to observe some predictable regularities in absolute poverty, or else provide some account of basic capabilities that will be likely to require support? Sen's work on basic capabilities in the context of absolute poverty, which will be explored here, employs but does not defend such an account.

1. ABSOLUTE POVERTY AND CAPABILITY

In *Poverty and Famines*, Sen discussed common approaches to poverty. His assessment at the time was that the *biological* approach to identifying the nutritional elements of poverty (which was under attack at that time due to difficulty in determining minimal nutritional requirements which were valid internationally) should be formulated to look at the nutritional status of persons not their incomes, but that this kind of investigation into poverty was incomplete, as not all determinants of poverty are primarily 'biological'. The *inequality* approach, on the other hand, being concerned with reducing inequalities within a society, paid insufficient attention to the fact that a society could retain its current level of 'inequality' yet, due to an economic decline, push the lower sectors into hunger; at the other extreme, incomes could increase such that the relatively poor could 'only' buy one Cadillac per year. In other words, reducing inequality is a separate (albeit sometimes overlapping) objective from that of reducing absolute poverty. Sen recognized that poverty will always have an element of context-dependence. 'It may indeed be the case that poverty, as Eric Hobsbawm (1968) puts it, "is always defined according to the conventions of the society in which it occurs"

---

[5] See also Penz (1991).   [6] Finnis (1998b: 63–4).
[7] e.g. WIEGO (Women in the Informal Economy Globalizing and Organizing).

(p. 398)'.[8] But Sen pointed out that the idea that poverty is simply a value judgement 'in the eye of the beholder' (as Mollie Orshansky had argued)[9] does not necessarily follow. Similarly, he argued that Townsend's argument for descriptions of *relative poverty*—which combine objective conditions with '*feelings* of deprivation'[10]—is incomplete. Sen concluded that 'there is an irreducible core of *absolute* deprivation in our idea of poverty, which translates reports of starvation, malnutrition and visible hardship into a diagnosis of poverty *without having to ascertain first the relative picture*. Thus the approach of relative deprivation supplements rather than supplants the analysis of poverty in terms of absolute dispossession'.[11]

This 'irreducible absolutist core in the idea of poverty'[12] has been carried forward in Sen's writings on capabilities. Sen argues that a better way of conceptualizing poverty than as income inadequacy is to understand poverty as basic 'capability failure', that is, as the *inability* of individuals and communities to choose some valuable 'doings or beings' which are basic to human life. This distinguishes his approach from the income approach, and also from the approach of relativists, egalitarians, and, he argues, basic needs approaches.

In other words, poverty can be seen as an *absolute inability* to pursue certain valuable functionings. This will usually be associated with *relative* poverty in the space of incomes or commodities.[13] Both the relative commodity requirements for capabilities, and also the identification of these 'necessaries of life' can change over time and across societies. Sen wrote,

[t]he characteristic feature of 'absoluteness' is neither constancy over time, nor invariance between different societies, nor concentration merely on food and nutrition. It is an approach of judging a person's deprivation in absolute terms (in the case of poverty study, in terms of certain specified minimum absolute levels), rather than in purely *relative* terms *vis-à-vis* the levels enjoyed by others in the society.[14]

Sen proposes, then, that (i) absolute poverty can be recognized even if one does not know the relative picture; (ii) absolute poverty is best conceived as a lack of capabilities (not commodities or functionings).

But what are these basic capabilities[15] which, if absent, constitute poverty—what are these basic capabilities that should be equally available to all persons? Sen gives examples rather than a systematic answer (as Williams *et al.* have complained),[16] and

---

[8] 1981a: 17.
[9] (1969: 37). See Sen's response at greater length in 'Description as Choice' (1982b: 432–49).
[10] (1981a: 16), citing Townsend (1974: 25–6). [11] 1981a: 17, emphasis added.
[12] 1983d: 332. [13] 1997a: 211 n. [14] Townsend (1985: 664), Sen (1985c: 673).

[15] It is of minor interest that Sen refrained from using the term 'basic capabilities' for a while. In *Quality of Life* he pointed out that he had not used the term 'basic capabilities' in his Dewey Lectures, nor in *Commodities and Capabilities*, in order to avoid confining the capability approach '*only* to the analysis of basic capabilities': Sen (1993a: 41 n. 33). Drèze and Sen's *Indian Development* (1997) takes up again the language of basic human capabilities as does *Development as Freedom* (Sen 1999a: 20).

[16] Ch. 1, Sect. 3, though see Doyal and Gough (1991). Sen and Anand (1994a) admit that there is an element of 'inescapable arbitrariness' to the project, but note that this is due to deficiencies in data, and *not* to conceptual unclarity.

appears to maintain what could only be a studied disinterest in such explanation.[17] In 'Poor, Relatively Speaking' Sen gave the example, in passing, of certain 'basic capabilities' which are very differently fulfilled in rich and poor countries. He listed six capabilities for which the commodity requirements were 'not tremendously variable between one community and another' and three others which had 'extremely variable resource requirements'.[18] Sen did not discuss this list either at the time (how it was generated; what status if any it had) or later. He has not set forward a definitive list of the capabilities that comprise absolute poverty.

There is a problem here. It is this: if absolute poverty can be recognized as such without having to ascertain the relative picture first, then it is necessary to give an account of how the basic capabilities are to be identified—what are the criteria of their selection. Such an account is especially necessary if the basic capabilities are selected on a country-by-country basis. Even a proposal (by Sen or any other person or group) of a particular set of basic capabilities would be insufficient unless it provided such an account, because some people would disagree with it, and it would be necessary to engage with them, and amend, refine, or uphold the proposed set.

I will focus on this problem of criteria to identify basic capabilities. It lies upstream of many more familiar technical problems. For example, after we identify basic capabilities, we still must identify minimum levels below which people are absolutely poor, and a procedure for identifying the goods and services required. But why is a 'conceptual' or philosophical account required? Are there no alternatives besides the biological or relative or inequality approaches?

One possible way of identifying basic capabilities, of course, would be to look for the area of *consensus*. Sen writes that 'Some functionings are very elementary, such as being adequately nourished, being in good health, etc., and these may be strongly valued by all, for obvious reasons'.[19] This seems likely. But *universal* agreement seems less plausible: some may think all who do not have spiritual richness to be 'poor' and those who have it to be 'flourishing' regardless of their material state, for example. A group of bilateral lenders may agree as to the constituents of absolute poverty, but their agreement may be mistaken or incomplete. Consensus seems an incomplete path.[20]

For economists concerned with the allocation of scarce resources, one requirement of relevant basic capabilities would be dependence on material resources. But in order for the resource requirements to be detailed (and they must be), it is necessary to have answered our first question, namely, whether and on what grounds we can *assume* that a commodity-dependent capability will be of value to the poor at all.

So consensus and material dependence relate to but do not demarcate basic capabilities. This section develops further a conception of basic need that relates closely to Sen's work. It defines basic need with reference to absolute harm rather than to wants, 'needs', desires, or preferences.

---

[17] 1996a: 56–7; see 1992a: 44–5, 108–16; 1993a: 31; 1985b: 30; 1999a: 20.
[18] (1983d: 337); see (1982b: 367–8) for the first discussion of the notion of basic capabilities.
[19] 1993a: 31; see 1985b: 30; 1988a: 20; 1999a: 20, 36.   [20] Finnis (1998b: 63–4).

Rawls's primary goods relate to things people are presumed to need regardless of their different conceptions of the good. While this might involve consensus and public provision, it also introduces the idea of enabling conditions, or *prerequisites* which Sen seems to share.[21] For example, in his discussion of mortality as an economic indicator, Sen argues that mortality (life expectancy) is a good indicator of capabilities not only at a pragmatic level,[22] because of its wide availability, but also at a foundational level. 'Being alive' is itself a valuable functioning. In addition, this particular functioning, 'being alive', has a very special status among functionings: it is central to the *capability* to achieve *any* other functioning.[23] For this reason (and also because, unlike perceptions of health which are themselves functions of knowledge, mortality is not dependent on any functioning besides itself), the statistic of mortality is itself a good indicator of capability. The idea that basic needs are 'preconditions' of a full life threads its way through the basic needs literature; for example, it was the primary argument used by Doyal and Gough.[24]

David Wiggins has given a rich and careful explication of basic human needs along these lines which is worth considering because it combines an account of absolute basic needs with an account of the relativity of basic needs to different communities and to a particular time frame. He notes that the connection between needs and rights is a difficult one and 'has proved elusive' but argues that 'it will be a great shame if the failure to be simple or hard and fast continues to stand in the way of our trying to understand the special force and political impact of a claim of serious need'.[25] Wiggins does not 'solve' the question of basic needs by providing a list of them. Yet his seems the most complete account to date, and it does articulate *the procedure* by which such a list might be identified.

1.1. *Criteria for identifying absolute needs and basic needs*

Wiggins works towards defining basic needs by first defining *absolute* and then *entrenched* needs. *Absolute*, or categorical needs (we will discuss how these are also relative shortly) refer to needs which, if unmet during a specified time period, *blight*

---

[21] 'As John Rawls noted in proposing concentration on the "primary goods" in the Difference Principle as part of his theory of "justice as fairness", there is more uniformity in the enabling conditions that are helpful for all than in the distinct achievements that different persons respectively value' (Sen 1998b: 318).

[22] (1998a). The pragmatic virtues of this indicator include availability and accuracy of data, interpersonal comparability, high degree of association with other valuable functionings (literacy, fertility rate, HDI, public expenditure on health), disaggregability by gender/age/race/occupation, and surprising sensitivity to external changes. For other discussions of life expectancy (LE) see Anand and Ravallion (1993), Dasgupta (1993). Stewart (1985: 61, 1995) preferred to use life expectancy as a single indicator rather than any others.

[23] Here I differ from Crocker (1992: 604). He writes, 'Sen's capability ethic . . . interpreting basic needs precisely as actual freedoms or capabilities, conceives these freedoms as part of the content of, rather than the conditions for or means to, a full life'. I will be arguing that Basic Needs are themselves valuable, but that they also enable other capabilities.

[24] (1991: 50 f.); Doyal and Gough, following Kant, defined physical health and autonomy as basic needs.   [25] 1998: 2.

one's life or cause serious harm. Consider *x* to be something that is needed, such as sanitation or shelter or clothing. Wiggins defines absolute needs in the following way:

(i) I need [absolutely] to have *x* if and only if
(ii) I need [instrumentally] to have *x* if I am to avoid being harmed if and only if
(iii) It is necessary, things being what they actually are, that if I avoid being harmed then I have *x*.[26]

So a person needs *x* absolutely 'if and only if, whatever morally and socially acceptable variation it is (economically, technologically, politically, historically . . . *etc.*) possible to envisage occurring within the relevant time-span, she will be harmed if she goes without'.[27] Wiggins gives the example of a man needing $200 to buy a suit. To test this claim one would first need to ascertain that $200 is the price of a suit (it could not be bought more cheaply or borrowed); secondly, one would need to ascertain whether the man would be harmed if he did not have a suit by time *t* (say, Sunday at 5 p.m.). Absolute needs satisfiers are a prerequisite for living an unharmed life.

Basic needs are a subset of absolute needs and entrenched needs. If Jason is lacking an *entrenched* need, say food, then no matter whether the political leaders assume that Jason's only possibility is to beg, or whether they assume that in fact there are many alternatives Jason could take to avoid being hungry (he could migrate and find work, or live with his cousins, or beg, or steal food), they will have to recognize that within the next three days (for example—any time period could be specified) *in all cases Jason will be harmed* if he does not get food.[28] This would not be the case, for example, if Jason had a need to sing because he was a tenor by profession and found fulfilment by singing well, because if he could and did change professions and found an alternative future in which he was fulfilled by carving and painting masks, the need to sing could disappear (note that the need to sing might still be absolute in the short term). An entrenched need is further defined as *basic* 'if what excludes futures in which *y* [the person, i.e. Jason] remains unharmed despite his not having *x* [the basic need-satisfier, i.e. food] are *laws of nature*, unalterable and invariable *environmental facts*, or facts about *human constitution*'.[29] We will come back to these. The value of Wiggins's account is (i) that needs are defined with respect to harm, rather than with respect to desires, wants, preferences, or pure biology as earlier basic needs writers had variously attempted to do[30] and (ii) that the relativity of these needs is clearly set out.

I would like to propose that basic capabilities could be specified according to Wiggins's basic needs account. This is a relatively straightforward proposal if basic capabilities are interpreted in the following way.

---

[26] ibid. 10.   [27] ibid. 14.
[28] Wiggins writes, '*y*'s need for *x* is *entrenched* if the question of whether *y* can remain unharmed without having *x* is rather insensitive to the placing of the . . . threshold of realistic envisage-ability-cum-political and moral acceptability of alternative futures' (ibid. 15)   [29] ibid. 15, emphasis added.
[30] See especially Fitzgerald (1977), which includes entries by Bay, Springborg, Renshon, Nielsen, and Fitzgerald. For an overview of the various previous attempts at defining basic needs see Gasper (1996*a* and *b*), Doyal and Gough (1991), Hettne (1995).

First, basic needs could be described relative to the substantive functioning that is harmed if the basic need is unmet rather than relative to the object that is instrumental to satisfying the need. While recognizing that unmet basic needs may cause multiple harms, Wiggins defines needs relative to the objects of need (which he calls 'x').[31] This *seems* to veer quite close to the opulence or commodity account of welfare, which we have already considered and discarded. But for Wiggins needs are 'general', so what is needed will be stated in a way sufficiently general to encompass relevant satisfiers. The mesh between Wiggins's basic needs and the capability approach (and, incidentally, the basic human needs approach) involves this generality. For also, in 'Capabilities and Well-Being'[32] Sen phrases some capabilities as the capability to meet nutritional requirements, to be educated, to be sheltered, to be clothed. These capabilities descriptions refer transparently to *what is needed at a general level* (nutritional diet, education, shelter, clothes). On these terms, if y has a basic need for x (defined generally, as above), and f is a functioning which entirely and only reflects the relationship between y and x, then f is a basic needs functioning. Likewise, if c is the capability to f then c would be a basic needs capability. It is these sorts of capabilities which will represent basic needs.

Secondly, it is worth reinforcing the point we already mentioned: basic capabilities or basic needs capabilities will comprise a band of functionings which are expressed at a sufficient level of generality to indicate basic needs (recall Sen's *general functionings* argument; see Ch. 3, Sect. 1). Sen's examples of capabilities vary in specificity—from the capability to eat caviar to the capability to be well-nourished; from the capability to read *Lady Chatterley's Lover* (or the street signs in Nicaragua) to the capability to be educated. Basic needs capabilities, whether identified at the local, regional, or national level, will be sufficiently general or, to use Nussbaum's term, vague (with respect to commodities etc.) to be true for all those to whom they refer. As Wiggins put it, 'Overspecificity in a "needs statement" makes it false'.[33]

1.2. *The relativity of basic needs: three kinds*

Stated in this fashion it might be possible to come up with a 'general' list of basic needs. But what kind of validity would a general set of basic needs have—would further information be required before implementing an activity aimed at addressing unmet basic needs? Wiggins identifies three ways in which basic needs are also relative. They are:

- *Relative to an account of well-being* As the words 'harm' and 'blighted' suggest, the particularization of what needs actually are, is not 'innocent of the metaphysics of personhood'[34] but requires some account(s) of human well-being or flourishing.

---

[31] 'Needs are *states of dependency* (*in respect of not being harmed*), which have as their proper objects things needed (or, more strictly, *having* or *using* . . . x)' (1998: 16; emphasis in original).
[32] 1993*a*: 36.   [33] Wiggins (1998: 23).   [34] ibid. 11.

- *Relative to culture and individual understanding* Harm (or suffering, or wretchedness) 'is an essentially contestable matter, and is to some extent relative to a culture, even to some extent relative to people's conceptions of suffering, wretchedness and harm'.[35] One might be particularly baffled by Scandinavian affinity for cold baths, for example, but not bothered by life in 'overcrowded' conditions. These kinds of individually or culturally relative differences might arise among groups that have the same *general* account of well-being and need.
- *Relative to feasible possibilities at the time* Needs are necessarily temporally indexed—need at time *t*. This limits consideration of alternatives to futures 'that (i) are economically or technologically realistically conceivable, given the actual state of things at *t*, [presumably in a particular place] and (ii) do not involve us in morally (or otherwise) unacceptable acts or interventions in the arrangements of particular human lives or society or whatever, and (iii) can be envisaged without our envisaging ourselves tolerating what we do not have to tolerate'.[36]

It is difficult to determine the depth of these relativities and how they are decided. And this is actually a key question, which will inform, for example, which indicators are constructed and thought to be valid at local, national, or international levels. Wiggins like Sen recognizes that the decision of which functionings are central and valuable is, to use his term, 'essentially contestable'. He also imagines 'that the agreement that can be reached about the truth or falsity of a wide variety of truth claims (when they are seriously and correctly construed as making the contextually much constrained but very strong claims they do make) is far more striking than the disagreement some others will arouse'.[37] Wiggins does not mean that consensus is a sufficient basis for determining the force and shape of moral claims.[38] This is significant, because it suggests that clarity could indeed emerge from a reopening of the discussion of what basic needs are. I return to this question in Section 1.4.

The second kind of relativity Wiggins identified has been widely recognized, for example, in basic needs literature, although its depth is unclear. Basic capabilities can be identified at a general level (recall Sen's *general functionings* argument); but further specification is required at a local level. In his first discussion of basic capabilities, Sen also stressed this point: 'The notion of the equality of basic capabilities is a very general one, but any application of it must be rather culture-dependent, especially in the weighting of different capabilities'.[39] Later, in discussing the selection of focal features of poverty Sen elaborates:

Just because [poverty identification] is a primarily descriptive exercise, we should not make the mistake of thinking that the analysis must be somehow *independent* of the society in which poverty is being assessed. Even the demand of 'objectivity' in description does not really require *social invariance* as it is sometimes supposed. What is seen as terrible deprivation can, of course, vary from

---

[35] ibid. 11. [36] ibid. 12. [37] ibid. 13–14. [38] ibid. 31. See also Penz (1991).
[39] 1982*b*: 368.

society to society, but from the point of view of the social analyst these variations *are* matters of objective study. We could, of course, debate about the exact ways in which normative judgements should take note of such social variations, but the primary exercise of diagnosing deprivation cannot but be sensitive to the way various types of hardships are viewed in the society in question. To deny that connection is not so much to be super-objective but to be super-dense.[40]

The third kind of relativity seems to have a constructive and a worrying interpretation. The worrying interpretation is that if at time t in place p it does not seem feasible to meet basic need x then absolute need x does not exist. I would find Sen's advocacy of a separation of the *description* of poverty (which will include all deprivation; whether or not one is able to envisage addressing it with presently available moral means) from the *choice* of what to do (which takes into account feasibility considerations) convincing in this regard.[41] The constructive interpretation gestures to the need to incorporate 'time' as a factor, that is, in the sequencing of responses to poverty. It might also include the hypothesis that people's account of their own needs is time-dependent; so people may only identify or recognize the most pressing need(s) at time t. Only when this need is filled, perhaps, will they identify a further set of needs.

1.3. *Definition of 'basic capability'*

What is the conclusion of the previous discussion? On the one hand, it can clarify the discussion of basic capabilities by showing how they relate to the full capability set (see Appendix). Furthermore, there is something to be said about the terminology used. Consider how the phrase 'this group does not have what they want' strikes the ear versus the phrase, 'this group has unmet basic needs'. David Wiggins argues that the difference between how the stark claims of 'need' strike the listener, in comparison with claims of 'want' or 'desire' or 'preference', explains, for example, the 'constant recourse to the idea of need' in Western political discourse.[42] Theoretically, he admits that the concept of need has been avoided because on the one hand, there really has not been a satisfactory philosophical account of what need is,[43] and on the other hand, the word 'need' may bring to mind public programmes which employed the language of needs but have had disappointing outcomes. But Wiggins makes the case that although the concept and conceptualization of need is difficult, it is none the less vital: 'given the special force carried by [the word] "need", we ought to try to grasp some special content that the word possesses in virtue of which that force accrues to it. It would be a sort of word-magic if so

---

[40] 1992*a*: 108.   [41] 1982*b*: 432–49.

[42] (1998: 4). This argument is common in basic needs literature: see also Doyal and Gough (1991), Fitzgerald (1977), Springborg (1981).

[43] This is despite, of course, significant attention to the concept. For some accounts which relate to the basic needs approach see Braybrooke (1987), Doyal and Gough (1991), Fitzgerald (1977), Gasper (1996*a*), Ghai *et al.* (1977), Heller (1976), Illich (1978), Lederer (1980), Maslow (1948*a,b*, 1954), Nielson (1963), Penz (1991), Springborg (1981), Streeten *et al.* (1981), Stewart (1985).

Basic Needs and Basic Capabilities 163

striking a difference as that between "want" and "need" could arise except from a difference of substance.'[44]

It might be argued that a parallel semantic difference exists between the force of the phrase 'this group is deprived of basic capabilities' and the phrase, 'this group has unmet basic needs'. The word 'capability' does not of itself carry the normative force of need. The difference is between 'need' which, in Wiggins's account, is 'not evidently an intentional verb' and 'capability' which, in Sen's account represents a potential for (intentional) choice. A strong sense of need (called, variously, objective, absolute, and universal need) seems to refer to things which are required precisely *despite* what one chooses, and however hard one struggles against the need (Susan fervently desired to run the marathon in six days, but on the fifth night, she just needed a twelve-hour sleep. Or, more to the point, Thomás keenly desired to subsist on the pineapples he was picking and send his entire wages home, but then he became very ill. The other pickers told him to buy real food from the canteen or he would be too weak to work at all).

This particular way of joining Wiggins's conception to the capability approach would suggest the following wordings. A basic capability is a capability to enjoy a functioning that is defined at a general level and refers to a basic need, in other words a *capability to meet a basic need* (a capability to avoid malnourishment; a capability to be educated, and so on). The set of basic capabilities might be thought of as capabilities to meet basic human needs. When it is necessary to refer to the set as a whole, it might be called the 'capability to meet basic human needs'.

This terminological change better reflects the link between basic capabilities and absolute poverty—a link that has, in addition to the valuational clarity, an ethical imperative we have not as yet discussed.

1.4. *Testing the definition: is it still too broad?*

Is there, at this stage, enough of a conceptual framework to identify basic needs? Consider an example. We might begin by trying to identify a need relating to nourishment. We could say, 'all people have a basic need for 1 kilo of bread per day'. But this would not be an absolute need, because Sarah could avoid being 'harmed' if she ate something else that was available; so one would need a more 'general' term, such as food. Furthermore, she needs food, instrumentally, in order to avoid the harm of hunger. So the relatively straightforward way of referring to a basic need might be a 'need to z' where z is the functioning that would be harmed if the need were not met—in this case, the functioning of being well-nourished. This moves the concept of basic needs towards capability, and retains its generality (the specification of commodities and strategies that are instrumental to meeting the need may be done at a lower level).

But does this make the approach too general? Consider a suggestion put forward by Denis Goulet, that 'having a meaningful existence may well be the most basic of

[44] 1998: 6.

all human needs'.[45] Could 'the capability to avoid a meaningless existence' be a basic need? In this scenario, Thomás would justify an instrumental need *y* by saying that *y* was crucially instrumental to having a meaningful life, and furthermore that if he were to avoid being harmed he must have a meaningful life. He might justify this further as an entrenched need, by saying that however feasible or otherwise it is for him to have a meaningful existence in political or other terms, if he does not within the next year, he will be harmed (e.g. sink into depression, become suicidal). Finally, he might say that his need for meaning is indeed *basic*. That is to say, he would not be able to avoid being harmed because of 'laws of nature, unalterable and invariable environmental facts, or facts about human constitution'. For, Thomás would say, it is a fact of human constitution that we need meaning. The frameworks of meaning may be philosophical or aesthetic or relational or religious or some combination of these. But, he would argue, any human being, by virtue of being constituted as a human being, has this kind of need.

If we are persuaded by Thomás, and there does not seem to be any particular difficulty in being so (the actual difficulty would be for Thomás to identify sharply what, instrumentally, was absolutely required in order to live a meaningful life), then the range of basic needs of individuals is quite broad. In particular, if the time frame is long enough there *could* be basic need(s) corresponding to each dimension of human flourishing raised in Chapter 3, for these are not substitutable one for another, and are all arguably constitutive aspects of human flourishing for some people.[46] This wide definition of human need was taken by Manfred Max-Neef, and has much to commend it. It is in keeping with the 'incommensurability' of the dimensions of human development and the potential each has to be of fundamental importance to an individual or society, and of primary importance at some point(s) in time. It also avoids the problem that more restricted basic material needs theories fall into, of undervaluing the other aspects of a human life.

Therefore I suggest that the *kinds* of basic capabilities might be associated with *any* of the dimensions of development—not just life and knowledge. A person or group which was not able to pursue or enjoy even a minimum 'level' of functionings in one dimension might say that they were harmed, their lives blighted, because they lack something which is constitutive of human flourishing.

This breadth of definition does seem the only fair way of recognizing the full range of basic needs. But it is unsatisfactory in two ways. The first is that the identification of needs entails a conception of human well-being for *prescriptive* not descriptive purposes, in order to pre-empt unmet needs; the second is that some needs are more relevant to economic decision-making than others.

As regards the first, one could write a set of generic basic needs that corresponded to each of the 'dimensions' argued for in Chapter 3 rather than, as Doyal and Gough

---

[45] Goulet (1995: 206).

[46] This is not to say that the dimensions are facts about the human constitution. They are reasons for action that are accessible to all. However, they might be thought of as a hypothesis about the human constitution.

did, only to the dimensions of 'life/health' and 'autonomy' or practical reasoning. But there are various problems with using this for prescriptive purposes (i.e. to generate an international code of poverty). As discussed in Chapter 3, the dimensions form a 'working' set—one which requires further discussion and debate, empirical testing, and refinement or perhaps reformulation of the 'conception of well-being' in relation to which harm is judged (Wiggins's first kind of relativity). There is sufficient uncertainty about whether this set is robust not to use it for prescriptive purposes.[47]

Also, and importantly, there are two quite different ways of understanding the complete set of dimensions:

Proposal I (weak)   If there is human flourishing, all valuable elements of flourishing will be understood with reference to the set of dimensions (there will be no human value that is not intelligible with reference to one or a combination of these).

Proposal II (strong)   Human flourishing entails some level of participation in *all* dimensions; participation in every dimension is necessary and sufficient for human flourishing.

Martha Nussbaum's proposition, recall, is the second: she argues that a life that lacks *any* of her central human capabilities is deprived. I have argued, rather, for the first, which is considerably weaker. It allows for the possibility that individuals may be 'flourishing' even if one or more dimension is not valued or present very much in their lives and commitments. If this is the case for individuals, it is possible that there are societies or communities in which some dimension or another of human development is hardly present. Yet if this position is taken one cannot propose that absolute poverty be framed mechanically as a set of basic capabilities that correspond to *each* dimension of human development, because some dimensions may simply be 'left out' by one group or another.

So, on these grounds, it does not seem possible to identify a full set of absolute basic needs.

1.5. *Identifying a subset of basic capabilities*

Let us return to the problem: we are looking for those basic needs that pertain to absolute poverty, that can be known *without having to ascertain first the relative picture*.

---

[47] An alternative way of distinguishing a subset of basic needs might be to distinguish between substantive and reflexive goods. Recall the distinction: '*Substantive goods* are [dimensions] [e]veryone shares in ... even before deliberately pursuing them' (Grisez *et al.* 1987: 107). *Reflexive goods* are [dimensions] which arise from humans exercising their deliberation and choice. In other words, substantive goods relate to persons' fulfilment as bodily beings, as intelligent beings, and as beings who make things. Furthermore, the characteristic of substantive goods is that they are participated in by human beings whether or not they are deliberately pursued (they may and often will be deliberately pursued as well). A busy mother may eat a banana without deliberately seeking nourishment; in fact any human being one runs into has generally eaten within the last 24 hours unless they have made a conscious decision not to, or not been able to. In this scenario, an outsider might identify basic needs more easily with respect to the dimensions of life/health/security, knowledge, and work, than in other dimensions.

Yet even if one is not prepared to say that *all* of the dimensions have corresponding basic needs in all countries, then it may still be possible to identify a subset of basic needs that constitute absolute poverty. One is looking for those capabilities which are indispensable to human flourishing but not sufficient for it. One simplification mentioned earlier may help to identify a relevant subset even without further knowledge about values. Economists, at least, are concerned with basic needs that go unmet in part because of an absence of necessary goods and services. And *minimal* levels of enjoyment of different dimensions may not be dependent upon goods and services (e.g. a more-than-minimal level of relationships, or 'frameworks of meaning and devotion' might regularly be enjoyed by those who are poor in material terms). Clearly life/health/security will always depend partially on material goods (and instrumentally on knowledge). Excellence in work and play normally also will. Dimensions such as relationships and spirituality and self-integration may be ruled out from consideration on the grounds that minimal levels of their enjoyment are not directly commodity-dependent (as evinced by the ability of some otherwise absolutely poor persons to enjoy these).

2. BASIC CAPABILITIES OR BASIC FUNCTIONINGS?

But this leaves a number of standing questions. One of these is whether, in these circumstances, it is actually relevant to talk about 'capabilities' rather than functionings— is our goal to have the capability to have that without which our life will be blighted, or simply to *have* that without which our life will be blighted? This is the primary issue between Sen's theory and the basic human needs theory. Furthermore, the capability approach seems unsettlingly difficult to apply at this point, such that some who have tried to work operationally on Sen's capability approach have focused on functionings instead.[48] Therefore I would like to explore this issue at some length.

2.1. *The capability approach and the basic human needs approach*

Sen argues that the capability approach can be seen as a replacement of the basic human needs approach. In 'Goods and People'[49] Sen outlines five critiques of basic needs approaches which may be summarized as follows:

1. Basic needs 'are defined in terms of commodities . . . even though the contingent nature of commodity requirements is fully acknowledged'.[50]
2. 'Individual commodity requirements for specific capabilities may not be independently decidable for each person, due to social interdependence'.[51]
3. The basic needs approach confines attention to minima, and is useful mainly for poor countries.

---

[48] See Chakraborty (1995, 1996), Pattanaik (1997), Pattanaik and McKinley in UNESCO (1998), Granaglia (1996), Balestrino (1996), Razavi (1996). *Politeia's* 1996 conference in Sen's honour was entitled 'Environment and society in a changing world: the perspective of *functioning theory*'. See Sen (1994b, 1996e).

[49] (1984b: 513–15). See also the commentary on this section in Crocker (1992: 603–7).

[50] 1984b: 513.   [51] ibid. 514.

4. '[N]eeds is a more passive concept than "capability", and it is arguable that the perspective of positive freedom links naturally with capabilities (what can the person *do*?) rather than with the fulfilment of their needs (what can be *done for* the person?)'.[52]
5. The basic needs approach neglects philosophical foundations—conceptions of 'the good life'.

That is, Sen might argue that the capability approach, by defining poverty with reference to human capabilities, and by highlighting the importance of choice, brings together considerations of the basic needs approaches which, as Streeten pointed out, were dealt with in a piecemeal fashion (and which included self-determination, participation, and so on) into one coherent philosophical framework. Furthermore it is equally relevant for developing and developed countries.

But there does not yet seem to be a consensus on this account of the relationship between basic human needs approach and the capability approach. Paul Streeten refers to 'the now somewhat unpopular Basic Needs Approach' as an important stage in the evolution of the currently popular goal of human development.[53] Sen writes that the basic needs approach can be seen 'as one part of the capabilities approach',[54] while Gough and Thomas write that 'we believe that our theory systematizes [Sen's] concept [of capabilities] and makes it directly operational'.[55] The question is, then, is the basic human needs approach (BNA) subsumed in and surpassed by the capability approach? Does BNA operationalize the capability approach? Does the capability approach misrepresent the BNA? Are they both variant systems to address the same end? (Obviously, both the capability approach and BNA have evolved and appear differently at different stages, and, in the case of BNA, as presented by different authors.)

Streeten voiced the prevalent view: that BNA had been incorporated into the capability approach. I shall examine the criticisms of BNA by Sen in this section, and relate them to writings in basic human needs. My assessment is that the capability approach is a wider, philosophically more rigorous way of conceiving the role of poverty reduction in relation to the full life, but that this does not mean that, when it addresses the operational tasks, it will recommend procedures which differ significantly from best-practice BNA. In fact, significant portions of the basic needs approach, such as attention to procedure and to getting results, to production systems and supply routes, and to targeting the poor, are not at all superseded by the capability approach. In addition there is still work to be done within both approaches, in identifying procedures for addressing Streeten's 'unsettled questions', and in clarifying

---

[52] ibid. 514.
[53] Streeten (1994). The 1990 HDR claimed that human development surpasses BNA because 'the basic needs approach usually concentrates on the bundle of goods and services that deprived population groups need: food, shelter, clothing, health care and water. It focuses on the provision of these goods and services rather than on the issue of human choices' (UNDP 1990: 11). Basic needs authors such as Stewart and Streeten recognize that in some practical applications of the basic needs approach, commodities were overemphasized.   [54] 1984b: 515.
[55] 1994: 41.

the level (local, regional, international) at which decisions are to be taken and indicators constructed.

To develop this suggestion, I return to Sen's five criticisms of basic needs mentioned above. Inspection of these, in the light of basic human needs literature and later commentary, reveals that numbers 1, 2, and 4 seem to misrepresent at least the basic human needs approach; 3 would be regarded as a true description and *positive* contribution of BNA. Item 5 was a true critique.

Sen's central critiques of basic needs have been the first two: it tends to define needs in terms of commodities, an identification which incurs the 'many-one problem' (that many different bundles of commodities could generate the same functionings), the problem of cultural appropriateness, and the problem of interpersonal variation in converting commodities into capabilities. While the problems with a commodity approach are beyond dispute, Sen's allegation, that the basic human needs approach necessarily made the commodity fetish mistake, is erroneous.[56] In Streeten's terms, the objective of the basic human needs approach is 'to provide all human beings with the opportunity for a full life'.[57] On the second page of *Basic Needs in Developing Countries* Stewart explicitly rejects the 'three acres and a cow' or 'chicken in every pot' view because 'the items are not wanted for themselves, but instrumentally as a means to improving the conditions of life'.[58] She recognizes that the metaproduction function—which converts food, health, education, shelter, and so on into the full life—varies at the level of the individual, depending on the person involved. Thus, she concludes, provision of sufficient entitlements to meet the needs of the household are 'only necessary, not sufficient conditions . . . to achieve an adequate Full Life'.[59] She argues that for economists who are engaged in the work (especially macroeconomic) of operationalizing a basic needs agenda (even assuming they advocate participation), 'it is necessary to assume actual patterns of consumption, intrahousehold distribution and metaproduction efficiency, to estimate the level of household entitlement necessary to achieve a particular level of the full life'. In other words, having recognized the interpersonal variability problem and the many-one problem, the basic human needs approach goes ahead and (somewhat bravely) assumes a particular, contingent, empirically testable position. Such specification is required if operationalization is to occur, but it is not tantamount to commodity fetishism.

Sen also argues that the basic needs approach cannot identify an internationally valid measure of indigence because the commodities vector can only be specified at a near-local level and even this varies between individuals. Basic capabilities refer to objective features of a person, rather than to goods. Thus, he argues, only the capability approach can support a conception of absolute poverty. Yet *both* the philosophical literature on basic needs and the basic human needs writings conceive of commodities

---

[56] The distinction between the basic material needs and basic human needs approaches is well established, and the appropriateness of Sen's allegations to the former alone is recognized. See Gasper (1996*a,b*) and the references therein; Stewart (1995).

[57] Streeten *et al.* (1981). Stewart (1989: 30) argues that commodities should not be given the status of human rights. [58] 1985: 2.

[59] Stewart (1989).

Basic Needs and Basic Capabilities 169

as necessary means to further human well-being. This is borne out in that the 'basic needs' indicators which have been used in inter-country comparisons of basic needs achievement are literacy and life expectancy,[60] while those for internal country studies tend to be more specific (material of housing construction, number of occupants per room, distance from paved road, and so on). Thus basic needs utilizes both culturally specific and culturally independent, both commodity-based and 'output', indicators of well-being. The value of collecting both kinds of information may be seen by noticing how deficient an analysis of any poverty alleviation strategy would be for policy purposes if it *only* collected outcome indicators (life expectancy, literacy) and had no record of the change of access to commodities.

The minimality criticism (item 3 above) is interesting. Simply put, the fact that the BNA is only useful for the deprived and focuses the attention of the rich on a finite task, is seen as precisely the strength of the approach. It is decidedly not open-ended. The BNA prioritizes the needs of the poorest in an operational way. It is concerned with procedural as much as with substantive theory, with strategy as much as with outcome.[61] It swings with 'nobility of purpose'[62] specifically against unacceptable poverty, with a commitment to fulfilling basic needs. In Chapters 1 and 2 we explored the breadth of human development (if human development is to take seriously the many claims of multidimensionality). Clearly the capability approach is more general. But if no core absolute needs are identified and prioritized, then human development might address claims for basic health care and claims for sending a town council to visit a twinned city on the same grounds. Drèze and Sen's identification, within the capability approach, of basic capabilities (that should be available to all) recaptures the basic human needs approach's focus on a closed set of variables.

Sen's criticism that the language of needs encouraged passivity (item 4) is valid, on the one hand—in so far as the language of needs attributes helplessness to the needy (and distracts from the value of their participation in identifying, specifying, and addressing the need). But on the other hand the criticism does not seem strong enough to validate rooting out the needs vocabulary for two reasons. First, the concept of active participation was a fixture in a number of basic human needs approaches (although the *conceptual* relationship between this and basic needs, as Streeten pointed out, was rather uneasy). Even the ILO World Employment Conference that endorsed the basic needs approach in June 1976 notionally assigned 'an important role to popular participation in decision making'.[63] This indicates that those who were introducing this language certainly did not have the mistaken notion that the poor were to be passive.

But secondly, the language of 'capabilities deprivation' lacks the moral force of the phrase 'unmet basic needs'. The phrase 'basic needs' accurately reflects the substantive difference between the limited set of functionings which people really need, almost despite themselves, to avoid harm (a Brahmin who fasts still *does* endure

---

[60] Rati (1992); Moon (1991); Stewart (1985, 1995).   [61] Stewart (1985: 14–35).
[62] Afxentiou (1990).   [63] See Lisk (1985).

physical harm) and other functionings (which they may or may not choose to enjoy, and be equally fulfilled). The language of capabilities obscures this real distinction.

The last criticism concerns the omission of a philosophical framework for the basic needs approach. It is uncontroversial that with respect to economic development the basic needs approach grew up first as a response to a problem, and the philosophy followed (or was assimilated) later. If one scrutinizes the framework implicit in the BNA the difference is less visible. Unlike Sen, and following Rawls's *Theory of Justice*, the BNA separates physical survival from autonomy and so tries to incorporate desirable choice into the framework as a separate variable (see Ch. 4, Sect. 2.1). Stewart, who thinks that participation is one functioning to be pursued alongside others, accepts straightforwardly that this is a difference between the two approaches: 'The metaproduction approach omits the capability step altogether while for Sen this is the prime objective'.[64]

It is at this juncture that we must return to examine again the relationship between basic human capabilities and basic human functionings. The remainder of this section and the next (Sects. 2 and 3), which close the conceptual part of this book, propose some simplifications of the capability approach, in light of the discussion thus far, to guide its application at the microeconomic level.

2.2. *One fundamental argument in favour of capability*

Why speak of capabilities when we are focused on 'meeting basic needs?' This question does bother people who try to compare the basic needs and the capability approaches and see what, if anything, is distinctive about the latter. I will argue that at an operational level the single most important function of the capability approach is to make *explicit* some *implicit* assumptions in the basic needs approach about the value of choice and participation (and the disvalue of coercion).

One significant stumbling block of the capability approach—besides the abstraction of the language it uses—is that it is very hard to picture at the micro level. For instance, consider the building of a health clinic in a remote rural area where traditional medicine is used, and persons visit hospitals infrequently. If a district government wished to be very sensitive to local values in an indigenous area, and not impose anything on the community, it might quietly arrange the building and staffing of a health clinic 'for those who wished to have access to modern medicine'. But if this counts as a capability expansion, then programmes to foster capabilities could proceed that were entirely inert with respect to people's *actual* valuations. This does not cohere with Sen's advocacy of public discussions.

Also, one might doubt that an idle staffed health clinic necessarily constitutes an expansion of capabilities. A person's capability is the set of n-tuples of functionings he or she could achieve. If Thomás lived in the village, *could* he achieve basic health care, or would his suspicion of, or lack of clarity about the clinic, mean that this was not a real option? The development of functional health clinics, cooperatives,

[64] 1990: 9.

Basic Needs and Basic Capabilities

schools, and better agricultural practices seems more often to *require* field staff to motivate communities, to provide information about the benefits of the initiatives, to demonstrate results and win confidence. This interaction may itself knead and alter the values of participants and/or decision-makers.[65]

As the example suggests, when there are limited resources, providing capabilities in the most spare and 'literal' sense may not be adequate even according to the definition of capabilities. The current question is whether there is a role, even so, for focusing operationally on capabilities rather than functionings.

Clearly, persons, whether poor or flourishing, might choose deliberately to refrain from meeting certain basic needs (although they have the capability to) in order to enjoy some different kind of good, and this deprivation may be occasional or systematic and long-term. For example, a hunger striker or a Brahmin may regularly refrain from eating, because they personally value the religious discipline or the exercise of justice-seeking agency, but the side-effect of pursuing these is that they will not be well-nourished (in the short or long-term, depending on the frequency and severity of their fasting). It would seem too strong to suggest that *people* will be blighted if they do not meet their basic need for nourishment because, while the Brahmin's 'functioning' of being well-fed would indeed be blighted by fasting, her *life* might be regal and radiant.[66] Hence the earlier discussion arriving at a definition of the capability to meet basic needs.

But if we took literally the goal only of 'meeting basic needs' and if our objective was to meet needs relating to health, education, sanitation, and shelter, and if country A had higher increases of health, education, sanitation, and shelter than country B, then we would say with utter certainty that the progress in A was better than B. If A had achieved these indicators by oppressive policies (outlawing fasting), we would *still* have to say that A was better than B (because A had come closer to our objective than B). In order to revise our conclusion consistently, we would need to change our objective.

Now perhaps we could focus on basic needs if we *always* added in the functioning of decision-making, participation, or autonomy among the co-realizable set of basic needs. Then our objective might be to increase *health, education, sanitation, shelter, and participation*. So, in evaluating the same situation, we could say that although A had done better in four variables than B, B had done better in participation than A.[67] This

---

[65] With Nussbaum I also think it significant 'that the endogeneity of preferences has been recognized by almost all the major writers on emotion and desire in the history of Western philosophy, including Plato, Aristotle, the Epicureans, the Stoics, Thomás Aquinas, Spinoza, and Adam Smith, not to mention countless contemporary writers in philosophy and in related fields (such as anthropology and cognitive psychology)' (Nussbaum 1997: 1198); see Nussbaum (2000a ch. 2).

[66] A fuller treatment of this point could draw upon Nussbaum's distinction between internal and external capabilities. See Crocker (1995).

[67] Stewart, (referring to Streeten *et al.* (1981), Lederer (1980), ILO (1976), and others) notes that BN *always* included 'certain standards of nutrition, and the universal provision of health and education services'. They sometimes included 'shelter and clothing and non-material needs such as employment, participation and political liberty' (Stewart 1985: 1). See Drèze and Sen (1989, 1995, 1997) and Sen (1998b), all of which view political participation as a basic capability.

or some similar sub-division between 'autonomy' or capability and other basic needs seems necessary at some stage along operationalization, in order to identify the information that must be collected and to identify trade-offs between well-being and agency. But there are critical difficulties in interpretation if one tracks aggregate 'participation' separately from other functionings. For autonomy or participation can increase on a number of levels—for example, in the political system, or in the implementation of basic needs activities, or in the participation of women within the household. Valuable increases in participation for subgroup B may occur during the same time period that coerced increases in basic functionings for subgroup A occur, but the overall indicators for $(B+A)$ may show uniformly positive change across all functionings. Of course this is true for any pair of functionings: there can always be progress on some fronts or for some groups and regress on others. But the *capability approach requires that changes in basic needs be valued with respect to the freedom of the same people whose needs are being affected.*

It may be that basic human needs writers have taken the need for participation and freedom in the development of basic needs strategies for granted all along. But the danger of not making this explicit (by, for example, gathering information on how participatory or otherwise a particular situation is) is that it will be overlooked by implementing institutions. The reason that it *must* be capabilities we are focusing on even in 'meeting basic needs', is that this approach makes the need for choice and participation at all stages explicit.

The simple distinction between functionings and capabilities potentially masks a number of differences that are quite important. It is one thing for a macro-level policy—which will require operationalization anyway—to aim for the 'capability of all women and men to have a basic education'. It is quite another thing operationally to provide the capability in a micro situation. For example, take the case of girls' education in Pakistan. South Asia as a region has the lowest literacy rate in the world, and Pakistan lags considerably behind the regional average. The combined first, second, and third level gross enrolment ratio of school-aged children is 27 per cent for girls, and 53 per cent for boys. There is, quite understandably, a government programme to provide for primary education in general and girls' education in particular. But how does this translate into the micro level? In practice, the need for girls' education is not uniformly understood *or valued*. So in some areas the social organizers have to motivate parents and teachers strongly to keep the schools open. This may be accomplished by the formation and support of men's and women's organizations, by the provision of teacher training, or by tireless discussions to convince parents of the value of girls' education. This is by no means an isolated example. Rather, energetic advocacy and mobilization accompany a great many participatory micro-projects. Social organizers *encourage* savings and micro-credit, the habit of tree-planting, the habit of pre-natal check-ups, good hygiene practices, the use of chlorine to clean flood waters, the spread of adult literacy classes, and so on. They create values as well as respect values. As the example of the health clinic in Chapter 2 suggested, if social organizers did not also inform persons of the potential value of an input or activity (i.e. clean water, female education) then demand might be low; an activity might fail.

I suggest it is this recognition of the micro-level reality that accounts for the basic needs writers' focus on functionings rather than capabilities.

There is no evidence that Drèze and Sen, who advocate the capability approach, envisage anything distinctive from basic needs at this level. For example, they argue against coercive family planning programmes, using data from China and from Kerala. They point out that in Kerala—where there was no coercion—female education, health care, contraceptive availability, and employment opportunities achieved an equivalent rate of increase without the social costs of coercive measures, and with the agency of educated women from Kerala itself. What is interesting to note is that they still consider 'success' to be a decrease in the overall fertility rate, which is a functioning.

This is, in fact, the thesis that makes its way through Drèze and Sen's monograph on India. In this book they analyse Indian economic development in terms of the expansion of basic capabilities such as 'the ability to live long, to read and write, to escape preventable illnesses, to work outside the family irrespective of gender, and to participate in collaborative as well as adversarial politics'.[68] They then develop the position that Indian development requires social investments (in health and education, for example), as well as liberalization. They substantiate the position by careful but ultimately simple comparisons between health and education-related indicators (literacy rates, life expectancy, infant mortality, fertility) in different regions and countries across time. The sustained attention to inequalities in health and education figures clearly establishes that the objective is for there to be equality in such indicators. This powerful analysis is easily comprehensible and has rather modest data requirements. But as interpreted, the goal of 'equality' regards the space of functionings (of which non-coercion is one), not capabilities.

In a 1988 article Sen described a concept of refined functioning that might be of use. He wrote that 'choosing to do x when one could have chosen any member of a set S, can be defined as a "refined functioning" x/S'.[69] If one applied the concept to the provision of basic needs, one would require information both about the basic need functioning x (female education, contraceptive prevalence, etc.) and also about the other possibilities for choice included in set S. However, it is not straightforward to obtain information on set S. Alternatively, one could consider the latitude of choice that was present in the *procedure* of delivering health care or education—how participatory or otherwise each sectoral programme was. Information on participation would also convert functioning information into capability information, because by definition participatory procedures allow members to consider alternatives and to affect development processes iteratively. Indicators of participation do exist and are being improved (see also Ch. 6, Sect. 3.2.5).

It would seem that the basic human needs approach, while perhaps lacking an adequate philosophical framework, did have all of the elements of the capability approach in view (this is not to say that all the so-called 'basic needs' programmes exemplified these elements). First, it was oriented to the whole human person not the provision of goods and services. Streeten *et al.* defined a BNA approach to

---

[68] 1995, p. vii.   [69] 1988a: 18.

development as one that 'attempts to provide the opportunities for the full physical, mental, and social development of the human personality and then derives the ways of achieving this objective'.[70] Secondly, it included an awareness of the need for public participation in the course of meeting basic needs, even if this was not fully spelled out and even if the mechanisms of participation were less developed. For example, Sheehan and Hopkins's 1979 book includes 'participation' as a non-material basic need. Streeten *et al.* consider it an 'unresolved issue' but do say that 'the basic needs approach points to actions that go beyond the delivery of a basic package to the poor and include political mobilization'.[71] All authors recognize the need for the basic needs to be specified at a local level. Stewart puts forward four reasons for organizing basic needs strategies such that they include the participation of local agents and give them 'some voice in decision-making and a commitment to the success of the institution'.[72] So how might this be made explicit?

2.3. *Three operational interpretations of basic capability*

There seem to be at least three ways of conceptualizing the relationship between basic functionings and capabilities in small poverty reduction activities.[73] Because *so much* discussion and debate regarding the capability approach relates to persons assuming different conceptualizations, I would like to spend some time exploring these. They might be written as follows:

Goal: to expand valuable capabilities: three possible operational interpretations

1. to increase the general basic functionings that are prerequisites to being able to exercise valuable capabilities;
2. to increase basic functionings on the assumption that nearly 100 per cent (or another empirically verifiable percentage) of persons would choose them;
3. to increase the basic capabilities people have, which requires one

   (*a*) to identify valued capability goals and strategies (e.g. using participation);
   (*b*) to work in the short term to establish functionings instrumental to these goals;
   (*c*) to use a procedure in the implementation that safeguards negative freedom.

The first assumes that at the micro level, 'the capability to meet basic needs' is equivalent to 'meeting basic needs' or having the associated functionings. The justification would be that some general basic human needs functionings (life expectancy,

---

[70] (1981: 33). See similarly Stewart's metaproduction function (1985: 17–19) which includes a consideration of interpersonal variation in conversion of goods into 'achievements with respect to the ultimate objectives' (1985: 19).   [71] 1981: 60–3, 25–6; second quote p. 56.

[72] (1985: 50–1). These reasons were: (i) enabling producer and consumer 'to exercise some general control and choice' about their felt needs; (ii) increasing sustainability; (iii) increasing 'the effectiveness of the BN-outputs in relation to full life indicators'; and (iv) simply providing participation, which may itself be an intrinsic part of a full life.

[73] See Sen's threefold description in (1994*b*: 339–40), Sen (1997*a*), and Sen (1999*a*: 82–3).

literacy) are prerequisites to other capabilities. *Having achieved* these threshold functionings one gains the positive freedom and *capability* to pursue a fulfilled life.

Consider again the situation in country A in which the basic needs functionings were fulfilled but the people were coerced. If one were solely interested in changes in capability, defined as the union of choice and function, one might give lexical priority to changes in capability, or not give *any* weight or value to an increase in functionings that occurred without choice. One could not distinguish between situation C in which basic needs were still unmet, and situation A in which all basic needs were met but with coercion. Yet surely there *is* a difference between situations A and C. One cannot reduce differences in capability to differences in freedom. The first approach described above considers information on *functionings alone*, in which terms the progress made in country A could be understood. Also, if participation were a functioning, the *differential* between A and C would be reflected by different indications of participation.

In the second alternative, one retains the goal of capability, but poses a counterfactual hypothesis that in the various sectors chosen, if people were asked, the 'uptake' of functionings provided would be nearly 100 per cent (the percentage of fasters and hunger strikers at any given time t would be insignificant or empirically predictable). In other words, basic needs operate in a manner similar to Sen's description of mosquito-eradication programmes for malaria control, or epidemic prevention: their provision expands people's freedom even though people have not chosen them directly, because people *would* choose to enjoy these functionings if they could. 'A public policy that eliminates epidemics is enhancing our freedom to lead the life—unbattered by epidemics—that we *would choose* to lead'.[74] If this counterfactual hypothesis can be defended, then a programme to expand basic functionings might be interpreted as a programme to expand basic capabilities. However innocent a set of counterfactual assumptions might or might not be at a 'general' level, the problem with employing this approach without further qualification was suggested in Chapter 4, which argued that participation may 'specify' general needs appropriately and facilitate sustainable and efficient activities, and also may have further intrinsic benefits in terms of ongoing self-direction.

The third is that 'capability' at the micro level simply refers to an absence of coercion and the ongoing possibility of choice. It parallels the informed choice procedure mentioned in the last chapter. I have attempted, in this alternative, to break down the capability approach into three component parts which might be implemented separately. It does allow for a period (b) in which the overriding energy is on basic functionings. For example if a broad goal, such as economic security, is validly shared by a group and forms the basis of a partnership, and if the institution of a mechanism to achieve this goal (such as a savings habit) requires considerable education and motivation, then the need to safeguard choice may be secondary for some period. But the activity develops in light of the goal of enabling participants to be able to choose critically whether or not they will continue to save. This precludes

---

[74] (1992a: 65), see Ch. 3, Sect. 2.2.

coercive measures that will not develop this capability to choose eventually but allows the temporary use of self-enforcement techniques. It argues for a participatory approach, and for a protection of negative freedom.

The problem with the first alternative is that it may overlook coercion, either overtly, as in the case of China, or more subtly, in a top-down planning approach that does not allow local specification of needs. In Drèze and Sen's family planning discussion the 'functionings' programme in China involved physical coercion and systematic enforcement; the 'capabilities' programme of Kerala involved efforts of policy and of persuasion by local actors. To correct this difficulty it may be necessary to specify the need for appropriate local activity, and also for an absence of coercion (although allowing commendation of a set of new practices). This transforms (1) into (3).

The second alternative was a counterfactual hypothesis which conceivably could be tested and, when valid, made. But in order to test whether or not this hypothesis is indeed valid one must maintain the *conceptual* distinction between functionings and capabilities, even when these are basic and most capabilities are realized. Furthermore even if the hypothesis were valid there may still be other benefits of participation besides the identification of valued functionings that would not be realized.

The third seems most coherent with the interpretation of the capability approach sketched here.

If one accepts this interpretation of the capability approach then *provided one was working within the framework of* (3a) *and* (3c) one could aim at improving functionings (3b) and still conceive of this as a 'capability' approach. I would argue that, as regards 'basic capabilities', that is, capabilities that pertain to absolute poverty, this interpretation is defensible and also seems consonant with Drèze and Sen's empirical work. It differs from the basic human needs approach in *formalizing* the need for local specification of needs, participation, and negative freedom, but does not introduce fundamentally new concerns. Rather, it crystallizes concerns that were already very much in debate in the basic human needs approach.

2.4. *Further questions: time 'competence' and advocacy*

I recognize that much of the capability approach is lost in this simplification of it. But even this interpretation leaves many operational issues unaddressed. One further question that will recur in our discussion of indicators is the time-relativity of choices that individuals and communities make about basic capabilities. How long does the community's decision remain in effect? This is an issue on which more work is required.

Another question is how one is to assess the basic capabilities of those who do not make many choices because others in their own family *must* choose on their behalf, such as babies, the mentally handicapped, and some old people—or because others in their family *do* choose on their behalf, such as some women?[75] The issue of

---

[75] This would entail a deeper discussion of 'competence' than is possible at this point. For instance, the capability of a competent woman for whom others made decisions should be evaluated differently from

'competence' may seem unproblematic, but much of the missionary and colonial energy derived from a presumption that people could not make informed choices, and this attitude has by no means become extinct.

A third question (there are certainly others) is whether provision of the economic or material requirements for the substantive, basic needs capabilities (3*b*) somehow skews or distorts the person's *capability* to choose by influencing their choice functions. Theoretically this question seems less complicated. Considering the 'unintentional' nature of need, for mature adults it is likely that a low level of functionings happen when either the objects of need are themselves unavailable (or unacceptable), or else the person has chosen (directly or indirectly) not to participate in them. If it is the former or if the choice not to participate was the indirect effect of another choice (such as to offer nourishing food to one's children and husband), then even if the person's preferences do not register deprivation, it is likely that if the supply of economic goods is increased, the level of achieved functioning will increase unreflectively. There is no reason for presuming that the widow who has reconciled herself to poverty and maintained her cheerfulness will none the less refuse clean water if it comes. In contrast, in the case of a deliberate reflective decision, for example, to fast for a certain period, the person's freedom of agency is not threatened by provision of the economic good (unless it proves a temptation or causes an endogenous value change, on which more below). Furthermore, if consulted, the (fasting) persons would be able to articulate their decision to endure temporary (nutritional) deprivation in order to enjoy another dimension of life.

This analysis does leave at least one significant issue standing, which is the problem of endogenous and unreflected value change—that, in fact, providing the capability to meet basic human needs may irreversibly change cultural and social institutions.

3. DEVELOPMENT: 'EQUALITY' OR 'EXPANSION' OF CAPABILITIES?

It is time to take this most difficult question on. Recall there are two different formulations that Sen gives regarding the prescriptive content of the capability approach. One reconceives of the goal of development as the 'promotion and expansion of valuable capabilities'.[76] This definition has taken root, for example, in the *Human Development Report* of the United Nations Development Programme and the human development school in general.[77] The second considers the justice claims and argues for equality in the space of basic capabilities. We see this demonstrated in Drèze and Sen's advocacy of equality in cross-national life expectancy, literacy, and health-care figures.

---

that of a small child; functionings are indeed a sufficient indicator of well-being for the latter during the period that they are unable to make choices.

[76] Sen (1990*a*). See also Drèze and Sen (1995: 9–13), Crocker (1995: 157).
[77] See e.g. Haq (1995).

But these two formulations are substantially different. If we conduct an informational analysis of the moral principles involved, the prescription of equality in basic capability space would definitively conclude that justice is accomplished if there is equality in basic capabilities, *regardless* of the effect the achievement of such equality might have had on other valuable capabilities (information on non-basic capabilities does not enter the justice consideration at all). Given the capability approach's stress on valuation, it seems strange that Drèze and Sen do not attend in any way to the possible 'contraction' in *other* valuable capabilities that might be associated with an expansion of the *basic* capabilities they identify. I am not suggesting, one way or another, that such contractions necessarily occur or would undermine their results. I am only pointing out that this is inconsistent with Sen's stress in other work on keeping track of the full menu of choices.[78] A lot may turn on this issue.

For example, Drèze and Sen point out that

> debates on such questions as the details of tax concessions to be given to multinationals, or whether Indians should drink Coca Cola ... tend to 'crowd out' the time that is left to discuss the abysmal situation of basic education and elementary health care, or the persistence of debilitating social inequalities, or other issues that have a crucial bearing on the well-being and freedom of the population (1995, p. vii).

Parts of these debates have to do with the contemporary politics of India (and it could well be these to which Drèze and Sen were alluding). But in addition, both within India and elsewhere, debates on multinationals and the symbolic Coca-Cola have had to do with a need to validate diverse forms of culture that are threatened. A person may agree that the public sector should spend more attention on 'debilitating social inequalities' (I happen to agree with this, for example). But this does not justify entirely disregarding the cultural considerations.

3.1. *Example: the mingling of basic and non-basic capabilities*

Let us consider an example from the Thar desert in Pakistan, where at the request of men in a large open meeting, an organization called Baanhn Beli formed 47 village groups to support the girls' education programme. One of the very poor villages in which they became active was Pari Hari. Pari Hari does not have electricity; the women in the women's organization there had not been to Diplo, the nearest market town, nor did they know the name of their country's prime minister. In Pari Hari, Baanhn Beli had supported the formation of male and female organizations. These groups were visited on a monthly basis by a male and female social organizer, who discussed issues such as savings, health, hygiene, and education. With the assistance of the NGO, the community had bored a sweet water well that saved hours each day from women's workload, and decreased outmigration in the dry season. They had also started a girls' school (there was already a government school in the village).

---

[78] Sen (1996*f*).

The men's and women's groups were asked to consider what changes—beneficial or harmful—had ensued from the Baanhn Beli's activity in Pari Hari.[79] The women identified six categories of beneficial impact (the order following is that in which the women identified the impacts chronologically): their daughters were going to school and becoming *educated*; *savings* had increased; their *health* and knowledge of healthcare had improved; women had not met together previously, and so after the formation of the women's organization, their *unity* with each other increased (before they had bickered often); when they met together, they learned the needs of others in the village—which family did not have enough money to buy a schoolbook for their daughter, who was ill, in which household someone had died—so were able to *help each other*; finally, their daughters and they themselves learned more about their *religious faith* from each other and from the school.

The women then compared the six different impacts they had identified, and discussed if they were more, less, or equally important relative to each other. They decided on the following ranking (impacts on the same horizontal level were 'equally' important):

Most important impacts:	Religion	Health	
Very important impacts:	Unity	Savings	Helping others
Less important impacts:	Girls' education		

What is interesting about this example, is that in Pari Hari, which by all accounts is very deprived, the women valued 'non-material' impacts (unity, helping others, religion) as well as impacts that affected their material poverty (health, savings, education). But what is even more interesting is that the material changes did not categorically outrank the non-material as more valuable nor vice versa; both were interspersed. Now as an isolated example, this pattern could be due to any number of factors: poor quality of education, a charismatic religious social organizer, a ranking in which the facilitator made leading suggestions, domination by one woman, and so on. Yet when this exercise was repeated in a number of different communities in Pakistan, by a number of different facilitators, in initiatives that ranged from agricultural to income generation to literacy to health clinics, using different ranking techniques and different ways of asking questions, a similar result emerged: respondents (men and women, urban and rural, young and old, poor and lower middle class) identified and valued both material and non-material impacts of development initiatives (the particulars varied), both impacts that directly affected their material quality of life and ones that had no effect whatsoever on it. Furthermore as it has been repeated throughout the world in participatory analyses, and also in the *Voices of the Poor* study mentioned earlier, the same results obtain. Material needs and impacts do not categorically outrank

---

[79] The details of this method are described in Ch. 6.

non-material needs, nor do non-material impacts categorically outrank material ones.[80]

The Pari Hari example is felicitous, because the capability set expanded *more* than in simple basic capabilities. But this is not always the case. In *Dominating Knowledge* Stephen Marglin and others articulate a strong anti-development critique. Their critique is not directed against basic needs:

> The chapters that follow have nothing to say against longer life-spans, healthier children, more and better-quality food and clothing, sturdier and more ample shelter, better amenities. Nor is any criticism leveled against the luxuries that people buy when their incomes grow enough to permit discretionary purchases, such as the radios and television sets that one sees even in very poor Third World villages.[81]

Rather, the major problem addressed by the book (and a great many others) is that development initiatives, whether focused on income or on basic needs, defined as exogenous and so undermined other valuable capabilities in the long term. This 'contraction' of the non-basic capability set accounts for Marglin *et al.*'s dissatisfaction with development: 'historically growth has expanded choice only in some dimensions while constricting choice in others'.[82]

This discussion introduces a significant operational concern into poverty alleviation projects, which is that the objectives for improving one's own material well-being, which are often held by international donors and NGOs, are not necessarily the most important objectives of local communities, and are certainly not the only important objectives.

3.2. *Attention to the full menu*

It seems, then, that the earlier formulation of capabilities really should be amended to incorporate consideration of the 'full menu' of choices that people face, perhaps in the following manner (amendments in italics).

3. Long-term goal: to increase the basic capabilities people have *without contracting their overall capability set*, which requires one

   (a) to identify long-term valued capability goals and strategies (i.e. using participation);

   (b) to work in the short term to establish functionings instrumental to these goals;

   (c) to implement a strategy such that negative freedoms are safeguarded;

---

[80] Impact diagrams and rankings have been documented by The Asia Foundation, and also in case studies of twenty-four Oxfam projects. Many similar studies have likewise found wider concepts of wealth than were anticipated—Jodha (1988), Narayan *et al.* (2000a,b), Dohad's example in Chambers (1995). For examples of collecting indicators of wealth see Jodha (1988) and de Kadt (1994). It is diverting to record that the *men* of Pari Hari identified the most valuable impact to be the decrease in bickering among women. [81] Apffel-Marglin and Marglin (1990: 1).

[82] ibid. 4. See also Apffel-Marglin and Marglin (1996); Escobar (1984–5, 1995); Illich (1978); Nandy (1994); Sachs (1992).

(d) to mitigate the contraction of wider capabilities that occur as a result of expanding basic capabilities (where possible, to allow both to expand).

I would suggest that the amendment of (3), above, represents a final 'operational' interpretation of the capability approach as it relates to capabilities to meet basic human needs.

4. INDICATORS AND BASIC CAPABILITIES

The abiding difficulty with the account developed above is that it does not address the issues of international comparability. How does the capability approach compare the capabilities between two very different cultural groups—how does it compare the rose growers' capability poverty with the capability poverty in Lima slums, for example? This section will argue for the collection of data that pertain to multiple dimensions of human life, including culture. However, it will argue *against* the interpretation of this data as 'indicators of capability' except in certain narrow cases that will be described. This chapter illustrates this analysis by arguing (a) that the DAC (Development Assistance Committee) indicators do not track capability poverty directly; additional information is required, and (b) that UNESCO culture indicators (which are argued to be developments of Sen's capability approach) do not track changes in culture-related capabilities.

Sen addresses the measurement problem directly a number of times.[83] The conclusion he reaches is that capabilities cannot be directly observed. In 'The Living Standard', he recognized that the data requirements for measuring capabilities were very great. He did not address this question further (recall: his primary concern in that paper was to advocate a move from measuring commodities to measuring functionings). He did note that, given the diversity of tastes, at higher levels of development 'it becomes harder to surmise about capability by simply observing achievement'. He writes that this problem is 'less serious' for extreme poverty.

In *Inequality Reexamined* the possibility that capabilities might be measured if sufficient data were made available is removed. Sen writes, 'the capability set is not directly observable, and has to be constructed on the basis of presumptions (just as the "budget set" in consumer analysis is also so constructed on the basis of data regarding income, prices and the presumed possibilities of exchange)'.[84] Theorization is an inescapable step in the construction of a 'capability set' comprising 'what functionings a person could have'.

So an evaluation of well-being achievement or poverty alleviation should consider a person's capability set, but this cannot be directly observed and must be surmised from empirical measures of that person's achieved functionings. How does

---

[83] Sen and Anand (1994b, 1997), Sen (1976, 1980a, 1983d, 1984a, 1985b, 1987b, 1991d, 1992c, 1993b, 1996g, 1997a,i).

[84] (1992a: 52). Later on he describes the data requirements as 'particularly hard' (seeming to suggest such data exist) and advocates practical compromises (p. 135) but does not give an example of what this hard-to-get data would be. Therefore we have elected to use his earlier assessment (p. 52) that capability sets are not directly observable.

182 Basic Needs and Basic Capabilities

one 'surmise' basic capabilities from achieved functionings? Put differently, what 'presumptions' and what data are necessary in order to construct a capability set? I will explore this question, again, by looking at empirical work associated with the capability approach.

4.1. *Achieved functioning indicators of capabilities*

As we have already seen, the first indicator of capabilities which Sen named was mortality rates. Sen and Anand noted that 'survival would seem to be a prerequisite for the enjoyment of any other capability or functioning'.[85] This 'prerequisites argument' justifies using primitive achieved functionings as a proxy for capabilities. Yet, being the prerequisite of *all* conceivable human capabilities, the information life expectancy figures can give as to the capability set of a particular range of functionings is limited. Furthermore, in countries which have already achieved a high life expectancy, the statistic ceases significantly to indicate all capabilities *per se*, but rather indicates a narrower range of health/diet-associated functionings. So other indicators are necessary.

Sen's empirical work on a capabilities deprivation measure identifies other functionings which pertain to the absolute core of poverty. Sen and Anand have set forward two indices of capabilities poverty, one of which relates to developing countries. This is the human poverty index of the UNDP that was introduced in the 1997 *Human Development Report*. It comprises three dimensions: survival, educational deprivation, and economic deprivation, and is written as the mean of three different proportions. These are represented, respectively, by

$s =$ *survival deprivation*: the expected incidence of mortality by age 40 (at current age-specific mortality rates)

$k =$ *deprivation of education and knowledge*: percentage of people who are illiterate

$e =$ *economic deprivation*: the mean of three sub-components: $\{(1/3)[h + w + n]\}$, where

$h =$ percentage of population without access to health care

$w =$ percentage without safe water

$n =$ percentage of children who are undernourished

The first indicator is the one discussed earlier, namely life expectancy.[86] The second is likewise itself a valuable functioning (pertaining to the dimension of 'knowledge'). Furthermore it is a prerequisite for the attainment of functionings in a number of other dimensions. The sub-components of the third indicator are, in developing countries, highly correlated with social as well as private income, but income does not appear as a discrete 'dimension of human development' or an intrinsically good

---

[85] (1997: 13). See also Sen (1993*b*, 1998*a*).

[86] The particular selection of age-specific mortality rates, and the decision to study these in a deprivational perspective, are very interestingly set out in Anand and Sen (1997), but will not be discussed here.

functioning. This being said, like life expectancy, income is instrumental to, and a prerequisite for, attaining a number of functionings. In addition, the particular variables Sen and Anand chose to represent economic deprivation themselves partially represent the dimension 'life—health, security, reproduction'. The percentage of children who are undernourished does so directly (by representing a shortfall in the capability to be nourished).[87] The other figures represent access to commodities which are both instrumental and essential to health (among other things). Because these are access figures and do not imply equality in amounts consumed, they are not susceptible to the same criticism Sen gives of primary goods: namely, that an equal distribution of rice portions will generate profound inequality in the nutritional status of different persons, depending on a number of characteristics including their age, gender, metabolic rate, and physical activity.[88] An analogue of Sen's criticism might still apply if, for example, regional variations in climate meant that different regions required different levels of health-care access in order to provide equivalent health-related capabilities. Still, there are good data on all these indicators, fulfilling the pragmatic need noted above.

Hence, generalizing the arguments Sen used in defence of life expectancy measures as a capability measure suggests why the new human poverty index is also an index of capabilities deprivation. These broad lines of argument might be further generalized in order to identify the criteria achieved functionings must satisfy in order to be considered as possible indicators of capabilities poverty.[89]

The criteria I propose are found in Table 5.1.

4.2. *Data availability and arbitrariness*

Suppose, using the concepts discussed earlier, we were to specify a number of general basic needs, such as Drèze and Sen or the basic human needs school have done. One subsequent task—on which the remainder of this chapter focuses—would be to discuss how to develop indicators that will help policy-makers to track the progress towards 'equality' in persons' capability to meet their basic needs. At this stage one is

---

[87] I am making the assumption that undernourishment of children under 5 is, categorically, not 'deliberately chosen' by the children, thus represents capability failure as well as achieved functioning failure. In this case, I suggest the achieved functionings are coincident with the capability. One might quarrel with this position either by arguing that children below 5 have the capability to exercise meaningful choice, or else that in their case, the choice is exercised by their guardian. In the latter case, undernourishment may in some families *be* deliberately chosen (i.e. the underfeeding of female children). That is, some children who are undernourished actually *could* be nourished; but their guardian makes a free choice to allocate the resources in a different way. Sen does not discuss how the distinction between capability and achieved functioning applies to young children or to the mentally infirm; here it is assumed that basic needs functionings and capabilities are coincident, not that the choice function is allocated to an independent guardian (see Nussbaum 2000a). However, this position has its own difficulties.

[88] Always, though, the question has to be raised whether the indicators of access really measure 'access' in the sense of positive ability of the poor, handicapped, etc. to use them (Sen's capability) or merely mark the existence of the institution (whatever its quality, appropriateness, or expense to users) on a map.

[89] Achieved functioning indicators could also be used in contexts where the policy variable (which may be affected) is not economic but, for example, political freedom.

Table 5.1. *Criteria for capability indicators*

An achieved functioning may be used as an indicator of basic capabilities if it satisfies six conditions:
  (i) the functioning belongs to the capability set (is itself valuable) OR the functioning is directly associated with the capability set (highly correlated, etc);
  (ii) the functioning pertains to a basic human need, i.e. that without which one's life may be blighted;
  (iii) the functioning is not significantly dependent on any non-basic prior functioning;
  (iv) the functioning is not dependent on the presence of uncommon ability or interest;
  (v) a level of achieved functioning which is widely acknowledged to be 'basic' can be specified and empirically observed;
  (vi) provision of the functioning does not necessarily compromise freedom to pursue other significant functionings in the long term.[1]

Note: [1] For some families, spending on education may in fact compromise their ability to spend on food, but this could be resolved if income increases.

moving firmly from conceptual to practical matters, and additional—at times arbitrary—considerations influence this transition. It might be helpful to bracket these off at the start of the discussion, so that their influence is explicit rather than implicit. Box 5.1 identifies several considerations which actually are and have been used to block off different kinds of needs, and it is important to be aware of each consideration, remembering that there is no guarantee that they will all coincide, nor are they all of equivalent importance.

Indicators may be found to track basic capabilities internationally. But the basic capabilities that such indicators track are most likely to be those that are commodity-dependent, whose threshold level can be specified and measured, which are relevant and agreed across cultures, and for which adequate data is available or could readily be obtained. But the fact that such basic needs are most amenable to international observation does not necessarily mean that they are more important than other basic capabilities. In fact some central basic capabilities might be left out. The degree of overlap between feasible basic capabilities and the full set of basic capabilities is

Box 5.1. *Considerations that may influence the choice of basic needs categories and indicators in practice*

1. Adequate data has been collected in the past.
2. Adequate data could begin to be collected.
3. International consensus exists that this is a basic need.
4. It would be possible to specify valid threshold levels.[1]
5. It would be possible to address the need by public action.
6. It would be possible to address the need by the provision of material resources.

Note. [1] The drawing of any line has a degree of arbitrariness to it; however, the magnitude of arbitrariness in the threshold regarding minimal caloric intake is significantly less than the arbitrariness might be if one attempted to specify a threshold of 'participation'.

4.3. *The ability to go about without shame*

Can indicators be found for all basic capabilities? In this section I turn to analyse directly one capability which Sen has repeatedly mentioned as pertaining to absolute poverty. The reason for doing so is that there seems to be a tension, at this stage, between Sen's writing on the subject of absolute poverty and Sen's recent work on indices and indicators of poverty. In this section I will argue that this stems not from a mere lack of data, but from a fundamental difference between the 'dimensions' of human fulfilment that are being considered. Consideration of this difference philosophically may be an efficient way of identifying the feasibility of indicators of non-material basic capabilities.

This problem comes to the fore because Sen has taken a great deal of care, in his conceptual work, consistently to argue that poverty, and in particular that *absolute* poverty, has both material and social dimensions. He repeatedly refers to Adam Smith's point that linen shirts and leather shoes were necessary, in nineteenth century Britain, in order to go about without shame.[90] Sen uses this example regularly to make one of two points. One point is that 'the ability to go about without shame' is a relevant basic capability which should figure in the 'absolutist core' of notions of absolute poverty.[91] This assertion was at the core of Sen's controversy with Townsend.[92] The other point is that 'the ability to go about without shame' is 'complex', that is

---

[90] Smith writes, 'By necessaries I understand not only the commodities which are indispensably necessary for the support of life, but whatever the custom of the country renders it indecent for creditable people, even the lowest order, to be without. A linen shirt, for example, is, strictly speaking, not a necessary of life. The Greeks and Romans lived, I suppose, very comfortably though they had no linen. But in the present times, through a greater part of Europe, a creditable day-labourer would be ashamed to appear in public without a linen shirt, the want of which would be supposed to denote that disgraceful degree of poverty which, it is presumed, nobody can well fall into without extreme bad conduct. Custom, in the same manner, has rendered leather shoes a necessary of life in England. The poorest creditable person of either sex would be ashamed to appear in public without them' (Sen 1981a: 18 quoting Adam Smith (1776) *An Inquiry into the Nature and Causes of the Wealth of Nations*, pp. 351–2). See Sen (1990a, 1984a.b: 332, 2000j).

[91] (1983d: 332–3), see (1993a: 36–7), where he lists other relevant complex functionings as 'being happy, achieving self-respect, taking part in the life of the community'. These are not new: Sen has referred readers to studies such as Rowntree's (1901) where 'secondary poverty' of this social nature was studied in Britain.

[92] Townsend argued that 'the problem of [Sen's] reiteration of the virtues of an "absolutist core" to the meaning of poverty is the underestimation of the importance of needs other than for food' (1985: 664). Sen clarified that absolute deprivation, while including hunger, also includes 'being ashamed to appear in public' and 'not being able to participate in the life of the community'. The distinction between absolute and relative poverty then is not in the elements that either may or may not contain, but rather in the criterion by which poverty is recognized (e.g. whether poverty is recognized according to relative disparity in certain capabilities, or according to an absolute lack of certain capabilities) (1985c: 673). See also Ch. 5, Sect. 1

to say, the commodity requirements to support this capability vary widely (evidently the Greeks and the Romans needed no linen shirts), but like the other basic capabilities it is also strongly dependent upon material resources.

We saw earlier how 'the ability to go about without shame' could figure as a basic need in Wiggins's approach, if it relates to how humans are constituted, and if this need persists in alternative futures and across persons. In addition, to be a basic need in Wiggins's account, it is also necessary to be able to specify x—that which is needed—in a sufficiently general way. We suggested in fact that basic needs could be re-specified as the capability to which they refer: that is, the capability to be respected by oneself; the capability to go about without shame.

The next consideration is whether there *can be* an indicator of capability deprivation, which is meaningful internationally/globally, and which adequately represents *all* of the dimensions of absolute poverty including the basic complex social ones (to go about without shame, to participate in the life of a community).

This point is most clearly discussed by referring to the elements of the discussion (reprinted in Table 5.2). What is evident from this table is that the social capabilities which Sen considers to be elements of absolute poverty may be expressed in highly diverse fashions across cultures.[93] This would suggest that *quantitative* international absolute poverty indicators of achieved functionings *will not be able satisfactorily to include the basic social capabilities*, and that this stems not from inadequate data, but from the nature of these kinds of capabilities, as having variable commodity requirements across communities and nations. To refer ahead to the discussion in Section 4.5, what the 'kilograms of reading material consumed' per capita tell us about culture varies from culture to culture.

4.4. *Implications for international poverty indicators*

At this stage some constructive conclusions can be made. The arguments in this section have suggested that

- indicators of functionings may, in certain circumstances, approximate indicators of capabilities;
- indicators of basic needs functionings will be less variable than indicators of basic needs commodities, hence could be more valid internationally (where commodity requirements are variable, focus on outcomes; where they are not, can specify inputs);
- it is rather unlikely that internationally valid commodity indicators will exist for the 'basic social capabilities' which Sen describes as co-constituents of absolute poverty with basic physical needs;
- there is a valid role for empirical, economic, and scientific information in:
  - determining the validity of indicators;

---

[93] There is also a problem of specifying the commodity dependence, but this itself does not preclude the generation of an indicator, because conceivably one could—and in fact would theoretically prefer to—gather indicators of capability, of output.

Basic Needs and Basic Capabilities

Table 5.2. *Needs and commodity requirements*

Sen: poor, relatively speaking[1] absolute poverty = inability	Sen and Anand:[2] HPI components	Drèze and Sen:[3]	Dimensions[4] of human development
Commodity requirements not too variable:	*Indicator components:*	*The ability:*	
to meet nutritional requirements	% who are undernourished	to live long	
to escape avoidable disease	% who will die before 40	to escape preventable illnesses	Life
to be educated	% without access to health care	to read and write	Knowledge
to be sheltered	% without safe water	to work outside the family irrespective of gender	Some degree of excellence in work and play
to be clothed	% who are illiterate		
to be able to travel			
Commodity requirements very variable:			
to live without shame		to participate in collaborative as well as adversarial politics	Friendship and sociability
			Self-expression
to participate in the activities of the community			Self-direction
to have self-respect (to be happy)[5]			Harmony with wider sources of meaning and value

Note: [1] 1983d: 337. [2] 1997. [3] 1995 p.vii. [4] Grisez *et al.* (1987). [5] 1993a: 36.

- checking the assumption that basic needs functionings are an adequate indicator of basic needs capabilities;
- specifying the basic needs and absolute poverty functioning (by research in physiology and cross-cultural psychology and so on);
- determining whether local or national indicators of basic social capabilities are valid;
- developing indicators on the social side.

At this stage, the question of whether poverty indicators can be improved upon is best carried forward by discussion of extant poverty, cultural, and social indicators.

4.5. *Indicators of culture*

The first topic is indicators of culture. The UNESCO *World Culture Report 1998* includes two chapters that develop indicators for international comparisons of culture on the basis of the capability approach.[94] In one of these Prasanta Pattanaik argues that it is possible to agree upon a set of fundamental goals relating to (i) physical functionings, (ii) political and social functionings, and (iii) intellectual and aesthetic functionings, although the relative weighting of these may vary. He proposes that these kinds of indicators inform international comparisons of different populations' human development:

> Indicators of human development . . . could evaluate, for example, whether the level of human development of one ethnic group is higher than that of another. They could thus be used to rank ethnic groups—or whole countries, for that matter—on the basis of their average level of human well-being.[95]

In a separate chapter Terry McKinley goes further and proposes indicators of culture—cultural freedom, creativity, and cultural dialogue—for the purpose of making international comparisons between cultural forms rather than only well-being:

> We are taking an explicitly ethical position: our concern is not only that a people's culture enables them to live together, but also that it enables them to live together *well*. What we seek are universally accepted ethical standards that can distinguish cultures that hamper human development from those that foster it . . . Our starting assumption is that the ultimate test of a particular culture is whether it fosters an expansion of human capabilities and choice.[96]

For example, he proposes that small teams of evaluators travel to all countries and evaluate cultural freedom in four dimensions—integrity of self, non-discrimination, freedom of thought and expression, and self-determination—on the scale of 0–10.[97] He proposes that creativity be measured by the publication of books, the production of long films, the consumption of music albums, films, and cultural paper, and the number of artists. Cultural dialogue might be measured by education and mass communication in the form of newspapers, telephone lines, televisions, and computers.

Sen, writing in the same publication, is rather more sceptical of the cultural indices. For cultures are deeply heterogeneous within as well as between countries, and this diversity is obscured by representing an entire country by one set of aggregate indicators. Furthermore he argues that cultural heterogeneity is not only actual; it is important. 'In a world constantly bombarded by the "imperialism" of the culture of the Western metropolis . . . surely what is needed is to strengthen resistance rather than look for uniform indicators of international cultural comparison'. Also, aggregation between different [incommensurable] kinds of cultural expression, such

---

[94] McKinley (1998) and Pattanaik (1998).
[95] Pattanaik (1998: 333). Note that he does not wish to assess well-being, and political, social, intellectual, and aesthetic functionings *per se* (i.e. not evaluate 'levels of culture') but 'only to the extent that they are constituent components of such well-being' (p. 334). [96] McKinley (1998: 322).
[97] This is a modification of Desai's Political Freedom Index; see Desai (1994a).

as, poetry, drama, and dance, 'cannot but be misleading'.[98] Sen suggests (i) that it may be possible to identify 'basic capabilities'—enabling conditions and human rights—that relate to the state and to cultural progress, but (ii) that the trade-offs between economic progress and social or cultural goods must be decided, chosen, perhaps with the participation of different groups: 'the challenges of globalization ... point to the need for equity in the development of human capabilities in political participation as well as in economic performance'.[99]

Pattanaik and McKinley both claim that their approaches explicitly develop Sen's capability approach. Yet they seem to overlook some issues of comparability and participation, and so misspecify the form that ethical standards about culture can reasonably take. This section will argue that their approaches to the ranking and evaluation of cultures augur against self-direction and participation, because each purports to compare functionings for *normative* purposes and to provide *incentives* for cultures to develop certain practices. Pattanaik and McKinley both begin from an admirable position, which is the recognition of valuable capabilities beyond those related to physical human functionings, and the recognition that an operational capability approach must relate to these elements of human development. But there are two difficulties in their work.

First, the move from 'goals' which are general dimensions of human functioning to 'indicators' that are particular practices, or expressions of a functioning, is problematic for two reasons in turn. On one hand the same 'indicator' may arise from different practices in different places. Drama ratings may be low, not because a particular society is not expressive, but because it has a convention against the deception that acting entails. In another society drama may be a trivial form of entertainment, in another a means of political communication, in another a central form of creative expression, in another a form of religious celebration. Pattanaik and McKinley each subsume indicators under particular goals (aesthetic fulfilment, in the case of plays).

Further, the 'normative' role of these indicators is particularly troublesome. Consider *A*, a bachelor philosopher who is fulfilled in solitary writing, in cooking thick soups, and in going for long city walks with his beagle. He might be far more flourishing than *B*, who is a divorced man of the same age who has just lost his job due to an alcohol addiction, who is estranged from his family and children, and is clinically depressed and overweight. But one might not, simply on the basis of this comparison, recommend that *B* enrol in classes of philosophy and cooking, and buy a beagle. In quite extreme cases one might identify an individual or culture that seemed to be flourishing more than another. But that does not mean that the less flourishing culture would be better off if (much less *only* if) it imitated the particular cultural practices of the other.

Both authors argue that cultural indicators can rank the intellectual and aesthetic functionings of different countries relative to each other. The world culture indicators convey, they argue, a *normative* message: if a country's cultural indicators improved, this would indicate higher human development. The problem is that the

---

[98] 1998b: 318, all quotes.   [99] ibid. 321.

particular *indicators* of intellectual and aesthetic functionings are *practices*. The normative use of the indicators creates an incentive for countries to encourage certain cultural practices (novel-writing, film production) that were chosen as indicators on the basis of rather arbitrary considerations such as data availability.

Pattanaik, recognizing this difficulty, recommends the construction of indices of cultural production and consumption, such as 'an index of production of music, dance, plays, operas, films, television programmes, paintings, and so on', and notes that such indices must include informal as well as formal cultural events 'e.g. dancing in tribal societies, choir music in churches, ritualistic wall paintings by housewives in rural India'.[100] In this case, the normative use of indicators would be for governments to *expand* the practices contained in their index. But this correction still confines valuable cultural progress to changes in *current* cultural practices. The index would increase if tribal dancing came into fashion; it would plummet if tribal dancing went out and people instead took to giving speeches on street corners for the first time. So even a fixed country-specific index of cultural practices is not useful for *normative* purposes across time. Finally, if the elements of the index change annually, there are deep problems for comparability.

The second fundamental difficulty with Pattanaik and McKinley is that they argue that cultures can be ranked. But how might one rank the flourishing of philosopher *A* above compared with successful human rights lawyer *C* who is happily married with two sons, one normal and one autistic, is an avid squash player, and goes through cycles in which she loves her work and then is devastated by the tragedy of her cases? How might one rank a culture in which the material conditions are poor but the relational, aesthetic, spiritual, and integrative dimensions are rich, as against a culture in which material and political conditions are well met but the other dimensions are impoverished? A deeper problem than simply the identification of suitable indicators and their interpretation is that the flourishing of many individuals and cultures may be intelligibly different—but *assertively* unrankable.

This raises the question of whether or not indicators should be collected at all or whether energy should be put into the development of better cultural indicators. There are actually good arguments for collecting such information. Such indicators could generate information to provoke 'explicit' public scrutiny of social changes—for instance, by tracking the change in communications technology. Also, a certain core of these indicators may represent 'basic capabilities' in economic, political, or social terms—capabilities that chart out the 'enabling conditions' for a rich cultural life but do not actually chart out cultural achievements. The indicators relating to negative freedom in each case may be of this kind.

4.6. *DAC indicators*

This final section considers the indicators of poverty identified by the Development Assistance Committee (DAC) of the Organization for Economic Cooperation and

---

[100] Pattanaik (1998: 338, 339 respectively).

Development (OECD).[101] The DAC indicators were chosen on two grounds: (i) they represent the largest current international consensus on the dimensions of poverty, and (ii) the DAC have given a public account of the reasoning that lies behind each indicator. This Committee has selected certain goals that they take to be central to international efforts to eradicate poverty, and chosen twenty-nine indicators by which to 'judge' their multilateral development efforts. The goals are 'economic well-being', 'social development', and 'environmental sustainability and re-generation'; the indicators appear in Table 5.3. The indicators were chosen on evaluative and technical grounds. 'The particular indicators we have chosen reflect our judgement of their importance in their own right and as meaningful proxies for broader development goals'.[102] These indicators represent 'aspirations for the entire development process, not just for co-operation efforts'. The indicators identified at this level have scope for relativity in the further specification and implementation of programmes to change the situations reflected in they indicate. Still, one might ask:

- Do these indicate basic functionings that are arguably valid internationally?
- Can some international 'priority' weighting be accorded to these indicators?
- Is concern for 'capability' indicated?
- How is consideration for the entire capability set (full menu) incorporated?

The first thing to notice is that a list of indicators *per se* does not inform one necessarily about the conceptualization of poverty that underlies them. This is very important because the same basic set of indicators (literacy, infant mortality, life expectancy, income) can inform quite different conceptions of poverty and different policy recommendations. Perhaps they are best understood as general functionings—incompletely theorized indicators. This being said, some observations can be made. DAC has specified the 'dimension captured' by each variable. For example, DAC describes the indicator 'population below $1 a day' as capturing the dimension 'incidence' of poverty: that is, 'the indicator measures the proportion of the population whose income/consumption levels fall below a prescribed poverty line. It reflects the purchasing power that households have over goods and services needed to escape poverty (food, clothing, housing and other nonfood essentials).' If the bundle of goods and services to which person *i* has access *includes* a bundle which would meet their basic needs, then they have the positive freedom to meet basic needs. One dollar a day does not necessarily confer this capability—disabled persons may need more; also if there is a food shortage, or no hospital, then $1 would be of scant use to meeting basic needs. But this indicator could also be *interpreted* rather as a partial proxy for people's positive freedom to choose the market commodities that are necessary to meet a variety of basic needs (which would need to be supplemented by further information regarding the availability of goods and services). In this interpretation, the proxy could be part of the set of indicators which present a capability

---

[101] The report containing these was approved on 6–7 May 1996.   [102] 1996: 7.

192   *Basic Needs and Basic Capabilities*

Table 5.3. *DAC indicators*

Goal	Indicator
Economic well-being	
Reducing extreme poverty	(1) Population below $1 per day
	(2) Poverty gap ratio: incidence × depth
	(3) Poorest fifth's share of national consumption
	(4) Prevalence of underweight under 5s
Social development	
Universal primary education	(5) Net enrolment in primary education
	(6) Completion of fourth grade of primary education
	(7) Literacy rate of 15- to 24- year olds
Gender equality	(8) Ratio of girls to boys in primary and secondary education
	(9) Ratio of literate females to males (15 to 24 year olds)
Infant and child mortality	(10) Infant mortality rate
	(11) Under 5 mortality rate
Maternal mortality	(12) Maternal mortality rate
	(13) Births attended by skilled health personnel
Reproductive health	(14) Contraceptive prevalence rate
	(15) HIV prevalence in 15- to 24- year-old pregnant women
Environmental sustainability and regeneration	
	(16) Countries with national sustainable development strategies
	(17) Population with access to safe water
	(18) Intensity of freshwater use
	(19) Biodiversity: land area protected
	(20) Energy efficiency: GDP per unit of energy use
	(21) Carbon dioxide emissions
General indicators	
	(22) GNP per capita
	(23) Adult literacy rate
	(24) Total fertility rate
	(25) Life expectancy at birth
	(26) Aid as % of GNP
	(27) External debt as % of GNP
	(28) Investment as % of GDP
	(29) Trade as % of GDP

approach to poverty measurement. The problem with interpreting the indicator this way is that a discussion might then turn to whether or not this is in fact the 'best' proxy indicator available for this purpose and conclude in the negative (because of the huge difference between this and poverty lines drawn as the income needed to fulfil minimum caloric requirements).

4.6.1. *International validity*
The first issue is whether these indicate basic functionings that are arguably valid internationally. Three categories do not appear to refer to functionings at all. 'Future generations' refers to a general concern that future generations will be able to meet their needs for food and energy; rate of material change refers to macro indications of the resources that will be available to affect the indicators. This concern is relevant for the capabilities approach—it has to do with the intertemporal distribution of capabilities—although it is not a functioning. Indicators related to contraceptive prevalence and total fertility are included for 'descriptive' content, but no 'target' is set for these. Purchasing power is not a valuable doing nor a valuable being but might be a proxy for the functionings that it gives one the power to pursue. Are the remaining functionings—health and basic education—'basic needs' in the sense defined before? To return to Wiggins

It is necessary, things being what they actually are, that if I[/we] avoid being harmed then I[/we] have [the capability to enjoy health/basic education]?

The only straightforward category is health. The basicness of 'education' turns on whether it is possible to suppose that, 'things being what they are' include 'a world such that persons without a basic education (*defined as literacy or a primary education*) will be harmed'. A person without any understanding whatever would be harmed, but whether the practice of literacy necessarily represents salient understanding is debatable. Still, because primary education may be specified to local situations and different ways of knowing, I will consider all of these to be valid internationally although this is (and all conclusions in this section are) 'essentially contestable'.

4.6.2. *International priority*
The second question is whether there is a case for focusing international attention and technical support on these indicators rather than others. I would suggest that there is, for three reasons: *basicness, feasibility, consensus*. First, all of the indicators are at 'basic' levels; they do specify functionings that are arguably prerequisites to other valuable functionings. And they do so at a general enough level to allow specification and adaptation at the national and local level. Secondly, the areas chosen are dependent upon material commodities that can be publicly provided. Thus it is feasible for international or outside actors to contribute constructively to this process using their own resources and comparative technical expertise, and to track their progress. Thirdly, the functionings (health, nutrition, education) focus on the basic physical and intellectual needs of human persons—on the subset of absolute poverty that relates to non-social needs. The area of consensus about the goal and about viable means may be larger for these functionings than for others. Furthermore, to return to the issue of purchasing power, income too can potentially contribute to people's ability to pursue other valuable functionings.

4.6.3. Concern for capability

One would have to notice that the DAC indicators could not be said to be indicators of capability according to the operational definition of capability given above. Consider the case of adult literacy. If there were forcible government measures to gather women and educate them in massive boarding schools whether or not they agreed, so long as their health was still good, one would see, in the next year, a strong increase in adult literacy and steady or improved measures in female health. Similarly, the DAC indicators would not be able to discriminate between country *A*, in which the primary education system was implemented using participatory measures, and country *B*, in which the education system was implemented in a top-down fashion. Country *A* may have increased people's capabilities for education more than country *B*, and also may be more sustainable. But this information would not be available by analysis of DAC indicators.

These could be indicators of basic capabilities if one could make the valid assumption that nearly 100 per cent of persons would indeed take up this freedom to achieve these particular functionings (although the likelihood of sustainability would still not be available), and that their having this particular choice between education, say, and an alternative is not particularly important. For in this case, the fact that people *would* take up the capability indicates that it is a valued functioning. Furthermore if the intrinsic value of choosing is not particularly important in this case then this could be one of the cases Sen identifies in which the freedom to exert agency is relatively unimportant (such as the malaria case). There could still be a difference from the malaria case in so far as the coercion involved, being more direct, might damage other capabilities. Such damage would have to be evaluated separately. Yet these assumptions about the relative importance of agency in these particular instances, which would need to be verified in order for the indicators to reflect basic capabilities, are neither discussed nor tested.

In order to make the DAC indicators reflect people's capability, albeit crudely and imperfectly, it would be necessary to have indications of how coercive or participatory the education, health, nutrition, and income generation or employment programmes had been.

4.6.4. Consideration of the entire capability set (full menu)

Related to the above point, one must notice that the DAC indicators could measure progress towards equality in the indicated functionings (health, basic education, nutrition, minimum purchasing power), but progress towards equality in this space not only does not reflect equality in basic capabilities, but also does not reflect whether or not the overall capability set of persons expanded or contracted. While there are at present no clear ways of tracking the 'overall capability set', an analysis of DAC indicators would need to bear in mind that they do *not* have this information, so the conclusions they could give on the basis of their indicators are limited.

The DAC effort is interesting to analyse because it represents an enthusiastic international consensus on measures of poverty, and because the linkage between the indicators and the goals is made explicit. Yet to comment on progress either towards equality in the space of basic capabilities, or the expansion of capabilities overall, additional discussion would be required.

5. CONCLUSION

This chapter has drawn the analyses of the preceding sections together with an account of basic capability, and proposed an operationalization of the capability approach. The conclusions of the various discussions of this chapter are:

(i) Operationalization of the capability approach with respect to absolute poverty entails the identification of basic capabilities, or basic needs.
(ii) Basic needs may be identified at a general level (i.e. relative to broad categories of harm and suffering); specification must occur at a lower level and in a particular temporal context.
(iii) The focus on capability rather than functionings, at the micro level, means operationally, that the goal is to develop a long-term capability to choose. This precludes violent coercion, and also precludes long-term systematic enforcement of functionings. It allows commendation of activities that may be expected to meet basic needs. But it also allows a community to choose to leave some basic needs unmet.
(iv) The goal of equality in the capability to meet basic human needs is insufficient unless it is nested within the goal of development as the expansion of valuable capabilities. The objective is equality in persons' capability to meet their basic needs that does not compromise their capability to enjoy non-basic valuable beings and doings. When there are conflicts or 'hard cases'—for example, when one could *only* meet basic needs by overriding or damaging other capabilities—these can only be resolved by a value judgement—if possible involving the participants. The 'capability to meet basic human needs' does not *necessarily* trump other capabilities.

This chapter concludes Part I. Part I has proposed a simplification and operational definition of the capability approach for its use at the microeconomic level. This operational definition, and the discussion which preceded it both in this chapter and others, offers a framework for the making of substantive value judgements (SVJ) in the process of pursuing equality in basic capabilities and of expanding human capabilities overall. I have not argued that this is a necessary interpretation of the capability approach.

Some of the distinctive features may be more clearly seen in Part II, which illustrates one particular application of this framework.

PART II

6

Assessing Capability Change

> I conclude that cost-benefit analysis is inescapable across a large range of policy decisions.[1]

1. INTRODUCTION TO PART II

The transition from a concept of human development to its practical application, such as the one these last two chapters undertake, is notably delicate. For practical assessments must make their way amid competing demands on the interest and time of all concerned. And they must adapt to an activity's logistical and social settings and to assessors' capacities. Rarely can all refined theoretical points be incorporated in an actual evaluation, so priorities are set and assumptions made—explicitly or implicitly, by design or by default.

It seems for this reason yet more important to bind the practical methodologies that prove feasible together with a fuller conceptual account of what would be desirable, so that the practical methods, however circumstantially valid, remain open to challenge, modification, and expansion on the grounds of their inconsistency with their own goal.

Given the very real constraints of the practical work faced in 1996: limited time, zero research budget for survey work, and the commitment to develop a methodology that Oxfam field staff could use, it was necessary to 'select, even select quite violently'.[2] The two chapters that follow can only be rightly understood if it is borne very clearly in mind what has been selected and why.

This study deliberately selected fieldwork on the Achilles' heel of the framework set out in the previous chapters. The Achilles' heel, the weakest spot, which if successfully attacked could bring the entire endeavour to naught, is the assumption that poor people *can* articulate and analyse their poverty and their valued freedoms in multiple dimensions, and further that if they do so the resulting analysis will be *different* from a sophisticated but narrower analysis that uses income as a proxy for poverty and freedom.

There is a regrettable cost in having such a focus, and in allocating limited time and resources to this analysis: we could not achieve significant progress on this problem *and* have a large sample size, collect quantitative data on the same dimensions and study the intercorrelations between these and the participatory data, have control and experimental groups or use a quasi-experimental setting and generate propensity

---

[1] Judge Richard Posner (2000: 1158). [2] Hicks (1983: 4).

scores. Even some of the work that was initially intended—analysing the robustness of the cardinal data we used, and the reliability of perceptual data on before-after changes (which can be notoriously unreliable)—could not be accomplished. However, on the positive side, those unrealized tasks, while essential and important, are also familiar. We know how to do them; they have well-developed literatures; we can do them next time. The purpose of this research was to demonstrate that it is worth having a 'next time'—that some of the key information on agency and functionings, without which capability assessment is impossible, can be obtained by simple facilitation, and assessed by the same communities.

A methodology for gaining systematic information regarding valuable changes in functioning and comparing these changes across activities was first developed and pilot-tested by this author in 1996 and subsequently used with seven Oxfam Pakistan activities in 1997. The three case studies in Chapter 7 were conducted at that time. Subsequently the methodology (with ongoing changes) was used on over twenty additional activities by Oxfam field staff. In addition a team of twenty-two persons used this method to evaluate the work of sixteen NGOs in Pakistan on behalf of The Asia Foundation and USAID. Also, Strengthening Participatory Organizations (SPO), a national NGO in Pakistan, assessed their women's activities using this methodology. The Oxfam field staff and The Asia Foundation's consultants separately evaluated the methodology at the close of their work, and their criticisms inform this discussion of it.[3]

The assessment methodology consciously builds upon the conceptual framework of the previous chapters but narrows its focus entirely to a concrete problem. In particular, the goal in developing a methodology was to enable field staff with a modest education to report the definition and relative importance of changes in empowerment,[4] income, and functionings as perceived by participants in these activities and by the institutions that implemented them. I will explain shortly that this focus was chosen in order to fill a gap in current participatory evaluation methodologies, and an assessment to which it contributed would also use many standard techniques without modification.

Chapter 7 returns to the rose cultivation activity and two other Oxfam projects and—tentatively but concretely—assesses and compares the expansions in capability that occurred as a result of these activities. In the first case study, a local NGO, Rural Women's Welfare Organization (RWWO) runs a revolving loan/micro-credit scheme that engages in social organization and provides loans to women for the purchase of a breeding goat in villages near Senghar, Sindh. The second activity involves Khoj, an initiative for women in the depressed peri-urban areas of Lahore that uses adult literacy classes as an entry point for community development and income generation. The third is the rose cultivation activity in Arabsolangi, Sindh, which involves men, women, and children in the cooperative cultivation, picking,

---

[3] See Narejo, Jabbar.
[4] Empowerment throughout Chapters 6 and 7 refers to an increase in autonomy—what Sen might call agency achievement or what Finnis might call self-direction—that is valued by the women who exercise it.

threading, and sale of rose garlands. All activities have an income generation component and are targeted at the poor; all have a social component (the formation of a class or group and the explicit intention to 'empower' participants, as well as to increase their income).

1.1. *Relation to previous chapters*

But how does this methodology arise out of the account of human development from Chapters 1 to 5? Connections emerge throughout this chapter, but the major linkages are signalled below.

Chapter 2 argued that dimensions of human development could be coherently specified and that the value of various capabilities could be articulated by reference to these dimensions. The dimensions form the spine of the participatory exercise used in these case studies to identify capability changes (and to minimize the dimensions of change that groups temporarily overlook).[5]

Chapter 3 argued that a practical-reason-based rationality, which includes technical rationality but is broader, is appropriate for decisions that require the decision-makers to weigh or value otherwise incommensurable ends—for example, empowerment and income. It suggested that in addition to information on the plural capabilities affected by the activities, information related to their procedures should be considered. The case studies use cost-benefit analysis to represent the principle of efficiency or 'technical' rationality that was introduced by John Finnis.

- *Employ efficient means to objectives* 'this is the requirement that one bring about good in the world (in one's own life and the lives of others) by actions that are efficient for their (reasonable) purpose(s)'.[6]

Efficiency here means achieving the most poverty reduction (income generation for poor producers) from Oxfam resources. Other moral principles will be mentioned but will *not* be systematically applied. A reflection on how such principles (or others like them) might be used when there are deep value conflicts between groups would be a valuable undertaking. Similarly, further discussion of what principles *must* be applied, or whether all can be, is required.

Chapter 4 scrutinized the relationship between the agent(s) who choose and the outcomes of the choice. It gave an account of the potential merits of participation.[7] It further discussed models for coordinating information transfer, effective activity, and participation. That chapter forms the underlying argument for the use of a participatory methodology (which the proposed assessment exercise is) and for an

---

[5] This relates to another principle, 'Do not leave out of account, or arbitrarily discount or exaggerate any of the dimensions'.   [6] Finnis (1980: 111).

[7] 'Best-Practice' Participation (and occasionally other participation) may relate to several principles: (i) *harmonize practices and commitments with each other* (groups may tailor activities to other local institutions); (ii) *foster the common good* (the discussion and common decisions may have transitive and intrinsic value); (iii) *do not overlook the foreseeable bad consequences of choices* (groups may scrutinize choices thoroughly); (iv) *do not act contrary to your conscience* (individuals may articulate their moral concerns within the discussion).

attention to the depth and kind of participation present at different stages of an activity.

Chapter 5 explored basic capabilities and basic needs. It proposed that the interaction between an external agent and a community, modelled on informed consent, would (i) develop mutual goals in a participatory manner; (ii) pursue agreed functionings efficiently; (iii) safeguard negative freedom; and (iv) mitigate the contraction of non-basic valuable capabilities (or facilitate their expansion). The methodology here (i) describes how the mutual goals were identified; (ii) evaluates the relative efficiency of the activities using cost-benefit analysis; and (iv) tracks the *changes* on the full set of capabilities—both those that were the direct goals (empowerment, health, education) and those that were not—and the relative *value* of these changes from several perspectives.

1.2. *Economic analysis*

The methodologies for evaluating the economic impact of development activities commonly use experimental or quasi-experimental designs. Experimental designs randomly assign the activity (or 'treatment') among eligible villages or beneficiaries. Quasi-experimental assessments compare the poverty of participants in an activity with comparison groups, which may be identified by purposive matching (either of an actual community or of a statistically created comparison group). Both allow the comparison with a counterfactual. However, in practice these evaluations are expensive, and not readily feasible for NGOs such as Oxfam Pakistan (and recall that our focal problem has been to develop methodologies suitable to the resources available to this kind of NGO).[8]

An alternative form that non-experimental economic analysis of development activities has commonly taken is cost-benefit analysis. Cost-benefit analysis (CBA) may be defined at a general level as a systematic valuation of the additional costs to be incurred by any proposed investment and the additional benefits it will generate. The general principle is the basic rationale: 'things are worth doing if the benefits resulting from doing them outweigh their costs'.[9] If impacts on a wide range of ends are integral to human development, then it is certainly necessary to incorporate these in any complete evaluation of the costs and benefits of a proposed investment. But we need to consider whether the *techniques* of social cost-benefit analysis can be expanded to incorporate all capability changes, and, if not, how the information from CBA may be incorporated into a capability framework.

I will argue that for all three of these activities, *techniques* of social cost-benefit analysis (SCBA) are not sufficient to evaluate the relevant capability vector. This is partly because of commonly recognized technical barriers: the derivation of existence values (i.e. for additional quality of life) is problematic and yields a large range of plausible values, but the error margins associated with such values may create an uncertainty coefficient sufficiently large to invalidate an analysis that employs them. Also, the common valuation methods all infer a price on an intangible benefit from

---

[8] See Roche (1999), Baker (2000).   [9] Sen (2000c: 934).

people's answers or behaviour with respect to quite different questions (determining the value of quiet from housing prices in an airway strip) or to speculative questions (if there were a market for *x* what would you be willing to pay?). The validity of this inference has been queried[10] as has the accuracy of the data it generates. In light of these difficulties, many advocate confining references to non-economic benefits to a *description* of qualitative impacts. But there is surprisingly little discussion of how to weight or manage these descriptions *vis-à-vis* economic benefits.[11] CBA is also insufficient for free choices, because these choices can only be made by consideration of the *reasons* for each alternative, as well as by consideration of the inclinations, tastes, and other factors of a group.[12] The practice of isolating and preserving the relative weights that past choices have implicitly ascribed to different variables (weights which are incidental, temporary, circumstantially valid by-products of such decisions—Ch. 4, Sect. 3) obscures this procedure. Also, the results of cost-benefit analyses are rarely shared with, and even more rarely understood by, the community managing the activity of concern. Finally and fundamentally, the 'decision' of how to respond to the CBA is usually institutionally located at or above the level of those doing the CBA. Informed consent is not obtained.[13]

I argue that an assessment of an investment's impact on human capability must contain the public *exercise* of scrutinizing the economic costs and benefits in the full range of dimensions (Ch. 3, Sect. 3) and of reporting qualitatively and systematically those impacts where they cannot be quantified. It must also contain a clear methodology for comparing different impacts in order to make a decision whether to invest.

The obvious must be noted: cost-benefit analysis and social assessment methodologies are not monolithic; each has internal debates and has developed significantly over time. No attempt will be made to interact with the entire corpus of their literatures. Furthermore there are alternative standard methodologies of assessment that cannot be considered for reasons of space. The next section recapitulates the importance of focusing on 'human impacts'; the following section will discuss cross-cutting parameters of CBA that are relevant to the three cases.

1.3. *Capability changes*

To be operational at the activity level, the capability approach must propose how the expansion and contraction of capabilities/functionings (Table 4.1) might enter systematic economic evaluation. If we recall our starting point in Chapter 1, which is that the 'goal' of development is the expansion of human capability rather than simply economic growth, and if we recognize that a full set of human capabilities is

---

[10] Sen (1995*a*), Richardson (2000).
[11] For two different approaches see Chiappero-Martinetti (1994, 1996) and Casini and Bernetti (1996). The most obvious early discussion of this was in UNIDO guidelines, and will be presented later in this chapter. [12] Richardson (2000), forthcoming.
[13] For these and other criticisms of cost-benefit analysis see the *Journal of Legal Studies* (2000) containing articles by Becker, Frank, Nussbaum (2000*c*), E. Posner, R. Posner, Richardson, Sen (2000*c*), Sunstein, and others.

multidimensional and includes not only health and literacy but also relationships and meaningful work, then the question arises, what use of scarce resources will best expand valuable human capabilities?

The 1972 UNIDO guidelines, which brought out the need to relate multiple valuable objectives to economic analysis most consistently and explicitly, describe social benefit-cost analysis as an approach that 'provides a rational framework for project choice using national objectives and values'.[14] The first question, then, is how to *identify* the objectives/values that should be used to evaluate capability expansion, whether these are intended or unintended (Ch. 3, Sect. 3.2.3). The second question is how to *compare* capabilities between persons and between activities. The third question is how to *combine* this information with information on the economic returns of the initiative in such a way as to inform a decision. The capability approach would suggest that the possible objectives might be wider than growth and equity (standard national objectives), may be framed in terms of human functionings or capabilities, and yet may be considered in aggregate. In this approach, the evaluation of development activities must systematically consider the relationship between investments and human impacts.

The class of real impacts that are of specific interest to the concerns of this chapter is of those that pertain to human and social capital,[15] norms, and institutions. There are several reasons for exploring the class of human impacts as a whole.

The ethical reason for studying these components is central: just as health and knowledge may be valued as *ends* as well as means to increasing productivity, so the abilities to enjoy other functionings (pertaining perhaps to participation, religion, art, human relationships) can be considered *intrinsically* valuable whether or not they are also instrumentally valuable.

The instrumental significance of human capital is well established.[16] In addition, the strong argument put forward by Putnam and taken up elsewhere is that 'social capital' in the form of norms and institutions is instrumental to high productivity; the presence of a strong social environment will decrease unit costs.[17] For example, participation may recruit such uncompensated resources as human capital (knowledge, skills), moral resources (commitment, charisma), or cultural resources (trust, social capital, volunteerism, institutions). Economic analyses have broadened to take into account side-effects that relate to the environment, to species diversity, and to human capital as a means of increasing productivity. But although variables such as

---

[14] (1972: 14). Note how quickly the reduction of these took place: Squire and van der Tak wrote, 'the objectives of any particular society clearly must be taken into account', but two sentences later we are told that at a general level, all countries have two objectives: growth and equity (1975: 4). Multiple objectives are treated again in Ward et al. (1991).

[15] Social capital is comprised of trust, cooperation, and the norms and institutions which are needed for collective action. See Putnam (1993), Harris and De Renzio (1997).

[16] Summers (1992) concludes, for example, that the social benefit of an extra year of schooling for 1,000 Pakistani girls is $42,600; the costs of this education would be $30,000. See also Sen (1997e), World Bank (1996b, ch. 8).

[17] Fukuyama (1995), Narayan-Parker and Pritchett (1997), Putnam (1993), *World Development* (1996) (issue on social capital), World Bank (1997), North (1993), Woolcock (1998).

'empowerment' and 'social capital' are also recognized to be important in increasing productivity, and although such variables may be positively or negatively affected by economic strategies in the medium to long term, the social and economic methodologies to address them are in the early stages.

Economic investments may also introduce cultural changes or (inadvertent) changes in common commitments. There has been a significant record of activity failure in terms of lower than estimated rates of return (or simple cessation of activities) due to conflicts of economic investments with certain cultural norms, which indicates that the previous common commitments are socially valued.[18] Such failures lead to correspondingly significant economic costs and inefficiency. Therefore mechanisms that anticipate, identify, and mitigate negative impacts would improve activity performance and decrease risk.

Also, development activities may deplete social resources, causing a long-term negative effect on productivity. Such negative effects could be very local (e.g. if participatory rural appraisal (PRA) 'uses' people's trust, hospitality, and cooperation for an exercise, but the result is unsatisfactory in people's eyes, this resource may not be available for future development teams). Similar effects may also be significantly larger.

One of the classes of information we discussed in Chapter 3, Section 3.2.3 was 'unintended but predictable consequences'. Many human impacts are of this nature, and Sen, recall, argued that these should be considered explicitly.

Finally, there is a need for methodologies that catalyse the 'explicit consideration of ends', by decision-makers.[19] The capability approach focuses on capabilities as the *ends* of development, rather than the *means* of productivity. Therefore a capability assessment would require a methodology of decision-making that transparently combines the economic criteria of efficiency, given political constraints, with other value judgements by the relevant group(s). Different methodologies will be required at different levels from the household to the national; this chapter considers methodologies appropriate for local participatory activities.

One final consideration relates to terminology. I have been using a handful of words quite loosely: capability expansion, human impacts, human externalities, valuable ends. Each of these terms has a resonance with different discussions, hence each is distinctly useful. *Impact* is a term currently favoured by development institutions and encompasses desirable and undesirable effects alike. *Externalities* draws attention to the cause–effect linkage between activities and unpriced side-effects that stand in danger of being overlooked. *Ends* and *functionings* both refocus the discussion on human 'beings and doings' and signal, at least implicitly, the need for periodic reflection on these. *Capability expansion* relates a particular activity and its accomplishments to human development considered as a whole. In the sections that follow I use the term 'human impact', and mean to indicate by this term, *'impact on a functioning or capability'* rather than on a

---

[18] See World Bank (1992c), North (1993), Cassen (1986), and Weiss in Kirkpatrick and Weiss (1996: 172 ff.), where he substantiates and discusses the stylized fact that 25 per cent of projects fail.
[19] See Ch. 3, Sect. 2.2.

commodity set or on a merely instrumental state of affairs. Defined in this way, impacts may be negative as well as positive (see Ch. 3, Sects. 3.1–3.2).[20]

2. COST-BENEFIT ANALYSIS

2.1. *History and current methods*

Social cost-benefit analysis is a technique for the systematic evaluation of social, fiscal, and, more recently, environmental impacts of activities, and the distribution of these impacts among different income strata. Although the task of considering the 'real' costs and benefits (e.g. consumer surplus) of public works activities traces back at least to Dupuit (1844), the technique was developed for use in developing economies in the mid-1960s and the 1970s in response to the widespread perception of pervasive market failures or missing markets, especially in credit, labour, and foreign exchange markets.[21] These market failures meant that key prices—such as foreign exchange rates, interest rates, and unskilled labour wages—were distorted. Furthermore certain benefits that might be believed to have priority, for instance, impacts on consumption poverty, were not given special weights. In other words, social, economic, and financial prices did not coincide.[22] A vigorous literature on cost-benefit analysis and shadow pricing emerged, discussing how to correct for risk and uncertainty, time preferences, wage rates, the opportunity cost of savings/capital, externalities, indirect benefits, distributional effects, social objectives, and changes in the macro climate. The ultimate aim was to obtain information regarding the social desirability of public investments that was not readily available from financial data due to market failures or incomplete markets.

As the World Bank was initially a lead advocate of CBA, its own history of evaluation methods is interesting. After a peak in 1981, the use of social cost-benefit analysis at the World Bank declined sharply.[23] A number of writers attribute this to the economic climate of the 1980s, which 'fostered the belief that the process of economic policy reform would allow market prices to reflect opportunity costs'.[24] The prevailing hypothesis was that 'getting prices right' was a necessary *and sufficient* condition for satisfactory activity selection. In a 1994 review article, Little and Mirrlees argue that in addition to the 1980s climate and a shift from project to programme funding, certain practical difficulties with CBA led to its decline. A thorough CBA requires considerable skill and confidence to address issues of technical uncertainty adequately.[25] Such issues include, for example, how to set distributional weights, how to value public

---

[20] Impact is sometimes defined as durable change, but the usage here does *not* imply long-term change.

[21] The key texts are Little and Mirrlees (1974), Squire and van der Tak (1975), UNIDO (1972) (Dasgupta, Sen, and Marglin).

[22] *Economic* prices correct financial prices for market imperfections by using shadow prices; *social* prices add in additional correctives such as distributional weights.

[23] Other donor agencies, regional banks, and governments have different records (Layard and Glaister 1994: 209–10).

[24] Kirkpatrick and Weiss (1996: 4), see Devarajan, Squire, and Suthiwart-Narueput in same volume, also Kaufmann (1991) and Salop (1992).

[25] Little and Mirrlees in Layard and Glaister (1994: 208). See also Ward *et al.* (1991: 153 f.).

versus private income and saving versus investment, how to calculate sectoral conversion rates, how to estimate shadow wage rates, how to set discount rates, and how to calculate multiple shadow exchange rates.

The 1990s have seen a partial resurgence of CBA as a method for assessing investments, albeit with significantly different emphases from the 1970s, especially in the development of mechanisms to price environmental externalities.[26] For example, in May 1996, the World Bank released a *Handbook on Economic Analysis of Investment Operations* that re-emphasized the importance of economic cost-benefit analysis in World Bank Projects (a reported one-third of staff appraisal reports of bank projects contained insufficient economic analysis). The *Handbook* reintroduces techniques of cost-benefit analysis, with significant simplifications and sensitivities. Simplifications include eliminating distributional weights for poverty[27] (though describing distributional implications of activities), using shadow prices selectively, and using a standard 10–12 per cent discount rate. The sensitivities include the recognition that some information may not be quantifiable so must be 'borne in mind'[28] in qualitative form: technical and institutional arrangements are 'taken for granted'; 'market prices seldom reflect the economic values of inputs and output';[29] winners and losers (the identification of which includes their economic status) must be identified; environmental externalities, among others, must be considered; and the CBA should 'factor into decision making' by policy-makers, rather than dictate a decision.[30] The overall goal of CBA *vis-à-vis* the social welfare function has not changed: 'A major aim of economic analysis is to assess the project's contribution to the society's welfare'.[31]

This chapter will evaluate the role that cost-benefit analysis has in the assessment of activities whose anticipated benefits are both poverty alleviation *and* some form of capability expansion. We will not consider environmental effects, about which there is already a substantial discussion.[32]

2.2. *Applicability of CBA to small NGO activities*

The first question is whether cost-benefit analysis techniques can legitimately be applied to the three Oxfam activities mentioned above. There are several dissuading points.

---

[26] Kirkpatrick and Weiss (1996), Little and Mirrlees (1991), Hausman and McPherson (1993), Sen (1995*a*), Oates (1992), Dasgupta and Mäler (1997).

[27] Distributional weights value income to the poor more than income to non-poor. Squire and van der Tak (1975).   [28] World Bank (1996*a*: 8). See also Ward *et al.* (1991).

[29] World Bank (1996*a*: 9).   [30] ibid. 10.

[31] ibid. 29; cf. 21–2. Contrast this with a competing and significant counter-objective found in Ward *et al.* (1991, p. ix): 'It is the contention of the authors that all project analysis and all policy analyses should begin with a return to the theory of the public sector . . . "What market failure is this intervention intended to address?" and "How is the intervention going to correct for that particular market failure." ' For simplicity, the 1996 objective alone is discussed in this chapter.

[32] Criticisms of EIA/CBA can be found in Casini and Bernetti (1996), Oates (1992, chs. 18–29), Sen (1995*a*).

First, CBA was designed to evaluate the prospective desirability of an investment at the planning stage. In contrast, the information on these three activities was gathered well into the implementation stage. But this need not concern us much for several reasons. First, the same techniques of CBA can be applied iteratively throughout the project cycle; indeed economists at the World Bank calculated the 're-estimated rates of return' or RERRs for over a thousand projects at the close of the project cycle.[33] Furthermore the use of CBA at this stage could elucidate the economic costs of achieving 'empowerment' and other objectives (e.g. participation), and this information is relevant to future project decisions. Finally, even well into implementation, the funding body may need to decide whether to channel additional resources to this activity and its implementing institution, in a second phase, or to allocate the resources elsewhere.

Secondly, it might be argued that while projections of empowerment and similar social 'benefits' are highly uncertain and notoriously difficult to predict, even the economic predictions themselves have a degree of uncertainty that will make any adjustments *vis-à-vis* shadow prices indecisive.[34] But in this analysis, estimations have been done using a range of plausible predictions and shadow prices.

Thirdly, it might be argued that activities of such a small scale are not suitable for CBA because (i) the cost of doing the analysis is too high, (ii) the activities are too isolated from markets to use nationally calculated shadow prices/discount rates/rates of time preference and the generation of shadow prices on a case-by-case basis is costly and has higher error margins, and (iii) activity appraisers at grass-roots level are less likely to be able to conduct such analyses. For example, Pohl and Mihaljek studied the relationship between the World Bank's re-estimated rates of return on estimated rates of return (among other independent variables). They found that of the CBAs that the World Bank had performed, those on *large-scale*, capital-intensive activities were most successful.[35] I have used CBA on small activities for the purposes of illustration. Whether these methods should be used regularly by field staff depends on their capacity and the complexity of the setting. Given the disclaimers in the analysis, the methods of CBA are applicable to the evaluation of small activities, especially because there are good financial and economic data in these cases.[36]

Fourthly, there could be legitimate worries about how human impacts will be figured. The estimation of shadow prices focuses on the *marginal* cost of the last unit. Recall that the problem is to maximize a social benefit/welfare function $f(x_1, x_2, \ldots, x_n)$ subject to the constraint $g(x_1, x_2, \ldots, x_n) \leq c$ where c is the constant (resource constraint). If $S(c)$ describes the relationship between changes in c and changes in the

---

[33] Pohl and Mihaljek (1992). Little and Mirrlees (1994: 214 f.) also discuss at length the (internal) document 'Project evaluation in practice: uncertainty at the World Bank' (Economic Advisory Staff, World Bank).

[34] Little and Mirrlees derived an improved formula for estimating whether the degree of uncertainty in errors which remains after the CBA outweighs the benefits of conducting the CBA, but the data for its estimation were not available. (1994: 225 f.).

[35] (1992: 32), discussed by Little in Layard and Glaister (1994).

[36] Drèze and Stern in Layard and Glaister (1994: 65 f.).

maximized benefits, then the shadow price of the constraint is $\delta S(c)/\delta c$. In other words, it is the rate of change of benefits per unit change in the constraint. Yet it might be argued that the *nature* of the benefits such as empowerment and social capital are not marginal kinds of things; their relationship to unit changes in capital investment may be discontinuous—a critical mass may be required before progress is evident. Thus the attempt to generate any kind of shadow prices for them is misplaced. Instead of generating shadow prices for empowerment and incorporating them into the cost-benefit analysis, I will examine the CBA together with an assessment of other human impacts at the close of the analysis and discuss the value judgement required in deciding how to 'combine' the information.

These four arguments aside, I return to the original insight which is that CBA at some general level is a useful tool for evaluating systematically the productivity of scarce resources, and this or a similar tool is a necessary component of an overall assessment of a human development activity.

2.3. *National parameters and cross-cutting issues*

This section will discuss the various considerations common to all the case studies: which set of prices to use, how to account for time and the opportunity cost of capital, foreign exchange constraints, whether to use distributional weights, and the general approach to shadow wages and shadow prices.

2.3.1. *Domestic/world/border prices*

An important issue in the social cost-benefit analysis is whether to conduct the analysis in local, border, or world prices. This is merely a matter of consistency, since local prices plus a shadow exchange rate will produce the same results as international prices and shadow wage rates. Little and Mirrlees had advocated the valuing of all goods at world prices even if they are not in fact traded. The purpose in this recommendation was to focus attention on the possible gains that could be made from international trade.[37] But in these three cases local prices are sufficient. One reason is that the investor does not have tools by which to affect trade strategy. Also, in general, small-scale informal sector activities are less likely to be subject to distorted prices than formal large-scale ones. And the products are not internationally traded in practice.[38] The rose garlands wither within one day so cannot be transported, while the paper bags were made of newspaper and were not of sufficient quality to be traded internationally. The goats are sold on a local market, and

---

[37] Layard and Glaister (1994: 18); see also Devarajan *et al.* in Kirkpatrick and Weiss (1996). A more subtle exploration of this recommendation and criticism of it as a theory of government action is found in Sen (1972), 'Shadow Prices and Markets', sect. 2 (reprinted in Layard and Glaister (1994: 102 f.) Sen argues that the use of world prices entails 'a rather extraordinary assumption about the project evaluator's areas of control' (ibid. 113).
[38] See, e.g. the World Bank's 1983 estimation of a border price for buffalo milk in Pakistan, which attributed a different economic value to milk retailed locally from that sold to a dairy industry. Ward *et al.* (1991: 247 f.) summarizes the results of this internal study of the first Agricultural Development Bank Project in Pakistan.

although goats are in theory tradables, goats of the breed normally used in the project are not of export quality. Therefore domestic prices will be used, with adjustments for a shadow foreign exchange rate if necessary.

2.3.2. Social discount rates

A second issue is how to discount future net benefits. One group of considerations relates to the real cost of raising capital (the real rate of interest on loans) and another to consumption decisions involving risk, preference for present consumption by current consumers (myopia), and diminishing marginal utility of increasing income (together underpinning the consumer real rate of interest). A third includes the value of consumption by future generations and socially optimal rates of savings (social rate of time preference) in the social welfare function. In a perfectly competitive equilibrium with a well-behaved social welfare function when all present and future individual utilities are additive and a government has complete taxation powers (e.g. regarding lump-sum transfers, 100 per cent profits tax, etc.), sometimes called a 'first-best' world, all three discount rates coincide. When these considerations are applied to CBA in a 'second-best' world, they generate different discount rates. Different theories hold that the annual discount rate of future net benefits (normally assumed to be constant) should be taken as the cost of borrowing and lending to consumers,[39] or to producers, or some estimated social rate of time preference (i.e. the marginal rate of substitution for the welfare function), or some weighted combination of the three.[40]

Identifying the correct social discount factor in the case studies is complex. The investing institution does not have any powers for lump-sum individual tax, for 100 per cent pure profits tax, to control the money supply, or to choose and differentiate tax rates. In Stiglitz's analysis, these common constraints (many of which would hold for government activities in Pakistan more generally) create a 'fifth-best' world, in which the social discount rate need not lie between the producer and consumer rates of interest, *nor* between the producer rate of interest and the social rate of time preference. Stiglitz argues that in these cases the social discount rate will differ for different activities and should be calculated therefore on a case-by-case basis.[41]

Yet this suggestion that the social rate of discount be calculated on a case-by-case basis for small NGO activities (rather than nationally) is unsatisfactory because of possible increased error margins that would have to be evaluated individually.[42] A common practice is to fix a social discount rate and do sensitivity analyses to determine the robustness of a positive result when the rate is varied. I have used an inflation-discounted discount rate of 12 per cent, the same rate that is used in public sector cost-benefit analyses (which are still undertaken) in Pakistan. Yet 12 per cent is quite a high rate, especially for social sector activities. These tend to have a much

---

[39] Dinwiddy and Teal showed, for example, that Little and Mirrlees's Accounting Rate of Interest (ARI), considered together with the shadow prices of wage and investment, is the consumption rate of interest (1996: 195).

[40] For a brief history of discounting theories see E. Kula in Kirkpatrick and Weiss (1996: 75 f.), also Dinwiddy and Teal (1996, ch. 10–11). [41] Stiglitz in Layard and Glaister (1994: 146–7).

[42] See UNIDO (1972, ch. 11).

lower discount rate, about 3 per cent, in order to reflect society-wide gains that result from health or education activities in particular.[43] Therefore I have done all net present values (NPV) estimations using 3, 8, and 12 per cent discount rates. Also, the methodology to be described, which specifies and compares the 'society-wide gains' that pertain to social investments, reflects an effort to account for these benefits more precisely and transparently than the use of a lower discount rate would. It would be possible to do such in-depth studies periodically in order to 'test' the assumption that lies behind a lower social discount rate.

2.3.3. Numeraire and point of view

The choice of numeraire is a matter of convenience rather than substantive significance, since values expressed in one numeraire can be converted into another (the UNIDO guidelines chose consumption as the numeraire; Little and Mirrlees, investment). It must be specified only in order to ascertain whether all values are expressed consistently. In this analysis, the numeraire is consumption, as it is the most direct unit for measuring the particular objective of poverty alleviation.

This analysis evaluates the costs and benefits from the point of view of a public investor. The common assumption is made that the investor is not able to influence taxes or money/debt supply.

2.3.4. Premium on savings/investment and distributive weighting

If savings are valued more highly than present consumption, an adjustment must be made to the proportion of extra earnings that is saved, to reflect the premium given to savings and investment (and each case study did have savings schemes). The adjustment should make savings (for investment) reflect the present value of the additional consumption that it would generate if invested. This is a function of a number of factors including the social rate of discount, productivity (return on marginal investment), a premium on public investment, and the propensity to reinvest.[44]

The difficulty is that this value is hard to fix, and it is not clear in the cases at hand whether it should be an inflator or a deflator. Savings are usually valued more highly than present consumption, even among the poor. In fact, there might be a case for valuing it even more highly among the poor: Qureshi *et al.* found that a lack of credit institutions meant that economic initiatives by the poor in Pakistan were generally credit constrained and that informal sector interest rates were higher than formal sector rates.[45] In this situation, the development of the habit of savings might enable the poor to decrease their need for credit. Also, savings might be socially valuable as families who save can smooth consumption throughout the year and so possibly decrease their vulnerability to absolute poverty in lean seasons.

But there might also be some point at which consumption by the poor was *more* socially valuable than savings. While this could be reflected by eliminating the

---

[43] Kim and Benton (1995).
[44] For a discussion of these considerations in the chosen numeraire see UNIDO (1972, ch. 14).
[45] Qureshi *et al.* (1996).

savings premium for income going to the poor, it might also be reflected in distributional weights.[46]

Technically, CBA may be carried out with or without distributional weights, the former being defined as 'efficiency' CBA and the latter as 'social' CBA by Squire and van der Tak.[47] A social CBA that uses distributional weights would make explicit two kinds of value judgements: the marginal value of income accruing to different income groups and the adjustment factor for an increase in consumption that arises from availability of real public resources.

The three Oxfam activities aimed to increase the well-being of poor participants. Hence they are particularly good candidates for distributional weighting. Distributional weights might be justified because the activities generate income among the poor (defined as those who are not capable of achieving nourishment, literacy, and other basic functionings) and income is generally one key constraint to enjoying such capabilities. Weights might also be justified because the income generated went to women, as an increase in women's income (defined simply as income over which women control spending decisions) is more strongly correlated with expenditure on basic needs and services that alleviate poverty than men's and is additionally correlated with women's empowerment. Hence the social value of poor women's income might arguably be at a premium (even be a 'merit good').[48]

Although advocated fairly widely, distributional weights have rarely been used by the World Bank or others.[49] If CBAs are done for a number of alternative proposals for the same activity, one might use dominance ranking to eliminate some possibilities that are worse both on distributional and efficiency terms. Alternatively, the distributional information might be kept aside until the very end and introduced explicitly as a separate consideration using a range of plausible weights.

In all cases, the need to make final *value judgements* regarding which sectors of a society should benefit, remains. For example, Harberger developed the example that if one used a plausible set of distributional weights, one might have an equity–efficiency trade-off such that it was more optimal to deliver ice cream to citizens in a poorer desert oasis, knowing that 75 per cent of it would melt *en route*, than consume it in the home oasis.[50] If the example was slightly less flippant—for example, the delivery of a staple food to a famine-prone area despite some spoilage or probable need for pay-offs—this kind of distributional information (on the extent or urgency of poverty)

---

[46] There might arguably be a third way, which is to estimate a premium on public income, because public income is raised through various taxes that have distributional effects (the premium also has the effect of spotlighting the need for effective cost-recovery in the private sector). Neglect of these effects leads to an overestimation of project NPV. Devarajan *et al.* (1996) argue that this premium should be re-introduced. But this analysis is conducted assuming no capacity to raise taxes, which obviates this premium as a distributional consideration.

[47] (1975, ch. 7). See UNIDO (1972, ch. 7), Dinwiddy and Teal (1996: 74 f.), Little and Mirrlees (1974, ch. 13).

[48] Corbett and Stewart (1994). The third possible argument for distributional weights is an employment objective, which values employment as a means to greater aggregate production. But this can be adequately treated by consideration of the aggregate production. See UNIDO (1972, ch. 8.2).

[49] This is analysed retrospectively by Squire *et al.* in Kirkpatrick and Weiss (1996).   [50] 1978.

Assessing Capability Change

might be decisive, as in early warning systems for famines. I shall discuss this need to make these kinds of judgements explicitly towards the end of this chapter, arguing that such judgements are inevitable and they are better made as choices between two transparent alternatives, rather than as choices of 'weights' that then determine a net present value and lead to activity acceptance or rejection.

2.3.5. *Shadow wages*

Shadow wages must be estimated for three types of labour: unskilled labour with low opportunity costs by the beneficiaries, skilled labour with significant opportunity costs by the local implementing partner, and skilled labour by donor staff. The estimation of unskilled shadow wages for beneficiaries is particularly difficult, and furthermore, as we shall see, the outcome of the analysis is highly sensitive to these estimations: slightly different plausible values could switch a clearly positive NPV to a clearly negative one. This section will present the considerations that underlie the selection of a shadow wage range. Before beginning it is helpful to note two contextual facts that simplify the wage analysis: there was no effective income tax mechanism in any of the three activities, nor is there minimum wage legislation. This means that the calculation of wages should not follow the methods of Squire, Little, and Durdag, whose shadow price for rural labour in Pakistan was significantly affected by export taxes and subsidies.[51]

In the surplus labour model, the shadow wage is argued to be zero (assuming savings and consumption to be equally valuable at the margin), since it is assumed that, in a situation of surplus labour, the employment of an individual will not lead to any decrease in the output of the peasant economy. In the case studies there was no significant effect on household output from this added work which would suggest the relevance of this approach.[52]

None the less, in each activity there are some seasonal employment opportunities that might suggest a positive opportunity cost of labour and a positive value for the shadow wage. Some women had minor alternative sources of income from agricultural labour and stitching or embroidery. It might be possible to identify one or more of these as alternative employment. For example, after the goat-raising initiative began, women carried on stitching quilts but their involvement in picking onions decreased (they expressed a preference for goat rearing because it was less demanding physically). Therefore one alternative to a wage rate of zero would be to take the hourly rate of onion picking as the 'opportunity cost' of their time. This wage is in the range of 4–7 Rs per hour. But onion picking was a seasonal activity, which occupied women for a few weeks full time, rather than year-round.[53] Similar

---

[51] 1979.

[52] Women from all three projects reported that had their household output declined they would not have been permitted to carry on with the projects, at least initially.

[53] The women were paid 40 Rs per maund of onions that they picked, dried, and packed into containers; this activity would be spread over at least three days, and amounted to less than half of a male labourer's standard wage of 70–100 Rs per day. The actual rate varied quite a bit depending on individual productivity; it amounted to an average hourly wage of 4–7 Rs.

problems held for other occupations. Hence alternative employment wage rates may not represent the true opportunity cost of labour, and one might consider a somewhat lower shadow wage rate, which reflected its seasonal nature.

Secondly, women typically engage in household and community work that is not valued by the market. A shadow wage of zero gives the impression that the women's opportunity cost of *any* level of employment is zero, so that if they were to work full time in goat rearing or rose cultivation it would not affect their aggregate output. This impression arises because of the invisibility or lack of market values for much of women's work. But there was in all cases an *absolute constraint* on women's time from non-market household activities. The activities were successful only *because* they did not require too much time. A shadow price of zero would not convey this information that is needed for activity-level planning and would represent a real undervaluation of the cost of labour. A common approach to this valuing of unpaid household work is to calculate costs on the basis of market rates for similar work that is compensated (paid child care, laundry services, housecleaning). Or else to stipulate the range of time at which the zero wage rate applies at the margin and use higher wages beyond this time.

Thirdly, one might simply use, as a shadow wage, the hourly wage of male labourers from the same locality. In each of the case studies, this was an unrealistic wage, but it may be of interest for the purposes of comparison and so has been included.

Fourthly, one might derive shadow wages from the valuation of leisure. As Sen notes, in the context of valuing the 'loss' of a migrant worker to a peasant economy, the premise of surplus labour (no change in household output) does require the further assumption that the increased 'sweat' or work burden on remaining workers (or in this case, on other hours of the day) is valued at zero, and some may wish to question that.[54] One could again return to the wage rate of onion picking or embroidery and take it as an upper limit on the value of leisure, because if women valued leisure *more* than this amount, they would not have undertaken the work.

Rosenweig's model of the 'autarchic' household valued the cost of migrant labour in terms of leisure time. It was assumed that a self-sufficient rural household has n members. N of these work on the farm, yielding consumption goods that are shared by all n members. Still, although the labour of N workers is uncompensated, their leisure time is valued and so must enter the welfare function of the household. The household welfare function can then be represented by a separable utility function representing the utility U from household consumption (not disaggregated) and the utility V for leisure.

$$W = nU(c) + NV(l)$$

where c is the per capita consumption for all household members, and l is the leisure time of the N workers.[55] Dinwiddy and Teal developed this into an equilibrium model that when solved gives the marginal product of labour as the ratio of the marginal utilities of leisure and output. Their conclusion is that surplus labour exists only if the marginal rate of substitution between consumption and leisure is a

[54] 1972.   [55] Rosenweig (1988); discussed in Dinwiddy and Teal (1996: 138 f.).

constant.[56] This model would suggest that the shadow wage of the goat owners would be zero if and only if other household members were willing to forgo their corresponding leisure. But such dual economy models discuss the benefit of alternative full-time, or migrant, labour. They do not apply to the current situation in which the cost of 'sweat' or 'leisure' is assumed to be borne fully by the women concerned, as was the case in all case studies, rather than by other household members.

In this case, the welfare function of the household would be:

$$W = nU(c) + gV(l) + gS(e) + nT(f)$$

where S, T, U, and V represent separable components of utility; c is current consumption; n refers to the complete household, of which g members receive loans for goats; e are the benefits that privately accrue to the goat owners (personal income, decision-making power, status), and f are the changes in consumption (if any) that accrue to the household from goat rearing. The variables c and f are recorded separately because of the assumption that household consumption effects of women's income are different from effects of male income.[57]

As was mentioned initially, all cases involve not one but three categories of workers: Oxfam staff, the staff of a local implementing NGO, and direct beneficiaries. The shadow wages of the first two categories of workers are treated in two ways. First, they are straightforwardly estimated on the basis of standard competitive salaries in their sector (the assumption being that these wage markets are competitive and that the salaries accurately represent the marginal social cost of labour). Secondly, it might be justifiably argued that the salaries of these groups have been artificially inflated by the presence of significant donor capital for this kind of work, above their social value. Therefore a second set of salaries is used that are based not on government salaries for comparable employment (these being widely acknowledged as artificially depressed) but on the average private sector wage levels in the relevant region.

It might appear at this point that the wage ranges identified above represent the opportunity cost of labour. But it may be necessary to incorporate some value for the social cost of consumption. The employment would have led to an increase in income, most of which, in all cases, was consumed. Therefore the issue arises whether a portion of the additional consumption should be conceived as a social cost because, as was suggested by Little and Mirrlees, for example, savings should be given a premium. Hence the increase in income from new employment that leads to additional consumption is ΔQ:

$$\Delta Q = Y^{t'}_{\omega} - Y^{t''}_{MPA}$$

which is the difference between $Y^{t'}_{\omega}$, the consumption due to new employment at wage rate ω, and $Y^{t'}_{MPA}$, the consumption earned at the wage rate equal to the

---

[56] ibid. 141. Rosenweig's empirical work suggested that this was not the case; that there was not in fact surplus labour in the rural household.   [57] See also Corbett and Stewart (1994).

marginal product of alternative employment (onion picking). This discounting in the shadow wage $(w)\star$ is reflected in the following formula:

$w\star$ = [net social cost of increased consumption] + [forgone marginal product][58]

The forgone marginal product is $Y^{t''}_{MPA}$, but as this is likewise assumed to be entirely consumed, its social value must be similarly discounted. Hence if d is the discount rate on consumption, then the shadow wage rate must be:

$$w\star = d\Delta Q + dY^t_{MPL}$$
$$= d(Y^t_\omega - Y^t_{MPA}) + dY^t_{MPL}$$
$$= d\{(Y^t_\omega - Y^t_{MPA}) + Y^t_{MPL}\}$$
$$= dY^t_\omega$$

As was discussed earlier, no discount rate will be used on the earnings; rather all weightings will be done at the end of an analysis.

In the case studies, the entire range of possible shadow wages is presented, from zero to the highest plausible shadow wage, adjusted if necessary for savings, and less the loss of output elsewhere. The SCBA is estimated using the different possible wages. Other inputs, such as utilities and transportation, are traded on a competitive market, so their financial prices are used.

It might be argued that the time of skilled donor staff should not be included. However, in practice the donor staff time is a lively consideration, as participatory projects 'take more time', and analyses that exclude these costs are not able to identify the incremental costs of supporting participatory processes to the NGO (which in practice choose to allocate some of their funding to an increased field staff rather than to additional activities).

2.3.6. Weighting of various objectives

The final stage in the cost-benefit analysis is integrating all of the information on different objectives (traditionally: consumption, distribution, savings, merit wants, employment) into one evaluative framework by assigning numerical relative weights to each. Despite the absolute centrality of this stage, it has been severely neglected in CBA (hence the heavy reliance on willingness-to-pay measures).[59] Even discussions that overtly recognize that weights represent 'value judgements', such as Squire and van der Tak's or the World Bank's 1996 *Handbook*, do not provide a clear procedure for making or obtaining such judgements.

The UNIDO guidelines described this assignment of weights as 'the difficulty at the heart of social benefit-cost analysis'.[60] They provide one of the more extensive discussions of this problem, which they describe as follows:

The difficulty of implementing benefit-cost analysis is not one of defining weights in principle, but of defining them operationally. We are roughly in the position of the mice of Aesop's fable who found their ingenious plan of putting a bell on the cat to warn them of his presence

---

[58] To this might be added the social cost of reduced leisure.
[59] See e.g. Dinwiddy and Teal (1996: 214–18), Kim and Benton (1995).   [60] 1972: 246.

foiled by the lack of a suitable means of implementing the plan. Who is to 'bell the cat?' It ought to be the political leadership that defines the weights, for the value judgements at issue are inherently political in nature, reflecting as they do conflicts and strains between various classes and sections of the population. But it is unlikely that the political leadership will of its own volition undertake the responsibilities envisioned for it, and we see no way of bypassing the political leadership that retains meaning for benefit-cost analysis.[61]

The UNIDO guidelines advocate a 'bottom-up' approach that involves economists 'extracting' political decisions from policy-makers by presenting alternative designs that vary the weights on different development objectives. The responses that emerge from policy-makers can be interpreted as setting bounds for relative weights on objectives. 'The long-run goal is to narrow the bounds on weights and shadow prices to a sufficiently small range that the top-down version of planning becomes feasible.'[62]

This might seem reminiscent of Miriam's assessment of the wild walled garden, but the above quotation from the UNIDO guidelines does not get *quite* to the heart of the matter when it comes to participatory local activities, at least.

For example, it might be argued that 'empowerment' benefits should not be priced and incorporated into the cost-benefit analysis but rather that Oxfam should treat empowerment as a primary objective. A cost-effectiveness (or least-cost) analysis could be done, and the most cost-effective activity chosen from among those in which 'empowerment' is an objective and a likely outcome. This has been the traditional practice in sectors where it is difficult to measure outputs, such as the health, education, and defence sectors. But this criterion would be insufficient to guide decisions in cases where there were two or more desired benefits (i.e. income generation and empowerment), only one of which can be adequately priced, because if one project is better for income, the other empowerment, then additional criteria such as the relative weights of income versus empowerment must be brought to bear.

And in this case Aesop's cat returns: who sets the weights? Oxfam and many other donors with national or international programs make allocative decisions about grants—they do not defer choices to national political leaders. Also, Oxfam and other NGOs supplement formal market and social sector systems; as such they have neither the need nor the authority to 'set' desired levels of, for example, literacy. Rather, the identification of needs and the choice of valuable functionings to pursue occurs by a participatory process with many different local communities (Ch. 5, Sect. 2.3). Thus it is not possible for Oxfam to derive a uniform set of national weights for its Pakistan CBAs. It might be possible to infer weights from the participatory discussions. But given the impermanence of the social commitments that generate those relative weights, and given the possible additional value of explicit discussion of the different ends and courses of action (Ch. 4, Sect. 2, Ch. 3, Sect. 2.2), it seems that the better way of employing CBAs is to use them as a source of

---

[61] ibid. 247; see the discussion at 135–53.
[62] (1972: 247; see also 140–1) and Sugden and Williams (1978: 181–6).

information on efficiency, predicted outcomes, and risk. The CBAs can then *factor into* rational decisions made jointly by Oxfam and a community.

3. CAPABILITY SET ANALYSIS

As Chapter 3 discussed extensively, Sen has drawn attention to the relationship between moral principles and information.[63] Some moral principles make use of an extremely limited set of information; others require more information than is in fact available. The capability approach clearly has deeper informational requirements than a social cost-benefit analysis, although decisions must be made in different contexts as to what information to consider.

Chapter 5 argued that an analysis that only tracked the expansion of basic capabilities/functionings was insufficient because *no information was gathered* or analysed as to whether or not other valuable capabilities had contracted (Chapter 3 had argued for collecting information on predictable if unintended impacts). To implement the capability approach more fully at the micro level, then, it is necessary to gather fuller information on the expansions and contractions of valuable functionings. This section will consider one methodology by which such information may be gathered and by which impacts on human ends can be identified, weighted, and compared between communities. The limitations of this methodology are critically discussed in the closing section of this chapter.

3.1. *Two methodologies and a gap*

Two widespread methodologies that aim to identify human impacts and to use this information to shape public and development activities to beneficiaries' values and institutions are 'social impact assessment' and participatory social assessments. I shall introduce these using Burdge's work as an example of social impact assessment and World Bank social assessment methodologies. I will then focus on the 'gap' each has in identifying a complete set of valued human impacts and comparing these across activities. Other features of each approach are very commendable although these features will not be much discussed here.

3.1.1. *Social impact assessment*

Social impact assessment (SIA) is one rough operational expression of 'informed choice' regarding public investments. It also broadly parallels cost-benefit analysis in that (i) it is typically done prior to making a public investment; (ii) it requires the estimation of projected costs and projected benefits (which are inherently uncertain); and (iii) it requires the formulation of both a baseline and counterfactuals. The key novelty of SIA methodology *vis-à-vis* CBA lies in its public focus on the social implications of activities and in particular on anticipated activity *disvalues*. This focus was introduced

---

[63] Especially Sen (1979*a*, 1985*a*, 1986*b*, 1996*f*); Ch. 3, Sects. 3–4.

because project planners nearly always underestimate negative human impacts.[64] In SIA, the evaluation explicitly identifies potential negative consequences of an investment, and explores alternative ways of 'mitigating' these consequences.

The impetus to assess social impacts of public investment was initiated by the National Environmental Policy Act enacted by the United States in 1969. 'Under that law, proponents of development activities and policies that involved U.S. federal land, federal tax dollars or federal jurisdictions were required to file an environmental impact statement detailing the impacts of the proposal, as well as alternatives, on the physical, *cultural and human environments.*'[65] Physical environmental impact assessments (EIAs) quickly became institutionalized, with nearly 12,000 being carried out in the first ten years (the public response was correspondingly vigorous: 1,200 lawsuits were filed which contested aspects of the assessments).[66] Unlike EIAs, SIAs took off much more slowly and unevenly. The first social impact assessment (SIA) was carried out on the Trans-Alaska pipeline in 1973. But the value of SIAs was less apparent, and the methodology and 'decision criteria' were less clear. Although extensive public participation was a mandatory component of SIAs, often a very minimal form of 'public involvement'[67]—such as formal public hearings—was used. This was unsatisfactory because the 'public involvement' lacked a structured procedure for identifying impacts 'in advance of the decision making process' and, although SIA laws were particularly designed to mitigate or alleviate foreseen negative social impacts, they did not initially achieve this.[68]

Subsequently SIA procedures were further developed. Burdge and others articulated key features of social impact assessment. First, SIA is a 'systematic effort to identify, analyze, and evaluate social impacts of a proposed activity or policy change on the individual, social groups within a community, or an entire community . . . in advance of the decision-making process . . . in order that the information derived from the SIA can actually influence decisions.' Secondly, it is a procedure for developing alternative courses of action that mitigate the negative social or human impacts. Thirdly, it increases the knowledge of both the community and the activity's proposer about the investment itself and its broader implications.[69]

SIA is similar to CBA in that it endeavours to identify and 'weigh' the social costs and social benefits of activities prior to their implementation and improve the benefit-cost ratio. In this sense it shares what Sen identified as the underlying principle of CBA (Ch. 3, Sect. 2). The focus is on identifying social costs because these are 'almost always borne at the community or local level' whereas economic outputs 'tend to be

---

[64] Environmental impact analysis or EIA, which is by far the better known branch of impact assessment, focuses on environmental values and disvalues of public investments.
[65] Burdge *et al.* (1994: 3, emphasis added).   [66] Freudenburg and Keaging (1982: 72).
[67] 'Public Involvement refers to the process whereby the community or larger society provides systematic input to a proposed policy or project through social impact assessment. The PI process continues for the entire life of the project. It serves as a means to educate the community about potential benefits and costs (hazards) of the proposed project' (Burdge *et al.* 1994: 183).
[68] Burdge *et al.* (1994: 178). See ibid. 1994: 177 f., Taylor *et al.* (1990: 3), Freudenburg and Olsen (1983).   [69] Burdge *et al.* (1994: 178–9).

sold on a multi-county or statewide level'.[70] In particular, Burge identified five categories of impacts (comprising twenty-three variables) for active study:

- population impacts;
- community/institutional arrangements;
- conflicts between local residents and newcomers;
- individual and family level impacts;
- community infrastructure needs.

SIA has attempted to acquire information regarding the human impacts that we identified earlier, and to communicate these in public fora in a manner that conduces to informed choice. Furthermore, the 'participatory' nature of discussion and the legal and procedural requirement of public involvement give a voice to those who are directly affected by decisions. Yet the methodology still has some deficiencies, which I will illustrate using Burdge's *Community Guide to Social Impact Assessment* (1995).

Despite the claim to be a systematic effort, the *Guide* contains no evident procedure for obtaining *comprehensive information* on valuable changes as evaluated by beneficiaries. Rather, the changes alleged to be valuable have been identified by the assessors (who scrutinize given, rather than open-ended, variables) and are not distilled from the relevant community. For example, variables studied in the category 'individual and family level impacts' are: daily living and movement patterns, religious practices, family structure, social networks, public health and safety, and leisure opportunities. In comparison with the categories of Chapter 2, these do not include dimensions such as meaningful work, knowledge and appreciation of beauty, self-integration, empowerment, or harmony with the non-human world. Whether there were or were not important impacts in these dimensions, it seems doubtful that one's questions should categorically exclude impacts of these kinds.

Furthermore even with regard to the categories that are included, the methodology proceeds to access objective information but leaves the definition and interpretation of important impacts to the assessor rather than the participants. For example, consideration of the category 'religious and cultural practices' is limited to 'the introduction into your community of a new group of persons with religious and cultural values, beliefs and practices dissimilar to those of the present population'.[71] Similarly the category 'family structure' is narrowly defined by age and marital status. This kind of factual information is important. But it would not pick up other sources of impact—such as impacts on cultural and religious values from sources *other* than immigration. In short, the SIA methodology of identifying *what impacts are significant* may be too narrowly defined *prior* to discussion with the community.

Moreover, the 'decision criteria' are not clear.[72] Taylor criticized SIA because the decision criteria for social assessments (which should reflect the basic values or social

---

[70] Burdge (1995: 49).   [71] Burdge (1995: 104).

[72] Decision criteria are the rules and principles for (i) deciding whether impacts are positive or negative, (ii) weighting them, (iii) combining the information, and (iv) generating a choice. See Taylor *et al.* (1990: 20 f.).

objectives of the community) are often not made explicit because of their contentious nature. In practice, assessors themselves normally 'rank' the strength of impacts and make recommendations based on their private rankings. While there may be an apparent efficiency in this, the previous discussion suggests that there are strong reasons for favouring the facilitation of this reflection and ranking by the participants in the activity.

SIA has made good progress in forging a consensus on the importance of assessing and mitigating negative social costs borne by the local community. But the SIA methodology to date may not be precise enough to carry out the aims of the assessments fully. In particular, a more systematic and explicit procedure is required for identifying impacts from the perspective of the participants and for making clear how information on human impacts feeds into choices—either by involving participants in the making of choices or by outlining a set of principles or decision criteria to be used by decision-makers.

3.1.2. Participatory social assessments

Social assessment methods have also found their way in modified form into World Bank procedures as beneficiary assessments,[73] participatory poverty assessments,[74] and social assessments,[75] all of which have been used to an increasing degree—with 125 social assessments being done between July 1997 and June 1998, for example.[76] The impetus is similar to SIA, in that the negative as well as positive impacts of a planned change are assessed using public participation. These assessments are also continuous with the methodologies of encouraging beneficiary participation now used within the World Bank and also with their underlying objective to focus on 'human' development or 'putting people first'.[77]

Participation is employed in social assessments as a procedure for obtaining local information and for tailoring activities and programmes to beneficiary values (it may also be an end in itself). Participation is said to increase the success, sustainability, ownership, and appropriateness of activities,[78] as well as the level of utilization, local enterprise, and the speedy diffusion of innovation. Community participation is said to improve the efficacy of decentralized activities.[79] Although the evidence is mixed, participation seems to have considerable economic potential as a method of

---

[73] Larry Salmen describes beneficiary assessment as follows: 'Beneficiary assessment is a systematic inquiry into people's values and behavior in relation to a planned or ongoing intervention for social and economic change . . . The ultimate goal of beneficiary assessment is to reveal the meaning people give to particular aspects of their lives so that development activities may better enhance people's ability to improve their own living conditions, as they see fit' (1995: 1; see also 1999).

[74] Norton and Stephens (1995).

[75] 'Social Assessment (SA) is a *process* which provides an integrated and participatory framework for prioritizing, gathering, analyzing, and incorporating *social information and participation* into the design and delivery of Bank-assisted operations' (World Bank 1996c).   [76] World Bank (1998c).

[77] For an introduction to social assessment, and a concise summary of is role and history in the Bank, see Cernea and Kudat (1997).

[78] 'There is considerable evidence that community involvement . . . [is] key to achieving sustainable improvements in poor people's welfare' (Narayan and Ebbe 1997: 1). See the references cited therein. Also University of Stockholm (1991).   [79] Klugman (1994).

increasing both allocative and X efficiency.[80] But does participation, as it is utilized in these assessments, fully capture capability change? This seems a question worth exploring directly.

One common difficulty is the exchange of information at the interface between the local community and outsiders. For example, Leach documents a case where an erroneous view of environmental change in Guyana's forest savannah was supported by wrong information from local people and entered the scientific canon. 'Villagers, faced by questions about deforestation and environmental change, have learned to confirm what they know the questioners expect to hear. This is not only through politeness and awareness that the truth will be met with incredulity, but also through the desire to maintain good relations.'[81] Similarly, Chambers observes that there is a regular pattern of beneficiaries ('lowers') reflecting back what they expect outsiders ('uppers') wish to hear: 'It has been a sobering experience to observe a charismatic outsider interrogate farmers who strain their minds and imaginations to say what they think he wants. Again and again they found the right words. The intelligent prudence of the lowers confirmed the conviction of the upper, unaware of his inadvertent ventriloquism.'[82]

A significant literature has arisen which addresses the problem of how 'outsiders' (persons from government, the public sector, NGOs, or donor agencies) can best 'listen to the people' (to borrow the title of Larry Salmen's book).[83]

Without de-emphasizing the need for charisma and commitment, some empirical studies of participation suggest that systematic methods increase the effectiveness of participation. For example, Jain's study of eleven successful development organizations in five Asian countries found that standardization and routinization of the activities, social messages, and analytical frameworks, improved performance.[84] Likewise, PRA approaches themselves are characterized by the flexible application of standardized 'tools' and 'exercises'. How could a systematic method reliably identify capability change?

One pervasive difficulty with information exchange in participatory meetings, even with standardized procedures for facilitating participation, is that there is no systematic methodology for obtaining the plural information represented earlier by Table 4.1 (indirect effects, side-effects, externalities) that is complementary to the other successful methodologies of participatory analysis. The methodology to be described shortly arose in an attempt to address this need among community groups. An adaptation of the basic approach could be used also to structure discussions at different levels.[85]

---

[80] Vivian and Maseko (1994), Insham et al. (1995), Cernea and Kudat (1997).
[81] Leach and Fairhead (1994: 86).   [82] Chambers (1994d).
[83] Salmen (1987), Blackburn and Holland (1998), Chambers (1994d, 1995, 1997), Dore (1994), Forester (1999), Geertz (1993), Holland and Blackburn (1998).
[84] (1994: 1368). See Tendler (1989).
[85] For example, The Asia Foundation also asked NGO staff to assess their perceived impacts, Oxfam staff assessed the impact that employment had on their own human development, and M. Phil. students in Development Studies assessed the impact of their course on their human development.

This kind of standardization is not found in the assessment methodologies. For example, 'beneficiary assessment' claims to be systematic, yet it does not have a system for asking about all of the dimensions of human flourishing. It is conceived as 'non-standardized',[86] which gives it the advantage of flexibility, but leaves it open to 'inadvertent ventriloquism', liable to overlook relevant information and liable to provide an incomplete account of key variables. As the example from Chambers suggested, 'open-ended' questions may produce responses that reflect respondents' perception of what the questioner wishes to hear. Social assessments likewise canvass demographic factors, socio-economic determinants, social organization, socio-political context, and individuals' needs and values. Yet these too have no tool for considering 'needs and values' systematically. Furthermore, their purpose is to assess impacts and risks and mitigate adverse impacts, but the 'decision criteria' as to whether or not an activity should proceed are not apparent.

Participatory poverty assessments (PPAs) are specific research techniques that are combined to give overall poverty assessments. 'The premise is that involving the poor in the process will contribute to ensuring that the strategies identified for poverty reduction will reflect their concerns, including the priorities and obstacles to progress as seen by the poor themselves.' PPAs cover a number of issues, of which two are of particular interest: (i) 'illustrating dimensions of the experience of poverty and vulnerability which conventional poverty analysis based on statistical outcomes tends to ignore' and (ii) eliciting perceptions of the poor on, for example, the availability of public services.[87]

The difficulty is, once again, that the participatory techniques that have been used have focused on a limited range of interpretations of poverty and vulnerability. In practice, reports from PPAs have included discussion of dimensions such as aesthetics, spirituality, and friendship, as in the *Voices of the Poor* work, and certainly have not had systematic methods for evaluating the relative importance of these impacts with respect to impacts on poverty or well-being. The following section presents a methodology for identifying locally valued impacts and their relative strengths, which may fill a gap in the wider methodology of both SIA and the World Bank's assessments.

3.2. *Valuing capability change or impacts*[88]

Both SIA and participatory social assessment methods are methodologies for accessing and analysing information on the human impacts of activities. Their explicit aim is to modify proposed investments that have undervalued human impacts and to make these investments cohere with communities' wider values.[89] Yet, as I have tried to point out, a weak area in both approaches is their ability to access and hence respond to

---

[86] Salmen (1995: 10; see 1999).   [87] Norton and Stephens (1995: 1), both quotes.
[88] This framework was written up separately for practitioners as an 'Impact Assessment Manual' for Oxfam in 1997, and has been translated into Sindhi. It has been distributed to country programmes by Oxfam and ActionAid, and via the Internet.
[89] As such, SIA might be thought of from the community's point of view as relating to the principle discussed in Ch. 3, Sect. 5.2 to 'harmonize' valuable commitments.

these values. This section will describe a methodology that focuses *only* on the small part of these assessments that is devoted to identifying valuable changes (positive or negative) in functionings/capabilities, and their relative strengths. The methodology could be incorporated in either of these assessments or in evaluations at a later stage.

To be constructive and intelligible, the identification of valued impacts was embedded in a larger assessment process. In each of the three Oxfam activities, beneficiaries described the history of the particular activity in their area, the economic impact (and how any income was spent), the mode of participation or decision-making, and the impacts on different dimensions of human development. Key informant interviews and site visits were conducted to assess the impact of the activity on consumption poverty. In other words, this particular tool (for getting information on valuable/negative impacts) was complemented by other kinds of analysis in assessment of the activity. But the following discussion focuses on the tool for identifying valuable capabilities rather than the standard tools which are presupposed.

The novel feature of the exercise is that rather than discussing impacts open-endedly (PRA) or by the use of closed categories (SIA), the discussions eventually incorporate all 'dimensions' of human development (Ch. 3). Similar work has been done by Manfred Max-Neef (Ch. 2, Sect. 4.1.2), but other assessment methodologies do not have such a system.

The conceptual basis for assessing the impacts systematically using a flexible matrix of categories was given in Chapter 3, which argued that the values which animate any person's or community's actions are not infinitely diverse but can be distilled into an irreducible set of simplest most basic reasons for action that are grasped by practical reason and used implicitly in planning actions and in evaluating the values and disvalues of past or proposed actions. It was further hypothesized that an adequate account of these most basic values or action-motivating reasons would be valid cross-culturally. Some preliminary data from cross-cultural psychology, anthropology, and philosophy was used, following a transparent procedure, to discuss elements of such a working set as a basis for further testing and discussion.

The operational value of specifying such a set of 'dimensions of human development' was argued to be the following: the capability approach cannot proceed to inform operational work until the especially valuable capabilities are identified and relative weights are assigned to the achievement of different capabilities.

In theory and practice such evaluative decisions could be made successfully without ever explicitly mentioning dimensions of development. Yet unsystematic public discussions and participatory exercises to date (at local and national levels) have often failed to consider key categories of valuable ends implicitly or explicitly. A set of dimensions such as that described in Chapter 3 could catalyse the missing discussions by providing 'an assemblage of reminders of the range of possibly worthwhile activities and orientations open to [a community]'.[90] In the exercise described below facilitators bring up the dimensions that have not 'risen to the eye' to provoke discussions on valued ends.

---

[90] Finnis (1980: 81). For a description of the need for 'catalysts' see Nussbaum and Sen (1989).

One final preliminary point is necessary before describing the exercise in detail. The exercise was conducted in a participatory manner, which means that to the greatest extent possible the facilitators or 'assessors' wore simple clothing, used the local language, adapted the methodology flexibly to the situation, respected traditional and religious customs, organized the meeting at a convenient time and place, came with the attitude of informal learning and openness, encouraged quieter persons to speak more and dominant persons to speak less. They also spent time both prior to and after the meeting talking informally, gathering other information necessary for a full assessment, and addressing immediate problems in the activity. Although these 'informal' features of best practice are not mentioned again, the methodology cannot be expected to generate accurate data *unless* these attitudes are also adopted. It might still generate richer information than that generated by alternative methods, but the accuracy of this information would be difficult to assess.

3.2.1. *Identification of impacts*
In all cases, the assessment was done well into the project cycle, with the end of identifying the complete set of important impacts the activity had had. There were two overt goals for the assessments:

(i) to access and report the multidimensional impacts of the activity to the funding institution such that these impacts were comparable across activities, and so could be factored into ongoing funding decisions by the donor and feed into 'best practices';
(ii) to assess impacts in such a way that the concerned community could (and did) reflect critically on *the relative value or desirability of different* impacts and formulate ongoing objectives (and on the basis of these select monitoring indicators). *The focus of the discussions in the next chapter will be on the first goal; but in practice this second goal is perhaps the more important.*

Two different methods of identifying human impacts, or changes in the capability set of participants, were used. The first was to describe each dimension individually, whenever possible drawing examples from recent discussions with participants and stressing that the examples were simply possibilities. Discussion followed immediately after each dimension was introduced and continued until the range of impacts seemed exhausted and the group moved to consider the next dimension. The second and eventually preferred method was to explain first the general intent of the assessment exercise (to think about the full range of impacts of an activity, good and bad, anticipated and unanticipated) and to begin by asking a purely open question 'what valuable and negative impacts have you noticed?' As people described them, the impacts would be explored as clusters (sometimes corresponding to the dimensions, sometimes not). If at the end of a discussion no impacts pertaining to a particular dimension had been mentioned, the facilitator would then inquire whether there were any impacts related to that dimension, in case that kind of impact had been forgotten or omitted because it was presumed to be of no interest (the facilitator also stressed that changes may *not* have occurred in each dimension).

Either method required, at some stage or another (usually), a question about whether an initiative had had impacts on a dimension. A critical issue was how to explain the dimensions in this setting. The objective of enabling others to reflect on valued capabilities would be foiled if the facilitator asked (or seemed to ask) a closed question about impacts on a fixed category of values that she chose (which was our criticism of SIA). But nor is it sufficient simply to ask entirely open-ended questions (see the criticism of PRA).[91] Rather, the goal is for participants to identify *all* valued benefits/disbenefits, by engaging with the chains of practical reasoning that they already use.[92] This seems to require (*a*) facilitators to communicate clearly what they mean by impact—that it relates to participants' own experience (on which they are experts) and their own reasons for doing things (which they already use), and (*b*) explaining the values (i) broadly or fully enough so that the descriptions serve as 'reminders' of impacts that have happened but might have been forgotten (e.g. impacts on 'relationship' can include impacts on relations with children, with spouses, with other members of the group, or with funders) and (ii) vaguely enough that people 'fill in the gaps' by describing the actual impacts that they have experienced and know very well, and do not feel confined to the examples. This method operationalizes Nussbaum's two ideas of a 'thick' and 'vague' account of the good and engages with what she calls 'internalist essentialist', or more simply, 'practical' reason.

In practice, dimensions were explored in a number of different ways. Initially, a symbol representing each category was drawn on a card that would be held up as its category was described and be used later in the ranking exercise. But the use of predrawn pictures was more confusing than helpful. Pictures seemed to impose a much narrower definition on the category than was intended and also caused anxiety as people struggled to understand what they meant (even though the pictures were drawn by local persons). Alternatively, groups would make an impact diagram showing the different impacts that an activity had had. This could be either on paper or using objects that symbolized impacts.

As the pilot tests had shown an underreporting of negative impacts, these were inquired after again separately, after the first discussion.

3.2.2. *Weighting the impacts*

Having identified a wide set of impacts, the next stage was to separate the relatively trivial impacts from the central ones. This was done in one of two ways. In one method, having discussed different dimensions of impact, the group would make a simple drawing or symbol to represent all the items of each cluster. These then would be ranked from strongest to weakest.[93] Some items were of relatively equal strength, so would have the same ranking. Some items were unrankable because they had affected

---

[91] Again, because respondents may try to come up with what pleases the asker, due to power imbalances.   [92] See Nussbaum (1986, ch. 10, sect. III).

[93] Ranking was chosen not only because it is a common tool in participatory exercises, but also because it is a good way to determine *value priorities*. For a discussion and empirical comparison of the difference between ranking and rating for this purpose, see Inglehart (1997: 117 ff.).

different participants very differently so no consensus could be reached. A strong attempt was made to get participation by all members in this ranking process.

The alternative method was for the facilitator and one or two participants (who had been trained beforehand) to ask each participant individually to identify the 'top three' categories of impact. These were used to obtain a partial ranking of key impacts. The logic of asking for the 'top three' impacts only was that there was a reason to doubt the robustness of this process (if the persons returned to do the same exercise the next day—i.e. when no impacts had changed, but the 'mood' might be different—would the rankings be the same?). It was hypothesized that the top three or four categories contained impacts that were clearly significant and tied to the activity; these were taken to be robust—at least enough to warrant further monitoring.

3.2.3. Explicit scrutiny

Finally, on the basis of issues that had been raised, the discussion was brought from reflection on the past to reflections on the present and future. Negative impacts that had been raised were discussed, as well as possible ways for mitigating them. Participants were encouraged to evaluate the impacts that had occurred: Were positive changes worth the effort? Was the 'mix' of impacts acceptable? Did participants want to make changes in the future and if so how? In the case studies, no attempt was made to identify indicators for participatory monitoring but this could have been done at this stage. The conversations of this part of the meetings are not presented, but these were intended to form the 'climax' of the group meeting, after which the meeting closed.

This activity also replaces, at the micro level, the 'bottom-up' weighting conversation between the planner and the minister that the UNIDO guidelines describe. A full methodological treatment of the selection of different objectives and the interplay between local priorities, national objectives, and the capabilities and priorities of an implementing agency (be it the World Bank or a line ministry or a local NGO) would be valuable but is beyond the limits of this discussion. Still, the potential constructive role of economic analysis in a discussion such as the one described above should not be overlooked.

The UNIDO approach was expressed as a dialogue between a minister and a planner. But in local level activities the locus of decision-making is not located in one agent but shared among an NGO and various community groups, male and female. The agents in this discussion, at the time of their conversation, have only identified and weighted the impacts that they have perceived from the project. They do not necessarily have information on the likely sustainability or predicted future life of the activity. At this point, the group's ability to make 'informed' choices would be greatly improved by a comprehensible economic analysis that, as Robbins described it, sketched the implications of the various alternatives under consideration and their associated risks and uncertainties.

One might also derive from the choices made by *de facto* actors in a certain region, a set of 'local objectives' regarding development that could be used in the future—much as early CBA analysts wished to obtain a set of national objectives and weights to inform their different analyses. Yet attributions of relative weighting to these decisions seem contrived, at least at the local level, for several reasons. Groups' objectives may change endogenously; they may come to value education or empowerment differently in different seasons. Similarly, the empirical situation may change: the group of persons who were deprived in Period I may be stable in Period II, and a different group may be on the margins. Many of the parameters (such as distributional weights, shadow wages, discounts for saving) depend on external features of the situation that may well undergo change. Thus there does not seem to be any value in *collecting* information that will allow one to calculate relative weights because these weights may not be relevant at a later point in time. An economic and social analysis that brings out the critical variables and contours of a decision clearly, so that the choices are as informed as possible, could be of use at a local level.

3.2.4. *Aggregating and comparing impacts*
The outstanding question was how these descriptions of impacts could be 'compared' across activities. A parallel question was how the degree of 'participation' of the process could be represented and indicated (Ch. 5, Sect. 3.2). Recall that this issue of how to aggregate 'valued' capabilities when communities disagree about social priorities still confronts the capabilities approach, even at the level of basic capabilities.

For this purpose a method of generating qualitative indicators from the impact assessment exercise was developed. It built upon the method for dealing with qualitative data sets developed by Insham, Narayan, and Pritchett.[94] Insham *et al.* were trying to determine the causal effect of participation on activity performance. Although this exercise is complex for several reasons (e.g. biased data and the fact that statistical associations do not prove causality), the central difficulty is that evaluating the depth of participation accurately, across a large sample of activities in which 'participation' took varied forms, seems to require subjective judgement rather than reliance on objective features (number of meetings, etc.) because the *practices* that such objective indicators record are *different* in different locations. So the same indicators may not be reliable proxies of participation in different settings (Ch. 4, Sect. 4). They argue that subjective judgements regarding participation (which in their study were gathered from the reading of evaluation reports of large-scale water activities) can be transformed into 'intersubjectively valid, cardinal measures' that are appropriate for statistical analysis.

The intuition behind their method is as follows:

When hogs, figure skaters, or bodybuilders compete, judges assign cardinal scores to subjective criteria: quality of coat for hogs; artistic impression for figure skaters; and muscle tone for bodybuilders. Grades for academic papers are another familiar example: a professor's subjective evaluation of a humanities paper is given a cardinal score. In each case, these subjectively assigned scores are added, averaged, and tabulated in ways only appropriate to cardinal data. This means that judging requires training to achieve this level of intersubjective agreement. For instance, judges of livestock contests are occasionally judged on the degree to which their subjective judgements conform to those of established judges. (Insham *et al.* 1995)

[94] (1995). See also Narayan (1995).

While there is a large tradition and literature for qualitative grading, and while it has been used in development, a methodology has not been developed that is clear enough to achieve relatively reliable results.[95]

In the three following case studies, the qualitative ranking was done in just one way; but subsequently two different ways of ranking were developed and are described. First, the impact of the activity on a particular capability or set of related capabilities is ranked relative to what was possible in that situation. That is, the question is asked as to what impact the goat loans or the literacy programme had relative to the potential impact they might have had *given* the circumstances such as time, social context, staff capacity, and so on. The ranking was given from zero to five, with zero being no change and five being intense change relative to the context. In particular, the following guidelines were employed:

5. Incredible. Used all of the potential and created more. Did a truly amazing job given the circumstances.
4. Excellent. Used every bit of potential that was offered.
3. Good. Made solid progress in expanding valuable ends.
2. Fair. Made certain progress but left quite a few possibilities unused.
1. Weak. Simply did not make adequate progress given the situation and its potential.
Null. No evident change in this area.
— Negative. Things got worse in this area.

The value of this assessment is that it enables comparisons in relative change between different activities. For example, the goat project had a score of three to four on impact on knowledge; the score for Khoj was five (see Table 7.20). This will be interpreted to say that Khoj had a relatively greater impact on something within the dimension of knowledge than RWWO's activity did. This information becomes meaningful for analysis when combined with other information. For example, it is difficult to know how important the impact was to participants. But recall that the ranking exercise described above does provide this information. So it is possible to combine these and say, for example, that Khoj had an impact on knowledge *and* that this was perceived as its most important impact by participants. RWWO had a strong if less fundamental impact on knowledge, but this was also perceived as one of the most valuable by participants.

Still, it is difficult to know the extent to which the assessment of relative impact is influenced by situational factors. For example, if women have not gathered together in a group before, the very process of forming a group is likely to be transformative; it would be very difficult for a project in a city with a plethora of women's groups to achieve similar impacts. So the relative impacts reflect the cultural and historical context in which activities take place. However, we may also wish to have a

---

[95] The Malcolm Baldrige National Quality Awards are given annually by the US president to private and more recently public initiatives, using a similar scoring of key qualitative variables. But their assessors receive intensive three-day training (for which significant preparation is required) and initial assessments are reviewed by senior 'examiners'.

description of the overall level of functioning, for example, participation, that a group had reached. For example, in a rural area, the process of meeting every week may have been transformative, because women had not previously had permission to meet in groups. So the relative ranking would be very high. But from a different perspective 'having a meeting' led by an external women's activist is a very basic form of participation, because the women do not spontaneously, for example, meet and discuss issues, nor do they manage the local activity, much less take positions of local leadership. In certain areas of cities this practice might not even constitute an impact, because it is part of how women normally interact. So we need a second measure that indicates that the current level of participation—no matter how locally transformative—is overall at a basic level.

To enable comparisons of overall functioning level, a second kind of qualitative scoring was developed (*after* the three case studies of Chapter 7 were completed). In this ranking, focal capabilities that activities were expected to have affected, either directly or indirectly, were identified. These were defined (by an evaluation team), and a scoring system was constructed that reflected the spectrum of possible levels of achievement for each functioning. The scores an activity had on this scale enabled comparison between the levels of achieved functioning in different communities. For example, the criteria for 'women's participation' were as shown in Table 6.1.

Several potential misunderstandings of this 'overall' capabilities indicator must be addressed immediately. First, that a person or group can identify a scale from the weakest to the strongest kinds of participation does not mean that the rankings are normative (in a normative ranking, more is better: ideally each community would have a high ranking in all variables). It may be that at time t community Z has a different relative weighting of functionings, and in order to maintain a high degree of social cohesion, for example, or family stability, they do not pursue the higher levels of

Table 6.1. *Criteria for women's participation*

Functioning	Criteria for overall ranking
Women's actual participation in community *Definition of participation* The inclusion and involvement of all stakeholders of a process in all stages of that process.	0 no awareness of activities 1 awareness of the activity and some surveys/consultation 2 some meetings/interaction with activity initiators; some 'contribution', responsibility by a few persons 3 some responsibilities in more than one stage/regular meetings 4 significant involvement in different stages/significant responsibilities and ownership/big 'contribution' 5 community working in more than one sector; taking initiatives; able to mobilize resources[1]

Note: [1] The Asia Foundation (1998: 139).

women's empowerment. Secondly, that one can identify a scale among communities in one nation does not mean that all levels of the stage are actually feasible for community Z at time t even if the community does wish to pursue them. Thirdly, one activity at different times may show different maximal levels of a functioning. Similarly if one organization works in multiple areas, these may have different levels of a functioning at the same time. The aggregate or average rankings in either case may be expressed as a range (or a mean). Fourthly, the 'scale' may change over time (although these changes should be minimized to facilitate comparisons across time).

When the above exercise had been carried out in a number of activities, the final stage was for the assessors to carry out qualitative assessments of key variables, using agreed upon and transparent criteria, on a ranking system (zero to five). While the case studies finished with this cross-activity comparison, it is noted that such 'fuzzy set' data (re-scaled from zero to one) could be used in complex analyses, as well as in modified cost-benefit analysis.[96] This might be an avenue to explore as a way of making qualitative or 'intangible' data available for large-scale empirical analysis.[97]

3.2.5. *Limitations*
The framework for identifying and valuing capabilities employs a focused tool designed to address a gap in other participatory assessment methodologies, and it accesses and processes richer information than other approaches. The exercise is a limited part of an overall assessment and requires further information. Also, the tool itself needs further study and refinement. For instance, the reflections of Oxfam staff and consultants to The Asia Foundation included the following:[98]

1. The methodology must be complemented by other tools for gaining information on topics such as an activity's history, objectives, process of implementation, economic, and financial information. Also, effects such as institutional strengthening and capacity building on the implementing agency must be noted and valued separately.
2. The methodology only directly accesses perceptions of change. In order to complete an understanding of the changes that are 'strongly valued', such as those which were of a greater duration or the magnitude of the changes, additional information must be gathered.
3. The methodology provides information on impact as perceived at one point in time. The validity of the methodology in tracking change over time is not known.
4. A method for 'attributing' the impact to the activity (rather than to broader social changes) is required.
5. The information and valuation of change is done only by the participants in the activity; positive or negative effects on the wider community are not included.
6. Some impacts identified will endure in the long term; others are short term. The method does not distinguish between them.

---
[96] Chiappero Martinetti (1994, 1996), and the references contained therein.
[97] Narayan-Parker and Pritchett (1997).
[98] See Jabbar (1998, sect. 4.2), complemented by discussion with Oxfam staff.

7. The methodology depends on strong communication abilities of the facilitator to make 'concepts' such as empowerment intelligible in relation to participants' own experience.

Despite these limitations, this methodology can be seen as an initial step towards applying the capability approach to local development activities.

4. CONCLUSION

This chapter has explored different methodologies for evaluating projects with objectives that include poverty alleviation and empowerment. It introduced cost-benefit analysis and social assessment techniques, the former being mostly used for conventional 'economic' objectives and the latter encompassing the range of human development objectives. It argued that the normal techniques of cost-benefit analysis were appropriate as a means of generating information on activity *efficiency* but were not appropriate when the costs and benefits could not be fully priced. It was argued that the explicit, systematic identification of costs and benefits, the demonstrative value of distributional weights and comparisons of 'intangible' outputs, and the impetus to identify the relative weights of these as precisely as possible by consideration of social objectives, were positive features of CBA.

If a systematic CBA does include descriptions and rankings of qualitative variables, but does not attempt to attribute prices to all variables, then the analysis presents the decision-maker with a basket of disaggregated characteristics of an activity. These include, but are not limited to, its economic efficiency, its distributional effects, its institutional effects, and its human impacts as valued by the beneficiary community. The World Bank's 1996 recommendation that these diverse considerations be 'borne in mind' by decision-makers is incontestable, but this procedure needs to be specified quite a bit. I have argued that these kinds of decisions require the use of practical reason, participation, and the consideration of ends (Chs. 2 to 5); technical optimization is not feasible. While I have not addressed the important question of how these can be 'borne in mind', an attempt has been made in this chapter to illustrate how the information necessary to do so could be obtained.

7

Three Case Studies

Among the most valuable impacts of Oxfam activities as described by participants:

> When relatives come, or someone has a problem, we talk. Or each woman will give an opinion about a marriage—whether it will work or not. If we get the opinion that the family is good, we will arrange the marriage; if someone says it is not a good family, we are glad to know. This is a very participatory process.
>
> Hakim Zaid, goat owner
>
> Women think they are like a bud—that they do not understand with their own eyes. But we are not buds, we are mountains. We can do anything with our lives. So I tried to open my eyes, and my eyes were opened.
>
> Shabnam, graduate of Khoj literacy course
>
> In the early morning, I pick flowers. When I do this, I feel I have done sawab—holy work. Inner peace comes.
>
> Dadi Taja, rose cultivator

The three case studies mentioned earlier will now be analysed using social cost-benefit analysis and the methodology of identifying and valuing human impacts described in Chapter 6, Section 3.2.

The structure of each case is the following. The activity is first introduced. All of the tangible costs and benefits that can be measured and analysed are then described, shadow prices applied where necessary, and a CBA completed. Finally, the key intangible impacts from the activity as described by beneficiaries are introduced, and rankings reported. The chapter closes with a discussion of the decision-making processes that an external agency should use in evaluating these three activities and others like them.

This chapter does not assess the comprehensive changes with respect to capability sets that have taken place. For that it might be necessary to present further information on the history and context of the activity, and the duration, and source of the 'intangible' benefits described. This information could be acquired by standard methods (Ch. 6, Sect. 3). Moreover it might be necessary to assess changes affecting other agents, including Oxfam, the partner NGOs, and other institutions.[1]

---

[1] This depends whether the goal of development (the expansion of valuable capabilities) refers uniquely to the capabilities of direct beneficiaries or whether it includes the capabilities of other 'stakeholders' either directly or indirectly. For example, many social development activities involve the funding of non-governmental organizations which then implement a desired activity. A further objective of this funding may be to strengthen the administrative processes and human capital of the organization such that it becomes more effective, and is also able to 'earn' donor support for future activities. Other activities

Instead this chapter will demonstrate that cost–benefit analysis is unable to provide a sufficient assessment of a development activity, but can provide a limited, useful input into such an assessment. Cost-benefit analysis is able to draw attention to costs and benefits not reflected in financial prices and thus to market failure. It does not provide a systematic way of identifying valuable costs and benefits (even if it were then to price these). Nor does it provide an adequate way of integrating 'intangible' effects into the analysis.

It will further demonstrate that the assessment of capability expansion of the participants in income generation activities should not be arbitrarily limited to 'basic capabilities' such as health, education, political participation, employment, and life expectancy. The set of valuable capabilities, even of very poor women, includes, often prominently, other capabilities. In the three case studies of Oxfam-supported participatory income generation activities, the activities' tangible income, and their associated effects on life, health, and economic security were never regarded as the *most* important impacts by participants. This was the case even for an activity that had significant economic returns, namely, goat rearing.

Pakistan was chosen as the location for all three case studies for two reasons. First, it has a poor record of human, as opposed to economic, development. Pakistan is often contrasted with its regional neighbour India because of the disparity between its GDP per capita[2] and its level of human development. According to the 2000 *Human Development Report*'s human poverty index,[3] 40.1 per cent of Pakistanis live in human poverty as against 34.6 per cent of Indian citizens. This contrasts with a GDP per capita measure, by which 31 per cent of Pakistan's population experience income poverty of less than one dollar a day, whereas the same figure for India is 44.2 per cent.[4] Pakistan's human development index (HDI)[5] rank is four places below its income ranking.

Secondly, the 'participation' of the poor in development activities is a relatively recent phenomenon, and one that is not reflected in broader society. This makes the effects of participatory activities and social organization relatively easier to trace than it would be for example in India, where participatory approaches have a much longer history and where the political structure has been a democracy since independence. Community development and human development interventions in Pakistan have proliferated only in the 1990s, although the roots these have built upon are older. The seminal contribution came from Akhtar Hamid Khan, who

---

have a particular 'advocacy' component, in which a funder intends that the social development activity will not only deliver social services, but also create pressure on local institutions to improve their performance, or motivate persons to spawn additional local activities. In either of these cases, the full set of 'capability expansion' would be wider than participants' own well-being, and would include agency aspects, and perhaps the capabilities of non-participants.

[2] Pakistan's 1998 real GDP per capita was $511 in 1995 US dollars, vs. India's at $444 (UNDP 2000: 180).   [3] UNDP (2000).

[4] UNDP (1998: 26, 170). The dollar per day figure refers to 1993 purchasing power parity in US dollars.

[5] UNDP (2000: 170). HDI combines life expectancy, adult literacy and school enrolment ratios, and real GDP per capita.

started the Komila Integrated Rural Development Project in then East Pakistan and subsequently established the Orangi Pilot Project in Karachi. This highly participatory approach was then taken to the Aga Khan Rural Support Programme (AKRSP) in the Northern Areas, by Shoaib Sultan Khan. A number of other non-governmental organizations, often founded by educated activists, have undertaken analogous programmes. Many donors and international NGOs—for example, Oxfam, Save the Children Fund, Catholic Relief Society, ActionAid, The Asia Foundation and some bilateral donors—have incorporated participatory methodologies into their programmes.

These programmes now focus on building capacity, and enhancing the capability of poor and marginal people to solve their own problems rather than simply providing services. They regard participatory methods as valuable in poverty alleviation on the grounds of efficiency as well as intrinsic worth. While an appreciation of participation did not necessarily emerge in response to the academic writings on basic needs and human development in the 1960s and 1970s, it did emerge out of the same intellectual environment. The three case studies that follow bring out the connections between the capability approach and the practical experience of certain NGOs in Pakistan, and in particular ask how the former can assist the latter.

1. LOANS FOR GOATS

1.1. *Introduction*

The Rural Women's Welfare Organization (RWWO), a local NGO based in Senghar, Sindh, received a single Oxfam grant in 1992 for the purposes of establishing and administering a revolving loan fund for goats. Using this grant, RWWO identifies village women who are poor, interested in receiving a goat loan, willing to repay, and willing to take the risk associated with a loan. These women decide how often they will pay instalments on the loan, and the amount of each instalment is calculated so that repayment in full occurs within one year. Then NGO staff together with the loanee attend a goat auction and the loanee chooses her goat. The NGO advances a fixed sum towards the purchase of a goat, for example, 2,000 Rs. If the woman chooses a goat that costs, say, 2,200 Rs, she pays the remaining 200 Rs. Periodically, representatives from each village bring the repayment instalments to the NGO office.

The beneficiaries of this loan scheme were poor women from four small villages near Senghar. The loan scheme was closely tied to a programme of social organization (group formation, health, and education meetings) and savings. In June 1997 the loan was still revolving and had just begun its fourth phase. The numbers of beneficiaries per phase had decreased from fifty to twenty-five due to inflation and some defaulting in the first phase. However, after the first phase, repayment rates had been 100 per cent. A total of 140 different women in four villages had received one goat each to date.

A goat provides an income stream of an estimated 3,000 Rs per year in 1997 prices. This is a welcome source of female income, as the only other sources are quilt making and, in two villages, onion picking. In addition, goat owners identified strong impacts on *knowledge, relationships,* and *empowerment* due to the frequent, regular meetings and the social mobilization component of RWWO's activity. The activity also impacted on *religion* (goats were killed for Eid sacrifices) and *empowerment* (women owned a productive asset for the first time and decided whether to sell goats or build a herd and how to use the income). There was significant *participation* in the sense that goat owners met regularly and discussed personal problems as well as goat care and sales. They decided on a repayment schedule. The goat owners also received instruction from RWWO on environmental awareness (this was not Oxfam-funded) and health/hygiene.

This activity is a typical Oxfam investment: targeted at the poor (and in this case at women), involving an intermediary local institution as a partner, and intending two kinds of benefits (to generate a sustainable income for beneficiaries and to increase local partner capacity). The 'social organization' component of the investment (the formation of a women's organization) was introduced in order to assure loan repayment, to offer training in goat care, and to motivate women to improve health and hygiene practices. This component also generated the other common impacts of participatory activities: it built relationships, provided a forum for communal problem-solving, and instigated an increase in collective action.

RWWO financial flows to date are given in Table 7.1. The partner received a one time grant of 65,400 Rs in 1992 for the purpose of setting up a revolving loan fund. They have to date given 140 goat loans. The first loans were given and repaid at 1,200 Rs; the second were given at 1,200 Rs and repaid at 1,300 Rs; the third were given at 2,000 Rs and repaid at 2,200 Rs; the current phase comprises loans of 2,000 Rs that will be repaid at 2,400 Rs plus a mandatory 60 Rs 'membership fee' to join the NGO for a total of 2,460 Rs.

1.2. *Cost-benefit analysis*

1.2.1. *Benefits*

Monetary benefits accrue to goat owners beginning about eighteen months after the purchase of a goat. The rupee amount of benefits and their duration depend on women's decisions as to the breed of goat and the use of offspring. However, some estimates may be made. In practice, records of the first pregnancy from goats in the first two phases showed a mean of 1.66 kids per year and an average value per 1-year-old kid of 1,800 Rs (1996 prices) each.[6] This meant that if all goat kids were sold (which was not necessarily the case),[7] the goat owner would have a steady income of $1,800 \times 1.66 = 3,000$ Rs per year. As the 1997 loan repayment was

---

[6] Reported prices ranged from 600–3,000 Rs.

[7] Some kids may be kept to build the herd. In practice, we found a range of practices were followed. One woman had a goat herd of 22 animals, from a Phase I Teddy goat. Several reported incomes of 10,000 and 18,000 Rs in total from the sale of kids. Some goats had died after one birth. There was significant variation in income, which made goat rearing a relatively insecure or unpredictable source of income until the herd was built up.

Table 7.1. *RWWO financial flows (in nominal rupees)*

Year	Oxfam grant	Loans granted to goat owners				Fees paid by goat owners to RWWO	Loan repayment by goat owners	Overhead expenses of RWWO	Net cash of RWWO
		Total capital loaned to goat owners	Goat loans given	Amount of each loan	Service charge on each loan*				
1992	−65,400	60,000	50	1,200	0			5,400	0
1993		48,000	40	1,200	100		−50,700	2,700	−48,000
1994									
1995		50,000	25	2,000	200		−52,000	2,000	−50,000
1996		50,000	25	2,000	400		−55,000	3,000	0
1997					(0–20%)	−1,500*			−3,500
	−65,400	208,000	140			−1,500	−157,700	13,100	−3,500

Note: *Service charges were fixed when the loan was issued, rather than being calculated as a percentage. They were initially too low, which led to capital erosion from inflation tax.

238   *Three Case Studies*

Table 7.2a. *Estimated benefits from one female goat (in constant 1996 rupees)*

Year	Goat population	Running income	Cum. Income
1	Female goat purchased	Loan taken out 2,000	−2,000
1.5	1.66 baby goats born		
2			
2.5	1.66 kids sold; 1.66 more baby goats born	1.66 * 1,800 = 3,000 Loan repaid = −2,460	540
3			
3.5	1.66 kids sold; 1.66 more baby goats born	1.66 * 1,800 = 3,000	3,540
4			
4.5	1.66 kids sold; 1.66 more baby goats born	1.66 * 1,800 = 3,000	6,540
5	Original female goat dies		
5.5	1.66 kids sold	1.66 * 1,800 = 3,000	9,540

2,460 Rs (all others have been smaller in real terms), this means that the loan would be fully recovered at the sale of the first two kids, and profits proceed from there. For projected benefits in time, a conservative estimate is that one goat would kid four times (bearing 6.7 kids) before death.

Based on these estimations, the aggregate annual financial benefits from the goat activity in constant 1992 prices are presented in Table 7.2b.[8]

Furthermore, if one makes the conservative estimate that loans will be given every two years for the next eight years beginning in 1999 and that with an estimated 90 per cent recovery rate plus 20 per cent service charges RWWO will be able to sustain the number of loans at twenty-five, then future income streams will be 96,300 Rs annually for ten years and 48,150 Rs for an additional two years.

The costs and benefits in constant 1992 prices are given in Table 7.4, with the inflation adjustment rates being taken from the consumer price index. Net benefits are shown as well as benefits discounted by using, as discussed earlier, a social discount rate of 12 per cent $(1/(1+0.12)^{n-1992})$. As this shows, the net benefits to goat owners are quite high.

The financial flows do not include any costs such as 'wages' for the goat owners, or Oxfam and RWWO staff time and transportation (RWWO staff provided their time and transportation costs voluntarily). It also does not include the erosion of loan capital from defaulters if there were to be defaults (after the first phase, in which there were significant defaults, the repayment rate has been 100 per cent). The valuation of these costs is discussed below.

---

[8] Note that the estimate of 3,000 Rs income per goat, when adjusted for inflation, using the consumer price index rates, is 1,926 Rs in 1992 prices.

Table 7.2b. *Goat owners' aggregate financial benefits (in constant 1992 rupees)*

	Goats	1992	1993	1994	1995	1996	1997	1998	1999	2000	2001	2002
Phase I	50	*		96,300	96,300	96,300	96,300					
Phase II	40			*		77,400	77,400	77,400	77,400			
Phase III	25					*		48,150	48,150	48,150	48,150	
Phase IV	25						*		48,150	48,150	48,150	48,150
Total	140			96,300	96,300	173,700	173,700	125,550	173,700	96,300	96,300	48,150

Note: * = year goat loans disbursed for each phase.

Three Case Studies

Table 7.3. *Projected financial benefits for goat owners (in constant 1992 rupees)*

Phase	1992	1993	1994	1995	1996	1997	1998	1999	2000	2001
I	★		96,300	96,300	96,300	96,300				
II		★			77,400	77,400	77,400	77,400		
III					★		48,150	48,150	48,150	48,150
IV						★		48,150	48,150	48,150
V								★		48,150
VI										★
VII										
VIII										
Yrly total	0	0	96,300	96,300	173,700	173,700	125,550	173,700	96,300	144,450
Total in 1000s	0	0	96.3	192.6	355.3	540	665.6	839.3	935.6	1,080

Phase	2002	2003	2004	2005	2006	2007	2008	2009	2010
I									
II									
III									
IV	48,150								
V	48,150	48,150	48,150						
VI		48,150	48,150	48,150	48,150				
VII		★		48,150	48,150	48,150	48,150		
VIII				★		48,150	48,150	48,150	48,150
Yrly total	96,300	96,300	96,300	96,300	96,300	96,300	96,300	48,150	48,150
Total in 1000s	1,176.3	1,272.6	1,368.9	1,465.2	1,561.5	1,657.8	1,754.1	1,802.3	1,850.4

1.2.2. Costs to goat owners

In the three villages, there is no *financial* cost for fodder; the women spend time but not money to gather it. One goat plus two kids requires a minimum of half an hour a day of work to clean, collect fodder, and, occasionally, milk or feed a baby. Four times a year, each goat will need an extra half day of attention for selling or breeding or birthing or veterinary treatment. Therefore there is a wage cost for 200 hours of care per goat per year.

Several different shadow prices will be used for labour: 0 Rs per hr., 7 Rs per hr. (which is the higher boundary of the range of onion-picking wages), and 10.5 Rs per hr. (which is the rate if the women were to earn the equivalent of a male wage). These wage rates were reported in 1996 and I will refer to them in tables as these rates, although in the analysis these and all figures are converted to 1992 rupees. As described earlier I have not estimated a separate discount rate for the proportion of income saved.

1.2.3. Costs to RWWO

The implementing agency, RWWO, that managed the Oxfam grant in this activity, contributed time, stationery, and transportation to this activity. In the first year, the

Table 7.4. *RWWO net discounted benefits (in constant 1992 rupees)*

	1992	1993	1994	1995	1996	1997	1998	1999	2000	2001	2002	Total
Costs	0	43,152	−38,160	35,900	−32,100	1,984.5						
Benefits	0		96,300	96,300	173,700	173,700	135,550	173,700	96,300	96,300	48,150	
Net benefits	0	43,152	58,140	132,200	141,600	175,684.5	135,550	173,700	96,300	96,300	48,150	1,100,776.5

Table 7.5. *Unremunerated costs of goat activity (in constant 1996 rupees)*

Cost	Wage rate Rs/hour L	M	H	Hours 1st yr.	Per yr.	1st yr. cost L	M	H	Est. cost/yr. L	M	H
Unskilled labour	0	7	10.5	100/goat	200/goat	0	700/goat	1,050/goat	0	1,400/goat	2,100/goat
Skilled labour	0	25	75[1]	528 (total)	190 (total)	0	13,200	39,600	0	4,750	14,250
Transport	/	/	/			9,600			6,000		
Administrator	/	/	/			5,400			3,600		
Loan defaulters	/	/	/			11,848[2]			Est. 2500[4]		
Oxfam support	/	/	/			18,000[3]			6,000		

Note: [1] This is equivalent to 12,000 Rs per month (taking a month to be twenty, eight-hour days). [2] Goat deaths. [3] Yr. 2 = 12,000. [4] 5,000/2 yrs.

time investment was significantly higher than all other years, at 528 hours total. This figure includes the time spent in setting up the loan administration and establishing the women's organizations. For subsequent years the total time spent in goat procurement, loan and repayment management, and 'motivating' visits to the women's organizations was estimated at 190 hours.

The shadow cost of labour in the case of the Rural Women's Welfare Organization can be estimated in three ways. RWWO offered their labour voluntarily, so perhaps their staff time could be considered to be a form of leisure that had an opportunity cost of zero (given that, as in the case of surplus labour, economic output did not decrease elsewhere). Indeed, volunteer opportunities might count as a social *benefit* if they generate satisfaction for the worker at no economic cost. Alternatively, their labour costs could be taken simply as the wage level for skilled labour in other NGOs. The reason for this would be that there is labour scarcity in this market; therefore the standard wage level could be assumed to reflect the marginal cost of labour. But although there is a scarcity of skilled labour, this market may not actually be competitive. For (as this example shows) some NGOs are characterized by volunteerism, while the wages of others are artificially high because the presence of foreign funds has distorted NGO salary structures. The wage rate for RWWO staff if employed by a national NGO would be 12,000 Rs per month (75 Rs per hr.), so one could use this as the shadow wage. Alternatively, if NGO partner salaries are artificially inflated above their social value, RWWO salaries could be taken as the wage level for skilled labour in the domestic private sector, which would be 4,000 Rs per month (25 Rs per hr.) in 1996 prices.

As with the goat owners, alternative values will be used. However, the findings were *not* sensitive to the wage used. So only two results are shown: those for 0 Rs per hr. and those for 75 Rs per hr.

The only additional costs were transportation and a variable payment for administrative assistance, for which the market prices adjusted to constant prices are sufficient.

1.2.4. *Cost to Oxfam*

In addition, the activity has had the equivalent of eight days of direct Oxfam field staff input over the time, plus a portion of overheads for accounting and reporting. This is a relatively low input of Oxfam time relative to operational activities (Ch. 7, Sect. 3). The daily cost for field staff, driver, and transport is estimated at 6,000 Rs (1996 prices), of which 12 per cent is the combined staff and driver salary; varying the shadow wages on these figures has therefore minimal effect on results, so only one rate is displayed. The annual overheads for reporting, accounting, communication, and administration are not included.

1.2.5. *Shadow prices of goats*

The market for the sale of goats is competitive, especially at the season of Eid Al Kurbani, which is when most of the goat sales from this activity take place (precisely because the increased demand pushes prices up). Therefore no adjustment to the sale price of the goats is made.

The resulting social cost-benefit analysis presents internal rates of return (IRRs) that reflect all the above factors (see Table 7.6).

1.2.6. *Conclusion of the cost-benefit analysis*

As Table 7.7 shows, the goat-rearing activity had a high internal rate of return when the wages were 0 Rs per hr. but this was reduced substantially by introducing alternative shadow wages for women's labour. Increasing the opportunity cost of labour to 7 Rs per hr. reduces the internal rate of return from 83 to 13 per cent. At 10.5 Rs per hr., which is equivalent to male wage labour in these same villages, the internal rate of return falls to −12 per cent. Similarly, if one projects this result over an additional four phases of goats, extending through the year 2010, the IRRs and NPVs are positive and negative at the same points. The final decision regarding the desirability of this activity (assessed on financial criteria only) rests on the value set for the unskilled wage labour of goat owners.

At this stage, it may also be appropriate to return to distributional weights (Ch. 6, Sect. 2.3.4). If one did introduce such weights, the social value of the financial benefits to goat owners would increase by the chosen weight. Such a weighting would reflect the public interest in creating income for the poorer sectors of society over others. Hence activities that offer such employment but have a lower internal rate of return could be chosen over activities in wealthier regions with higher rates of return. Even a mild distributional weight would make the investment clearly desirable. For example, a distributional weight of 1.5 on income to these women over the national standard switches the internal rate of return for the first four phases (at 10.5 Rs per hr., unskilled; 75 Rs per hr., skilled) from −12 to +24 per cent. The switching point of distributional weighting to a positive value is 1.1 (at 1.2, the IRR is 7 per cent, which would still be below a 12 per cent SDR). If one considers the projected eight phase programme, the switching point of distributional weights to a positive IRR (at 10.5 Rs per hr., unskilled; 75 Rs per hr., skilled) increases to 1.23.

It might be helpful, in considering distributional weights, to contextualize the amount of income that is being generated. With one goat earning 3,000 Rs per yr. from the sale of kids (on average), the total gross income is roughly the income needed for a household of seven members to subsist at the poverty level for one month. This can increase quite rapidly, however, if the owner keeps female kids for breeding purposes rather than selling them. A herd with four additional female goats would earn an average gross of 1,250 Rs per month (1996 rupees), making a substantial contribution towards household expenses (as well as producing up to 6 lbs. of goat milk per day).

The cost-benefit analysis was undertaken with conservative estimates of financial benefit to goat owners. The fact that mild distributional weights move even the most stringent cost-benefit analysis (in which the women's shadow wage is estimated, unrealistically, to be equal to a male wage) to a positive internal rate of return, suggests that the goat-rearing programme is a sound economic investment. This is especially the case given its potential to increase women's income in the medium term by building a goat herd.

Table 7.6. *RWWO running costs and present values under various assumptions (1992–end of current phase)*

	1992	1993	1994	1995
Total active goats	50	50	90	90
Unskilled labour	(100 hrs/goat)			
@7 Rs * 200 hrs/goat	−35,000	−70,000	−126,000	−126,000
Adjusted to 1992 prices	−22,470	−44,940	−80,892	−80,892
@10.5 Rs * 200 hrs/goat	−52,500	−105,000	−189,000	−189,000
Adjusted to 1992 prices	−33,705	−67,410	−121,338	−121,338
Skilled labour				
No. hours worked	528	190	190	190
@75 Rs/hr	−39,600	−14,250	−14,250	−14,250
Adjusted to 1992 prices	−25,423.2	−9,148.5	−9,148.5	−9,148.5
Admin. costs	−5,400	−2,700	0	−2,000
Adjusted to 1992 prices	−3,466.8	−1,733.4	0	−1,284
Transport costs	−9,600	−6,000	−6,000	−6,000
Adjusted to 1992 prices	−6,163.2	−3,852	−3,852	−3,852
Financial benefits from				
goat sales	0	0	96,300	96,300
dist. wt. = 1.5 * 135	0	0	144,450	144,450
Loan costs				
Actual, to 1997	−65,400	43,152	−38,160	35,900
Future repayment@90%				
Oxfam costs				
Sum of Oxfam costs	18,000	12,000	6,000	6,000
Adjusted to 1992 prices	−11,556	−7,704	−3,852	−3,852
IRR/NPVs:				
All wages = 0 Rs	−86,586	37,566.6	54,288	127,064
IRR	**83%**			
NPV@3%	Rs 845,838.06			
NPV@8%	Rs 636,345.32			
NPV@12%	Rs 512,818.49			
Unsk. = 7/Skilled = 0	−109,056	−7,373.4	−26,604	46,172
IRR	**21%**			
NPV@3%	Rs 208,924.31			
NPV@8%	Rs 121,740.16			
NPV@12%	Rs 71,905.78			
Unsk. = 7/Skilled = 75	−134,479.2	−16,521.9	−35,752.5	37,023.5
IRR	**13%**			
NPV@3%	Rs 126,503.37			
NPV@8%	Rs 48,686.48			
NPV@12%	Rs 4,731.05			
Unsk. = 10.5/Skilled = 0	−120,291	−37,547.4	−70,902	1,874
IRR	**−12%**			
NPV@3%	−134,139.39			
NPV@12%	−167,827.01			

1996	1997	1998	1999	2000	2001	2002
115	140	90	90	50	50	25
−161,000	−196,000	−126,000	−126,000	−70,000	−70,000	−35,000
−103,362	−125,832	−80,892	−80,892	−44,940	−44,940	−22,470
−241,500	−294,000	−189,000	−189,000	−105,000	−105,000	−52,500
−155,043	−188,748	−121,338	−121,338	−67,410	−67,410	−33,705
		0				
190	190	190	190			
−14,250	−14,250	−14,250	−14,250	0	0	0
−9,148.5	−9,148.5	−9,148.5	−9,148.5	0	0	0
0	−3,000	−3,600	−3,600	0	0	0
0	−1,926	−2,311.2	−2,311.2	0	0	0
−6,000	−6,000	−6,000	−6,000	0	0	0
−3,852	−3,852	−3,852	−3,852	0	0	0
173,700	173,700	125,550	173,700	96,300	96,300	48,150
260,550	260,550	188,325	260,550	144,450	144,450	72,225
−32,100	1,984.5	0	0	0	0	0
		45,000	0			
6,000	6,000	6,000	0			
−3,852	−3,852	−3,852	0	0	0	0
137,748	169,906.5	164,386.8	167,536.8	96,300		48,150
34,386	44,074.5	83,494.8	86,644.8	51,360		25,680
25,237.5	34,926	74,346.3	77,496.3	51,360		25,680
−21,147	−22,693.5	39,196.8	46,198.8	28,890		14,445

246   *Three Case Studies*

Table 7.6. (*cont.*)

	1992	1993	1994	1995
Unsk. = 10.5/Skilled = 75	−145,714.2	−38,991.9	−76,198.5	−3,422.5
IRR	12%			
NPV@3%	−191,953.51			
Unsk. = 10.5/Skilled = 75, Distributional wt. of 1.5	−120,291	−37,547.4	−22,752	50,024
IRR	24%			

Table 7.7. *RWWO projected NPV and IRR at various rates of unskilled labour (in constant 1992 rupees)*

Shadow wage rate For unskilled (Skilled = Rs 75/hr)	NPV 12% discount rate	NPV 3% discount rate	IRR
W★ = 0	659,529	1,310,158	83%
W★ = 7 Rs/hr	81,042	299,262	13%
W★ = 10.5 Rs/hr	−237,875	−255,910	−12%

1.3. *Efficiency considerations*

It is clear from the CBA that goats are very profitable and the loan capital is recovered quickly, so the question is why women are not buying goats on their own; why outside intervention is required.

One factor seems to be risk. There is no insurance market so if a goat is purchased that dies or does not kid, the capital costs are lost. This risk would provide a strong disincentive to poor buyers. After losing 50 per cent of its real loan capital due to a combination of inflation and defaulters (from goat deaths), RWWO itself began to charge a service fee sufficient to provide for both inflation and insurance. One might suggest that RWWO's resources might be more efficiently placed if instead of offering credit it offered insurance. The same resources might benefit a significantly greater population. This kind of intervention might also target the poor effectively, because (given the sensitivity of the returns from goats to the shadow price of labour) presumably those with the lowest labour costs would come forward to buy insurance, whereas loans may also attract people with higher labour costs.

This analysis, while arguably sensible in the longer term, would not have been feasible initially for two reasons. First, the women did not have ownership of productive assets prior to the RWWO programme, nor the habit of savings, so they could not have gathered the capital necessary to buy a goat or to purchase insurance. Also, in this region, household assets belong to the men. Although some women still care for livestock or help in the fields, the marketing is performed by male members of the household, who generally control the income. The twin goals of this activity

1996	1997	1998	1999	2000	2001	2002
−26,443.5	−27,990	33,900.3	37,050.3	28,890		14,445
65,703	64,156.5	101,971.8	133,048.8	77,040		38,520

were to generate income and to 'empower' women which meant, among other things, to generate an income stream over which the woman had control. In this case it required changing practices regarding property rights and marketing. Without the social organization component the women would not have owned and sold goats. An analysis of insurance markets alone would overlook this.

The other reason an RWWO insurance programme might not have been effective initially relates to knowledge and information. A considerable proportion of the RWWO investment in terms of time involved training women about goat care, goat health, goat sales, and also about saving, health, and other topics. This training transferred the skills necessary for women to raise and manage a goat herd and through this they also learned how to interact with institutions outside their village. As mentioned above, it is likely that this input also increased the productivity of the goat project. Clearly it would be possible for RWWO to provide training, group formation, and to offer insurance rather than credit. Still, before this training had taken place, before the incentive of credit had been given and profit been made, and before the trust with RWWO had been developed, the demand for insurance might have been very low indeed.

1.4. *Market viability*

A final 'efficiency' consideration, which is different from the question addressed by cost-benefit analysis but readily available from the same information and important in terms of sustainability of projects, is whether or not the activity would be financially viable without further donor support. In order to estimate this, one uses actual nominal flows and actual, rather than shadow, prices. If 90 per cent of the current goat loanees repay their current loan and no additional grants are made, the programme will continue into the fifth phase, but then the number of loans given will decrease to fifteen in the sixth phase. If the repayment rate remains 100 per cent (although recall the service charge now includes insurance for goat deaths), the number of loans will remain constant except in the eighth phase, when they will decrease by one loan to twenty-four.

The financial flows show that if RWWO continues to be willing to provide *voluntary* support for women's organizations and loan administration, the undertaking would be financially viable. The programme would not be sustainable if estimated RWWO labour and transport were to be remunerated at market prices.

1.5. *Further costs and benefits*

Although we have concluded that the social cost-benefit analysis of the goat activity is positive, this information is of limited use in an assessment of capability expansion. An internal rate of return above the social discount rate means that overall social welfare will increase, but this 'welfare' is narrowly defined. The capability approach would require the institution to gather additional information besides return rates.

Table 7.8 notes additional costs and benefits from the goat loan activity that may not be able to be priced accurately but might be considered in an evaluation. The section that follows presents a sequence by which some of the goat owners' impacts may be incorporated into activity-level assessment.

Before discussing how these costs and benefits can enter an evaluation, it is necessary to ask where the knowledge of these benefits came from and how accurate and complete knowledge about them might be.

1.6. *Identifying the impacts*

As mentioned above, these case studies include only the further impacts that accrued directly to the goat-owners.[9] The novel impact assessment exercise described earlier (Ch. 6, Sect. 3.2) was conducted in three villages. The following discussion describes, step by step, the process of identification and weighting of the impacts.

In June 1997, five years after the first goat loan was given, the population of women who had received goat loans in any year in each of three of the four villages (twenty-five to forty per village) came together for a meeting at which, among other things, they reflected on the impacts that the goat activity had had on all dimensions of human development. The discussion from one village is synthesized below. The three villages were of similar size; inhabitants were of the same caste and socio-economic level, and responses in different villages varied only slightly.[10]

At the close of this discussion, a great range of impacts had been identified, but the relative importance of each impact was unspecified. An evaluation must fathom how important these impacts are in relation to the impact from income from goat sales, and how the goat activity generated or reinforced each impact. In Ravat Goth, both ranking methods described earlier were used. First, each woman was asked

---

[9] Additional work is required on the question of how to evaluate accurately the economic benefits of institutional strengthening and staff capacity-building. See Edwards and Hulme (1992, 1995); The World Bank (1997) for accounts of the value of such strengthening; The Asia Foundation (1998) for one evaluation methodology.

[10] A trip to the fourth village was planned so that the sample would be the entire population, but was not possible because of time constraints.

Table 7.8. *Additional RWWO costs and benefits*

	Costs	Benefits
RWWO		Reputation
		Institutional knowledge
		Institutional capacity
Local goat group		Job satisfaction
		Existence
		Collective action
Goat owners	Relationships	Relationships
	Leisure	Knowledge
	Motivational and emotional cost if goat dies	Health
		Empowerment
		Religion
Society		Women's status
		Social capital

individually to select the most valuable three impacts of the initiative.[11] This was in part an error-reduction mechanism: a complete ranking of impacts would probably change if the women did the ranking on a different day (the facilitators tried it themselves in training with this result). However, the three strongest impacts would plausibly be relatively more robust.[12] Next, the group was asked to rank the impacts collectively. They generated the group ranking also shown below.

At a later point in time, having used this assessment exercise on seven Oxfam activities, the assessors independently rated the impact each activity had had on each dimension relative to the context, based on their recollection of the group meeting (they did not have the women's ranking to refer to) together with the other information they had gathered while in the communities and from discussions with the NGO staff (Table 7.20). The ranking of the participants individually, the group as a whole, and the assessors converged on the same four or five dimensions, although the order differed.

Thus impacts on knowledge, empowerment, life/health/security, and religion were identified as the strongest, with relationships being the fifth significant category (it was difficult to separate relationships and empowerment because as the above descriptions reflect, the formation and ongoing operation of a women's group was valued under both titles). If, then, we are interested in assessing the direct impact of the activity on the 'expansion of valuable capabilities' we will need to include in our

---

[11] These did not necessarily correspond with the biggest or more enduring impacts. Further work is needed to distinguish 'importance' from 'magnitude'.

[12] This could be verified by returning to the project and repeating the exercise quite soon after the first assessment—before the project had itself changed. This was not possible in the current study.

Box 7.1. *Descriptions of human impacts from RWWO goat loans—village: Ravat Goth*

Dimension	Summary	Examples
Knowledge	Veterinary services	We had a workshop in livestock. I learned about inoculating livestock, about the medicines to be used for worms, and about injections for sick animals.
	Treatment of sick animals	We learned to keep the fodder of sick goats away from that of well goats.
	Good milking practices	I learned that when I milk a goat, I should not have a ring on my finger, because its metal could hurt the udder.
		When you are milking a buffalo and the buffalo walks away, we used to pull the animal back by its udder. We learned this was no good; we should go with them.
Religion	Kurbani	There is no effect of this activity on our namaz (prayer).
Spirituality	Eid offering	The goat activity gave very positive help in religion. At first, we were too poor to give offering at Kurbani Eid. Now we are able to offer the goats.
		After eleven months the kids are ready, and we sell them for Eid al-Azhar.
	Break Ramazan fasts with milky tea.	The fasting of Ramazan is not made more difficult because of the goats. Before, we worried that if we fast, we would not be able to cut fodder; but it is not a problem.
		There is the benefit at Ramazan times too. Before, we cooked black tea. Now there is milk, so to open our fast we can cook tea with milk.
Relationships	Collective grazing of goats 'love and unity'	There is a basic unity and love between us, and our work is founded on this. We cooperate with each other more than we did before.
		When we got the first goats, we acted individually. We did not know how to provide their food. Then we saw that we could gather the goats in the morning and graze all together. [They do collective grazing of the goat herd.]
		You see, today you were late in coming. We sat together anyway, and sang folk songs to pass the time. Would we do this if we were not friendly with each other?

Three Case Studies 251

Box 7.1. (*cont.*)

Dimension	Summary	Examples
Participation, empowerment, self-direction	Discussion on personal decisions	When relatives come, or someone has a problem, we talk. Each woman will give an opinion about a marriage – whether it will work in their house or not. If we get the opinion that the family is good, we will arrange the marriage; if someone says it is not a good family, we are glad to know. This is a very participatory process. If there is a sick man, we tell each other; if someone needs money, we all gather some and provide. All sorrows we tell to each other, and share. We sit together … and whoever gives the best opinion, we do this.
Life/health/ security	Milk income	Life is better than before. I earned 10,000 Rs in three years by selling goat kids. I sold the goat kids and made a house. I did not have milk for tea or children; I am a widow. I get 1.5 lbs of milk a day from the goats.
Inner peace	Joy at birth of kids Glad for income source	When our goat is pregnant, we wait so strongly for the kids. We are so so happy to hold the baby in our hands. Sometimes we go out and buy 10 Rs of sweets to offer to celebrate the birth. When the kids are born, all of the family is happy and the children jump for joy. Obviously, our family needs money, so if the number of livestock increase, we are very happy.
Work/play	Little effect on workload Satisfaction is great	Our goats are few—I have about six or seven. If you gave us a goat every day we would be too busy; this number is no problem.

assessment reference to the key capabilities in these four (or five) dimensions. The impacts that participants associated with the dimensions varied somewhat between the women and among communities. Yet despite the legitimate concerns in participatory literature about 'whose' definitions predominate, the relative homogeneity of these villages in social and socio-economic terms, and the discussions, made the identification of modal definitions of impact seem plausible (this again requires further study). So based on the information from this participatory exercise, and limited further key informant interviews, the dominant 'definitions' or sense(s) of each impact were clarified by assessors and are related below.

1.7. Explanations of impacts

1.7.1. Empowerment

There were two significant senses of empowerment.

First, women had not met together in groups before the RWWO activity began. The group that was created provided a forum in which they could discuss other problems—ranging from the sale of goats to their children's marriages, to who was ill or poor, to personal griefs. The ability to discuss choices they had to make was satisfying and built confidence—and better choices.

Secondly, the nature of the activity—goat breeding—puts decisions into the woman's hand. Will she sell the goats or keep them to build the herd? Will she sell them now (and get less money) or later? Is there a 'goat glut' in the market? How will profits be spent? The decision-making process was educational and built confidence in the women's individual and collective capacities and cognitive abilities.

1.7.2. Knowledge

The dominant definition of knowledge seemed to be 'education' or the acquisition of new information. The women also valued the new tacit knowledge about group organization and collective decision-making mentioned under 'empowerment'. New information was gained through the high-quality training provided by or through RWWO in the group meetings. In contrast to other programmes, the training was well remembered and learning was accurate. In addition, knowledge increased in a way that would not be captured by animal health data. For example, participants learned about oral rehydration therapy, about tree-planting, and other topics. It is to be noted that RWWO did environmental training funded by UNDP (as a result of which the women voluntarily discussed global warming), but the other training (i.e. nutrition and health) was provided as part of RWWO's group formation procedure.

1.7.3. Life/health/security

Impacts on life/health/security derived from goat products in the form of milk or money. There were also impacts on health and hygiene that derived from the training component of social organization. Impacts on life, health, and security are not a substitute for income. Income is fungible and may have been used on other dimensions, but impacts on life, health, and security represent impacts on human functionings themselves. Yet in this case, the income and milk from the goat-rearing activity were directly instrumental to expansion of capabilities related to life and health. It is quite interesting to note, then, that if the ranking process is accurate and if all of the income was spent on this dimension, then women still valued RWWO's successful income generation activity relatively more for its impacts on knowledge and empowerment than for its direct impact on life/health/security (Table 7.9).

Three Case Studies 253

Table 7.9. *Rankings of RWWO human impacts*

Individual ranking: top three variables	Group ranking: strongest to weakest	Assessors' ranking: top three variables
Empowerment	Knowledge	Relationships
Knowledge	Religion	Empowerment
Life/health/security	Relationships	Life/health/security
	Empowerment	
(Fourth: religion)	Life/health/security	(Fourth: tie between religion, knowledge, and work)
	Inner peace	
	Art	
	Work	

1.7.4. *Religion*

The goats were related to religious experience in two ways. One is that most women prepare goats for sale at Eid al-Azhar, and this adds a different layer of significance to the goat rearing because they are used for sacrifice. The other (which was a stronger felt impact) is that in two villages, because of the goats, the families were able to sacrifice a goat at Kurbani Eid, whereas previously they had not been able to.

1.7.5. *Negative impacts*

Participants also identified the following negative impacts:

- *Relationships* While the women's relationships with each other had strengthened, some faced tension with male relations. The tension arose from the women's group meetings rather than from the acquisition of a goat and was to some extent counterbalanced by goat income.
- *Leisure* The women had less time just to sit and relax because of the meetings and need to collect additional fodder.
- *Emotional/motivational cost if a goat dies* In Phase I a number of goats had died; a few others had died after giving birth only once. The women who had received loans for these goats were quite upset by this. The group activity was not a sufficient end in itself; successful goat breeding was necessary to give the group direction and motivation.

It was not easy to know how important these negative impacts were in comparison with positive impacts. A ranking exercise that included both positive and negative impacts did not seem feasible (The question 'how *dis*-valuable is "emotional disappointment" in comparison to the "values" of empowerment or increased economic security?' is flawed, because the impacts are rationally incommensurable, either because they differ in kind or because they are different practices that relate to the same dimension(s) of value.[13] Thus we could only ask that the rankings of positive

---

[13] See Finnis (1997: 216 and 227–32).

254 *Three Case Studies*

impacts be done by feelings while keeping the 'negative' aspects in mind. For example, the positive impact on life/health/security might be tempered by the risk associated with goat fatalities and the emotional cost this would entail. Similarly, the loss in leisure did not seem very important at all (perhaps it was constructed only in response to a sense that assessors wanted to identify negative impacts). And the tensions with the men may have been inherently linked with the advances in empowerment. Given the importance and difficulty of knowing whether or not information on negative effects *is* reflected in the rankings, further work on this issue is necessary.

1.8. *Interpretation of rankings*

Thus far the assessors have (i) asked questions about the activity, (ii) obtained information about particular practices or sets of practices or sets of human ends that (ii*a*) pertain to various dimensions and (ii*b*) were impacted by the activity, and (iii) facilitated a ranking of these impacts by three different groups (participants, NGO staff, assessors). But how is this information to be interpreted? *Are* these identified impacts necessarily enhancements of valuable capabilities? What is the status of this ranking? Can it be used in the future or only at present? Does it provide theoretical information *about* a community's values or is it the facilitation *of* a decision-making process that would need to be re-done on each occasion? Clearly responses to these questions can only be preliminary and significant further research is required. However, a set of hypotheses might be constructed as follows.

The rankings are contingent, changing, internally plural value ascriptions. Participatory rankings probably partly reflect the *magnitude* of change that has occurred (how much was learned); partly the *importance* of this change with respect to the common commitments (e.g. the importance of religion) and in terms of the local *context* (the presence or absence of previous activities, the degree of interest in the activity, the relative disempowerment of women). But rankings do not give a full description of common commitments or values because they mostly evaluate the changes exemplified by the particular activity in question. Furthermore, there are conflicts between individuals within a group, and the changes in ranking might reflect internal group dynamics rather than changes in values. The validity of the rankings *across time* will evolve as the impacts of the activity change *form* and *magnitude* (more income is earned or the group dynamics shift) and as the surrounding context and the *values* of the community shift. It would be possible to disaggregate these components somewhat by tracking the form and magnitude of tangible impacts (as has been done for income); however, rankings such as those done by RWWO participants embrace all three, and thus a change in ranking from one period to the next could reflect a change of any kind.

1.9. *Incorporating additional benefits*

The last query is how to evaluate the further costs and benefits. They might be divided into two classes: those for which some sort of price may be attributed (whether or not the price represents the *entire* value of the cost/benefit) and those that cannot be priced. Before addressing this issue it may be worth noting that had the social impact assessment not been carried out, the question of how to price these further effects would not have arisen because this information itself would not have been obtained.

In terms of the former class, there are the benefits of information regarding inoculation, worming, the treatment of sick animals, and general goat care. Value might be attributed to such increase in knowledge or human capital in several ways. First, the survival rate of both breeding goats and kids in this region could be compared with the rates for regions that have not received training and veterinary support. Secondly, the returns to training might be estimated in a way similar to the returns for education more generally, by comparing the average income of trained women with untrained women in the region. But it is difficult to do so for returns to informal training in a small sample, and no comparison group was constructed. Thirdly, one could argue that the financial benefits *already* incorporate returns to goat-related training, because goat productivity would have been lower had training in animal care not been provided. This position will be adopted, on the understanding that some unpriced residual knowledge-benefits remain.

The other benefits—relating to relationships, empowerment, and religion—are 'intangible' although these outcomes, as any others, might be attributed temporary prices or weights on several grounds, such as their contribution to social capital[14] or indeed the rankings of participants themselves presented above. But, besides the arbitrariness of this pricing exercise, it seems to obscure rather than clarify the question of whether or not capabilities have expanded, because if benefits are priced and aggregated then information about what these benefits *were* is lost, and might only be represented by a total sum. Rather, such outcomes may be described and explained (as above) and further indicators of their nature provided. Section 7.4, below, will make use of the information in this form.

The RWWO activity was a worthwhile investment in economic terms, although the fragility of this conclusion was shown by the large error margins of the shadow wage rate, which were broad enough to include both positive and negative net present values. Therefore in this case the further information on human impacts would not necessarily have affected an evaluation in economic terms.

In the next two case studies the cost-benefit analysis and social impact assessment go in two different directions. The impact assessments from these cases generate the information on changes in functionings that has none the less occurred.

2. LITERACY AND COMMUNITY DEVELOPMENT

2.1. *Introduction*

The Khoj literacy activity is carried by the strength of its impacts on empowerment rather than income. It is a prime example of an activity that, if evaluated only by traditional criteria, would no longer be funded. An analysis based on criteria such as

---

[14] See Narayan-Parker and Pritchett (1997).

the total number of graduates who have achieved literacy since 1994 (forty) or are now studying (twenty-six), the unit cost per graduate, the income generated by the income generation component, the projected future socio-economic benefits of this human capital improvement, or the institutional strengthening of Khoj as an institution would conclude that Khoj is too expensive, too risky, and too 'weak' institutionally to merit funding.

Khoj is a prime example of the value of assessing 'intangible' human impacts of activities. For in light of these, it becomes *entirely clear* that Khoj has had a fundamental and transformative impact on the women students. Had an assessment of Khoj only reported on economic, or even 'literacy' impacts, it would have omitted the most significant impact.

Also, Khoj strongly raises the problem of weighing incommensurable objectives. For given the rarity of such strong impacts of women's empowerment and their relevance to literacy participants' own objectives as well as Oxfam's, this grant, which was eight times larger than the goat loan, benefited less than half the number of women, and failed to generate income, can still not be summarily dismissed. Clearly if an alternative proposal had a similarly strong effect on empowerment *and* also had a successful income generation component, that proposal would be preferable to Khoj. Also, if it had a similar outcome at lower cost it would be much preferred. But, if Oxfam had to choose narrowly between all alternative activities that *only* generated literacy and/or income, and Khoj, it is a matter of judgement, I argue, which of the two proposals would be more suitable investments.

The following sections elaborate these findings. First, the activity is introduced. Secondly, a cost-benefit analysis is done. Thirdly, further benefits and costs and their weighting are discussed. Finally, the possible ways of making a decision in light of both the economic and intangible impacts are discussed.

Between 1994 and 1997, Khoj literacy activity received 717,000 Rs (£14,416) for the purposes of setting up pilot projects of literacy and income generation. The literacy programme was conceived as an entry point into community development. It was based on the 'phonetic' method of Paolo Freire. This method employed the use of 'code' words to teach the students different sounds and to begin a discussion on how the word relates to the women's lives. Examples of (Urdu) code words were: reading, rights, cleanliness, abuse, health, divorce, and food. After learning the code words, the women could that very day generate other written words using the same letters, simply by thinking about the sounds and trying to figure out how to write the new words down. So in addition to literacy, the programme taught *topics* that were of relevance to the women's lives and the *process* of independent thought and discovery of one's own knowledge. Both were intended to bring about women's empowerment. After women attained literacy, the activity intended them to learn and immediately implement an income-generating skill and thus concretize their empowerment. This expectation of future income was the primary incentive used to attract and maintain enrolment.

Khoj opened pilot literacy centres in three areas near Lahore: Sadhpur, Badrwala, and Ghaziabad. Of these centres, Sadhpur closed after one class attained literacy but did not succeed in the income generation component. Badrwala was suspended due to logistical difficulties (the cost of taxis to transport the literacy instructor) rather than to a lack of community interest. In Ghaziabad, sixteen women completed the literacy course on 17 November 1996. Ten new students started class in July 1997, and the centre also began teaching twenty-five primary school children using the same method. In March 1997 Khoj opened a second centre in a different section of Ghaziabad, which was attended by one class of sixteen women and one additional primary school class. Two of the three teachers of these classes were themselves graduates of the first class in Ghaziabad. Box 7.2 describes the activity in context.

2.2. *Reasons for attending literacy classes*

The students begin to attend the literacy programme for several different reasons. Most women want to be able to read the bills and know how to discuss their cases with electricity officials if they are overcharged. Many (most) of the initial students had fathers or husbands who were heroin addicts and felt that if they were educated, their ability to address this problem would increase. In addition, the male income was not stable, so additional income was necessary for subsistence. One woman was married to a science teacher who has two masters' degrees. He would not walk with her or talk with her because she was illiterate and uninteresting. Her goal from this course was to be able to talk with her husband and to walk with him.

In contrast quite a few of the students at the new centre were unmarried. They thought that if they became educated, they would be able to marry a better husband, and might be able to tutor children in their new homes, thus contribute to household income. The younger women also realized that if they were literate, they would be able to write letters to their family from their husband's house.

2.3. *Current income*

Most women hoped to be able to earn a better income and hoped that literacy would permit this. Nearly all students did some form of handiwork for cash—either embroidery or making infant clothes out of second-hand sweaters. But women's wages were depressed. For example Sabra, 35 years old, was married to a man who was also a heroin addict. To supplement his erratic income, she embroidered dupattas (headscarves). One dupatta earned 12 to 13 Rs and took two to four days, spending two to three hours per day, to complete. Her income per month was 100 Rs (or one day's expenses or one male's *daily* wage) on average. This was normal: Zeenat, her mother, and two sisters all embroidered dupattas and wove chairs, and together earned 500 Rs per month.

2.4. *Poverty assessment*

All women involved in the literacy course came from poor or marginally non-poor families. This observation was based on questions asked about income and on home

Box 7.2. *Descriptions of human impacts by graduates of Khoj literacy class*

In Ghaziabad, a peri-urban slum area near Lahore, living conditions are crowded. Families share houses, renting one room each with a common courtyard; some do not have electricity for fans in the summer; children play around open sewers; many husbands are heroin addicts. Yet in this neighbourhood, a quiet transformation is taking place: women are learning to read.

They come, in classes of ten to sixteen, to a room of someone's house, six days a week for two hours. That is a lot of time for a poor woman in a busy household. But as one student told a neighbour, trying to convince her to come to the school, 'your work will never be over—mine isn't; so just leave it for two hours'. Many women bring their primary school aged children, who are taught in a separate room using the same method. Classes are taught by women from their very neighbourhood—more often than not the teacher just recently attained literacy herself.

Many people say that literacy is just instrumental. And it is surely instrumental—literate women can read the numbers of buses or the labels on foods; they can open bank accounts and read electricity bills. But in Ghaziabad literacy is much more. 'Graduates' from the literacy class gather weekly to read together and so continue to deepen their knowledge about everything from the nutritional value of carrots and chick peas to the causes of breast cancer to the etiquette of discussions. Perhaps more significantly, though, the literacy programme has brought about deep changes in their sense of themselves as women.

For example, take the case of Shabnam, 32 years old, who was illiterate and is now a teacher at the school. She was married at 16, has two sons and two daughters, and lived with her husband and mother-in-law. She poetically described the effect the programme had had on her life as overturning the assumption that only men can make decisions: 'Women think they are like a bud—that they do not understand with our own eyes. But we are not buds, we are mountains. We can do anything with our lives. So I tried to open my eyes, and my eyes were opened. From this kind of experience, one's very humanity becomes energetic.'

Another significant example is a graduate called Nargis.[1] Nargis is a woman who was illiterate and wanted to be a doctor. She is now literate and teaches primary school children to read. But perhaps more significantly, like Shabnam her family situation is transformed. Prior to her class, neighbours reported that Nargis was unusually badly treated at home. She was very frightened of her husband and would often be absent from class if her husband was sleeping—she did not know if he might wake up and need a glass of water. Subsequently she has gained confidence—her classmate explained that all of them had learned one very important thing, which is that 'We are equals with men. Someone should not beat us; if they do, with love, politeness, we should suggest that this is not a good road, this is to be retreated from.'

In one incident, the ability to read was dramatic. Four to five months after Nargis had begun the course, she was washing clothes at home. She took down her husband's suit to wash it, and, noticing that there were papers in its pocket, removed them before soaking it. But when she took the papers from his pocket, she realized that these were divorce papers; they had been prepared in a registry office and her thumbprint had been forged. She was very nervous to have discovered these but took them swiftly to the elders of her family. These elders met with the elders of the husband's family, and the situation was eventually resolved without a divorce. But when all was over, her husband asked her, 'How did you *know* what these papers said?' 'I can read now,' she replied quietly.

Note: [1] Name has been changed.

visits to each of the students' homes. The average family size was nine persons and incomes varied, with the highest being nearly 6,000 Rs per month. Drug addiction was a problem, hence incomes were difficult to specify because the men did not work regularly. If a man were to work regularly—six days a week at 100 Rs per day (reported earnings were 80–150 Rs per day)—he would earn about 2,400 Rs per month. For example, Shumaila's brother earned 2,400 Rs per month cutting mirrors; her other brother earned 1,500 Rs per month from making and marketing envelopes. Given that in 1995–6 the per capita poverty line was roughly 500 Rs per person, a family of nine would require 4,500 Rs, or two regular male salaries, to function above the income poverty line. Traditional female employment would not support a family.

2.5. *Cost–benefit analysis*

The costs of Khoj are wages, training, stationery, travel, utilities, rent, and miscellaneous expenses associated with the administration of the literacy activity. Table 7.10 shows the financial costs of Khoj.

2.5.1. *Wages*

Khoj has employed four to six persons continually since its inception in 1994; it does not have a voluntary component. These persons include one or two teachers (paid 1,000 Rs per month for four hrs. per day), one secretary (paid 1,000–1,500 Rs per month, part time), one supervisor (paid 2,500–6,000 Rs per month, part time), and a project coordinator (paid 7,000–8,000 Rs per month, part time).[15] The breakdown of the wages between this staff is shown in Table 7.11. The teachers' salaries are slightly low in comparison with other urban teachers (which would be nearer to 1,200 Rs in 1997) and also with the unskilled male wage. The supervisor and project coordinator were hired on a competitive market, and no shadow wage is necessary in principle, although it is unclear why the secretary's wage varied so much. The project coordinator's wage might be artificially inflated, as we discussed for RWWO, so a shadow wage of 5,500 Rs per month, part time could also be estimated. The teacher salaries sometimes directly benefited a teacher who was previously beneath the poverty line; it might therefore be asked if these costs should be discounted to indicate their social value.

The above figures are in nominal terms; real salaries fell during the project due to inflation. For the remainder of this section, references to wages are given in 1997 prices (as this was the time when the study was carried out); however, in the analysis all figures were then converted to constant 1994 prices using the consumer price index.

---

[15] Oxfam justified the significant expenditure on the secretary, supervisor, and coordinator's salaries by the nature of the project as a 'pilot' project, and by the significant hope that Khoj would develop a methodology that could be scaled up at a later stage. It is worth mentioning that Oxfam does not usually support administrative salaries to this level.

Table 7.10. *Financial costs of Khoj (in nominal rupees)*

	Wages	Training	Stationery	Travel	Utilities	Rent	Misc.	Total	In 1994 Rs
1994	122,000	0	19,965	19,496	1,159	35,500	7,423	205,543	205,543
1995	166,000	6,867	11,945	25,756		35,658	5,004	244,363	212,596
1996	199,100		10,420	36,275		35,450	4,774	286,019	223,953
1997	30,000		4,000	9,273		22,200		65,473	43,139
Total									685,231

Table 7.11. *Khoj staff and salaries (in nominal rupees)*

	1994			1995			1996			1997
	Salary	Months	Total	Salary	Months	Total	Salary	Months	Total	Total
Coordinator				8,000	12	96,000	8,000	12	96,000	
Supervisor	7,000	12	84,000	3,083	12	37,000	5,925	12	71,100	26,000
Secretary	1,500	12	18,000	1,000	12	12,000	1,000	12	12,000	
Teacher	1,000	12	12,000	1,000	12	12,000	1,000	12	12,000	4,000
Teacher	1,000	5.5	5,500	1,000	9	9,000	1,000	8	8,000	
Surveyor	2,500	1	2,500							
Total			122,000			166,000			199,100	30,000

The women participants in the literacy programme also faced the opportunity cost of giving up two hours a day in order to study. In practice this time was difficult for women to find, and those who did attend had to sacrifice leisure activities, and negotiate with male household members. Initially teachers went door to door to persuade students to come. Valuing this opportunity cost of time is difficult.[16] These women do sell hand-embroidered scarves or knitted infants' clothes to middlemen. One dupatta earns 12–13 Rs and takes two to four days, spending two to three hours per day, to complete, which nets an actual wage of 1.6–2 Rs per hour. Alternatively, the wage could be zero, to reflect the fact that the household output did not decrease from literacy. Or (unrealistically, but in the same manner as for the goats activity), the shadow wage for women's time could be equivalent to the local unskilled male hourly wage of 12.5 Rs per hour. The alternative shadow wages of 0, 2, and 12.5 per will be used.

Khoj began by renting one location and since the end of the first six months has rented two locations for its activities, at 500 Rs per month. The rent goes to relatively well-off families in a depressed area, that is, persons who were marginally above the poverty line. In addition, the activity contributes 2,000 Rs per month to the cost of an office rent in a wealthy neighbourhood of Lahore, which Oxfam justifies by the 'pilot' nature of this activity.

2.5.2. *Economic benefits to literacy graduates*

The intention of Khoj's non-formal literacy programme was for students to attain literacy in twelve to eighteen months and subsequently to begin an income generation activity that would provide a sustainable income. This was a common understanding between the Khoj staff and students and was a significant factor motivating most students. However, there were no functional income generation activities at the time of assessment. Paper-bag-making was tried in both Sadhpur and Ghaziabad; it failed outright at Sadhpur, because the work was perceived as difficult and low-paying. In Ghaziabad several women temporarily earned 1,000 Rs per month, which was a strong improvement, but then prices dropped due to the popularity of plastic bags so the initiative had to be abandoned. A plan was under way at the time of the assessment to pilot-test the use of an elastic-making machine.

It is often argued that 'human capital formation' such as the building up of literacy skills will increase the potential income a woman can gain by external employment. Thus education can be valued by its social and private economic returns. For example, Psacharopoulos estimated social and private returns to education by region.[17] Using data from 1975, Psacharopoulos estimated that the private returns to primary education in Pakistan were 20 per cent and the social returns were 13 per cent. Burki and Ubaidullah estimated the returns to primary education in the informal

---

[16] See Corbett and Stewart (1994).
[17] 1994 (these figures are controversial because of the data on which they are based; see e.g. the discussions in *Journal of International Development*, 8/3 (1996)).

sector of the nearby area, Gujranwala, to be 4.69 per cent (they estimated returns per year of schooling at 5 per cent).[18] Their rates could be taken as the most accurate local estimation available. If the 5 per cent figure were accurate, then one might estimate the mean annual income of a woman graduate.

$$\frac{\text{mean annual income of literate woman} - \text{mean annual income before literacy class}}{15 \text{ months} \times \text{income loss/month} + \text{cost of study}} \Rightarrow 5\%$$

But there is a fundamental problem: these estimations are not for *adult* literacy students who will then enter the *female* labour market.[19] On the one hand literacy is likely to have a higher opportunity cost for a woman than for children, even though this is difficult to value. On the other hand, a number of studies, including Psacharopoulos's, argue that the returns to education are higher for females, even after adjusting for the selectivity bias (that the girls or women who seek education may have made a prior decision to work after their studies). Yet local indications in Ghaziabad showed that the market for female employment was effectively missing. This means that a simple adjustment of the male rate of return will be inaccurate, as the women's economic returns will be sensitive to the low rate of female participation in the labour force, which was 7.15 per cent in Pakistan's urban areas in 1993–4.[20] In Ghaziabad, women mostly keep quite strict purdah and could not walk more than a few hundred metres from their home even with a burqah or full-length veil (which is why a second centre had to be opened only a half mile from the first, because the women in the new area were not permitted to walk as far as the first school). The only graduates of the first literacy class in Ghaziabad, eight months after finishing, who had employment other than handicrafts (which they had done before literacy training), were the two teachers employed by Khoj. The earnings functions of those doing handicrafts had not changed since they became literate nor had their output increased.

In this setting, the returns to literacy will depend not only on women's actual productivity, entrepreneurship, and signals to employers, but also on the creation of an appropriate female job market. Burki and Ubaidullah's study in Gujranwala found that earnings from self-employment in the informal sector increased sharply with age and experience (the study focused on skilled work in the informal sector, such as craftsmen, repairmen, construction workers, and so on). This finding might underscore the potential value of Khoj exploring self-employment activities for

---

[18] (1992); see also Burki and Abbas's (1991) study of 1,058 men which found that human capital investments are rewarded similarly in the informal and formal sectors.

[19] For a discussion of the distinctive concerns of women in South Asia see S. R. Khan (1993), Haq and Haq (1998).

[20] From the Government of Pakistan's Economic Survey (1996: 104). This is the percentage of women over the age of 10 who are in the labour force. The comparable figure for males is 64.66 per cent. Nationally, women comprise 13 per cent of the labour force and earn 20 per cent of all earned income (UNDP 1998). See also Schultz in King and Hill (1993).

women. But the primary barrier to female employment is their inability either to work outside the home (if they wish) or to undertake lucrative employment that can be done within the home.

Given that the expected economic benefits of women from the literacy programme are not clear, and are highly dependent on external circumstances, I have estimated the internal rate of return using different assumptions:

1. that graduates' *average* income would increase from 160 Rs to a mean of 500 Rs per month and that that increase would remain in effect for five, ten, or twenty years (i.e. some graduates may earn more; others will not increase earned income although they may still improve health/children's education);
2. that graduates' average income would increase from 160 Rs to a mean of 1,000 Rs per month (as it had, briefly, for teachers and those who produced paper bags in their homes) and remain in effect for three or five years;
3. the graduates' income would increase from 160 Rs to 2,400 Rs per month (the unskilled male wage), and that increase would remain in effect for one or two years (highly unrealistic, but included for the purposes of comparison).

The actual economic benefits were that one graduate of the first class had obtained employment of 1,000 Rs per month for approximately 60 per cent of the time since completing her course; several graduates had earned 500–1,000 Rs for several months only; the rest had seen no change in income. The average current income of women graduates interviewed was 124 Rs, but there seemed to be some underreporting, as women had not always included income from knitting baby clothes in this figure, so it has been adjusted to 160 Rs per month.

As Table 7.12 shows, in situation *A*, the internal rate of return at all wage levels is negative over a five-year period but positive over ten or twenty years, such that the programme would be beneficial at a social discount rate of 3 per cent. In *B*, if the

Table 7.12. *Internal rates of return under varied wage and benefit estimations*

Assumptions	A[1]			B		C	
Additional income and time	*5 yrs.*	10 yrs.	20 yrs.	3 yrs.	5 yrs.	1 yr.	2 yrs.
	Rs 500	Rs 500	Rs 500	Rs 1,000	Rs 1,000	Rs 2,400	Rs 2,400
IRRs							
High shadow wages	*−10%*	8%	14%	5%	23%	−4%	71%
Med. shadow wages	*−6%*	12%	17%	14%	36%	16%	93%
Low shadow wages	*−5%*	12%	17%	16%	37%	20%	95%

Note: [1] Column *A* (entries in italics) is most likely.

income lasts only three years, the IRR at the highest wage frame is zero; returns to the other wages are at 14 per cent and 16 per cent; at five years all wage levels have very strong IRRs. If all women earn the male wage for one year, the IRR is still negative at high wages, but positive at low and medium wages. In the unlikely event that all women were to earn a male wage for two years only, the IRR would be strongly positive. By far the likeliest best-case situation is a relatively modest increase in average income (the first column of A, which is in italics). Its internal rate of return is negative. If one instead assumes a ten year increase in income and wages, the switching point at a 3 per cent social discount rate is for each woman to earn an extra 240 Rs per month. If there is a distributional weighting of 1.1 (10 per cent), then the switching point is 216 Rs. To put this in context, the daily expenses of an average household are 150 Rs; a woman would only have to earn enough for a day and a half of household expenses each month for the literacy approach to generate net economic benefit. But in a different context, at current wage levels, she would have to embroider over sixteen dupattas, taking nearly 100 hours, or four half-time weeks, to earn this money.

2.5.3. Conclusion of the cost-benefit analysis

The conclusion of the cost-benefit analysis is highly dependent upon future income streams. Present data suggest that even the most mild assumption (an increase to an average of 500 Rs, over five years) was not met, nor will be met without further input from Khoj or a change in the female labour market. In this case, the result of the cost-benefit analysis is clearly negative. The activity does not yield net economic benefit, hence should not be funded.

But is this an appropriate use of CBA? A more common approach to the economic evaluation of social activities such as literacy or health clinics—that recommended by the 1996 World Bank *Handbook on Economic Analysis*, for example—is to identify the desirable level of cover and then analyse alternative options for providing the desired cover of service using a least-cost analysis (to identify which is the most cost-effective). In setting a desired level for literacy, one still considers the social benefits of literacy *vis-à-vis* the benefits of alternative investment possibilities such as income generation activities, but literacy is seen as a 'good', a product, valuable in itself.

A least-cost analysis would not actually be accurate in the present case because the women were motivated to join the literacy course in the expectation of economic benefit. Where there is such a divergence between individual and social utility functions, it would be difficult to create demand for literacy on its own. In practice, the women might not choose, or might not be permitted to join a course if they knew this would not affect their productivity.

But if literacy were only instrumental to income generation, then the benefits from resources devoted to literacy would have to be compared with the possible benefits from other more direct or more successful income generation activities (the urban equivalent of goats). One way forward would be to return to the observation that women's returns to literacy were blocked by the social constraints to female employment. For example, consider that the earning potential of literate women is x times higher than the earning potential of illiterate women, which is (w). However, literate women face a social constraint to realizing these potential returns, *s*. If the constraint is in place, their earning function is the same as illiterate women; if it is removed, the potential returns may be realized.

Earning function of illiterate women:	(w)
Potential earning function of literate women	$x(w)$
Social constraints on female employment	s
Earning function of literate women in presence of s	(w)
Earning function of literate women without s	$x(w)$

If this is the case, then clearly the only way for Khoj itself to assist the women in generating income and give the overall activity a positive IRR (leaving aside for now the question of alternative uses of resources) would be for Khoj to assist women in addressing *s*. It may be that non-formal education provides one component of addressing *s*, because this method of literacy has changed (as we shall see) women's self-understanding and generated curiosity about the authority of social conventions, and generated local leadership. But likewise there may be imperfect information regarding female self-employment, or regarding opportunities for within-household employment, or regarding the effective marketing of handicrafts, that also contribute to the social constraint, and that Khoj could address more directly.

2.6. *Further benefits and costs*

Table 7.13 sets out significant additional costs and benefits from the literacy classes.

In addition, female education might be valued not for its prospective economic returns but rather for its social returns, such as the effect on child's health and attitudes towards children's education (which did change), or on contraception prevalence. For instance, some students expressed the hope that they would be able to help their children with their homework. Others discussed the changes of their understanding of nutritional and hygiene practices. It is difficult to predict, much less value, such changes accurately, however, and to do so requires value judgements. Therefore they will be treated discretely in the following section, together with the other valuable impacts, and the values of participants will be employed.

Table 7.13. *Additional Khoj costs and benefits*

	Costs	Benefits
Khoj		Develop curriculum
		Pilot-test method
		Increase capacity
		Job satisfaction
Graduates	Relationships	Empowerment
	Leisure	Inner voice
		Knowledge
		Relationships
Society		Women's status
		Female human capital

2.7. Identifying Khoj impacts

The participatory impact assessment exercises were conducted twice. The first time was with the students who had graduated (twelve out of sixteen came; one was ill; three had moved away). The second time was with all of the students who had begun one month before. Their responses are given in Boxes 7.3 and 7.4, in their own words. The graduates identified the strongest two impacts as being *knowledge* and *empowerment*. Knowledge in this case meant being able to read, the knowledge they had gained from classroom discussions of code topics, and also their new ability to communicate with others. Empowerment indicated their awareness of what they themselves could do and be.[21] The new class identified the strongest two impacts as *knowledge* (with the same appreciation of learning how to communicate, as well as learning to read) and *inner peace* or heart's voice (their sense of satisfaction at being able to study). The impacts are described in Boxes 7.3 and 7.4.

Box 7.4 shows the impacts of a class that had been in progress for a month. Note that these students are much younger; only a few are married.

2.8. Ranking Khoj impacts

The impacts were ranked by students from both literacy classes. In contrast to the goat programme, the ranking was done by the group, which was not in this case dominated by one or several women. When two items could not be ranked above or below the others, they were both given the same value (e.g 1*a*, 1*b*). The director, who was not present during this meeting, was asked, separately, to rank what she thought the impacts of the course had been on participants. After the study was complete, and without referring back to any previous rankings, the assessors themselves also ranked the impacts of the activity (in relation to other activities assessed). Please note that 'abuse' was added by the graduate class as a variable which was perceived as distinct from the others (empowerment and relationships).

Each of these rankings is presented in Table 7.14. The rankings show that the activity was perceived to impact knowledge, inner peace (or, as they put it, the heart's voice), and empowerment very strongly. It is also clear that there was substantial effect on life/health, and in the category of 'friendships or relationships' (which the graduates did *not* understand as including the marital relationship—hence their addition of 'abuse' as a separate category). 'Heart's voice' and 'empowerment' are two sides of the same coin; the first largely inner; the second largely outer.[22]

---

[21] It is an interesting footnote that the empowerment impacts have persisted. For example, four years later the woman referred to as Nargis in the above story has since claimed title to her ancestral lands and is a candidate in the local bodies election (personal communication, 19 April 2001).

[22] The literacy classes perceived the categories 'heart's voice' and 'empowerment' to be quite similar. Facilitators suggested that empowerment referred to the (external) ability to make valuable decisions; heart's voice to the (internal) integration of thoughts, feelings, and actions and sense of peace with oneself.

Three Case Studies 267

Box 7.3. *Graduates*

Category	Schematic description	Examples
Empowerment	That women are equal to men; daughters to sons	SHABNAM. Women think they are like a bud—that they do not understand with our own eyes. But we are not buds, we are mountains. We can do anything with our lives. So I tried to open my eyes, and my eyes were opened.
	That women do not need to suffer abuse	ZEENAT. When we came here, we did not talk about our problems. After coming here, we learned how to discuss things, not to quarrel.
		ZARINA. I learned I could do something about abuse; before I had fallen a lot.
	That women can decide what is good and bad	REEFAT. My mother and father did not allow girls to speak; they would beat us. Now I have learned to trust my own talk, and ability to judge that this is good and this is bad …
	Literate women can solve own problems	My heart has become strong. I can speak about my rights, can even slowly, politely, tell my parents that they have done something wrong. We have begun now to talk with them about the difference between sons and daughters, that we are equal. 'Literate people can solve their own problems'.
		ZEENAT. When I read I realized that women are as prepared as men to make decisions … Before they didn't let us say even one word. But now we notice it doesn't feel good. I can decide for myself … We are equals with men. Someone should not beat; if they do, with love, politeness, we should suggest that this is not a good road, this is to be retreated from.
Knowledge	How to read About 'code' topics Time management	ANVARI. I am very happy. Learned to save money, to save time. People in the house waste time. They waste money. We ourselves work hard, come to the centre, give the husband time, and give time to the kids.
Work	If income increased …	NARGIS. Now I am a teacher

Box 7.3. (*cont.*)

Life	Knowledge of health, nutrition, good food preparation and water treatment, and hygiene practices	NARGIS. We read the code khorak (food). We knew that we are poor, we cannot drink milk, eat many foods; we eat little meat. We learned that it was not necessary; there are not as many vitamins in such things. Chick peas are 4 rupees a pound, and they have many vitamins. Apples are expensive; carrots are not. But carrots are good for health—as good as expensive things ... About the code 'cleanliness': they talked about sweeping and washing dishes and keeping the house clean ... Before our house was not clean—people used to spit where they were, and flies would sit in it and then come to the food. So this was not clean. Now, before we do any work, we wash our hands, and keep our nails short. Since my child was born, there were always skin problems; I learned about them. I learned about dangerous diseases from flies and bugs. We should put lids on food so flies don't sit on it. We should wash vegetables.
Relationships	Good among centre Many had to struggle to attend classes	My Auntie is mad sometimes that I come. I say that I respect her, but I want to bring some good changes in our own lives. ZEENAT. Unity is essential for all humans; we have unity here in this centre.
Inner peace	Satisfied with being able to study and be educated	ZEENAT. My brothers used to sit on a chair and read. I wanted to be like that. The heart's voice said that if you will learn and write, and want to, you can. SHABNAM. It is also in our religion, that if you are educated, and you educate another (or help the sick or ill), this is sawab (a holy act).
Religion	Jinns leave the educated alone	SHANNAB. Our prophet said that we could study, and that for educated people, jinns (spirits) go far away and have a tough time coming back. They get tired.

	Box 7.3. (*cont.*)	
	Can read religious books/challenge religious practices	NARGIS. We have more knowledge now, because we have read books about the religion—like which religious leaders are saying bad things, and which good. Our people say that in our religion, women cannot go out. We reply: 'Show us'. It is not written. We have gotten this knowledge from this centre. Observation: There was quite an active and informed discussion on whether or not religion required the burkah (heavy veil). SHABNAM. First I prayed five times a day. Now it is so busy I can't even pray one time. I praise with my life. I think this is what we must do.

Box 7.4. *Descriptions of human impacts by new students in Khoj literacy class*

Category	Schematic description	Examples
Empowerment	For some (not others) the decision to attend class had been a first independent choice	GOSHI. I think that after studying I will be able to decide for myself what is good and bad. BUKSHA. I told my father I would come here—he was at first angry, then said go. I decided first for myself. RAJIA. In our house there are difficulties, because the old people make all the decisions. I had to get permission to come here.
	Hope to develop own judgement	NUXANA. Now I am little (16 years)—I cannot decide for myself. My brothers and parents decide.
	Learn to interact with strangers	SHAMSHA. Confidence is being born after a bit—I can talk to others now. Before I could not. GULNAZ would not speak, so her classmate explained, 'Before she was always taught to be silent. Now she speaks a little bit. It comes, slowly slowly.'

Box 7.4. (*cont.*)

Knowledge	Are learning to read	BUSHRA. I can make ten words from one code—I make them up from my own mind.
Work	Time management	GOSHI. Before we worked all day. Now we work harder, till 11, and save lots of time—time easily is made.
	Study is satisfying	NAZIA. Now because there is a responsibility to study, so we do our work quickly and come to the centre to work. That is why they opened the centre. So we make the time to study. I am very satisfied with the studies.
Life	Students have done the code 'cleanliness'	NAZIA. I learned to keep things clean. This is good.
Relationships	Learning to speak softly and to discuss not fight.	SHAMSHA. I have learned to speak with love to the other, and to speak slowly and make sure I am understood.
		NAZIA. I have learned . . . how to speak with my in-laws. Before we spoke very quickly, and fought. We learned to speak slowly, give an answer instead of fighting. Do not fight. Do not fight with them. Educated women do not fight—it is a thing of understanding.
	Relationships with classmates	RAJIA. Before we did not sit together; now we sit and hear the other's griefs. [MAFIA: '. . . and talk about clothes.'] It seems good to me.
		SHAMSHA. Here it is nice but when we go back to the home we are stressed again. Because of stressful problems at home with relationships—and things are very expensive, and so even to make ends meet is very difficult.
Inner peace	Strong	MAFIA. There is a very big change in my inner voice since when I did not study. I want to be a teacher. And I try hard. I want to do it, and I surely will do it. This is my desire.
		NUXANA. My heart's voice is happy. Reading is a good work for my life.
		SHAMSHA. My heart tells me to read, to write. To be able to talk to someone out of your own understanding, that will be a good thing. It is a good thing that each should do this work.

	Box 7.4. (cont.)	
Art	(no impact)	Kanisa. My heart wants to read.
Religion	(no impact)	Shamsha. God does not give us cooked food. We could not cook it by prayer. With our own hands, we cook. Without our own hands, nothing can be done. So we should work hard and then ask God to help us.

Table 7.14. *Rankings of Khoj impacts by different groups (from strongest to weakest)*

Khoj coordinator rankings	Graduate class's rankings	New class's rankings	Assessors' rankings
Inner peace	Empowerment =	Inner peace =	Empowerment =
Empowerment	Knowledge	Knowledge	Knowledge
Knowledge	Life/health/security	Empowerment	Inner peace
Life/health/security	Abuse	Relationships	Life/health/
Work/play	Inner peace	Life/health/security	security =
Relationships	Religion		Relationships
Abuse	Relationships		Religion
Religion	(Work varied)		(Work varied)

Therefore it can be taken as an overall sign of empowerment that one or the other were in all cases taken as the strongest impact of the literacy programme.

While ranking does serve to order the perceived 'impacts' very roughly *vis-à-vis* each other, it does not give a good idea of how deep in fact these impacts were compared to the impacts of similar activities in other areas. This would have been simpler to evaluate had we studied other non-formal literacy programmes among women. Therefore in order to evaluate the comparable depth of very different impacts, we conducted a qualitative ranking across activities along the 'dimensions' of development to which participants responded, as described in Chapter 6, Section 3.2.2.

3. ROSE CULTIVATION

This final case study is the one with which the reader is by now familiar, involving Dadi Taja and others in the village of Arabsolangi, Sindh.

3.1. *Activity and participants*

In 1994 Oxfam allocated 23,645 Rs for an income generation activity in Arabsolangi. Unlike the two other case studies, this activity was 'operational' in that rather than allocating funding to a local organization directly, an Oxfam Program Officer, in this case Safia Ali Nawaz, undertook direct responsibility for generating the funding proposal, overseeing the activity and, in the process, for building the capacity of the local Women's Organization. Part of the initial grant was a revolving loan to be repaid by the participants in the initial income generation activity, and managed in the future by the Women's Organization.

Arabsolangi is an agricultural village of 280 Muslim and Hindu households located near a main road. It has a male Village Organization (VO) founded in 1983 that had 160 members in 1996, and a Women's Organization (Marvi WO) founded in 1994 that had 105 members of whom 30 to 40 were active. Both organizations required monthly savings, and had received assistance from NGORC (NGO Resource Centre), a national NGO that strengthens local non-governmental organizations.

Oxfam selected the Marvi Women's Organization because Oxfam wished to support income generation activities, and Marvi WO had indicated in a conference of local organizations that (i) they wished to begin income generation activities for women, and (ii) they wished to expand their institutional capacity to manage this type of activity. The specification of the activity and the identification of participants was undertaken jointly by the WO, one Oxfam officer, and others in a series of public meetings.

At the initial public meetings, participants (at this point there was no defined group) decided what kind of income generation activity they wished to initiate, and who to invite as participants. Roses were proposed, and after soil tests, cultivation of roses was selected as the activity. Participants were selected on grounds of economic need (the lowest income, most children, other family members unemployed), with the exception of a male and female activist, who were involved to manage (learn to manage) the activity. The final group included six women and four men, aged 20 to 38. Two men and two women were married; two women were widowed and one divorced; all were unemployed. Three of the ten persons were not WO/VO members, for they were unable to pay the membership fee. All women were illiterate except the female activist, who had a BA. Two of the male members had passed metric (one was later replaced by his sister, who again was illiterate), one could write Sindhi, and one, the VO activist, had a BA. Half of the members lived in mud houses; seven households were landless; two farmed 1 acre each; one had leased 2.5 acres but had harvested no crop from it. The two activists were not among the poor; the other members of the rose group were.[23]

---

[23] This, and much other information, was cross-checked, in this case by informal discussion and house visits to each member and to other households that WO members and others identified as the 'very poorest' in the village.

3.2. Technical implementation

As roses had not been cultivated in Arabsolangi previously, Safia first arranged for the soil to be tested by an agronomist from Khaipur/Sukkur, who found that the activity was viable. She arranged for the two male members to visit a 60-acre rose plantation to the south, and also a Hyderabad plantation, from which they procured the first 200 rose bushes (at that point women other than the female organizer were not able to travel). A tractor was hired for the levelling of land. The bushes were planted in the first week of March 1995. Consultants came and trained the tanzeem members in the care and picking of roses.

3.3. Participation

Although Oxfam was directly involved in this activity, its involvement had facilitated rather than hindered local participation, especially of the poorest, at all stages of the activity.[24] One very rough indication of the depth of participation was the degree to which the initiative was taken locally. When two or three of the rose plants were diseased, two male members went into Khairpur and sought assistance to treat the disease and prevent its spread. Also, the making and selling of garlands was not originally planned. This initiative and the decision as to how the profit would be divided (40 per cent for salesmen; 10 per cent for thread and threaders; 50 per cent for tanzeem and members' shares) was managed internally by the group, between Safia's visits. Also, there was adequate management of work even when membership fluctuated. At certain times members were unable to work due to ill health or pregnancy. They arranged their own substitutes. For example, the husband of one woman did his wife's share of fieldwork during her pregnancy. In another case, when one man found a job elsewhere, his sister (who fitted the original criteria) took his place.

3.4. Cost-benefit analysis

Land for the rose field was leased for two and a half years from 1995–8; at the close of this time in June 1998 Oxfam formally ended their involvement with the rose cultivation activity. The financial figures used below are those given at the end of this period, were verified, and have informed the cost-benefit analysis. I last visited the activity in June 1997; the woman's project officer then visited Arabsolangi twice after the close of the activity in 1998 and did a final impact assessment using the method described earlier.

---

[24] Sindhi-speaking Safia, who grew up in Khairpur and Hyderabad in an academic family, was often referred to as 'one of us', meaning of the Solangi caste and village. She considered the factors that contributed to this to be her use of simple clothes, her practice, at the initial stage, of staying overnight in the village; her willingness to speak about personal and political as well as project issues, her genuine interest in the activity. She also spoke 'country' Sindhi and would sit on the floor or the charpai, not on a chair. People compared Safia favourably to other visitors who had come for survey purposes, and wore city clothes, sat in chairs, and did not stay or eat in the village.

3.4.1. Material costs

The activity received Oxfam support of 23,645 Rs (£529) of which 16,000 Rs was intended to be a revolving loan that the WO could then re-use for other purposes. The support was used to pay for land levelling, to procure the rose bushes and purchase tube roses (which were lost due to poor storage conditions), to lease the land, and purchase stationery and fertilizer.

The costs are itemized in Table 7.15. The costs of thread were borne by the threaders; water was free, and the initial cultivation expenses included sufficient fertilizer for the period.

3.4.2. Wages

Four overlapping groups of persons were involved in the rose cultivation activity. The tanzeem members were supposed to maintain the rose plot, weed it, and periodically water it (this was physically demanding). This took about one hour a week. Every morning during some months, and periodically during others, two 'harvesters' would go to the plot just before dawn and pick the rosebuds—this took 20 to 30 minutes. These were brought to a home, where children and adults sat together and threaded the roses to make garlands—these people are called 'threaders'. The whole process took an hour to an hour and a half. Finally, male 'sellers' would hang the garlands on a stick, wrap them with a wet cloth, and take them by bus to a market to sell, averaging an hour and a half per trip.

Wages were paid to the threaders and to the sellers. The tanzeem had decided among themselves that sellers were to keep 40 per cent of their profits from garland sales and return 60 per cent as profits. The threaders were paid 5 Rs for their help—which generally lasted less than an hour. The rose tanzeem members (who included the two pickers) did not receive any wages for their part in weeding and maintaining the rose field; rather, the activity was set up such that profits would be shared equally among the ten rose tanzeem members, with an eleventh share going to the Women's Organization, as mentioned earlier.

Table 7.16 shows the actual wages paid over the course of three years, and the shares returned to tanzeem members. For purposes of comparison, I have calculated shadow wages based on the price of 10 Rs per hr. in 1995 prices, and re-converted these to nominal prices. Keeping in mind that this converts to 11 Rs per hr. in 1996 (which was the year of the goat-rearing figures), this seems a standard low male

Table 7.15. *Rose project expenses*

Cost	1995	1996	1997
Cultivation expenses	14,064	5,360	0
Stationery expenses	286	0	0
Lease of land	5,400	0	0
Tax	0	0	200
Loan repayment to WO		10,000	0
Total	19,750	15,360	200

Three Case Studies

Table 7.16. *Wages from rose garland production*

	1995	1996	1997	1998[1]
Sellers				
Actual payment received	0	12,003	18,149	17,920
If at 10 Rs/hr, 1.5 hrs/day, 2 people	0	8,736	9,707	10,920
Threaders				
Actual payment received	0	2,317	3,650	4,480
If at 10 Rs/hr, 4 hrs/wk, 3 people	0	4,992	5,547	6,240
Pickers				
Actual payment received	0	0	0	0
If at 10 Rs/hr, 2 hrs/wk, 2 people		2,496	2,773	3,120
Members				
Actual payment received	0	0	0	0
If at 10 Rs/hr, 1 hr/wk, 10 people		4,160	4,622	5,200

Note: Until June. [1] By all accounts the first six months in 1998 produced more roses than the previous two years, so I have doubled the number of hours estimated (which is a bit generous) in comparision with 1996 and 1997.

shadow wage (the same considerations apply here as there). As the contrast between actual and shadow wages shows, the sellers were paid relatively more than the shadow wage, whereas threaders, pickers, and cultivators were paid less.

While the income was small, the relative economic impact for sellers has been significant. One of the teenage 'sellers', Waheed, is the sole support of his family. Another seller and tanzeem member (who, like Dadi Taja, also picks roses and threads garlands), Ibrahim, supports his wife and mother largely on this income. In several other households the rose income from boys is the only regular source of cash, the other sources being livestock or income-in-kind such as food for work.

3.4.3. *Oxfam costs*

The Oxfam input into the rose activity was substantial and, it will be seen, expensive. In the initial three months (introductory meetings, needs assessment, technical feasibility, land levelling), Safia visited once a month, for an average of three days per visit (Arabsolangi is about a five-hour drive from the Oxfam Sindh Office). From March 1995 (planting of rose bushes) until November, she visited every six weeks. After December 1995, Oxfam held one quarterly meeting of about three hours. After Safia moved offices, her replacement, Hidayat, led these meetings. Oxfam did tend to send visitors often to this activity and funded additional activities with the WO and the VO, although the creative input into the rose activity stopped when Safia left. The Oxfam costs for transportation, salaries, and per diem averaged 16,000 Rs for three-day visits; and 6,000 Rs for all other visits in 1996 prices. As before, the cost of transportation and food was competitive; the salary component for Safia and the driver were a relatively small proportion of the total costs, and shadow prices for these components did not affect the sign of the IRR so only actual values were used.

3.4.4. Income and profit-sharing from roses

Table 7.17 shows the income stream from March 1995, when the rose bushes were planted, until June 1998, when the activity closed. The income increased as the rose bushes matured and also because the practice of selling fresh garlands rather than drying the flowers was very profitable (initially the group had dried bushels and bushels of rose petals and made paste and rose-water, but they could not sell it). In practice, the income was also much more seasonal than had been anticipated. For example, rose sales during the month of April 1997 produced 17,618 Rs, which was 48 per cent of the annual income in 1997.

It will be expected that the activity gives a satisfactory internal rate of return. However, this depends crucially upon not the shadow wages of unskilled labour, this time, but on the inclusion or exclusion of Oxfam input. Recall from above that the entire loan was 23,645 Rs, but in 1995 alone Oxfam's in-kind support was valued at 68,040 Rs.

The internal rate of return based upon the actual costs and actual income to the rose cultivation group was 54 per cent. If one replaces the actual wages paid with the shadow wages described earlier, in which the labour time is (generously) estimated, the internal rates of return remain safely above any estimated social rate of discount. For example, at 10 Rs per hour (in 1995), the internal rate of return is 36 per cent. However, when one includes Oxfam costs, the internal rates of return become strongly negative. One might wish to apply distributional weighting, as this activity involved the poorest of the poor. Still, one would need to apply strong weights to reverse this result: at a distributional weighting of two and a half and

Table 7.17. *Income and profit-sharing from roses (in nominal rupees)*

	1995	1996	1997	1998
Income	2,000	31,140	36,797	62,880
Shares distributed	2,000	886	0	53,000[1]

Note: [1] At the time of writing this there was some uncertainty as to whether or not this final figure had actually been distributed to the participants. Oxfam was engaged in verifying that this had in fact happened or else in enforcing its distribution.

Table 7.18. *Rose cultivation internal rates of return (1995–1998)*

Wage level Actual payments	IRR 54%		
Shadow wages	Excluding Oxfam costs	Including Oxfam costs	Including Oxfam and distributional weight of 2.5
Rs 7 per hour	64%	−41%	14%
Rs 10 per hour	36%	−52%	7%
Rs 12 per hour	20%	−60%	2%

Three Case Studies

shadow wages of 7 Rs, the internal rate of return rises again to 14 per cent, which would be above the plausible social discount rate.

The conclusion of the cost-benefit analysis, then, is that while the income generation activity for roses would be viable and indeed lucrative as an economic investment, and while this income would have had a significant social premium because it would have accrued to the poorest households in the village, the high cost of Oxfam support turned what would have been a highly positive social cost-benefit analysis into a strongly negative one.

3.5. *Further human impacts*

The method described in Chapter 6 was initially tried with the rose tanzeem in 1996 and generated significant enthusiasm. Rather than hurrying the process, the women dispersed after a few hours and reconvened to carry the discussion late into the night. A briefer assessment was done again, this time by the new women's project officer in Oxfam, in October 1998. The analysis shown in Box 7.5 builds upon the information from both assessments and also from an interim visit to Arabsolangi in 1997. The box contains selected responses from the first visit in 1996.[25]

Because this was the earliest case study, the qualitative scoring was relatively undeveloped and the ranking was not done. However, the two facilitators later did a rough qualitative scoring on the scale from one to three of the relative impact within different dimensions. These are re-scaled and reported in Table 7.20. Participants ranked impacts at the close of the project.

As that table shows, the strongest impacts of the rose cultivation activity at midterm were on relationships between the women, on art in the sense that the work with roses was creative and aesthetically pleasing, and on inner peace—for the sellers, because they were supporting their families, and for the threaders, because they were expanding what they could do and because the roses were used for shrines and for the Qur'an. In the retrospective assessment in 1998, three dimensions still had a strong impact: relationships, knowledge, and the environment.

4. COMPARISON OF ACTIVITIES

Oxfam has a limited budget and allocates this among competing demands for funds. If Oxfam undertook to use the capability approach, its goal would be to expand the set of valuable capabilities of participants in *each* activity to the fullest extent possible, and to target participants who are deprived of basic capabilities. The further goal would be to choose activities that, taken together, expand participants' basic capabilities relatively more than alternative sets of activities might. This chapter has demonstrated some different kinds of information that would be of relevance to the assessment of three individual Oxfam activities. It has not undertaken a comparative

---

[25] In the final assessment in October 1998 by Hidayat Narejo, the three top impacts were (1) relationships; (2) knowledge; (3) environment (from the 'beautiful' rose garden).

Box 7.5. *Sample comments on activity impact*

'Inner peace' = harmony within self (under ki Avaz)

SASUI. I get satisfaction when people purchase the garlands for holy or religious places. We earn something, and so meet the expenses of children's education.

DADI TAJA. In the early morning, I pick flowers. When I do this, I feel I have done sawab—holy work. Inner peace comes.

Religion

SUGRAH. Each Friday, persons go to Shen Shah [the shrine]. They purchase the garlands. This is sawab. They also purchase garlands for the Qu'ran Sharif.

NUZAKAT. We sell garlands to shopkeepers. Hindus purchase garlands for their Motis and string them over these photos. Muslims use garlands for the Qu'ran Sharif.

Knowledge

SASUI. We want to know—we have expectations—how to save money and reinvest it in others, to teach about our activity. We got training from the consultant. Also, the Hakkim came and told us about rose remedies using water and gulkand.

DADI TAJA. I didn't know how to make garlands, or to keep a rose garden. Now it feels easy. We are the only ones [in the area] who know how to keep roses.

IBRAHIM. I did not know how to use a spade, how to plant, the season of flowers, the care for flowers and protection from diseases. We got training. At the beginning, we prepared only four garlands and no one bought them, because there were only four or five flowers on each and they were crooked.

MIR GUL. We learned that you have to be in a good mood in order to enter and sell in the market—no matter how you feel inside. The first day, I was very shy, serious. I came back—the women told me to change my mood. Now I am successful.

Environment

ASHIQ. There was no park for entertainment. Now we walk in the garden. In these days of pollution we are selling flowers. People feel the fragrance; it puts them in a good mood.

Relationships

NUZAKAT. In the market, before we didn't know the shopkeepers or the bus people.

MIR GUL. In my market, in Bangla, I have contacts with Muslims and Hindus; before I did not. My mother is happy—my father has died, and we now help each other. Sometimes I come late to school from selling. The teachers are understanding because they know my problem—Ashiq spoke to them.

IBRAHIM. My wife and my mother make the garlands and they are happy.

BOYS. Our friendship has become very strong. The unity and love with each other has increased.

DADI TAJA. People in the village now respect me. Before I'd not go into their houses [she sells garlands in the village].

ASHIQ. People from other organizations and villages come to visit our activity. When I go out, often the roses are my introduction to an NGO.

SUGRAH. The relations with Oxfam have increased. They invited me to a workshop; I have met with different NGOs, and gone for an exposure visit to Hyderabad. We also met with Hakims, with gardeners, shopkeepers, and a rose plantation owner.

> **Box 7.5.** (cont.)
>
> SASUI. I have only one son. Before this, I did not allow him to go to the market, for fear of an accident. Now I wake him up myself, and send him away saying, 'Go, may God look after you'.
>
> *Art and aesthetic experience*
> MIR GUL. We make garlands. While we thread them, we feel happy.
> WAHEED. Before, we were just selling dry flowers. Now we sell finished products that we have made.
> SASUI. When I feel sad, when I have a problem at home, I walk in the roses.
> SUGRAH. Whenever guests come we visit the rose garden.
> DADI TAJA. People tell me that the fragrance of roses is always in my clothes.
>
> *Participation*
> BOYS. We four [boys] return from the market and go to school at the same time. Before that we came individually. Now we all work together. If we work alone, it is boring. When we sit together, we discuss things too. We are happy to be together.
> DADI TAJA. It is good. Suppose a woman is not feeling well, we can do each other's work. We have done so many times, to help each other out.
> SUGRAH. When we sit together, we talk of many things. During the meeting of the rose cultivation, for example, we discussed family planning. Two women said they were ready.
>
> *Work*
> BOYS. Sometimes we go late to school. We have work!
> The women thought the activity had no impact on work.

analysis of the three activities. This section will illustrate how such an analysis might be undertaken. The concluding section will relate the case studies back to the theory as expounded in Chapters 1 to 5. It will also point out outstanding issues on which further work is required.

4.1. *Cost-benefit comparisons*

Table 7.19 shows what the information available for comparison across activities would have been if Oxfam had only done a careful cost-benefit analysis of these activities.

On the basis of this analysis, technical comparison between the three activities *would* identify a dominant or optimal alternative. If Oxfam were interested solely in supporting the activity with the highest economic rate of return, it would shift *all* of its resources into goat loans for poor women. Distributional considerations would not affect this decision, because the participants of all activities were poor women.

If Oxfam were interested in *increasing* the rate of return in each of these same activities it might build into this analysis some further considerations regarding the possible market failures identified in the course of cost-benefit analysis. For example,

280   *Three Case Studies*

Table 7.19. *Comparative efficiency indicators (all prices in constant 1992 rupees)*

	Goats	Literacy	Roses[1]
Total Oxfam grant	63,400	506,329	16,764
Number of direct beneficiaries	140	66	10
Number of years in operation	5	3	2
Plausible IRR without distributional weights	20%	−6%	−52%
Total estimated income per beneficiary from project	6,058	190 (?)	3,630
Annual estimated income per beneficiary	1,102	190 (?)	2,286
Socio-economic status of women	Poor	Poor	Poor
Market viability	Yes	No	Possibly

Note: [1] I have counted as beneficiaries only the ten members of the rose cultivation group, and assumed all profits to be distributed. The threaders' income in constant 1992 rupees was a total of 2,211 Rs or an annual income of 885 Rs. The sellers' income was a total of 7,339 each for an average of four sellers, or 2,936 Rs each per year (in 1996 rupees, the threaders' income was a total of 3,482 Rs, or an annual income of 1,393 Rs. The sellers' income was a total of 11,558 each for an average of four sellers, or 4,623 Rs each per year).

it might encourage RWWO to shift its support for goats, after an initial phase, from credit to insurance. Similarly it might devolve responsibility for the rose cultivation project to the local WO (making the IRR positive), and provide technical support as necessary. It would endeavour to assist Khoj to (i) decrease costs or expand operations to reduce overhead costs per graduate, and (ii) add a functional income generation component.

If Oxfam were interested only in providing social investments that corrected for clear market failure, it might shift funds out of goat rearing and rose cultivation, both of which might arguably become financially sustainable, to female literacy. The rationale for doing so might be that the 'output' of the literacy activity—empowerment—was a 'good' itself, and also that it could be a means of reducing the social constraints that blocked female participation in the labour market, so might lead to private economic returns in the long term. Literacy, unlike the other activities, would *not* attract private investment, so required outside support.

Yet the impact assessment exercise also in all cases identified additional impacts that were not reflected, or were only partly reflected, in the quantifiable costs and benefits. Therefore if Oxfam were evaluating the three activities against its goal (of expanding the set of valuable capabilities of disadvantaged participants in *each* activity to the fullest extent possible) these changes in capabilities would also need to be considered.

These capabilities changes were diverse. There are clear problems in translating these benefits—which include nutrition, security from saving, friendships with goat owners, knowledge, and the aesthetic value of a newborn goat—into quantifiable and commensurate measures. The impact assessment methodology can only go beyond social cost-benefit analysis if it provides a way to combine the quantitative information with the qualitative information on wider impacts in a way that is more

Three Case Studies

structured and durable than 'keeping in mind' intangible effects (Ch. 6, Sect. 2.1). How can a comparison of activities on the basis of capability change proceed?

4.2. *Comparison of capability expansion*

4.2.1. *Operational definition of capability*

In Chapter 5, Section 3.2, I proposed the following operational definition of capability:

Long-term goal: to increase the basic capabilities people have without contracting their overall capability set, which requires one

(a) to identify long-term valued capability goals and strategies (e.g. with participation);
(b) to work in the short term to establish functionings instrumental to these goals;
(c) to implement a strategy such that negative freedoms are safeguarded;
(d) to mitigate the contraction of wider capabilities that occur as a result of expanding basic capabilities (where possible, to allow both to expand).

Thus I proposed that an assessment of capability expansion would be incomplete if it did not include information regarding: change in functionings, the valuation of that change, freedom, and plural principles including efficiency and attention to the full menu of capability expansion and contraction.

If this definition is applied to the three case studies, then, I suggest, one will identify relevant grounds for activity comparison. How does the information raised in the three case studies feed into such an assessment? The next four sections describe information that relates to each sub-component.

4.2.2. *Identification of changes in functionings*

The impact assessment exercise gathered information on changes that had occurred. Some information was about functionings; other information related to instrumentally valuable changes. The 'reported' changes from the impact exercise were positionally objective perceptions of change. These reported changes were further investigated quantitatively and anecdotally.[26]

The changes were reported in two ways. First, the functionings were identified, and descriptions of these functionings in the participants' own words were noted.

---

[26] For example, the magnitude and projected income generated by the goat activity was estimated on the basis of both the kidding rates and sale prices women recalled, and on outside investigation of the breeding patterns and market value of the relevant goat breeds in that region. The impact this income had on basic functionings was tracked by asking women how it was spent (and by whom). Examples ranged from the purchase of foodstuffs to the construction of a house, or the purchase of coloured paint for a house to the purchase of a goat for sacrifice. Some goat owners preferred to build up a herd of goats, thus increasing their economic security by retaining the kids. The magnitude of change in income was put into perspective by inquiries about male and female earning functions in the participant households, and by obtaining local present market prices for a consumption basket of food to compare with nationally published data.

These have already been presented in the case studies. But it would not be possible or relevant to compare changes in particular practices or functionings between the activities because few particular functionings if any had changed in all three activities. Hence, the impacts that related to each dimension of human flourishing were compared. The procedure of this comparison was described in Chapter 6, Section 3.2.5.

The qualitative ranking of the three case studies by the assessors appears in Table 7.20. The starred numbers indicate the three most significant impacts as identified by the participants and reported in the case studies above.

This information complements the cost-benefit analysis. How? From the cost-benefit analysis, we identified whether or not income was generated, and also, if it was, how it was spent. Nearly all expenditure related to functionings that were valued because they contributed to the dimension of life/health/security (food, shelter, more goats for economic security, education in so far as it would increase earning potential), with a small proportion going to functionings that were valued for other reasons (knowledge, beauty, relationships). And indeed we notice that for the goat activity, which was the most lucrative, the functioning changes related to life/health/security were among the most valued. But the other functionings—relating to empowerment, or relationships, or knowledge for example—are much less strongly associated with income. The earlier discussion argued that they were not fully incorporated in the cost-benefit analysis. Yet these functionings did change, and their change was positively valued by participants, and also perceived as significant by assessors comparing different activities. So at a minimum the table conveys information about the kinds of functionings that the project most affected. It enables one to see at a glance which areas were most strongly impacted in each activity.

Table 7.20. *Qualitative ranking of impacts by facilitators (5 = intense impact; 0 = no impact)*

Category	Goats RWWO	Literacy Khoj	Roses Oxfam[1]
Life/health/security	4*	3–4	1
Knowledge	3–4*	5*	5*
Work/play	3–4	1–5	0–5
Relationships	4–5	4–5	5*
Beauty/environment	2	0–1	5**
Self-integration/inner peace	4	4*	5**
Religion	3–4	2–3	3
Empowerment	3–5*	5*	3

Notes: [1] This case study was the first to be graded, and used a scale of 1 to 3. I have recorded a value of 1 as 1, a value of 2 as 3, and a value of 3 as 5, in order to translate it roughly to the later scale.
* These impacts were the top three ranked by participants.
** The three rose impacts at mid-term included inner peace; at final term this was replaced by the environment.

4.2.3. Identification of valued capability change

Long-term valued capability goals and strategies are identified by the group(s) whose capabilities will be affected, or in such a way that they give informed consent to these goals, and can re-evaluate the goals and strategies at different points in time.

The 'freedom to choose' might be operationally expressed at two levels: group and individual or subgroup. The first regards the freedom a group has to exert self-direction: to create and sustain their identity even if it differs from the identity of the funding agency, for example. Thus if they genuinely regard public education as undesirable, understand the implications this choice will have on their community, and re-evaluate this position periodically (as the Amish in the United States, for example), they would be free to opt out of public education. The second regards the ongoing freedom a participant has to go against the stream and fast, for example, even though the community wants to be well-nourished, or even though someone's identity differs from the identity attributed to a group by a funding agency. The lines between these are blurred, because clearly the abilities to choose are interdependent. If the majority enjoys rock music, then although the individual may not be coerced into listening or partaking of this kind of music, her capability to enjoy traditional musical forms will be severely curtailed because public performances of this music will decrease.

In each of the case studies, the ongoing discussion of the value or otherwise of the particular initiatives was partly represented by 'participation'. There are various ways of characterizing participation—who participates, at what stages—represented, for example, by records of meeting frequency and attendance. And there are various ways of exercising participation—in the choice of objectives, sequencing and strategies, in the administrative responsibility, in the provision of property and human resources, or in other ways. The focus of the three case study assessments was on the extent to which participation institutionalized a process of communication about values, such that activities focusing on basic capabilities were tailored to participants' wider values.

The qualitative indicators piloted in the three case studies (Ch. 6, Sect. 3.2.5) were quite simple overall assessments of actual participation in an activity, as well as of the degree to which implementing agencies were interested in and able to encourage participation. When more than one level was expressed by an activity, either in different places or by different parts of the organization, or when facilitators' responses differed, the ranking was expressed as a range.

Table 7.21 suggests that although participation was a procedural component of each of the case studies, its exercise differed in degree. The rose cultivation activity dominates the others: it was the most participatory, it involved the greatest spectrum of village groups; the capacity for and interest in participation of the implementing agency was the greatest. The goat-rearing activity was more participatory than the literacy activity.

A simple comparison of these degrees of participation is not equivalent to an indicator of capability. For example, the women may not have valued the need to make

284   *Three Case Studies*

Table 7.21. *Qualitative ranking of participation (5 = very participatory)*

Category	Goats RWWO	Literacy Khoj	Roses Oxfam
Implementing partner's capacity for participation	4–5	2–3	5
Interest in participation	4	2–5	5
Actual participation			
Who *significantly* influenced the choice and form of activities besides the NGO	Participants	Participants	Participants, women's group, men's group, community leaders
Women	4	3	5
Men	1	n.a.	5

choices and to participate.[27] Also, as mentioned earlier (Ch. 6, Sect. 3.2.5) the indicators here are a work in progress; qualitative variables would be better expressed by giving both context-dependent and context-independent scales.

Yet this information (informed by site visits and interviews) does enable one to affirm that none of the three case studies involved coercion or project initiation without consultation of the local group(s). They indicate that some system was in place for ongoing communication between the agency and the participant group, such that participants could modify their activity. These indicators are rough and should be improved, but even at this level of crudeness, they may be useful. For example, a simple comparison of family planning systems between China and Kerala would have reflected the very stark differences regarding the 'capacity' and 'interest' in participation, as well as in the 'actual' levels of participation.

4.2.4. *Efficient expansion of functionings*

The efficiency of each activity in terms of income generation has already been discussed in the cost-benefit analyses. One might undertake further analyses of the efficiency of capability expansions by using least-cost analyses or unit-cost comparisons, for example. The outcome of the capability assessment in this aspect would commend the same kinds of efficiency-enhancing measures as the CBA.

4.2.5. *Capability contraction*

During activity planning and implementation, there was no explicit procedure for suggesting that the expansion of the directly intended capability or capabilities might cause other capabilities to contract. In some Oxfam activities this issue may have been attended to inadvertently. For example, Oxfam occasionally funds 'visits' by one community which is interested in beginning a women's organization or a

---

[27] In other case studies, not included here, participants complained precisely because so much of their time was spent just talking and planning activities. In such cases, a 'high' indicator of participation would not capture the dissatisfaction participants expressed.

micro-credit initiative, for example, to another village which already has one in place so that they can hear about the village's experience of an activity and ask questions about any of their possibly wide ranging concerns. However, in the three case studies, site visits did not take place. Rather, women's and men's concerns were answered, to the extent that they were raised explicitly, by the social organizers.

This being said, participants did in all cases identify some functionings that had been negatively impacted by the initiatives.[28] In so far as these impinged upon the capabilities of participants, these might indicate capability 'contractions' that had occurred within the time frame of the activity (recall that many 'contractions' in capability may not be visible immediately, and may have a cumulative rather than immediately apparent effect on cultural and institutional forms). The extent to which negative impacts were understated is not clear.

4.2.6. *Capability comparison*
How can these different forms of information inform a decision? An assessor who was comparing two activities aimed at capability expansion could base his or her decision on the following information:

1. a social cost-benefit analysis, which accounts for all economic costs and benefits that can be accurately estimated;
2. the description of positive and negative changes in valued functionings from the holistic impact exercise, which is assumed to be a relatively complete account of the change in the overall capability set;
3. the ranking values of the most significant functionings and their associated dimensions of value, which identify the relative strength of the impact in the eyes of beneficiaries. This is to be done separately for positive and negative impacts;
4. the qualitative ranking values of these impacts by facilitators, which can be used in cross-activity analysis;
5. the degree and kind of 'participation' and self-direction exercised in the activity;
6. further information from standard assessment tools and activity history that would clarify the activity's relationship to other principles of evaluation.

To illustrate the above points, in the goat-rearing activity, the assessor would notice:

1. The internal rate of return for the activity was greater than the range of plausible social discount rates. It fell beneath the SDR, when the shadow cost of labour for the women equalled the male unskilled wage rate, although the switching value of distributional weighting was 1.1. In the segmented labour market at present, alternative employment opportunities for women do not have this wage rate. Therefore, if one either adopts the mild distributional weighting or the middle wage, the internal rate of return is highly positive.

---

[28] Examples of negative impacts were: goat deaths, the loss of tube roses, the moulding of rose petals from moisture, the conflict with family members in the literacy activity.

2. The participants identified a range of benefits other than the generated income.
3. The participants strongly valued benefits that related to knowledge, empowerment, life/health/security, religion, and relationships. While some of each of these may have been correlated with income, income does not fully represent these benefits.
4. The qualitative rankings showed that the activities' impacts on knowledge and empowerment and life remained strong when compared with other activities.
5. The qualitative rankings showed that RWWO had had a high degree of participation.[29]

How does this information help in comparing activities? One way is that it draws attention to aspects of that activity which might be improved. For example Khoj is a clear example of the kind of project the World Bank *Handbook* describes as an activity in which the intangible or qualitative benefits are significant but evade accurate pricing and so must be 'borne in mind'. The Khoj literacy programme had the strongest impact on empowerment of the three case studies (and indeed of all the Oxfam activities evaluated), and also had a strong impact on knowledge, but failed to generate significant income (although there were some exceptions, such as the two women employed by Khoj as teachers). This underscores the need to incorporate empowerment impacts into Khoj's assessment, as the cost-benefit analysis excludes these benefits altogether (benefits can only be correlated with income if income is generated). But how is this incorporation or 'taking into account' to occur? In the present case, there seem to be two clear conclusions:

1. Khoj's work would clearly be improved if it impacted the earnings function as well as empowerment. Therefore if an alternative were available that had a positive economic assessment while still evidencing the same empowerment impacts, or if the current initiative could be modified such that its income generation component were improved (and the other impacts did not decrease), this alternative would dominate the current one.
2. If there were a choice between Khoj and a clearly successful income generation activity that did not have the same projected impacts on knowledge and relationships and empowerment, and if Oxfam had itself the capacity to support either equally, then *neither option would clearly dominate the other.*

The other way that the information assists comparisons is more subtle and more significant. It relates back to the distinction between technical and moral reasoning (Ch. 3, Sect. 2). For if neither option clearly dominates another, as perhaps in these three cases, then these three activities represent a case of 'fundamental (or assertive) incompleteness' (Ch. 1, Sect. 2.4). That is, more information will not lead to a unique optimum; the choice cannot be made on technical grounds but rather is a morally significant choice. In this case the additional considerations that can enter are 'feelings', that is, of fairness, and considerations of identity (Ch. 4, Sect. 2.4). If

---

[29] This information was corroborated by comparison with four additional Oxfam activities, in relation to all of which RWWO's qualitative impacts remained strong.

Oxfam had to choose between alternatives of this kind—some of which were better for efficiency, some of which were better for empowerment, it could (i) decide arbitrarily or (ii) make a policy decision to prefer one objective (cost-effectiveness) over another (empowerment) when they conflict and, consistent with this, develop appropriate expertise, or (iii) choose activities on different grounds—for example, choose to work with 'the poorest' and allow these groups to identify the activities they wish—and develop broad expertise. In any of these cases, the identification and relative valuation of the impacts by several agents has more clearly identified the implications of different courses of action. This clarity is the subtle and significant function of the capability assessment described here. To return to Robbins's quote:

There is nothing in Economics which relieves *us* of the obligation to choose. But, to be rational, we . . . must be aware of the objective implications of the alternatives of choice. For rationality in choice is nothing more and nothing less than choice with complete awareness of the alternatives rejected. And it is just here that Economics acquires its practical significance. It can make clear to us the implications of the different ends we may choose.[30]

Although the choice remains underdetermined, the identification of valuable capabilities did bring to bear more complete information regarding each of the three activities than alternative methodologies of assessment might have.

5. RELATING PART I AND PART II

Chapter 1, Section 1 argued that 'without some specification—and simplification—the capability approach cannot be used efficiently. The challenge is to simplify it without introducing significant distortions in the process.' It also offered to make those simplifications explicit, in order to invite criticism and modification of them. This final section re-contextualizes the methodology presented in Part II within the framework of Part I. It identifies and begins to evaluate the simplifications which were introduced. It also notes the extent to which the case studies illuminate the strengths and weaknesses of the framework.

5.1. *Practical reason and plural principles*

Chapter 3 discussed the concept of 'ethical' rationality proposed by Sen. It suggested that the pursuit of human development could be represented in the principle 'in voluntarily acting for human goods and avoiding what is opposed to them, one ought to choose and otherwise will those and only those possibilities whose willing is compatible with a will toward integral human fulfilment'.[31] It further proposed that plural specifications of these principles, such as 'efficiency within reason', be used in the assessment of human development activities. These principles could rule out certain options if 'dominant' options existed which generated the same benefits more efficiently, for example. The principles could also clarify the considerations

---

[30] 1932: 135–6.   [31] Grisez *et al.* (1987: 128).

that are to be taken into account in any fully rational free choice. They could not act as an 'umpire' principle and remove fundamental incompleteness.

Chapter 3 then proposed that the principles be 'starting points' for dialogue regarding the value or otherwise of development activities (Ch. 3, Sect. 3.3). An assessment of the adequacy of the methodology needs to look at (1) which rules it employs (and what assumptions it makes in areas where principles are not employed), (2) how adequately it employs the rules it does, and (3) whether the value of employing a rule justifies its cost.

The impact assessment methodology made a limited use of these principles. The operational definition of capability focused on two principles. It drew attention to the efficiency with which functionings were provided. In the case studies the cost-benefit analyses (in other cases these could have been least-cost analyses) provided information by which to assess whether an activity had *employed efficient means to objectives*. Secondly, the operational definition drew attention to the effects that the provision of a new capability had on extant capabilities. Knowledge of these effects would enable a community to judge whether the activity enabled them to '*have a harmonious set of purposes and orientations*',[32] or whether it displaced other significant activities, or caused the capability menu to contract.

This focus on two principles to the neglect of others is insufficient, because, on Finnis's approach, an alternative for action could satisfy several principles but be deeply unethical on other grounds. Therefore it might be helpful to reconsider the full set of principles of practical reasonableness—even if it is not feasible or necessary to study each of them—in order to clarify the assumptions one is making, or the information that one has, in relation to each of them (Ch. 3, Sect. 5.2).

It would be inaccurate to say that no information on other principles was generated by the impact assessment exercises. For example, the information on the full range of functioning changes helped to operationalize the principle, *do not leave out of account, or arbitrarily discount or exaggerate any of the dimensions*. This is because it brought into view dimensions of changes that otherwise might have been left out of account or arbitrarily discounted (it was not a full operationalization, because while advocating this community discussion of goals in light of the identification of valuable impacts as a 'climax' it did not require or report on it—Ch. 6, Sect. 3.2.4). In so far as this methodology successfully identifies capabilities that had been negatively affected, it would help to evaluate the principle prohibiting *deliberate harm to any dimension of human well-being*. Finally, if (and only if) the identification of changes in capabilities or functionings catalysed a discussion of the value conflicts or inconsistencies, and of the evolving local identity, then this discussion process could have further enabled communities to *harmonize practices and commitments with each other*.

The process of participation itself also could, in the best cases, embody other principles. For instance, in so far as participation is used to tailor basic needs activities to local priorities and sequences, it helps to operationalize the principle *not to attribute*

---

[32] Finnis (1980: 103); emphasis added.

to any particular project the overriding and unconditional significance which only a dimension of human flourishing and a general commitment can claim. This is because situating a basic needs activity such as a health clinic within the other priorities of the community (for a cemetery, a road, and a secondary school perhaps) helps to temper any overriding enthusiasm to devote *all* local resources to health if in fact this is not the most urgent need. Participation may also *foster the common good*, by stimulating reflection and collective action on common issues, and helping to bring into or keep in the picture people whose needs and interests might otherwise have been overlooked. It may also enable participants to act according to their *conscience*. At times the opposite could occur (as when a participatory decision fractures a community, or requires an individual to act against her conscience in order to implement it). Indeed, none of these potentially positive occurrences may in fact occur, which is why such scrutiny may be very valuable.

The methodology does not have any systematic mechanism for assessing *sustainability* or *discrimination*. Rather, it was assumed, and partly observed, that Oxfam would sustain its activities and would not discriminate arbitrarily (a targeting of disadvantaged groups is not arbitrary).

These linkages between the participatory procedures, NGO procedures, and the principles that are not systematically studied in the assessment methodology will vary on a case-by-case basis.

Still, as Chapter 3 argued, none of the principles is an 'umpire' principle, and it could be that, all relevant information will not identify an optimum alternative, but rather there will be incompleteness. This is not a new problem.[33] For example, the social impact assessment methodology described earlier (Ch. 6, Sect. 3.1.1) was criticized because it raised a number of issues without having clear 'decision criteria' that coordinate them. And clearly 'trade-offs' between sustainability, growth, and distribution, for example, represent the need to make decisions informed by three principles when there is not one dominant outcome. One deep weakness of SIA was its inability to provide decision criteria. Does the methodology proposed here do any better?

The methodology focused on generating information about valuable capability change, and using cost-benefit analysis as only one component of an assessment of human development activities. It did not treat in depth the problem of combining this information to reach a decision. The criteria discussed earlier were understood to apply. Also Chapter 4 worked towards decision criteria by articulating the value of self-direction and the principle of subsidiarity. Information about the extent to which decision-making was localized is indicated in the qualitative indicators of participation. But evidently many issues are left unresolved, such as how considerations of 'feelings' and 'identity' enter when the decision taken is on behalf of a community, and what to do when one agent's choice is contested.

---

[33] The 'basic principles' of an environmental impact assessment, for example, evaluate whether an initiative is: purposive, rigorous, practical, relevant, cost-effective, efficient, focused, adaptive, participative, interdisciplinary, credible, integrated, transparent, and systematic.

The depth of this problem is likely to be cross-cutting and significant. The case studies exemplify an 'incomplete' ordering. And they also demonstrate how even inefficient options could be defended by virtue of what they do contain that competing options do not. One suspects that in practice the information could merely provide a tool for rationalizing a decision made arbitrarily or on other grounds.

But what would fill the gap? We have argued that the purpose of plural principles is to rule out alternatives, although in many cases incomplete orderings will still result. The 'gap' might instead be filled by a decision-making procedure, as Finnis suggests.

... much remains to be settled by individual and group commitment in accordance with discernment of feelings and fair procedures of collective or representative decision making. The essential role of feelings and emotions in individual life and action is closely paralleled by the essential role of procedures for decision making in the life and action of communities; in each case, that role is beneficial so long as subordinated to the fundamental reasons for action (basic human goods) and to the standards of unfettered practical reasoning (moral principles and norms).[34]

Earlier I criticized Nussbaum because her account of capabilities required a theory of political obligation that may not be uniquely required, and that certainly did not take into consideration the institutional capabilities of different states (Ch. 2, Sect. 2.2). It would be a similar error to propose any particular 'decision-making procedure' here. One can, however, recommend that such a procedure be developed, and that it respect the principle of subsidiarity, and the requirements of practical reasonableness.

To conclude, the methodology simplified the framework in Part I by operationalizing only two of the possible principles of practical reasonableness. I have argued that in order for this simplification to be adequate to assess the 'practical reasonableness' of alternative options, one would need to state clearly (and if possible substantiate) the assumptions one was making regarding the other principles, relating, for example, to sustainability, equity, and fostering the common good. Furthermore, the methodology does not specify (i) which agent(s) are to make a decision regarding the activities to be funded after the capability information is collected, nor (ii) by what procedure this decision is to be made. I have argued that one should not specify these processes universally. One can only specify that the issue can be addressed by the development of an appropriate procedure, and that an appropriate procedure should respect the reasons mentioned by Finnis in the quotation above, and also the principle of subsidiarity discussed earlier.

5.2. *Dimensions of development*

Chapter 2 proposed that one way to identify the relevant valuable capabilities for the assessment of an activity is to focus on the 'value' term. Finnis proposes that human

---

[34] Finnis (1997: 233).

values are not infinitely diverse; rather, the intelligible values that people actually hold (whether or not these are moral all things considered) reflect combinations of fundamental reasons for action that can be grasped by reflection on one's practical experience. I called these reasons for action 'dimensions of human development'. The pursuit of these dimensions, or the actualization of human potentialities that they express, contributes in its own unique way to the well-being or meaning of a human life. I proposed that the *value* of any valued functioning could thus be represented as a coordinate in *n*-dimensional space, where the dimensions (axes) are the dimensions of human development (or integral human flourishing), the *n* countable elements of d_i. Chapter 2 proceeded to discuss various lists of human needs, values, and capabilities in order to study what the dimensions might be, but did not put forward a single list.

The methodology employed in the field used a working list of dimensions that included: life/health/security, knowledge, relationships, meaningful work and play, empowerment/participation/practical reason, religion/spirituality, the environment, and self-integration/inner peace. Clearly the value of many local practices and functionings would be a combination of these dimensions. Yet the methodology involved asking systematically about each dimension of value (recognizing that there would be multiple interpretations of the dimension, and that few if any practices would relate neatly only to one dimension), in order not to overlook any kind of valuable capabilities. How do we assess this 'simplification' and specification?

Clearly the three case studies do not comprise an empirical 'test' of whether or not these dimensions adequately represent incommensurable kinds of value. The number of people was too small and the exercise was designed to use the dimensions to generate information about capability change—not to test the dimensions (which would be a valuable but distinct undertaking). Furthermore, as the dimensions represent the *reasons for acting* that are used and recognized by persons, the provision of empirical data could not 'prove' the completeness or otherwise of the reasons (Ch. 2, Sect. 3) although it could support or challenge the list in the manner described by Grisez, Boyle, and Finnis.[35] That being said, two observations can be noted.

5.2.1. *Is a complete set of valuable capabilities necessary, or is a subset of 'crucially important' capabilities sufficient for evaluation of capability expansion?*

First and most importantly, the impact rankings constructed by participants highlighted the need to consider not only the 'set' of basic capabilities that were the direct focus of activities, but also the expansion or contraction of other capabilities. For the rankings showed that changes in the subset of capabilities related to material deprivation (which was a direct focus of income generation activities among the poor) were not uniformly valued more than changes in other capabilities. The descriptions of impacts by participants reinforce the suggestion in Chapter 4 that the introduction of novel practices has a number of related effects. This is by no means a

---

[35] 1987, sects. IVA and IVC.

new thought and has been postulated by basic needs writers consistently.[36] Yet the overriding importance of certain basic capabilities has often been assumed anyway for convenience, and thus empirical data about wider impacts has not been collected. Sen distinguishes his capability approach from basic needs precisely on the grounds that it is applicable to developed as well as developing countries, to situations in which the capabilities of interest are complex or refined rather than basic. Yet he writes 'for some evaluative exercises, it may be useful to identify a subset of crucially important capabilities dealing with what have come to be known as "basic needs" '.[37] But if the valuable capabilities of the absolutely poor are wider than 'crucially important' capabilities, *and* if the goal of development is to expand valuable capabilities, then information about the change in 'crucially important' capabilities is insufficient to evaluate whether or not the capability set has expanded or contracted.[38] The evidence from the case studies highlighted the need to consider both the changes in the income-related subset of capabilities that were the direct focus of activities, and the changes in the capability set overall.

5.2.2. *Do the dimensions impose values?*
Secondly, although no general conclusions are possible, the case studies did indicate that the dimensions of development seemed intelligible to participants, and enabled facilitators to identify and report valuable capabilities that they would not have thought to inquire about otherwise. In this way it seems that the methodology enriched the information used in analysing activities. The methodology aimed to identify a 'complete' set of valuable capabilities. It is not possible to state whether the identified set was 'complete' or 'complete enough' for the evaluation (further testing would be necessary to assess this); it is only possible to say that it enriched the capabilities information.

The use of the dimensions in this methodology might be challenged further. For example, it will be argued that this method of presentation used for qualitative rankings—that is, ranking impacts according to the 'dimension' of value with which they were predominantly associated (Table 7.21)—'imposes' the taxonomy of the evaluators on participants, and/or suggests to them the values they 'should' have. Two responses might be made. First, this criticism is partially acknowledged, in that assessments done subsequent to the case studies began by asking open-ended questions, and only introduced the strategic questions about unmentioned dimensions of impact if the respondents had systematically excluded them.[39] But the widespread assumption that open-ended questioning is sufficient for identifying changes was

---

[36] e.g. Stewart (1985, ch. 1). 'Contrary to Maslow's theory of a hierarchy of wants ... even people who are deprived of very basic physiological needs do consume non-basic goods and services.'

[37] 1993*a*: 40.

[38] As Salmen put it, 'a key challenge of poverty reduction is to penetrate the institutional web of the poor, which encompasses legal and religious practices, the role of the family and its effect on child rearing and education in order to assist the poor in achieving what they consider a better life' (Salmen 1992: 3).

[39] Ch. 6, Sect. 3.2.2, the second method described—the change was also made partly because it was faster this way, and partly because beginning with open-ended questions made for an easier atmosphere.

challenged by the studies. The dimensions were introduced when they were not mentioned spontaneously because it was hypothesized that participants may have 'assumed' that facilitators were not interested in this particular kind of impact (Ch. 6, Sect. 3.1). Therefore while this introduction *may* lead to biased information (for then participants might 'generate' impacts in order to 'please' the facilitator), the *absence* of strategic questions may also have included a bias, which the strategic questions aimed to correct. Further empirical tests are necessary to see how to minimize both kinds of bias.

For example, in one assessment (of a training workshop), participants had been engaged in animated discussion about impacts for about a half an hour. The facilitator then began to ask strategically about other possible dimensions of impact that had not been mentioned, and began with 'knowledge'. Participants realized immediately that in the intensity of the conversation they had forgotten this impact altogether. Their final ranking showed knowledge to be one of the three most valued impacts.

Furthermore, the fact that participants in some case studies reported 'no impact' on certain dimensions that had been inquired about directly (i.e. 'work' and 'environment'), suggests that at least in these cases, positive examples of impact were not fabricated to 'please' facilitators.

Secondly, in the absence of a consistent taxonomy it is hard to see how projects can be compared. The clear alternative would be to have participants generate categories themselves. However, because these categories will not be the same, the information would not be useful for cross-project comparison without some transformation. Furthermore, the task of generating categories takes time and it is a question worth asking whether the information is worth the time of (poor) participants who have other concerns to attend to. Finally, there is the issue of feasibility of analysis. In one study, participants were asked in an open-ended manner to identify variables by which they assessed the same institutional process. Fifteen participating NGOs generated 139 variables. A careful scrutiny of the definitions of each variable enabled these to be collapsed into seventeen broad categories in which the activities had been compared by at least four institutions, with a residual category that included thirty items. The time necessary to make and analyse these comparisons from locally generated categories suggests that such comparisons should be reserved for situations in which it is of utmost significance to study the local categorizing process. I would argue that the case studies and similar activities do not require this information in order to evaluate capability expansion, hence that the use of a working set of dimensions is appropriate for small NGOs with limited resources.

To conclude, the methodology simplified the framework in Part I by using a working set of dimensions of human development as the basis of questions about the kinds of valuable human impacts that had occurred. The values of different changes in functionings were ranked by both participants and assessors, and the rankings were reported under the 'dimensions' of development with which the functioning was most closely associated. I have argued that this methodology enriched the information about valued capability change. I further argued that the working set of dimensions did seem intelligible to communities, and did not necessarily impose values on communities. The methodology would benefit from considerable further study, for example, about how complete the capability sets generated are, what kind of bias the explicit introduction of dimensions does introduce, and whether or not rankings are most accurate and analytically useful if they are done across dimensions (as here), across general functioning (as for participation), or across different categories still.

5.3. *Culture and basic needs*

Sen has espoused participatory approaches with increasing clarity, although these links have not necessarily been appreciated by those working in participatory development. Chapter 4 argued that decisions regarding changes in practices—which will in the end affect identity—should be governed by the principle of subsidiarity, which holds that the most local agent(s) capable of making a choice should make it, or give informed consent to it. The application of this principle is more difficult than it sounds. For example, decisions about which activity Oxfam undertakes to support will affect Oxfam's institutional identity, as well as that of the local community(ies). Also, decisions are constrained by financial and institutional resources: a community may 'value' a maternal health clinic more than a sanitation supply, but only obtain a grant for building a sanitation supply. In this case, the open-menu nature of Oxfam projects allowed for a deep kind of participation.

Chapter 5 further studied the relationship between functionings, capabilities, and basic needs. It argued that basic needs could be identified at a general level, although their specification would be relative to a spatio-temporal context, and to the commitments of the community in question. It also argued that a programme to meet basic needs should focus on expanding people's capability to meet basic needs (rather than on meeting their basic needs), one of which might be the need to participate in active and collaborative politics. The principal reason for a focus on capability overall—and not only on participation or freedom as a basic need among others—is that if participation is studied as a distinct functioning, then Sonia may be judged 'able to participate' because she has a legal right to vote, even though she may not be able to choose whether or not to be educated—the capability to make *each* choice she would value making, is absent.

The impact assessment methodology used 'participation' to represent the decision-making capability of a group, which may not only be intrinsically valuable in itself, but have valuable transitive and intransitive effects. It provided qualitative ranking of this variable in different activities, and anecdotal information about how choices were made. The need for improvements in the ranking mechanisms has already been acknowledged (Ch. 6, Sect. 3.2.5, Ch. 7, Sect. 4.2.3). Also, the simple use of participation to represent decision-making did not treat systematically several difficult issues such as whether capabilities are expanded when a group does not intentionally choose, nor would have chosen, to pursue a functioning they subsequently value. Yet the measure was still useful.

One residual issue about capability and participation remains. In the context of the case studies, the rose cultivation group 'chose' their activity from a set of possibilities they generated. Both Khoj and RWWO selected and developed a technical competence (literacy and micro credit), and then identified groups of participants who would be interested. In the case of RWWO there was a coincidence between intended and actual results (income generation), although additional impacts were also generated. In Khoj, this was not the case. Participants understood that literacy would be a means to income generation. They became literate but largely failed to generate income. But the secondary benefit (women's empowerment—which was an explicit objective in Khoj documentation) was not necessarily explained to prospective students, although it was subsequently highly valued by the participants. One might ask, then, whether the women had the 'capability' to be empowered or whether their functioning of empowerment was realized without their choice. As this is a debated issue, especially in women's activities that have a further agenda of 'conscientization' or empowerment, it bears some reflection as to how the criteria of 'free choice' or 'informed consent' apply.

One possibility would be to say that it was not feasible accurately to predict and then to communicate *what* empowerment would arise from the activity to the first few classes. 'Informed consent' was not possible because information on side-effects was not available. Khoj could only surmise how women would value the effects. But after the possible range of empowerment impacts had been observed—that is, in future literacy initiatives—Khoj would introduce these impacts to future participants, and these would factor into their choice of whether to study.

A second possibility would be to say that the communication difficulty was permanent, due to the inherently limited capacities of illiterate/unempowered women in that cultural context. That is, even literacy initiatives with sufficient information on side-effects would not be able to obtain informed consent. But the intervention was justified as advancing valuable capabilities none the less because *after* they had become educated, participants valued their empowerment—as the graduates themselves testified. Before the intervention women could not imagine this was possible—again, as the graduates had testified.

The problem with this 'incompetence' argument is that it cannot be refuted. The same 'form' of argument might be used to justify intensive religious or political proselytization, for example, or the introduction of consumer habits such as computer games; moreover, the avowed praise of graduates (consumers) one year later would similarly be argued to legitimize them. While this praise may be a *component* of a justification it is not itself sufficient to distinguish between the value of conversion to a dogma or practice, and the value of a basic capability.

A third possibility would be to argue that the barrier was political. Even had future students been themselves convinced of the benefit of empowerment, authority figures (husbands, parents, community leaders) would have opposed the activity had they known that this functioning would ensue. The opposition might have come from a misperception of what empowerment would entail in their context, which could be corrected in theory by enough trust, flexibility, and accurate information (which is a version of the argument above). Or the opposition might have come from systematic disagreements between authority figures and participants as to the value of this functioning. In either case the only feasible way for women to *realize* empowerment was for the activity to be run under the public guise of income generation. While this is plausible as an account of local conditions, the question remains: how could Oxfam (and Khoj) distinguish between censored functionings that were (i) essential to well-being, (ii) possible expressions of well-being, and (iii) detrimental to well-being? And what role did discussions with future participants play in this process?

However one may answer these questions conceptually (Ch. 5), the methodology that was used in the impact assessment clearly leaves them unaddressed. To this extent the methodology does not provide a way to distinguish activities which use informed consent from activities in which consent is built during the process. If this oversight is significant at the micro level, then an additional tool must be developed to complement the indicators of participation.

To conclude, this methodology simplified the framework in Part I by using participation as representation of the principle of subsidiarity, and by comparing the levels of participation in different activities. As the discussion above illustrates, this is a very partial representation of subsidiarity, and sidesteps many of the issues that Oxfam and others have identified as perplexing (Ch. 4, Sect. 2.4.1). I have argued that the ranking mechanism needs to be improved and possibly supplemented by other tools, but that the approach is quite parsimonious with data, and that it is useful, if only because the alternative—of not recording whether or not any freedom of choice was available—is incompatible with the capabilities approach in this interpretation of it.

6. CONCLUSION

Before a garment is stitched the roughly cut shapes of cloth are tacked together to make sure the general fit is satisfactory and to keep the pieces of fabric from sliding apart. These last two chapters have been given to the task of tacking between Sen's capability approach, the methodologies of microeconomic project assessment, and the framework for identifying valuable capabilities presented in Part I.

Appendix

In *Commodities and Capabilities*, Sen formalized the following relationships:

- Given the following terms:

    x_i = person i's vector of commodities
    $c(\cdot)$ = a function (not necessarily linear) converting x_i into a vector of characteristics
    $f_i(\cdot)$ = the personal utilization function of i, by which they convert characteristics into functionings
    F_i = the set of f_i from which person i can choose one

- An *achieved functioning* is:

    $b_i = f_i(c(x_i))$.

- Person i's feasible functioning set, for a given vector of commodities is the set:

    $P_i(x_i) = [b_i \mid b_i = f_i(c(x_i)),$ for some $f_i(\cdot) \in F_i]$.

- Person i's *capability set*, if the choice of commodities is restricted to the set X_i, is:

    $Q_i(X_i) = [b_i \mid b_i = f_i(c(x_i)),$ for some $f_i(\cdot) \in F_i$ and some $x_i \in X_i]$.

- Finally, if v_i is the valuation of the ith person, then there exists a set of possible values V_i

    $V_i = [v_i \mid v_i = v_i(b_i),$ for some b_i in $Q_i]$.

I am proposing the following:

- The set of possible values has a small number of n elements: $d_1, d_2, \ldots, d_n$.
- Any reasonable valuation of a functioning by the ith person (any reasonable $v_i(b_i)$, for some b_i in Q_i) can be completely resolved into a combination of these several orthogonal elements: $v_i = (d_1, d_2, d_3, \ldots, d_n)$.

And, in terms of basic needs:

- Given the following terms:

    $x_{i,bn}$ = person i's vector or goods/services/freedoms needed to fulfil basic needs
    $c(\cdot)$ = a function (not necessarily linear) converting x_i into a vector of characteristics
    $f_{i,bn}(\cdot)$ = the personal utilization function of i, by which he or she converts characteristics of $x_{i,bn}$ into basic functionings
    F_i = the set of f_i from which person i can choose one

- An *achieved basic functioning* is:

    $b_{i,bn} = f_{i,bn}(c(x_{i,bn}))$.

- Person i's feasible functioning set, for a vector of basic needs $g/s/f$ is the set:

    $P_i(x_i) = [b_i \mid b_i = f_i(c(x_{i,bn})),$ for some $f_i(\cdot) \in F_i]$.

- Person i's *capability set*, if the choice of $g/s/f$ is restricted to the set X_i, is:

    $Q_i(X_i) = [b_i \mid b_i = f_i(c(x_i))$, for some $f_i(\cdot) \in F_i$ and some $x_i \in X_i]$.

- Person i, then, has the *capability to fulfil basic needs* if the set X_i includes $x_{i,bn}$, hence if the set b_i includes $b_{i,bn}$.[1]

[1] See Desai (1990).

References

Afxentiou, Panayiotis C. 1990. 'Basic Needs: A Survey of the Literature'. *Canadian Journal of Development Studies*. 11/2: 241–57.
Akerlof, George, and Rachel Kranton. 2000. 'Economics and Identity'. *Quarterly Journal of Economics*. 115/3: 715–53.
Alderfer, C. D. 1969. 'An Empirical Test of a New Theory of Human Needs'. *Organizational Behavior and Human Performance*. 4: 142–75.
Alkire, Sabina. 1997. 'Impact Assessment: Oxfam vs Poverty'. Mimeo manual.
—— 2001. 'The Basic Dimensions of Human Flourishing: A Comparison of Accounts'. In Biggar and Black 2001.
—— and Rufus Black. 1997. 'A Practical Reasoning Theory of Development Ethics: Furthering the Capabilities Approach'. *Journal of International Development*. 9/2: 263–79.
—— and Severine Deneulin. 2000. 'Individual Motivation, its Nature, Determinants and Consequences for within Group Behaviour'. WIDER Working Papers, No. 184. United Nations University.
Allardt, E. 1993. 'Having, Loving, Being: An Alternative to the Swedish Model of Welfare Research'. In Nussbaum and Sen 1993: 88–94.
Alston, L. J., T. Eggertsson, and D. North, eds. 1996. *Empirical Studies in Institutional Change*. Cambridge: Cambridge University Press.
Aman, K., ed. 1991. *Ethical Principles for Development: Needs, Capabilities or Rights*. Montclair State, NJ: Institute for Critical Thinking.
Anand, S., and C. Harris. 1994. 'Choosing a Welfare Indicator'. *American Economic Association Papers and Proceedings*. 84/2: 226–49.
—— and M. Ravallion. 1993. 'Development in Poor Countries: On the Role of Private Incomes and Public Services'. *Journal of Economic Perspectives*. 7/1: 113–50.
—— and Amartya Sen. 1997. 'Concepts of Human Development and Poverty: A Multidimensional Perspective'. In *Poverty and Human Development*. Human Development Papers 1997. Human Development Report Office, the United Nations Development Programme, New York.
Andrews, Frank M., and Stephen B. Withey. 1976. *Social Indicators of Well-Being: Americans' Perceptions of Life Quality*. New York: Plenum Press.
Antony, Louise M. 2000. 'Natures and Norms'. *Ethics*. 111: 8–36.
Apffel-Marglin, F., and S. Marglin. 1990. *Dominating Knowledge: Development, Culture, and Resistance*. Oxford: Clarendon Press.
—— —— 1996. *Decolonizing Knowledge: From Development to Dialogue*. Oxford: Clarendon Press.
Appadurai, Arjun. 1996. *Modernity at Large: Cultural Dimensions of Globalization*. Minneapolis: University of Minnesota Press.
Argyle, Michael, and Maryanne Martin. 1991. 'The Psychological Causes of Happiness'. In Argyle *et al*. 1991.
—— F. Strack, and N. Schwartz. 1991. *Subjective Well-being: An Interdisciplinary Perspective*. Oxford: Pergamon Press.

Aristotle. 1980. *The Nicomachean Ethics*, ed. J. L. Ackrill, W. D. Ross, and J. O. Urmson. Oxford: Oxford University Press.

Arneson, Richard J. 1989. 'Equality and Equal Opportunity for Welfare'. *Philosophical Studies*. 56: 77–93.

—— 2000. 'Perfectionism and Politics'. *Ethics*. 111: 37–63.

Arrow, Kenneth J. 1995. 'Returns to Scale, Information and Economic Growth'. In B. H. Koo and D. H. Perkins, eds. *Social Capability and Long Term Economic Growth*. New York: St Martin's Press. 11–18.

—— 1997. 'Invaluable Goods'. *Journal of Economic Literature*. 35: 757–65.

—— A. K. Sen, and K. Suzumura. 1997. *Social Choice Reexamined*. i and ii. Basingstoke: Macmillan.

Axelrod, L. J. 1994. 'Balancing Personal Needs with Environmental Preservation: Identifying the Values that Guide Decisions in Ecological Dilemmas'. *Journal of Social Issues*. 50/3: 85–104.

Baker, Judy L. 2000. *Evaluating the Impacts of Development Projects on Poverty: A Handbook for Practitioners*. Washington: World Bank.

Balestrino, Alessandro. 1996. 'A Note on Functioning-Poverty in Affluent Societies'. *Politeia*. 12/43–4: 97–106.

Bamberger, Michael. 1988. 'The Role of Community Participation in Development Planning and Project Management: Report of a Workshop on Community Participation held in Washington D. C., September 22–25, 1986'. *EDI Policy Seminar Report*. 13. The World Bank.

——, ed. 2000. *Integrating Quantitative and Qualitative Research in Development Projects*. Washington: World Bank.

Bangura, Yusuf. 1995. 'The Search for Identity: Ethnicity, Religion and Political Violence'. *UNRISD Occasional Paper*, No. 6. World Summit for Social Development.

Banuri, Tariq. 1990a. 'Development and the Politics of Knowledge: A Critical Interpretation of the Social Role of Modernization Theories in the Development of the Third World'. In Apffel-Marglin and Marglin 1990.

—— 1990b. 'Modernization and its Discontents: A Cultural Perspective on the Theories of Development'. In Apffel-Marglin and Marglin 1990.

Barber, Benjamin. 1995. *Jihad versus McWorld*. New York: Times Books.

Basu, Kaushik. 1987. 'Achievement, Capabilities, and the Concept of Well-Being'. *Social Choice and Welfare*. 4: 69–76.

—— P. Pattanaik, and K. Suzumura, eds. 1995. *Choice, Welfare, and Development: A Festschrift in Honour of Amartya K. Sen*. Oxford: Clarendon Press.

Bay, Christian. 1968. 'Needs, Wants and Political Legitimacy'. *Canadian Journal of Political Science*. 1: 241–60.

Beauchamp, Tom, and James Childress. 1994. *Principles of Biomedical Ethics*. Oxford: Oxford University Press.

Becker, G. 1996. *Accounting for Tastes*. Cambridge, Mass.: Harvard University Press.

Beitz, C. R. 1986. 'Amartya Sen's *Resources, Values and Development*'. *Economics and Philosophy*, 2.

Bell, D. E., H. Raiffa, and A. Tversky. 1988. *Decision-Making: Descriptive, Normative, and Prescriptive Interactions*. Cambridge: Cambridge University Press.

Bell, Simon. 1994. 'Methods and Mindsets: Towards an Understanding of the Tyranny of Methodology'. *Public Administration*. 14: 323–38.

Belli, Pedro, Jack Anderson, Howard Barnum, John Dixon, and Jee-Peng Tan. 2001. *Economic Analysis of Investment Operations: Analytical Tools and Practical Applications*. Washington: The World Bank.

Beteille, Andre. 1993. 'Amartya Sen's Utopia'. *Economic and Political Weekly*. 17 Apr.: 753–6.

Bhatnagar, Bhuvan, and Aubrey Williams. 1992. 'Participatory Development and the World Bank'. *World Bank Discussion Paper,* No 183. Washington.

Biggar, Nigel, and Rufus Black, eds. 2001. *The Revival of Natural Law: Philosophical, Theological and Ethical Responses to the Finnis-Grisez School*. Aldershot: Ashgate Publishers.

Bishop, John, John Formby, and W. James Smith. 1993. 'International Comparisons of Welfare and Poverty: Dominance Orderings for Ten Countries'. *Canadian Journal of Economics*. 16/3: 707–26.

Biswas-Diener, Robert, and Ed Diener. 2000. 'Making the Best of a Bad Situation: Satisfaction in the Slums of Calcutta'. *Social Indicators Research*. 55/3: 329–52.

Black, Rufus. 1996. 'Towards an Ecumenical Ethic: Reconciling the Work of Germain Grisez, Stanley Hauerwas and Oliver O'Donovan'. D. Phil. thesis. Magdalen College, Oxford.

Blackburn, James with Jeremy Holland, eds. 1998. *Who Changes? Institutionalizing Participation in Development*. London: Intermediate Technology Publications Ltd.

Blackwood, D. L. and R. G. Lynch. 1994. 'The Measurement of Inequality and Poverty: A Policy Maker's Guide to the Literature'. *World Development*. 22/4: 567–78.

Blair, Harry. 2000. 'Participation and Accountability at the Periphery: Democratic Local Governance in Six Countries'. *World Development*. 28/1: 21–39.

Bohman, James. 2000. *Public Deliberation: Pluralism, Complexity, and Democracy*. Cambridge: MIT Press.

Bohnet, I. and Frey, B. S. 1994. 'Direct Democratic Rules: The Role of Discussion'. *Kyklos*. 47: 341–54.

Bond, Michael Harris. 1988. 'Finding Universal Dimensions of Individual Variation in Multicultural Studies of Values: The Rokeach and Chinese Value Surveys'. *Journal of Personality and Social Psychology*. 55/6: 1009–15.

Bond, Richard, and David Hulme. 1999. 'Process Approaches to Development: Theory and Sri Lankan Practice'. *World Development*. 27/8: 1339–58.

Braithwaite, V. A., and H. G. Law. 1985. 'Structure of Human Values: Testing the Adequacy of the Rokeach Value Survey'. *Journal of Personality and Social Psychology*. 49/1: 250–63.

Braybrooke, David. 1987. *Meeting Needs*. Princeton: Princeton University Press.

Brentano, Franz. 1973. *Psychology from an Empirical Standpoint*, trans. Antos C. Rancurello, D. B. Terrell, and Linda McAlister. New York: Humanities Press.

Burdge, Rabel. 1995. *A Community Guide to Social Impact Assessment*. Middleton, Wis.: Social Ecology Press.

—— et al. 1994. *A Conceptual Approach to Social Impact Assessment*. Middleton, Wis.: Social Ecology Press.

Burki, A. A., and Q. Abbas. 1991. 'Earnings Functions in Pakistan's Urban Informal Sector: A Case Study'. *The Pakistan Development Review*. 30/4: 695–706.

—— and Ubaidullah, A. 1992. 'Earnings, Training and Employment in Gujranwala's Urban Informal Sector: Evolution or Involution?' *Pakistan Economic and Social Review*. 30/1: 49–66.

Carmen, Raff. 2000. 'Prima Mangiare, Poi Filosofare'. *Journal of International Development*. 12: 1019–30.

Carvalho, Soniya, and Howard White. 1997. 'Combining the Quantitative and Qualitative Approaches to Poverty Measurement and Analysis'. *World Bank Technical Paper*, No. 366.

Casini, L., and I. Bernetti. 1996. 'Public Project Evaluation, Environment and Sen's Theory'. *Politeia*. 12/43–4: 55–78.

Cassen, Robert. 1986. *Does Aid Work?* Oxford: Clarendon Press.

Cernea, Michael M. 1982. 'Indigenous Anthropologists and Development-Oriented Anthropology'. In H. Fahim, ed. *Indigenous Anthropology in Non-Western Countries*. Durham, NC: Carolina Academic Press.
—— ed. 1991. *Putting People First: Sociological Variables in Development*. 2nd edn. Oxford: Oxford University Press.
—— and Ayse Kudat, eds. 1997. 'Social Assessments for Better Development: Case Studies in Russia and Central Asia'. *Environmentally Sustainable Development Studies and Monographs Series*. 16. The World Bank.
Chakraborty, Achin. 1995. 'The Concept and Measurement of the Standard of Living'. Ph.D. Thesis. University of California at Riverside.
—— 1996. 'On the Possibility of a Weighting System for Functionings'. Centre for Development Studies, Working Paper, No. 270. Thiruvananthapuram, Kerala, India.
—— 1998. 'The Irrelevance of Methodology and the Art of the Possible: Reading Sen and Hirschman'. Centre for Development Studies, Working Paper, No. 286. Thiruvananthapuram, Kerala, India.
Chambers, Robert. 1992. 'Rural Appraisal: Rapid, Relaxed and Participatory'. *IDS Discussion Paper*. 311.
—— 1993. *Challenging the Professions: Frontiers for Rural Development*. London: Intermediate Technology.
—— 1994a. 'Participatory Rural Appraisal (PRA): Challenges, Potentials and Paradigm'. *World Development*. 22/1: 1437–54.
—— 1994b. 'The Origins and Practice of Participatory Rural Appraisal'. *World Development*. 22/7: 953–69.
—— 1994c. 'Participatory Rural Appraisal (PRA): Analysis of Experience'. *World Development* 22/9: 1253–68.
—— 1994d. 'All Power Deceives'. *IDS Bulletin*. 25/2
—— 1995. 'Poverty and Livelihoods: Whose Reality Counts?' *IDS Discussion Paper*. 347.
—— 1997. *Whose Reality Counts?: Putting the First Last*. London: Intermediate Technology Publications.
Chang, Ruth, ed. 1997. *Incommensurability, Incomparability, and Practical Reason*. Boston: Harvard University Press.
Charlesworth, Hilary. 2000. 'Martha Nussbaum's Feminist Internationalism'. *Ethics*. 111: 64–78.
Chenery, Hollis. 1974. *Redistribution with Growth: Policies to Improve Income Distribution in Developing Countries in the Context of Economic Growth*. A joint study by the World Bank's Development Research Center and the Institute of Development Studies, University of Sussex. Oxford: Oxford University Press.
Chiappero-Martinetti, Enrica. 1994. 'A New Approach to Evaluation of Well-Being and Poverty by Fuzzy Set Theory'. *Il Giornale degli economisti e annali di economia*. 7–9.
—— 1996. 'Standard of Living Evaluation based on Sen's Approach: Some Methodological Questions'. *Politeia*. 12/43–4: 47–53.
Chinese Culture Connection. 1987. 'Chinese Values and the Search for Culture-Free Dimensions of Culture'. *Journal of Cross-Cultural Psychology*. 18: 143–64.
Christopher, John Chambers. 1999. 'Situating Psychological Well-Being: Exploring the Cultural Roots of Its Theory and Research'. *Journal of Counseling and Development*. 77 (Spring): 141–52.
—— 1995. 'A Poverty-Oriented Cost-Benefit Approach to the Analysis of Development Projects'. *World Development*. 23/4: 577–92.
Coase, R. 1960. 'The Problem of Social Cost'. *Journal of Law and Economics*. 3: 1–44.

Cohen, G. A. 1993. 'Amartya Sen's Unequal World'. *Economic and Political Weekly*. Oct. 2: 2156–60.
Cook, K. S., and M. Levi. 1990. *The Limits of Rationality*. Chicago: Chicago University Press.
Cooke, Bill, and Uma Kothari. 2001. *Participation: The New Tyranny?* London: Zed Books.
Corbett, Jane, and Frances Stewart. 1994. 'Putting Gender into Cost Benefit Analysis'. Background paper for the 1995 Human Development Report.
Corbridge, S. 1993. 'Ethics in Development Studies: the Example of Debt'. In F. Schuurman, ed. *Beyond the Impasse: New Directions in Development Theory*. London: Zed Books. 123–39.
Cornia, Giovanni Andrea, Richard Jolly, and Frances Stewart, eds. 1987. *Adjustment with a Human Face: Protecting the Vulnerable and Promoting Growth*. i. Oxford: Clarendon Press.
Cox, James C. 1997. 'On Testing the Utility Hypothesis'. *Economic Journal*. 107 (July): 1054–78.
Crocker, David A. 1991. 'Toward Development Ethics'. *World Development*. 19/5: 457–83.
—— 1992. 'Functioning and Capability: The Foundations of Sen's and Nussbaum's Development Ethic'. *Political Theory*. 20/4: 584–612.
—— 1995. 'Functioning and Capability: The Foundations of Sen's and Nussbaum's Development Ethic, Part 2'. In Nussbaum and Glover 1995: 153–99.
—— and Toby Linden. 1998. *Ethics of Consumption: The Good Life, Justice and Global Stewardship*. Oxford: Rowman and Littlefield.
Crosswell, Michael J. 1981. 'Basic Human Needs: A Development Planning Approach'. In Danny M. Leipziger, ed. *Basic Needs and Development*. Cambridge, Mass.: Oelgeschlager, Gunn & Hain.
Crush, Jonathan. 1995. *Power of Development*. London: Routledge.
Csikszentmihalyi, Mihaly. 1997*a*. 'Happiness and Creativity: Going with the Flow'. *Futurist*. Sept–Oct.: 8–12.
—— 1997*b*. 'Finding Flow'. *Psychology Today*. July–Aug.: 46–8, 70–1.
Cummins, Robert A. 1996. 'The Domains of Life Satisfaction: An Attempt to Order Chaos'. *Social Indicators Research*. 38/3: 303–28.
Curry, S. and J. Weiss. 1993. *Project Analysis in Developing Countries*. London: Macmillan.
Daniels, Norman. 1990. 'Equality of What: Welfare, Resources or Capabilities?' *Philosophy of Phenomenological Research*. 50: 273–96.
Dasgupta, Partha. 1990. 'Well-Being in Poor Countries'. *Economic and Political Weekly*. 25 (4 Aug.): 1713–20.
—— 1993. *An Inquiry into Well-Being and Destitution*. Oxford: Oxford University Press.
—— and Karl-Göran Mäler. 1997. *The Environment and Emerging Development Issues*. i and ii. Oxford: Clarendon Press.
—— and Martin Weale. 1992. 'On Measuring the Quality of Life'. *World Development*. 20/1: 119–31.
Davies, James C. 1963. *Human Nature in Politics*. New York: Wiley.
Davis, Shelton H. and Lars T. Soeftestad. 1995. 'Participation and Indigenous Peoples'. Social Development Papers No. 9. Washington DC: The World Bank.
Davitt, T. E. 1968. 'The Basic Values in Law: A Study of the Ethico-legal Implications of Psychology and Anthropology'. *Transactions of the American Philosophical Society*. 58/5.
de Kadt, Emanuel, 1994. 'Getting and Using Knowledge about the Poor? *IDS Bulletin*. 125/2: 100–9.
Deneulin, Severine. Forthcoming. 'Paternalism, Perfectionism, and Liberalism, in Sen's and Nussbaum's Capability Approach'. Manuscript.

Desai, Meghnad. 1990. 'Poverty and Capability: Towards an Empirically Implementable Measure'. *Suntory-Toyota International Centre Discussion Paper*, No. 27. London School of Economics Development Economics Research Programme.
—— 1994a. 'Measuring Political Freedom'. *The Centre for the Study of Global Governance*. Discussion Paper No. 10.
—— 1994b. 'The Measurement Problem in Economics'. *Scottish Journal of Political Economy*. 41/1: 34–42.
Devarajan, Shanta, Lyn Squire, and Sethaput Narueput. 1996. 'Project Appraisal at the World Bank'. In Kirkpatrick and Weiss 1996: 35–53.
Devereux, John A. 1993. 'Competence to Consent to Medical Treatment in England and Australia'. D. Phil. Thesis. University of Oxford.
Dia, Mamadou, ed. 1996. *Africa's Management in the 1990s and Beyond: Reconciling Indigenous and Transplanted Institutions*. Washington DC: The World Bank.
Diener, Ed and Robert Biswas-Diener. 1999. 'Income and Subjective Well-being: Will Money Make us Happy'. Draft.
—— —— 2000. 'New Directions in Subjective Well-Being Research: The Cutting Edge'. Draft.
—— and M. Diener. 1995. 'Cross-Cultural Correlates of Life Satisfaction and Self-Esteem'. *Journal of Personality and Social Psychology*. 68: 653–63.
—— —— and C. Diener. 1995. 'Factors Predicting the Subjective Well-Being of Nations'. *Journal of Personality and Social Psychology*. 69: 851–64.
—— and E. M. Suh, eds. 2000. *Culture and Subjective Well-Being*. Cambridge: MIT Press.
DiMaggio, Paul. 1994. 'Culture and Economy'. Chapter 2 in Neil Smelser and Richard Svedberg, eds. *The Handbook of Economic Sociology*. Princeton: Princeton University Press. 27–57.
Dinwiddy, C., and F. Teal. 1996. *Principles of Cost-Benefit Analysis for Developing Countries*. Cambridge: Cambridge University Press.
Dobb, Maurice. 1973. *Theories of Value and Distribution since Adam Smith: Ideology and Economic Theory*. Cambridge: Cambridge University Press.
Dore, Ronald. 1994. 'Why Visiting Sociologists Fail'. Sixth Dudley Seers Memorial Lecture. *IDS Discussion Paper*. 341.
Dörner, Dietrich. 1996. *The Logic of Failure*. New York: Free Press.
Doyal, Len and Ian Gough. 1991. *A Theory of Human Need*. Basingstoke: Macmillan.
—— —— 1993. 'Need Satisfaction as a Measure of Human Welfare'. In Wolfgang Blass and John Foster, eds. *Mixed Economies in Europe*. Brookfield, Vt.: Edward Elgar.
Drèze, Jean. 1994. 'Economic Development, Public Action and Social Progress'. *Canadian Journal of Development Studies*. 15/3: 329–46.
—— and Amartya Sen. 1989. *Hunger and Public Action*. Oxford: Clarendon Press.
—— —— eds. 1990. *The Political Economy of Hunger*. Oxford: Clarendon Press.
—— —— 1991. 'Public Action for Social Security: Foundations and Strategy'. In Ehtisham Ahmad, Jean Drèze, John Hills, and Amartya Sen, eds. *Social Security in Developing Countries*. Oxford: Clarendon Press.
—— —— 1995. *India: Economic Development and Social Opportunity*. Delhi: Oxford University Press.
—— —— eds. 1997. *Indian Development: Selected Regional Perspectives*. New York: Oxford University Press.
Duch, Raymond M., and Michael A. Taylor. 1993. 'Postmaterialism and the Economic Condition'. *American Journal of Political Science*. 37: 747–89.

Dupuit, J. 1844. 'On the Measurement of Utility of Public Works', translated from the French in *International Economic Papers*. 2. 1952.
Dworkin, Ronald. 1986. *Law's Empire*. Cambridge, Mass.: Harvard University Press.
Eade, D., and Williams, S. 1995. *The Oxfam Handbook of Development and Relief*. Oxford: Oxfam Publications.
Edwards, Michael, and David Hulme, eds. 1992. *Making a Difference: NGOs and Development in a Changing World*. London: Earthscan.
—— —— eds. 1995. *Non-governmental Organizations' Performance and Accountability: Beyond the Magic Bullet*. London: Earthscan.
Ellerman, David. Forthcoming. 'Helping Others to Help Themselves'. Manuscript.
Ellerman, David. 2001. 'Helping People Help Themselves: Autonomy-Compatible Assistance'. In Nagy Hanna and Robert Picciotto, eds. *The New Development Compact: Toward a Comprehensive Strategy*. Washington: The World Bank.
Ensminger, J. 1992. *Making the Market: The Institutional Transformation of an African Society*. Cambridge: Cambridge University Press.
Escobar, Arturo. 1984–5. 'Discourse and Power in Development: Michel Foucault and the Relevance of his Work to the Third World'. *Alternatives*. 10: 377–400.
—— —— 1995. *Encountering Development*. Princeton: Princeton University Press.
Esman, M. J., and Uphoff, N. T. 1984. *Local Organizations: Intermediaries in Rural Development*. Ithaca, NY: Cornell University Press.
Eunkook, S., E. Diener, S. Oishi, and H. Triandis. 1998. 'The Shifting Basis of Life Satisfaction Judgements across Cultures: Emotions versus Norms'. *Journal of Personality and Social Psychology*. 74/2: 482–93.
Fabel, A. J. 1994. 'Environmental Ethics and the Question of Cosmic Purpose'. *Environmental Ethics*. 16/3: 303–14.
Farina, Francesco, F. Hahn, and S. Vannucci, eds. 1996. *Ethics, Rationality and Economic Behaviour*. Oxford: Clarendon Press.
Fields, Gary S. 1994. 'Poverty and Income Distribution: Data for Measuring Poverty and Inequality Changes in the Developing Countries'. *Journal of Development Economics*. 44: 87–102.
Finnis, John. 1980. *Natural Law and Natural Rights*. Oxford: Clarendon Press.
—— 1983. *The Fundamentals of Ethics*. Oxford: Oxford University Press.
—— 1987. 'Legal Enforcement of "Duties to Oneself": Kant v. neo-Kantians'. *Columbia Law Review*. 87: 433–56.
—— 1990a. 'Allocating Risks and Suffering: Some Hidden Traps'. *Cleveland State Law Review*. 38/1–2: 193–207.
—— 1990b. 'Concluding Reflections'. *Cleveland State Law Review*. 38/1–2: 231–50.
—— 1991. *Moral Absolutes: Tradition, Revision and Truth*. Washington: Catholic University Press of America.
—— 1992a. 'Natural Law and Legal Reasoning'. In George 1992.
—— 1992b. 'Economics, Justice and the Value of Life: Concluding Remarks'. In L. Gormally. *The Dependent Elderly: Autonomy, Justice and Quality of Care*. Cambridge: Cambridge University Press. 189–98.
—— 1994. 'Liberalism and Natural Law Theory'. *Mercer Law Review*. 45: 687–704.
—— 1995a. 'Law, Morality, and "Sexual Orientation" '. *Notre Dame Journal of Law, Ethics & Public Policy*. 9: 11–39.
—— 1995b. 'Unjust Laws in a Democratic Society: Some Philosophical and Theological Reflections'. *Notre Dame Law Review*. 71/4: 595–604.

Finnis, John. 1996. 'Is Natural Law Theory Compatible with Limited Government?' In Robert P. George, ed. *Natural Law, Liberalism, and Morality*. Oxford and New York: Oxford University Press. 1–26.
—— 1997. 'Commensuration and Public Reason'. In Chang 1997: 215–33.
—— 1998a. *Aquinas: Moral, Political, and Legal Theory*. Oxford: Oxford University Press.
—— 1998b. 'Natural Law and the Ethics of Discourse'. *American Journal of Jurisprudence*. 43: 53–74.
—— 1999. 'Natural Law and the Ethics of Discourse'. *Ratio Juris*. 12/4: 354–73.
—— J. Boyle, and G. Grisez. 1987. *Nuclear Deterrence, Morality, and Realism*. Oxford: Oxford University Press. 1987.
Finsterbusch, K., J. Ingersoll, and L. Llewellyn, eds. 1990. *Methods for Social Analysis in Developing Countries*. Social Impact Assessment Series, No. 17. Oxford: Westview Press.
Fisher, Anthony. 1994. 'The Principles of Distributive Justice considered with respect to the Allocation of Health Care'. D. Phil. Thesis. Blackfriars. University of Oxford.
Fitzgerald, Ross, ed. 1977. *Human Needs and Politics*. Sydney: Pergamon.
Forester, John. 1999. *The Deliberative Practitioner: Engaging Participatory Planning Processes*. Cambridge, Mass.: MIT Press.
Foster, James. 1994. 'Normative Measurement: Is Theory Relevant?' *American Economic Review*. 84/2: 365–70.
Frank, Robert H. 1997. 'The Frame of Reference as a Public Good'. *Economic Journal*. 107: 1832–47.
Freudenburg and Keaging. 1982. 'Increasing the Impact of Sociology on Social Impact Assessment: Toward Ending the Inattention'. *The American Sociologist*. 17: 71–80.
Freudenburg and Olsen. 1983. *Journal of the Community Development Society*. 14/2: 67–82.
Frey, Bruno. 1997. *Not Just for Money: An Economic Theory of Personal Motivation*. Aldershot: Edward Elgar.
Fromm, Erich. 1949. *Man for Himself, An Enquiry into the Psychology of Ethics*. London: Routledge & Kegan Paul.
—— 1956. *The Sane Society*. London: Routledge & Kegan Paul.
Fukuyama, Francis. 1995. *Trust: The Social Virtues and the Creation of Prosperity*. New York: Free Press.
Galtung, Johan. 1980. *The True Worlds: A Transnational Perspective*. New York: Free Press.
—— 1994. *Human Rights in Another Key*. Cambridge: Polity Press.
Gasper, Des. 1996a. 'Culture and Development Ethics: Needs, Women's Rights, and Western Theories'. *Development and Change*. 27: 627–61.
—— 1996b. 'Needs and Basic Needs: A Clarification of Meanings, Levels and Different Streams of Work'. Institute of Social Studies Working Paper, No. 210. The Hague: Institute of Social Studies.
—— 1997. 'Sen's Capability Approach and Nussbaum's Capabilities Ethic'. *Journal of International Development*. 9/2: 281–302.
—— 2000a. 'Development as Freedom: Taking Economics Beyond Commodities—the Cautious Boldness of Amartya Sen'. *Journal of International Development*. 12: 989–1001.
—— 2000b. 'Evaluating the "Logical Framework Approach"—Towards Learning-Oriented Development Evaluation'. *Public Administration and Development*. 20/1: 17–28.
—— 2000c. 'Logical Frameworks: Problems and Potentials'. Manuscript.
Geertz, Clifford. 1973. *The Interpretation of Cultures*. New York: Basic Books.
—— 1993. *Local Knowledge: Further Essays in Interpretive Anthropology*. London: Fontana Press.

George, Robert P. 1988. 'Recent Criticism of Natural Law Theory'. *University of Chicago Law Review.* 55: 1371–1427.
—— 1989. 'Human Flourishing as a Criterion of Morality: A Critique of Perry's Naturalism'. *Tulane Law Review.* 63: 1455–74.
—— ed. 1992. *Natural Law Theory: Contemporary Essays.* Oxford: Clarendon Press.
—— 1993. *Making Men Moral.* Oxford: Clarendon Press.
Gerrard, Bill, ed. 1993. *The Economics of Rationality.* London: Routledge.
Gezelius, H., and D. Millwood. 1988. 'NGOs in Development and Participation in Practice: An Initial Inquiry'. Popular Participation Programme. Working Paper No. 3. University of Stockholm.
Ghai, Dharam. 1988. 'Participatory Development: Some Perspectives from Grass-Roots experiences'. *UNRISD Discussion Paper*, No. 5.
—— ed. 1994. *Development and Environment: Sustaining People and Nature.* London: Basil Blackwell.
—— A. R. Khan, E. L. H. Lee, and T. Alfthan. 1977. *The Basic-Needs Approach to Development: Some Issues Regarding Concepts and Methodology.* Geneva: ILO.
Ginsberg, Morris. 1953. 'On the Diversity of Morals: The Huxley Memorial Lecture 1953'. *Journal of the Royal Anthropological Institute.* 83/2.
Goetz, Anne Marie, and David O'Brien. 1995. 'Governing for the Common Wealth? The World Bank's Approach to Poverty and Governance'. *IDS Bulletin.* 26/2: 17–26.
Gough, Ian, and Theo Thomas. 1994. 'Need Satisfaction and Welfare Outcomes: Theory and Explanation'. *Social Policy & Administration.* 28/1: 33–56.
Gould, Jeremy. 1997. *Localizing Modernity: Action, Interests & Association in Rural Zambia.* Helsinki: Suomen Antropologinen Seura (TAFAS 40).
Goulet, Denis. 1992. 'Development: Creator and Destroyer of Values'. *World Development.* 20/3: 467–75.
—— 1995. *Development Ethics: A Guide to Theory and Practice.* London: Zed Books.
Granaglia, Elena. 1996. 'Two Questions to Amartya Sen'. *Politeia.* 43–4: 31–5.
Granato, J., Ronald Inglehart, and D. Leblang. 1996a. 'Cultural Values, Stable Democracy, and Economic Development: A Reply'. *American Political Science Review.* 40/3: 680–96.
—— —— —— 1996b. 'The Effect of Cultural Values on Economic Development: Theory, Hypotheses, and Some Empirical Tests'. *American Political Science Review.* 40/3: 607–31.
Greif, Avner. 1994. 'Cultural Beliefs and the Organization of Society: A Historical and Theoretical Reflection of Collectivist and Individualist Societies'. *Journal of Political Economy.* 102/5: 912–50.
—— 1998. 'Historical and Comparative Institutional Analysis'. *American Economic Review.* 88/2: 80–84.
Griffin, James. 1986. *Well-Being: Its Meaning, Measurement and Moral Importance.* Oxford: Clarendon Press.
—— 1991. 'Mixing Values'. *Proceedings of the Aristotelian Society* (suppl.). vol. 65: 101–18.
Griffin, James. 1996. *Value Judgement: Improving our Ethical Beliefs.* Oxford: Clarendon Press.
Griffin, Keith. 1989. *Alternative Strategies for Economic Development.* London: Macmillan.
—— and Terry McKinley. 1994. *Implementing a Human Development Strategy.* London: Macmillan.
Grisez, Germain. 1967. 'Methods of Ethical Inquiry'. *Proceeds of the American Catholic Philosophical Association.* 41: 160–8.
—— 1975. *Beyond the New Theism: A Philosophy of Religion.* Notre Dame, Ind.: University of Notre Dame Press.

Grisez, Germain. 1978. 'Against Consequentialism'. *American Journal of Jurisprudence*. 23: 21–72.
—— 1983. *The Way of the Lord Jesus: Christian Moral Principles*. i. Chicago: Franciscan Herald Press.
—— 1993. *The Way of the Lord Jesus: Living a Christian Life*. ii. Quincy, Il.: Franciscan Herald Press.
—— 1997. *The Way of the Lord Jesus: Difficult Moral Questions*. iii. Quincy, Il: Franciscan Herald Press.
—— and Joseph Boyle. 1979. *Life and Death with Liberty and Justice*. Notre Dame, Ind.: University of Notre Dame Press.
—— —— and John Finnis. 1987. 'Practical Principles, Moral Truth and Ultimate Ends'. *American Journal of Jurisprudence*. 32: 99–151.
Hacking, Ian. 1996. 'In Pursuit of Fairness'. *New York Review*. 19 Sept.: 40–3.
Haq, Mahbubul. 1995. *Reflections on Human Development*. New York: Oxford University Press.
—— and Khadija Haq. 1998. *Human Development in South Asia*. Karachi: Oxford University Press.
Harberger, Arnold C. 1978, 'On the Use of Distributional Weights in Social Cost-Benefit Analysis'. *Journal of Political Economy*. 82.2, part 11, S87–S120.
Harris, J., and De Renzio, P. 1997. 'Missing Link or Analytically Missing: The Concept of Social Capital'. *Journal of International Development*. 9/7: 919–37.
Harrison, Lawrence E. 1983. Underdevelopment is a State of Mind: The Latin American Case. Lanham, Md.: University Press of America/Madison Books.
—— and Samuel, P. Huntington, eds. 2000. *Culture Matters: How Values Shape Human Progress*. New York: Basic Books.
Hausman, Daniel M., and Michael S. McPherson. 1993. 'Why Economists Should Take Ethics Seriously'. In D. Bos, ed. *Economics in a Changing World*. iii. New York: St Martin's Press.
—— —— 1996. *Economics Analysis and Moral Philosophy*. Cambridge: Cambridge University Press.
Heller, Agnes. 1976. *The Theory of Need in Marx*. London: Allison and Busby.
Hentschel, Jesko. 1999. 'Contextuality and Data Collection Methods: A Framework and Application to Health Service Utilisation'. *The Journal of Development Studies*. 35: 64–94.
Hettne, Björn. 1995. *Development Theory and the Three Worlds: Towards an International Political Economy of Development*. 2nd edn. Essex: Longman Group Ltd.
Hicks, John. 1983. *Classics and Moderns: Collected Essays on Economic Theory, Volume III*. Oxford: Basil Blackwell.
Hicks, Norman, and Paul Streeten. 1979. 'Indicators of Development: The Search for a Basic Needs Yardstick'. *World Development*. 7: 567–80.
Hofstede, G. 1980. *Culture's Consequences: International Differences in Work-Related Values*. Beverly Hills, Calif.: Sage Press.
Holland, Jeremy with James Blackburn, eds. 1998. *Whose Voice? Participatory Research and Policy Change*. London: Intermediate Technology Publications Ltd.
Hopkins, Michael. 1991. 'Human Development Revisited: A New UNDP Report'. *World Development*. 19/10: 1469–73.
Huntington, Samuel. 1996. *The Clash of Civilizations and the Remaking of World Order*. New York: Simon & Schuster.
Illich, Evan. 1978. *Toward a History of Needs*. New York: Pantheon Press.
Inglehart, Ronald. 1997. *Modernization and Postmodernization: Cultural, Economic, and Political Change in 43 Societies*. Princeton: Princeton University Press.

—— 2000. 'Globalization and Postmodern Values'. *The Washington Quarterly*. 23/1: 215–28.

—— and Wayne Baker. 2000. 'Modernization, Cultural Change, and the Persistence of Traditional Values'. *American Sociological Review*. 65: 19–51.

Insham, Jonathan, Deepa Narayan, and Lant Pritchett. 1995. 'Does Participation Improve Performance? Establishing Causality with Subjective Data'. *The World Bank Economic Review*. 9/3: 173–200.

International Labour Organization, 1976. *Employment, Growth and Basic Needs*. Geneva: International Labour Organization.

Jain, Pankaj. 1994. 'Managing for Success: Lessons from Asian Development Programs'. *World Development*. 22/9: 1363–77.

James, J., and F. Stewart, 1981. 'New Products: A Discussion of the Welfare Effects of the Introduction of New Products in Developing Countries'. *Oxford Economic Papers*. 81–107.

Jimenez, E. 1986. 'The Public Subsidization of Education and Health in Developing Countries: A Review of Equity and Efficiency'. *The World Bank Research Observer*. 1: 111–29.

Jodha, N. S. 1988. 'Poverty Debate in India: A Minority View'. *Economic and Political Weekly*. Nov.: 2421–8.

Kahneman, Daniel, Ed Diener, and Norbert Schwarz, eds. 1999. *Well-Being: The Foundations of Hedonic Psychology*. New York: Russell Sage Foundation.

Kakwani, N. 1993. 'Performance in Living Standards: An International Comparison'. *Journal of Development Economics*. 41: 307–36.

Kanbur, Ravi, ed. 2001. 'Qual-Quant: Qualitative and Quantitative Poverty Appraisal-Complementarities, Tensions, and the Way Forward'. Manuscript. May.

Kaufmann, Daniel. 1991. 'Determinants of the Productivity of Projects in Developing Countries: Evidence from 1,200 Projects'. Background paper for the *World Development Report 1991*. Mimeo.

Kennedy, Terence. 1992. 'The Originality of John Finnis' Conception of the Natural Law'. In C. Curran and R. McCormick. *Readings in Moral Theology No. 7*. New York: Paulist Press. 124–38.

Kenny, Charles. 2000. 'Subjective Wellbeing and Economic Growth in Developing Countries'. Draft.

Khan, Janbaz. 1990. 'Social Impact Assessment: A Critique from the Perspective of the Third World Countries with Special Reference to the Construction of Chashma Right Bank Canal in the Dera Ismail Khan District of Pakistan'. *The Journal of Development Studies, Peshawar*. 10: 71–89.

Khan, Minhajuddin. 1995. 'Participatory Approaches in Rural Development Planning in Pakistan'. *Journal of Rural Development & Administration*. 27/1.

Khan, Shahrukh R. 1993. 'South Asia'. In King and Hill 1993.

—— and Mohammad Irfan. 1985. 'Rates of Returns to Education and the Determinants of Earnings in Pakistan'. *Pakistan Development Review*. 24/3–4: 671–80.

Khwaja, Asim Ijaz. 2001. 'Can Good Projects Succeed in Bad Communities? Collective Action in the Himalayas'. Paper presented at the Annual Bank Conference on Development Economics. Washington DC. 2 May.

Kim, Aehyung, and Bruce Benton. 1995. 'Cost Benefit Analysis of the Onchocerciasis Control Program'. *World Bank Technical Paper*, 282. The World Bank.

King, Elizabeth, and M. Anne Hill, eds. 1993. *Women's Education in Developing Countries: Barriers, Benefits, and Policies*. Washington DC: The World Bank.

Kirkpatrick, C. H., and John Weiss, eds. 1996. *Cost Benefit Analysis and Project Appraisal in Developing Countries*. Cheltenham: Edward Elgar.

Klamer, Arjo. 1989. 'A Conversation with Amartya Sen'. *Journal of Economic Perspectives*. 3/1: 135–50.

Klemisch-Ahlert, Marlies. 1993. 'Freedom of Choice: A Comparison of Different Rankings of Opportunity Sets'. *Social Choice and Welfare*. 10: 189–207.

Kluckhohn, Clyde. 1951. 'Values and Value-Orientations in the Theory of Action'. In Talcott Parsons and Edward Shils, eds. *Toward a General Theory of Action*. Cambridge, Mass: 388–433.

—— and A. L. Kroeber. 1963. *Culture: A Critical Review of Concepts and Definitions*. New York: Vintage Books. Originally published in 1952 *Papers of the Peabody Museum of American Archaeology and Ethnology*, 47/1 (1952). Harvard University.

Klugman, Jeni. 1994. 'Decentralization: A Survey of Literature from a Human Development Perspective'. *Human Development Report Office. Occasional Papers* No. 13. UNDP.

Koh, Harold Hongju, and Ronald C. Slye, eds. 1999. *Deliberative Democracy and Human Rights*. New Haven and London: Yale University Press.

Korten, D. 1980. 'Community Organization and Local Development: A Learning Process Approach'. *Public Administration Review*. 40: 480–512.

Krech, David, Richard S. Crutchfield, and Norman Livson. 1969. *Elements of Psychology*. 2nd edn. New York: Alfred Knopf.

Kuper, Adam. 1999. *Culture: The Anthropologists' Account*. Cambridge, Mass.: Harvard University Press.

Kurien, P. A. 1994. 'Non-economic Bases of Economic Behavior: The Consumption, Investment and Exchange Patterns of Three Emigrant Communities in Kerala, India'. *Development and Change*. 25: 757–83.

Kynch, Jocelyn, and Amartya Sen. 1983. 'Indian Women: Well-being and Survival'. *Cambridge Journal of Economics*. 7: 363–80.

Lancaster, Kevin. 1971. *A New Approach to Consumer Theory*. New York: Columbia University Press.

Lane, Robert E. 1969. *Political Thinking and Consciousness*. Chicago: Markham Publishers.

Larson, James S. 1996. 'The World Health Organisation's Definition of Health: Social versus Spiritual Health'. *Social Indicators Research*. 38/2: 181–92.

Lasswell, Harold D., and Allan R. Holmberg. 1969. 'Toward a General Theory of Directed Value Accumulation and Institutional Development'. In Ralph Braibanti, ed. *Political and Administrative Development*. Durham, NC: Duke University Press. 354–99.

Layard, R., and S. Glaister. 1994. *Cost-Benefit Analysis*. 2nd edn. Cambridge: Cambridge University Press.

Leach, M., and J. Fairhead. 1994. 'Natural Resource Management: The Reproduction and Use of Environmental Misinformation in Guinea's Forest-Savanna Transition Zone'. *IDS Bulletin*. 25/2: 81–7.

Lederer, Karin, ed. 1980. *Human Needs: A Contribution to the Current Debate*. Cambridge, Mass.: Oelgeschlager, Gunn, and Hain.

Levy, S., and Guttman, L. 1974. *Values and Attitudes of Israeli High School Youth*. Jerusalem: Israel Institute of Applied Social Research.

Lewin, Shira B. 1996. 'Economics and Psychology: Lessons For Our Own Day From the Early Twentieth Century'. *Journal of Economic Literature*. 34: 1293–323.

Lewis, W. Arthur. 1955. *The Theory of Economic Growth*. London: Allen & Unwin.

Lind, Niels C. 1992. 'Some Thoughts on the Human Development Index'. *Social Indicators Research*. 27: 89–101.

Lindbeck, Assar, Sten Nyberg, and Jörgen W. Weibull. 1999. 'Social Norms and Economic Incentives in the Welfare State'. *The Quarterly Journal of Economics*. 114/1.

Lipton, M., and R. Longhurst. 1989. *New Seeds and Poor People*. London: Unwin Hyman.
Lisk, Franklyn, ed. 1985. *Popular Participation in Planning for Basic Needs*. A study prepared for the ILO. Aldershot: Gower.
Lisska, Anthony J. 1996. *Aquinas' Natural Law: An Analytical Reconstruction*. Oxford: Clarendon Press.
Little, I. M. D. 1957. *A Critique of Welfare Economics*. 2nd edn. Oxford: Oxford University Press.
—— and J. A. Mirrlees. 1974. *Project Appraisal and Planning for Developing Countries*. London: Heinemann Educational Books.
—— —— 1994. 'Project Appraisal and Planning Twenty Years On'. Reprinted in Layard, R. and S. Glaister 1994.
McGillivray, Mark. 1991. 'The Human Development Index: Yet Another Redundant Composite Development Indicator?' *World Development*. 19/10: 1461–8.
—— and Howard White. 1993. 'Measuring Development: The UNDP's Human Development Index'. *Journal of International Development*. 5: 183–92.
MacIntyre, Alisdair. 1981. *After Virtue*. Notre Dame, Ind.: University of Notre Dame Press.
McKinley, Terry. 1998. 'Measuring the Contribution of Culture to Human Well-Being: Cultural Indicators of Development'. In UNESCO 1998: 322–32.
McLean, I., and A. B. Unken. 1995. 'What Is Social Choice?' In I. McLean and A. B. Unken, trans. and eds. *Classics of Social Choice*. Ann Arbor: University of Michigan Press. 1–63.
Malan, Naude. 1999. 'Participation in Research and Development at the Tshikonelo Agricultural Project, Northern Province'. *Development Southern Africa*. 16/3: 501–18.
Marc, Alexandre, Carol Graham, Mark Schacter, and Mary Schmidt. 1995. 'Social Action Programs and Social Funds: A Review of Design and Implementation in Sub-Saharan Africa'. *World Bank Discussion Paper*, 274. The World Bank.
Marcuse, Herbert. 1964. *One Dimensional Man: Studies in the Ideology of Advanced Industrial Society*. Boston: Beacon Press.
Marx, Karl. 1887. Capital: *A Critical Analysis of Capitalist Production*. i, ed. S. Moore and E. Aveling, trans. F. Engels. London: Allen and Unwin. 1938.
—— 1943. 'A Theory of Human Motivation'. *Psychology Review*. 50: 370–96.
—— 1948a. ' "Higher" and "Lower" Needs'. *Journal of Psychology*. 25: 433–6.
—— 1948b. 'Some Theoretical Consequences of Basic Need Gratification'. *Journal of Personality*. 16: 402–16.
—— 1954. 'The Instinctoid Nature of Basic Needs'. *Journal of Personality*. 22: 326–47.
—— 1956. 'Criteria for Judging needs to be Instinctoid'. In M. R. Jones, ed. *Human Motivation: A Symposium*. Lincoln, Nebr.: Nebraska University Press. 33–48.
—— 1963. 'Fusion of Facts and Values'. *American Journal of Psychoanalysis*. 23/2: 117–31.
—— ed. 1959. *New Knowledge in Human Values*. New York: Harper and Row.
Max-Neef, Manfred. 1989. 'Human Scale Development: An Option for the Future'. *Development Dialogue*. 5–81.
—— 1992. *From the Outside Looking In: Experiences in Barefoot Economics*. London: Zed Press.
—— 1993. *Human Scale Development: Conception, Application, and Further Reflections*. London: Apex Press.
Michener, Victoria J. 1998. 'The Participatory Approach: Contradition and Co-option in Burkina Faso'. *World Development*. 26/12: 2105–18.
Moon, Bruce E. E. 1991. *The Political Economy of Basic Human Needs*. Ithaca, NY: Cornell University Press.

Mosse, David. 1994. 'Authority, Gender and Knowledge: Theoretical Reflections on the Practice of Participatory Rural Appraisal'. *Development and Change*. 25: 497–526.

Mulgan, Richard. 2000. 'Was Aristotle an "Aristotelian Social Democrat"?' *Ethics*. 111: 79–101.

Munene, J., and S. H. Schwartz, eds. 2001. *Cultural Values and Development in Uganda*. Amsterdam: KIT Publishers.

—— —— G. Kibanja, and J. Kikooma. Forthcoming. *Poverty and Moving Out of Poverty: The Role of Culture and Social Capital*. Kampala: Fountain Publishers.

Munro, D. 1985. 'A Free-Format Values Inventory: Explorations with Zimbabwean Student Teachers'. *South African Journal of Psychology*. 15: 33–41.

Murphy, Mark. 2001. *Natural Law and Practical Rationality*. Cambridge: Cambridge University Press.

Murray, Christopher, and L. C. Chen. 1992. 'Understanding Morbidity Change, *Population and Development Review*. 18/3: 481–503.

Murray, H. A. 1938. *Explorations in Personality*. New York: Oxford University Press.

Myers, David G., and Ed Diener. 1995. *Psychological Science*. 6/1 (Jan.): 10–19.

—— —— 1997. 'The Science of Happiness'. *Futurist*. Sept–Oct. 1–7.

Myrdal, Gunnar. 1968. *Asian Drama: An Inquiry into the Poverty of Nations*. New York: Twentieth Century Fund.

Nandy, Ashish. 1994. 'Culture, Voice and Development: A Primer for the Unsuspecting'. *Thesis Eleven*. 39: 1–18.

Narayan, Deepa. 1993. 'Participatory Evaluation: Tools for Managing Change in Water and Sanitation'. *World Bank Technical Paper*, 207. The World Bank.

—— 1995. 'Designing Community Based Development'. *Environment Department Working Paper*. 7. The World Bank.

—— with Raj Patel, Kai Schafft, Anne Rademacher, and Sarah Koch-Schutte. 2000a. *Voices of the Poor: Can Anyone Hear Us?* New York: Oxford University Press for the World Bank.

—— Robert Chambers, Meera K. Shah, and Patti Petesch. 2000b. *Voices of the Poor: Crying Out for Change*. New York: Oxford University Press for the World Bank.

—— and Katrinka Ebbe. 1997. 'Design of Social Funds: Participation, Demand Orientation and Local Organizational Capacity'. *World Bank Discussion Paper*, No. 375. The World Bank.

Narayan-Parker, Deepa, and Lant Pritchett. 1997. 'Cents and Sociability: Household Income and Social Capital in Rural Tanzania'. Policy Research Working Paper. 1796. The World Bank Social Development and Development Research Group.

Nelson, N., and S. Wright, eds. 1995. *Power and Participatory Development: Theory and Practice*. London: IT Publications.

Ng, Yew-Kwang. 1997. 'A Case for Happiness, Cardinalism, and Interpersonal Comparability'. *The Economic Journal*. 107: 1848–58.

Nielsen, Kai. 1963. 'On Human Needs and Moral Appraisals'. *Inquiry*. 6: 170–83.

—— 1969. 'Morality and Needs'. In J. J. McIntosh and S. Coval, eds. *The Business of Reason*. London: Routledge and Kegan Paul. 186–206.

—— 1977. 'True Needs, Rationality and Emancipation'. In Ross Fitzgerald. *Human Needs and Politics*. Oxford: Pergamon Press. 142–56.

North, Douglass. 1989. 'Institutions and Economic Growth: An Historical Introduction'. *World Development*. 17/9: 1319–32.

—— 1990. *Institutions, Institutional Change and Economic Performance*. Cambridge: Cambridge University Press.

—— 1993. 'Institutions and Credible Commitment'. *Journal of Institutional and Theoretical Economics*. 149: 11–23.

Norton, Andrew, and Thomas Stephens. 1995. 'Participation in Poverty Assessments'. *Environment Department Papers Participation Series*. 20. The World Bank.

Nozick, Richard. 1974. *Anarchy, State and Utopia*. Oxford: Basil Blackwell.

Nussbaum, Martha C. 1986. *The Fragility of Goodness: Luck and Ethics in Greek Tragedy and Philosophy*. Cambridge: Cambridge University Press.

—— 1988. 'Nature, Function and Capability: Aristotle on Political Distribution'. *Oxford Studies in Ancient Philosophy*. 6, suppl. vol. Oxford: Clarendon Press. 145–84.

—— 1990a. 'Aristotelian Social Democracy'. In Bruce Douglass, Gerald Mara, and Henry Richardson, eds. *Liberalism and the Good*. London: Routledge. 203–52.

—— 1990b. *Love's Knowledge: Essays on Philosophy and Literature*. Oxford: Oxford University Press.

—— 1992. 'Human Functioning and Social Justice: In Defense of Aristotelian Essentialism'. *Political Theory*. 20/2: 202–46.

—— 1993. 'Non-relative Virtues: An Aristotelian Approach'. In Nussbaum and Sen 1993: 242–69.

—— 1994a. 'Scepticism about Practical Reason in Literature and the Law'. *Harvard Law Review*. 10: 714–44.

—— 1994b. 'Platonic Love and Colorado Law: The Relevance of Ancient Greek Norms to Modern Sexual Controversies'. *Virginia Law Review*. 80/7: 1515–651.

—— 1995a. 'Aristotle on Human Nature and the Foundations of Ethics'. In J. Altham and R. Harrison, eds. *World Mind and Ethics: Essays on the Ethical Philosophy of Bernard Williams*. Cambridge: Cambridge University Press. 86–131.

—— 1995b. 'Human Capabilities, Female Human Being'. In Nussbaum and Glover 1995: 61–104.

—— 1995c. 'Emotions and Women's Capabilities?' In Nussbaum and Glover 1995: 360–95.

—— 1996. 'Compassion—The Basic Social Emotion'. *Social Philosophy and Policy*. 13/1: 27–58.

—— 1997. 'Flawed Foundations: The Philosophical Critique of (a Particular Type of) Economics'. *University of Chicago Law Review*. 1197–214.

—— 1998a. 'Good as Discipline Good as Freedom'. In Crocker and Linden 1998.

—— 1998b. 'Public Philosophy and International Feminism'. *Ethics*. 108/4: 762–96.

—— 2000a. *Women and Human Development: The Capabilities Approach*. Cambridge: Cambridge University Press.

—— 2000b. 'Aristotle, Politics, and Human Capabilities: A Response to Antony, Arneson, Charlesworth, and Mulgan'. *Ethics*. 111: 102–40.

—— 2000c. 'The Costs of Tragedy: Some Moral Limits of Cost-Benefit Analysis'. *Journal of Legal Studies*. 29: 1005–36.

—— and J. Glover, eds. 1995. *Women, Culture and Development A Study of Human Capabilities*. Oxford: Clarendon Press.

—— and A. Sen. 1989. 'Internal Criticism and Indian Rationalist Traditions'. In M. Krausz, ed. *Relativism, Interpretation and Confrontation*. Notre Dame, Ind.: University of Notre Dame Press. 229–325.

—— —— eds. 1993. *The Quality of Life*. Oxford: Clarendon Press.

Oakley, Allen. 1994. *Classical Economic Man: Human Agency and Methodology in the Political Economy of Adam Smith and J. S. Mill*. Aldershot: Edward Elgar.

Oakley, P., and D. Marsden. 1984. *Approaches to Participation in Rural Development*. Geneva: ILO.

Oates, W. E., ed. 1992. *The Economics of the Environment*. Aldershot: Edward Elgar.

OECD. 1996. *Shaping the 21st Century: The Contribution of Development Cooperation*. Paris: OECD.

Offer, Avner, ed. 1996. *In Pursuit of the Quality of Life.* Oxford: Oxford University Press.

Okin, Susan Moller, Joshua Cohen, Matthew Howard, and Martha C. Nussbaum. 1999. *Is Multiculturalism Bad for Women?* Princeton: Princeton University Press.

Omkarnath, G. 1997. 'Capabilities and the Process of Development'. Centre for Development Studies Working Paper, No. 275. Thiruvananthapuram, Kerala, India.

O'Neill, Onora. 1996. *Towards Justice and Virtue: A Constructive Account of Practical Reasoning.* Cambridge: Cambridge University Press.

Oostendorp, Remco. 1995. 'Adam Smith, Social Norms and Economic Behavior'. Ph.D. Thesis. Harvard.

Orshansky, M. 1969. 'How Poverty is Measured'. *Monthly Labor Review.*

Oswald, Andrew J. 1997. 'Happiness and Economic Performance'. *Economic Journal.* 107: 1815–31.

Overseas Development Administration. 1995. *A Guide to Social Analysis for Projects in Developing Countries.* London: HMSO.

Oxfam Pakistan. 1996. '1995–1996 Annual Report'. Mimeo.

Packard, Vance. 1960. *The Wastemaker.* New York: D. McKay Co.

Pakistan, Government of. 1996. *Economic Survey 1995–1996.* Islamabad: Government of Pakistan.

Pattanaik, Prasanta. 1997. 'Cultural Indicators of Well-Being: Some Conceptual Issues'. *UNRISD Occasional Paper Series on Culture and Development.* 2. Geneva: UNRISD and Paris: UNESCO.

—— 1998. 'Cultural Indicators of Well-Being: Some Conceptual Issues'. In UNESCO. 1998. 333–9.

Paul, S. 1989. 'Community Participation in Development Projects'. World Bank Discussion Paper No. 6. The World Bank.

Peerzade, Sayed Afzal. 1997. 'The Definition and Measurement of Poverty: An Integrated Islamic Approach'. *The Pakistan Development Review.* 36/1: 87–97.

Penz, G. Peter. 1991. 'The Priority of Basic Needs: Toward a Consensus in Development Ethics for Political Engagement'. In Aman, 1991.

Perlman, Mark. 1996. 'Assessing the Reprinting of Schumpeter's *History of Economic Analysis*'. In L. S. Moss, ed. *Joseph A. Schumpeter, Historian of Economics.* London and New York: Routledge.

Perry, Michael. 1989. 'A Brief Comment'. *Tulane Law Review.* 63: 1673–8.

Petit, Philip. 1993. *Consequentialism.* Aldershot: Dartmouth.

Pitt, Mark M., and Shahidur R. Khandker, 1998. 'The Impact of Group-Based Credit Programs on Poor Households in Bangladesh. Does the Gender of Participants matter?' *Journal of Political Economy.* 106/5 (Oct.): 958–96.

Pohl, Gerhard, and Dubravko Mihaljeck. 1992. 'Project Evaluation and Uncertainty in Practice: A Statistical Analysis of Rate-of-Return Divergences of 1,015 World Bank Projects'. *World Bank Economic Review.* 6/2: 255–77.

Posner, Richard. 2000. 'Cost-Benefit Analysis: Definition, Justification and Comment on Conference Papers'. *The Journal of Legal Studies.* 29/2: 1153–77.

Pratt, Brian, and Jo Boyden. 1985. *The Field Director's Handbook: An Oxfam Manual for Development Workers.* Oxford: Oxfam Publications.

Psacharopoulos, George. 1994. 'Returns to Investment in Education: A Global Update'. *World Development.* 22. 1324–43.

Putnam, Hilary. 1995. 'Pragmatism and Moral Objectivity'. In Nussbaum and Glover 1995: 199–224.

Putnam, Robert D. 1993. *Making Democracy Work: Civic Traditions in Modern Italy*. Princeton: Princeton University Press.

Qizilbash, Mozaffar. 1996a. 'Capabilities, Well-Being and Human Development: A Survey'. *Journal of Development Studies*. 33/2: 143–62.

—— 1996b. 'Ethical Development'. *World Development*. 24/7: 1209–21.

—— 1997a. 'Needs, Incommensurability and Well-being'. *Review of Political Economy*. 9: 261–76.

—— 1997b. 'Pluralism and Well-Being Indices'. *World Development*. 25: 2009–26.

—— 1998a. 'Poverty: Concept and Measurement'. *Sustainable Development Policy Institute Research Report Series*. 12. Islamabad: SDPI.

—— 1998b. 'The Concept of Well-Being'. *Economics and Philosophy*. 14: 51–73.

Qureshi, Saeed, Ijaz Nabi, and Rashid Faruqee. 1996. 'Rural Finance for Growth and Poverty Alleviation in Pakistan'. Policy Research Working Paper No. 1593. The World Bank.

Rahman, M. D. Anisur. 1988. *People's Self-Development: Perspectives on Participatory Action Research*. London: Zed Books.

Ram, Rati. 1992. 'Intercountry Inequalities in Income and Basic-Needs Indicators: A Recent Perspective'. *World Development*. 20: 899–905.

Ramsay, Maureen. 1992. *Human Needs and the Market*. Aldershot: Avebury.

Ranis, Gustav, Frances Stewart, and Alejandro Ramirez. 2000. 'Economic Growth and Human Development'. *World Development*. 28/2: 197–219.

Rati, Ram. 1992. 'Intercountry Inequalities in Income and Basic Needs Indicators: A Recent Perspective'. *World Development*. 20/6: 899–906.

Ravallion, Martin. 1994a. 'Measuring Social Welfare With and Without Poverty Lines'. *American Economic Association Papers and Proceedings*. 359–63.

—— 1994b. 'Poverty Rankings Using Noisy Data on Living Standards'. *Economics Letters*. 45: 481–5.

Rawls, John. 1971. *A Theory of Justice*. Cambridge, Mass.: Harvard University Press.

—— 1980. 'Kantian Constructivism in Moral Theory'. *The Journal of Philosophy*. 77/9: 515–72.

—— 1982. 'Social Unity and Primary Goods'. In Sen and Williams, 1982.

—— 1988. 'The Priority of Right and Ideas of the Good'. *Philosophy and Public Affairs*. 17/4: 251–76.

—— 1993. *Political Liberalism*. New York: Columbia University Press.

—— 1997. 'The Idea of Public Reason Revisited'. *The University of Chicago Law Review*. 64/3: 765–807.

Razavi, Shahrashoub. 1996. 'Excess Female Mortality: An Indicator of Female Subordination? A Note Drawing on Village-Level Evidence from Southeastern Iran'. *Politeia*. 12/43–4: 79–96.

Renshon, Stanley A. 1974. *Psychological Needs and Political Behavior*. New York: Free Press.

Richardson, Henry. 1997. *Practical Reasoning about Final Ends*. Cambridge Studies in Philosophy. Cambridge: Cambridge University Press.

—— 1999. 'Institutionally Divided Moral Responsibility'. *Social Philosophy and Policy*. 218–49.

—— 2000. 'The Stupidity of the Cost-Benefit Standard'. *Journal of Legal Studies*. 29: 971–1004.

—— Forthcoming. *Democratic Autonomy*.

Riddell, Roger. 1990. 'Judging Success: Evaluating NGO Approaches to Alleviating Poverty in Developing countries'. ODI Working Paper No. 37.

Rietbergen-McCracken, Jennifer, and Deepa Narayan. 1997. 'Participatory Tools and Techniques: A Resource Kit for Participation and Social Assessment'. Washington: The World Bank.

Ringen, Stein. 1995. 'Well-Being, Measurement, and Preferences'. *Acta Sociologica*. 38/3: 3–15.
Robbins, L. 1932. *An Essay on the Nature & Significance of Economic Science*. London: Macmillan.
—— 1935. *An Essay on the Nature and Significance of Economic Science*. 2nd edn. London: Macmillan.
—— 1938. 'Interpersonal Comparisons of Utility'. *Economic Journal*. 48.
Roche, Chris. 1999. *Impact Assessment for Development Agencies: Learning to Value Change*. Oxford: Oxfam GB with NOVIB.
Rodgers, J. R. 1991. 'Does the Choice of Poverty Index Matter in Practice?' *Social Indicators Research*. 24: 233–52.
Rokeach, Milton. 1969. *Beliefs, Attitudes, and Values*. San Francisco: Jossey-Bass.
—— 1973. *The Nature of Human Values*. New York: Free Press.
Rosenweig, Mark R. 1988. 'Risk, Implicit Contracts and the Family in Rural Areas of Low Income Countries'. *Economic Journal*. 98: 1148–79.
Rowntree, B. Seebohm. 1901. *Poverty: A Study of Town Life*. Bristol: Policy Press.
Ryff, Carol D. 1989. 'Happiness is Everything, or Is It? Explorations on the Meaning of Psychological Well-Being'. *Journal of Personality and Social Psychology*. 57/6: 1069–81.
—— and Susan M. Heidrick. 1997. 'Experience and Well-Being: Explorations on Domains of Life and How they Matter'. *International Journal of Behavioral Development*. 20/2: 193–206.
—— and Corey Lee M. Keyes. 1995. 'The Structure of Psychological Well-Being Revisited'. *Journal of Personality and Social Psychology*. 69/4: 719–27.
Sachs, Wolfgang. 1992. *The Development Dictionary*. London: Zed Press.
Sah, R. J. and J. E. Stiglitz. 1985. 'The Social Cost of Labor and Project Evaluation: A General Approach'. *Journal of Public Economics*. 28: 135–63.
Salmen, Lawrence F. 1987. *Listen to the People: A Participant–Observer Evaluation of Development Projects*. New York: Oxford University Press for the World Bank.
—— 1992. 'Reducing Poverty: An Institutional Perspective'. Poverty and Social Policy Series. No. 1. The World Bank.
—— 1995. 'Beneficiary Assessment: An Approach Described'. Environment Department Papers Social Assessment Series. 23. The World Bank.
—— 1999. 'Beneficiary Assessment Manual for Social Funds'. Social Protection Discussion Paper, 9930. The World Bank.
Salop, Joanne. 1992. *Economic Analysis of Projects: Towards a Results-Oriented Approach to Evaluation*. Washington: The World Bank.
Samuelson, Paul. 1938. 'A Note on the Pure Theory of Consumer's Behaviour'. *Economica*. 5.
Sandbrook, Richard. 1982. *The Politics of Basic Needs: Urban Aspects of Assaulting Poverty in Africa*. London: Heinemann.
Sandel, Michael. 1998. Tanner Lectures on Human Values. Oxford [own notes].
Schoeffel, Penelope. 1995. 'Cultural and Institutional Issues in the Appraisal of Projects in Developing Countries: South Pacific Water Resources'. *Project Appraisal*. 10/3.
Schumpeter, Joseph A. 1952. *Ten Great Economists: From Marx to Keynes*. London: George Allen & Unwin.
—— 1954. *History of Economic Analysis*. New York: Oxford University Press.
Schwartz, S. H. 1992. 'Universals in the Content and Structure of Values: Theoretical Advances and Empirical Tests in 20 Countries'. *Advances in Experimental Social Psychology*. 25: 1–65.
—— 1994. 'Are There Universal Aspects in the Structure and Contents of Human Values?' *Journal of Social Issues*. 50/4: 19–45.
—— 1997. 'Values and Culture'. In Donald Munro, John Schumaker, and Staurt C. Carr, eds. *Motivation and Culture*. New York: Routledge.

—— and Wolfgang Bilsky. 1987. 'Toward a Universal Psychological Structure of Human Values'. *Journal of Personality and Social Psychology.* 53/3: 550–62.

—— —— 1990. 'Toward a Theory of the Universal Content and Structure of Values: Extensions and Cross-Cultural Replications'. *Journal of Personality and Social Psychology.* 58/5: 878–91.

Sen, Amartya K. 1959*a*. 'Choice of Capital-Intensity Further Considered'. *Quarterly Journal of Economics.* 73: 466–84.

—— 1959*b*. 'The Choice of Agricultural Techniques in Underdeveloped Countries'. *Economic Development and Cultural Change.* 7: 279–85.

—— 1966*a*. 'Hume's Law and Hare's Rule'. *Philosophy.* 41: 75–9.

—— 1966*b*. 'Peasants and Dualism with or without Surplus Labour'. *Journal of Public Economy.* 74: 425–50.

—— 1966*c*. 'Labour Allocation in a Cooperative Enterprise'. *Review of Economic Studies.* 34(4)/96: 361–71. Reprinted as ch. 2 in D. Prychitko and J. Vanek, eds. 1996. *Producer Cooperatives and Labor-Managed Systems, Volume I.* Cheltenham: Edward Elgar.

—— 1966*d*. 'Education, Vintage and Learning by Doing'. *Journal of Human Resources.* 1: 3–21.

—— 1967. 'The Nature and Classes of Prescriptive Judgments'. *Philosophical Quarterly.* 17/66: 46–62.

—— 1970. *Collective Choice and Social Welfare.* San Francisco: Holden-Day.

—— 1972. With Steve Marglin and Partha Dasgupta. Part I. 'Introduction to the Methodology of National Benefit-Cost Analysis'. *Guidelines for Project Evaluation.* UNIDO. New York: United Nations.

—— 1973. 'Choice Functions and Revealed Preference'. *Econometrica.* 41.

—— 1974*a*. 'Choice, Orderings and Morality'. In Stephan Körner, ed. *Practical Reason.* Oxford: Basil Blackwell.

—— 1974*b*. 'Informational Bases of Alternative Welfare Approaches: Aggregation and Income Distribution'. *Journal of Public Economics.* 3: 387–403.

—— 1975. *Employment, Technology and Development.* Oxford: Clarendon Press.

—— 1976. 'Poverty: An Ordinal Approach to Measurement'. *Econometrica.* 44/2: 219–31.

—— 1977. 'Rational Fools: A Critique of the Behavioral Foundations of Economic Theory'. *Philosophy and Public Affairs.* 6: 317–44.

—— 1979*a*. 'Informational Analysis of Moral Principles'. In Ross Harrison, ed. *Rational Action.* Cambridge: Cambridge University Press. 115–32.

—— 1979*b*. 'Utilitarianism and Welfarism'. *The Journal of Philosophy.* 76/9: 463–89.

—— 1980*a*. 'Equality of What?' In S. McMurrin, ed. *Tanner Lectures on Human Values.* Cambridge: Cambridge University Press.

—— 1980*b*. 'Famines'. *World Development.* 8: 613–21.

—— 1980*c*. 'Labor and Technology'. In J. Cody, H. Hughes, and D. Walls, eds. *Policies for Industrial Progress in Developing Countries.* New York: Oxford University Press. 121–58.

—— 1980/1. 'Plural Utility'. *Proceedings of the Aristotelian Society.* 81: 193–215.

—— 1981*a*. *Poverty and Famines: An Essay on Entitlement and Deprivation.* Oxford: Clarendon Press.

—— 1981*b*. 'Ingredients of Famine Analysis: Availability and Entitlements'. *Quarterly Journal of Economics.* 96/3 (Aug.): 433–64.

—— 1981*c*. 'A Positive Concept of Negative Freedom'. In E. Morscher and R. Stanzinger, eds. *Ethics: Foundations, Problems and Applications.* Vienna: Holder-Pichler-Tempsky.

—— 1981*d*. 'Public Action and the Quality of Life in Developing Countries'. *Oxford Bulletin of Economics and Statistics.* 43: 287–319.

Sen, Amartya K. 1982a. 'Rights and Agency'. *Philosophy and Public Affairs*. 11/1: 5–29.
—— 1982b. *Choice, Welfare and Measurement*. Oxford: Basil Blackwell.
—— 1982c. 'Liberty as Control: An Appraisal'. *Midwest Studies in Philosophy*. 7: 207–21.
—— 1982d. 'The Food Problem: Theory and Policy'. *Third World Quarterly*. 4: 447–59.
—— 1982e. 'The Right Not To Be Hungry'. In G. Floistad, ed. *Contemporary Philosophy*. ii. The Hague: Martinus Nijhoff.
—— 1983a. 'Accounts, Actions and Values: Objectivity of Social Science'. In Chris Lloyd, ed. *Social Theory and Political Practice*. Oxford: Clarendon Press.
—— 1983b. 'Evaluator Relativity and Consequential Evaluation'. *Philosophy & Public Affairs*. 12: 113–32.
—— 1983c. 'Liberty and Social Choice'. *The Journal of Philosophy*. 80/1: 5–28.
—— 1983d. 'Poor, Relatively Speaking'. *Oxford Economic Papers*. 35: 153–69. Reprinted as chapter 14 in Sen 1984b: 325–45.
—— 1983e. 'The Profit Motive'. *Lloyds Bank Review*. 147 (Jan.): 1–20.
—— 1983f. 'Carrots, Sticks and Economics: Perception Problems in Economics'. *Indian Economic Review*. 18: 1–16.
—— 1983g. 'Economics and the Family'. *Asian Development Review*. 1: 14–26.
—— 1984a. 'The Living Standard'. *Oxford Economic Papers*. 36: 74–90.
—— 1984b. *Resources, Values and Development*. Oxford: Basil Blackwell.
—— 1984c. 'Money and Value: On the Ethics and Economics of Finance'. *Economics and Philosophy*. 9: 203–27.
—— 1985a. 'Well-Being Agency and Freedom: The Dewey Lectures 1984'. *Journal of Philosophy*. 82/4: 169–221.
—— 1985b. *Commodities and Capabilities*. Amsterdam: Elsevier.
—— 1985c. 'A Sociological Approach to the Measurement of Poverty: A Reply to Professor Peter Townsend'. *Oxford Economic Papers*. 37: 669–76.
—— 1985d. 'Rights and Capabilities'. In T. Honderich, ed. *Morality and Objectivity*. London: Routledge. 130–48.
—— 1985e. 'Rationality and Uncertainty'. *Theory and Decision*. 18: 109–27.
—— 1985f. 'Social Choice and Justice: A Review Article'. *Journal of Economic Literature*. 23: 1764–76.
—— 1985g. 'The Moral Standing of the Market'. *Social Philosophy and Policy*. 2: 1–19.
—— 1986a. 'Behaviour and the Concept of Preference'. In J. Elster, ed. *Rational Choice*. Oxford: Basil Blackwell.
—— 1986b. 'Information and Invariance in Normative Choice'. In W. Heller, Ross Starr, and David Starrett, eds. *Social Choice and Public Decision-Making: Essays in Honor of K. J. Arrow, Vol I*. Cambridge: Cambridge University Press.
—— 1986c. 'Rationality, Interest, and Identity'. In Alejandro Foxley, ed. *Development, Democracy and the Art of Trespassing*. Notre Dame, Ind.: University of Notre Dame Press. 343–53.
—— 1986d. 'Social Choice Theory'. In K. J. Arrow and M. D. Intriligator, eds. *Handbook of Mathematical Economics, Volume III*. North-Holland: Elsevier Science Publishers.
—— 1986e. 'Food, Economics and Entitlements'. In WIDER Working Papers. WP1 (Feb.).
—— 1986f. 'Adam Smith's Prudence'. In S. Lall and Frances Stewart, eds. *Theory and Reality in Development*. London: Macmillan.
—— 1987a. *On Ethics and Economics*. New York: Basil Blackwell.
—— 1987b. 'The Standard of Living'. In Sen *et al.* 1987.
—— 1988a. 'The Concept of Development'. In H. Chenery and T. N. Srinivasan, eds. *The Handbook of Development Economics Volume I*. Amsterdam: Elsevier Publishers.

—— 1988b. 'Freedom of Choice'. *European Economic Review*. 32: 269–94.
—— 1988c. 'Family and Food: Sex-Bias in Poverty'. In P. Bardhan and T. N. Srinivasan, eds. *Rural Poverty in South Asia*. New York: Columbia University Press.
—— 1988d. 'Property and Hunger'. *Economics and Philosophy*. 4: 57–68.
—— 1989a. 'Women's Survival as a Development Problem'. *Bulletin of the American Academy of Arts and Science*. 43.
—— 1989b. 'Economic Methodology: Heterogeneity and Relevance'. *Social Research*. 56/2: 299–329.
—— 1989c. 'The Territory of Justice'. Discussion Paper 1425. Harvard Institute of Economic Research.
—— 1989d. 'Food and Freedom'. Text of Sir John Crawford Memorial Lecture, Washington, 1987, reprinted in *World Development*. 17: 769–81.
—— 1989e. 'Indian Development: Lessons and Non-Lessons'. *Daedalus*. 118: 369–92.
—— 1989f. 'Sri Lanka's Achievements: How and When'. In P. Bardhan and T. N. Srinivasan, eds. *Rural Poverty in South Asia*. New York: Columbia University Press.
—— 1990a. 'Development as Capability Expansion'. In K. Griffin and J. Knight, eds. *Human Development and the International Development Strategy for the 1990s*. London: Macmillan.
—— 1990b. 'Justice: Means versus Freedoms'. *Philosophy & Public Affairs*. 19: 107–21.
—— 1990c. 'Gender and Cooperative Conflict'. In Irene Tinker, ed. *Persistent Inequalities*. New York: Oxford University Press.
—— 1990d. 'Public Action to Remedy Hunger'. *Arturo Tanco Lecture* delivered 2 August 1990 at Queen Elizabeth II Conference Centre, London: The Global Hunger Project.
—— 1991a. 'Economic Development: Objectives and Obstacles'. In Kurt Martin, ed. *Strategies of Economic Development*. New York: St Martin's Press.
—— 1991b. 'Wars and Famines: On Divisions and Incentives'. *Suntory-Toyota International Centre Discussion Paper*, No. 33. London School of Economics Development Economics Research Program.
—— 1991c. 'Welfare, Preference and Freedom'. *Journal of Econometrics*. 50: 15–29.
—— 1991d. 'The Nature of Inequality'. In K. J. Arrow, ed. *Issues in Contemporary Economics: Markets and Welfare*. London: Macmillan.
—— 1991e. 'What Did You Learn in the World Today?' *American Behavioral Scientist*. 34: 530–48.
—— 1991f. 'Utility: Ideas and Terminology'. *Economics and Philosophy*. 7/2: 277–83.
—— 1991g. 'Beneconfusion'. In J. G. T. Meeks, ed. *Thoughtful Economic Man: Essays on Rationality, Moral Rules and Benevolence*. Cambridge: Cambridge University Press.
—— 1992a. *Inequality Reexamined*. Cambridge, Mass.: Harvard University Press.
—— 1992b. 'Markets and Governments'. Boston University Institute for Economic Development. Discussion Paper. 28: 1–19.
—— 1992c. 'Progress and Social Deficit: Some Methodological Issues'. In M. Desai, A. Sen, and J. Boltvinik, *Social Progress Index: A Proposal*. Regional Project to Overcome Poverty in Latin America and the Caribbean (RLA/86/004). Bogota: UNDP.
—— 1992d. 'Minimal Liberty'. *Economica*. 59: 139–59.
—— 1993a. 'Capability and Well-Being'. In Nussbaum and Sen 1993: 30–53.
—— 1993b. 'Life Expectancy and Inequality: Some Conceptual Issues'. In P. Bardhan, Mrinal Datta-Chaudhuri, and T. N. Krishnan, eds. *Development and Change: Essays in Honour of K. N. Raj*. Bombay: Oxford University Press.
—— 1993c. 'Markets and Freedoms: Achievements and Limitations of the Market Mechanism in Promoting Individual Freedoms'. *Oxford Economic Papers*. 45: 519–41.

Sen, Amartya K. 1993d. 'Positional Objectivity'. *Philosophy and Public Affairs*. 22: 126–45.
—— 1993e. 'Internal Consistency of Choice'. *Econometrica*. 61/3: 495–521.
—— 1993f. 'Money and Value: On the Ethics and Economics of Finance'. *Economics and Philosophy*. 9: 203–27.
—— 1993g. 'The Economics of Life and Death'. *Scientific American*. 266.
—— 1993h. 'On the Darwinian View of Progress'. *Population and Development Review*. 19/1: 130–7.
—— 1993i. 'The Idea of India'. Nehru Lecture given at Trinity College, Cambridge, on 5 Feb. 1993.
—— 1993j. 'India and the West'. *The New Republic*. 208/23: 27–34.
—— 1993k. 'Markets and Freedoms'. *Oxford Economic Papers*. 45/4: 519–41.
—— 1994a. 'Rational Choice and Monitoring: Facts and Theory'. Paper presented at American Economic Association Annual Meeting.
—— 1994b. 'Well-Being, Capability and Public Policy'. *Giornale degli economisti et Annali di economia*. 53: 334–47.
—— 1994c. 'Economic Wealth and Moral Sentiments'. Lecture held in Zurich on 28 Apr. 1994 on invitation of Bank Hofmann A. G., Zurich, and the Faculty of Economics at the University of Zurich.
—— 1994d. 'Population and Reasoned Agency: Food, Fertility, and Economic Development'. In K. Lindahl-Kiessling and H. Landberg, eds. *Population, Economic Development, and the Environment*. Oxford: Oxford University Press.
—— 1994e. 'The Formulation of Rational Choice'. *AEA Papers and Proceedings*. 385–90.
—— 1994f. 'Markets and the Freedom to Choose'. In Siebert 1994.
—— 1995a. 'Environmental Evaluation and Social Choice: Contingent Valuation and the Market Analogy'. *The Japanese Economic Review*. 23–37.
—— 1995b. 'Rationality and Social Choice'. Presidential address delivered at the 107th meeting of the American Economic Association, 7 Jan. 1995. *American Economic Review*. 85/1: 1–24.
—— 1995c. 'Gender Inequality and Theories of Justice'. In Nussbaum and Glover 1995: 259–73.
—— 1995d. 'Is the Idea of Purely Internal Consistency of Choice Bizarre?' In J. Altham and R. Harrison, eds. *World, Mind, and Ethics: Essays on the Ethical Philosophy of Bernard Williams*. Cambridge: Cambridge University Press. 19–31.
—— 1995e. 'Demography and Welfare Economics' *Empirica*. 22: 1–21.
—— 1995f. 'The Political Economy of Targeting'. In Van de Walle, D. and K. Nead, eds. *Public Spending and the Poor: Theory and Evidence*. Baltimore: Johns Hopkins University Press for the World Bank.
—— 1995g. 'Varieties of Deprivation: Comments on Chapters by Pujol and Hutchinson'. In Edith Kuiper, ed. *Out of the Margin: Feminist Perspectives on Economics*. London: Routledge.
—— 1995h. 'Agency and Well-Being: The Development Agenda'. In Noeleen Heyzer, S. Kapoor, and J. Sandler, eds. *A Commitment to the World's Women: Perspectives on Development for Beijing and Beyond*. New York: UNIFEM.
—— 1995i. 'Economic Regress: Concepts and Features'. *Proceedings of the World Bank Annual Conference on Development Economics 1993*. Washington: The World Bank. 315–54.
—— 1996a. 'On the Foundations of Welfare Economics: Utility, Capability and Practical Reason'. In Farina *et al.* 1996: 50–65.
—— 1996b. 'Welfare Economics and Two Approaches to Rights'. In Jose Casas Pardo and Friedrich Schneider, eds. *Current Issues in Public Choice*. Cheltenham: Edward Elgar.

—— 1996c. 'Social Commitment and Democracy: The Demands of Equity and Financial Conservatism'. In Paul Barker, ed. *Living as Equals: The Eva Colorni Memorial Lectures*. Oxford: Oxford University Press.

—— 1996d. 'Rationality, Joy and Freedom'. *Critical Review*. 10/4: 481–94.

—— 1996e. 'Freedom, Capabilities and Public Action: A Response'. *Politeia*. 12/43–4: 107–25.

—— 1996f. 'Our Culture, Their Culture'. *The New Republic*. 1 April: 27–34.

—— 1996g. 'On the Status of Equality'. *Political Theory*. 24/3: 394–400.

—— 1996h. 'The Concept of Wealth'. In Ramon H. Myers, ed. *The Wealth of Nations in the Twentieth Century: The Policies and Institutional Determinants of Economic Development*. Stanford, Calif.: Hoover Institution Press.

—— 1997a. *On Economic Inequality*. With a substantial annexe 'After a Quarter Century' by J. Foster and A. Sen. 2nd edn. Oxford: Clarendon Press.

—— 1997b. 'What's the Point of a Development Strategy?' In E. Malinvaud *et al. Development Strategy and the Management of the Market Economy*. Oxford: Clarendon Press.

—— 1997c. 'Development Thinking at the Beginning of the 21st Century'. In Luis Emmerij, ed. *Economic and Social Development in the XXI Century*. Washington: Inter-American Development Bank and Johns Hopkins University Press.

—— 1997d. 'Maximization and the Act of Choice'. *Econometrica*. 65/4: 745–79.

—— 1997e. 'Radical Needs and Moderate Reforms'. In Drèze and Sen 1997: 1–32.

—— 1997f. 'Indian Traditions and the Western Imagination'. *Daedalus*. 126/2: 1–26.

—— 1997g. 'Poverty in the Human Development Perspective: Concept and Measurement'. In UNDP 1997: 15–23.

—— 1997h. 'Individual Preference as the Basis of Social Choice'. In Arrow *et al.* 1997.

—— 1997i. 'Economics, Business Principles and Moral Sentiments'. *Business Ethics Quarterly*. 7/3: 5–15.

—— 1997j. 'From Income Inequality to Economic Inequality'. *Southern Economic Journal*. 64/2: 384–401.

—— 1997k. 'Human Rights and Asian Values'. Sixteenth Morgenthau Memorial Lecture on Ethics & Foreign Policy.

—— 1997l. 'Human Rights and Asian Values: What Lee Kuan Yew and Le Peng don't understand about Asia'. *The New Republic*. 217 (14 July): n. 2–3.

—— 1997m. 'Inequality, Unemployment and Contemporary Europe'. *International Labour Review*. 136/2: 155–72.

—— 1997n. 'Maximization and the Act of Choice'. *Econometrica*. 65/4: 745–79.

—— 1997o. 'The Penalties of Unemployment'. *Temi di Discussione del Servizio Studi*. 307 (June). Rome: Banca d'Italia.

—— 1998a. 'Mortality as an Indicator of Economic Success and Failure'. *Economic Journal*. 108/447: 1–25.

—— 1998b. 'Culture, Freedom and Independence'. In UNESCO 1998: 317–21.

—— 1998c. 'Reason Before Identity'. Romanes Lecture given in Oxford on 17 Nov. 1998.

—— 1998d. 'Economic Policy and Equity: An Overview'. Prepared for Conference on Economic Policy and Equity, IMF, 8–9 June.

—— 1998e. 'Individual Freedom: Basis for a Social Commitment'. Excerpt from the address delivered at the award ceremony for the Giovanni Agnelli International Prize, 16 Oct.

—— 1998f. 'The Possibility of Social Choice'. *American Economic Review*. 89/3: 349–78.

—— 1998g. 'Universal Truths: Human Rights and the Westernizing Illusion'. *Harvard International Review*. 40–3.

—— 1999a. *Development as Freedom*. New York: Knopf Press.

Sen, Amartya K. 1999*b*. 'Democracy as a Universal Value'. *Journal of Democracy*. 10/3: 3–17.
—— 1999*c*. 'The Possibility of Social Choice'. *American Economic Review*. 89/3: 349–78.
—— 1999*d*. 'Health in Development'. Keynote address to the Fifty-Second World Health Assembly, Geneva, 18 May.
—— 1999*e*. 'Foreword'. In Jacques Silber, ed. *Handbook of Income Inequality Management*. Boston: Kluwer Academic Publishers.
—— 2000*a*. 'Consequential Evaluation and Practical Reason'. *The Journal of Philosophy*. 97/9: 477–502.
—— 2000*b*. 'Population and Gender Equity'. *Nation*. 271/4: 16–8.
—— 2000*c*. 'The Discipline of Cost-Benefit Analysis'. *Journal of Legal Studies*. 29: 931–53.
—— 2000*d*. 'India through Its Calendars'. *The Little Magazine*. 1 (1 May): 5–12.
—— 2000*e*. 'Beyond Identity: Other People'. *The New Republic*. 223/25: 23–30.
—— 2000*f*. 'India and the Bomb'. *The New Republic*. 25 Sept.: 32–8.
—— 2000*g*. 'East and West: The Reach of Reason'. *The Atlantic Online*. July: 1–3.
—— 2000*h*. 'Work and Rights'. *International Labour Review*. Geneva. 119–28.
—— 2000*i*. 'What Difference can Ethics Make?' Presented at the International Meeting on 'Ethics and Development' of the Inter-American Development Bank in collaboration with the Norwegian government.
—— 2000*j*. 'Social Exclusion: Concept, Application, and Scrutiny'. Social Development Papers, No. 1. Office of Environment and Social Development, Asian Development Bank.
—— 2001. 'Apocalypse Then'. *The New York Times*. 18 Feb.
—— and S. Anand. 1994*a*. 'Sustainable Human Development: Concepts and Priorities'. Occasional Paper, No. 8, Human Development Report Office. New York: UNDP.
—— —— 1994*b*. 'Human Development Index: Methodology and Measurement'. Occasional Paper, No. 12, Human Development Report Office. New York: UNDP.
—— —— 1997. 'Concepts of Human Development and Poverty: A Multidimensional Perspective'. Background Paper for UNDP 1997.
—— —— 2000*a*. 'Human Development and Economic Sustainability'. *World Development*. 28/12: 2029–49.
—— —— 2000*b*. 'The Income Component of the Human Development Index'. *Journal of Human Development*. 1/1: 83–106.
—— J. Muellbauer, R. Kanbur, K. Hart, and B. Williams. 1987. *The Standard of Living: The Tanner Lectures on Human Values*. Cambridge: Cambridge University Press.
—— and Bernard Williams, eds. 1982. *Utilitarianism and Beyond*. Cambridge: Cambridge University Press.
Shaffer, Paul. 1996. 'Beneath the Poverty Debate'. *IDS Bulletin*. 27/1.
Sheehan, G., and M. Hopkins. 1979. *Basic Needs Performance: An Analysis of some International Data*. Geneva: ILO.
Siebert, Horst, ed. 1994. *The Ethical Foundations of the Market*. Tübingen: Mohr.
Sikkink, Kathryn. 1991. *Ideas and Institutions: Developmentalism in Brazil and Argentina*. Ithaca, NY: Cornell University Press.
Singer, P. 1995. 'Is there a Universal Moral Sense?' *Critical Review*. 9/3: 325–39.
Smith, Adam. 1776. *An Inquiry into the Nature and Causes of the Wealth of Nations*. Edinburgh, 1997.
Smith, Peter B., and Michael Harriss Bond. 1993. *Social Psychology across Cultures: Analysis and Perspectives*. Hemel Hempstead: Harvester Wheatsheaf.
Spelman, Elizabeth. 2000. 'How do they see you?' *London Review of Books*. 16 Nov.

Springborg, Patricia. 1981. *The Problem of Human Needs and the Critique of Civilisation*. London: George Allen & Unwin.
Squire, Lyn, I. M. D. Little, and Mete Durdag. 1979. 'Application of Shadow Pricing to Country Economic Analysis with an Illustration from Pakistan'. World Bank Staff Working Paper, No. 330. Washington: The World Bank.
—— and H. G. van der Tak. 1975. *Economic Analysis of Projects*. Baltimore: Johns Hopkins University Press.
Srinivasan, T. N. 1994a. 'Destitution: A Discourse'. *Journal of Economic Literature*. 32: 1842–55.
—— 1994b. 'Human Development: A New Paradigm or Reinvention of the Wheel?' *American Economic Review*. 84/2: 238–43.
Stark, Oded. 1995. *Altruism and Beyond*. Cambridge: Cambridge University Press.
Stewart, Frances. 1985. *Basic Needs in Developing Countries*. Baltimore: Johns Hopkins University Press.
Stewart, Frances. 1986. 'The Human Dimension in Development: Objective and Resource'. In Khadija Haq and Uner Kirdar. *Human Development: The Neglected Dimension*. North–South Round Table. New York: United Nations. 28–45.
—— 1989. 'Basic Needs Strategies, Human Rights and the Right to Development'. *Human Rights Quarterly*. 11: 347–74.
—— 1995. 'Groups for Good or Ill'. Paper presented at 1995 QEH Conference.
—— 1996. 'Basic Needs, Capabilities, and Human Development'. In Offer, 1996.
—— Henk Thomas, and Ton de Wilde, eds. 1990. *The Other Policy: The Influence of Policies on Technology Choice and Small Enterprise Development*. London: IT Publications.
—— and Ejaz Ghani. 1991. 'How Significant are Externalities for Development?' *World Development*. 19/6: 569–94.
Stiefel, Matthis, and Marshall Wolfe. 1994. *A Voice for the Excluded: Popular Participation in Development Utopia or Necessity?* London: Zed Books in association with UNRISD.
Streeten, Paul. 1984. 'Basic Needs: Some Unsettled Questions'. *World Development*. 12/9: 973–8.
—— 1994. 'Human Development Means and Ends'. *American Economic Association Papers and Proceedings*. 84/2: 85–97.
—— Shaid Javed Burki, Mahbub ul Haq, Norman Hicks, and Frances Stewart, et al. 1981. *First Things First: Meeting Basic Human Needs in Developing Countries*. London: Oxford University Press for the World Bank.
Sugden, Robert. 1993. 'Welfare, Resources and Capabilities: *A Review of Inequality Reexamined* by Amartya Sen'. *Journal of Economic Literature*. 31: 1947–62.
—— and A. Williams. 1978. *The Principles of Cost-Benefit Analysis*. Oxford: Oxford University Press.
Summers, L. 1992. 'Investing in All the People'. Policy Research Working Paper, No. 905. The World Bank.
Sunstein, Cass R. 1996. *Legal Reasoning and Political Conflict*. New York: Oxford University Press.
—— 2000. 'Cognition and Cost-Benefit Analysis'. *The Journal of Legal Studies*. 29/2: 1059–104.
Tashakkori, Abbas, and Charles Teddlie. 1998. *Mixed Methodologies: Combining Qualitative and Quantitative Approaches*. London: Sage Publications.
Taylor, C. N., C. H. Bryan, and Colin G. Goodrich. 1990. *Social Assessment: Theory, Process and Techniques*. Studies in Resource Management No. 7. New Zealand: Centre for Resource Management.
Taylor, Charles. 1993. 'Explanation and Practical Reason'. In Nussbaum and Sen 1993.

Tendler, Judith. 1989. 'What Ever Happened to Poverty Alleviation?' *World Development*. 17/7: 1033–44.

Therkildsen, Ole. 1988. *Watering White Elephants*. Uppsala: Scandinavian Institute of African Studies.

Townsend, Peter. 1974. 'Poverty as Relative Deprivation: Resources and Styles of Living'. In Dorothy Wedderburn, ed. *Poverty, Inequality and Class Structure*. Cambridge: Cambridge University Press.

—— 1985. 'A Sociological Approach to the Measurement of Poverty—A Rejoinder to Professor Amartya Sen'. *Oxford Economic Papers*. 37: 659–68.

Trump, Thomas M. 1991. 'Value Formation and Postmaterialism: Inglehart's Theory of Value Change Reconsidered'. *Comparative Political Studies*. 24: 365–90.

UNDP. 1990–2001 (annually). *The Human Development Report*. New York: United Nations Development Programme.

UNESCO. 1995. *Our Creative Diversity: Report of the World Commission on Culture and Development*. Paris: UNESCO Publishing.

—— 1998. *World Culture Report 1998: Culture, Creativity and Markets*. Paris: UNESCO Publishing.

UNIDO. 1972. (P. Dasgupta, A. Sen, and S. Marglin) *Guidelines for Project Evaluation*. New York: United Nations Industrial Development Organization.

United Nations Research Institute for Social Development. 1995. 'Social Integration: Approaches and Issues'. UNRISD Briefing Paper Series. 1. World Summit for Social Development.

University of Stockholm. 1991. 'Guidelines for Consultations and Popular Participation in Development Processes and Projects'. Popular Participation Programme. Mimeo.

UNRISD and UNESCO. 1997. 'Towards a World Report on Culture and Development: Constructing Cultural Statistics and Indicators'. Report of the Workshop on Cultural Indicators of Development. Royaumont Foundation, France, 4–7 Jan. UNRISD Occasional Paper series on Culture and Development. 1. Geneva: UNRISD and Paris: UNESCO.

Uphoff, Norman. 1998. 'Learning about and for Participation: From Theoretical and Empirical Studies to Practical Experience, and Back to Theory'. *Canadian Journal of Development Studies*. 19/3: 439–60.

Van der Hoeven, Rolph. 1988. *Planning for Basic Needs: A Soft Option or a Solid Policy? A Basic Needs Simulation Model applied to Kenya*. Aldershot: Gower for ILO/WEP.

Veenhoven, Ruut. 1993. *Happiness in Nations: Subjective Appreciation of Life in 56 Nations 1946–1992*. Rotterdam: RISBO, Erasmus University, Rotterdam.

—— Carla Den Buitlar, and Henk de Heer. 1994. *World Database of Happiness: Correlates of Happiness*. Rotterdam: RISBO.

Vivian, Jessica. 1993. 'NGOs and Sustainable Development in Zimbabwe: No Magic Bullets'. *Development and Change*. 25/1: 167–94.

—— and G. Maseko. 1994. 'NGOs, Participation, and Rural Development: Testing the Assumptions with Evidence from Zimbabwe'. UNRISD Discussion Paper, No. 49.

Wade, Robert. 1988. *Village Republics: Economic Conditions for Collective Action in South India*. Cambridge: Cambridge University Press.

Wainryb, Cecelia. 1993. 'The Application of Moral Judgements to other Cultures: Relativism and Universality'. *Child Development*. 64/3: 924–33.

Ward, William, Barry Deren, and Emmanuel D'Silva. 1991. *The Economics of Project Analysis: A Practitioner's Guide*. EDI Technical Materials. Washington: The World Bank.

Welbourn, Alice. 1992. 'Rapid Rural Appraisal, Gender and Health: Alternative Ways of Listening to Needs'. *IDS Bulletin*. 23/1: 8–18.

Westendorff, David G., and Dharam Ghai. 1993. *Monitoring Social Progress in the 1990s*. Aldershot: Avebury.

Wiggins, David. 1998. *Needs, Values, Truth*. 3rd edn. Oxford: Clarendon Press.

Wignaraja, Ponna. 1993. *New Social Movements in the South: Empowering the People*. London: Zed Books.

Wilson, W. 1967. 'Correlates of Avowed Happiness'. *Psychological Bulletin*. 67: 294–306.

Woolcock, Michael. 1998. 'Social Capital and Economic Development: Toward a Theoretical Synthesis and Policy Framework'. *Theory and Society*. 27: 151–208.

World Bank. 1989. *Sub-Saharan Africa: From Crisis to Sustainable Growth: A Long-Term Perspective Study*. Washington DC: The World Bank.

—— 1991. 'Operational Directive 4.15: Poverty Reduction'. 31 Dec. The World Bank Operation Manual.

—— 1992*a*. 'Reducing Poverty: An Institutional Perspective'. *Poverty and Social Policy Series*. No. 1.

—— 1992*b*. *Poverty Reduction Handbook*. Washington DC: The World Bank.

—— 1992*c*. *Effective Implementation: Key to Development Impact*. Washington DC: The World Bank.

—— 1993. *Implementing the World Bank's Strategy to Reduce Poverty: Progress and Challenges*. Washington DC: The World Bank.

—— 1996*a*. *Handbook on Economic Analysis of Investment Operations*. May. Washington DC: The World Bank.

—— 1996*b*. *Ethics and Spiritual Values: Promoting Environmentally Sustainable Development*. Washington DC: The World Bank.

—— 1996*c*. *Introduction to Social Assessment (SA): Incorporating Participation and Social Analysis in to the Bank's Work*. July. Washington DC: The World Bank Social Policy and Resettlement Division.

—— 1996*d*. *The World Bank Participation Source Book*. Washington DC: The World Bank.

—— 1997. *World Development Report: The State in a Changing World*. Washington DC: The World Bank.

—— 1998*a*. *World Development Report 1998*. Washington DC: The World Bank.

—— 1998*b*. *Assessing Aid: What Works, What Doesn't, and Why*. New York: Oxford University Press for the World Bank.

—— 1998*c*. *Social Development Update*. Washington DC: The World Bank.

—— 1998*d*. *Social Assessment Guidelines*. Washington DC: The World Bank.

—— 2000. *World Development Report 2000/2001*. Washington DC: The World Bank.

Wunsch, J., and D. Olowu, eds. 1990. *The Failure of the Centralised State*. Colorado: Westview Press.

Index of Names

Note: Page numbers followed by '*n*' refer to footnotes and those followed by '*t*' refer to tables.

Alinsky, Saul 149
Allardt, E. 77*t*
Anand, S., with A. K. Sen 10*n*, 83*t*, 182–3
Andrews, Frank M., with S. B. Withey 77*t*
Apffel-Marglin, F. 150
  with S. Marglin 125
Aquinas, St Thomas 17, 46*n*
Argyle, Michael 77*t*
Aristotle 5, 6, 17, 18, 29, 32, 36, 44, 58, 95, 108, 136
Arrow, Kenneth J. 90, 94, 127
Ayer, Sir Alfred J. 135

Banuri, Tariq 120, 142*n*
Beauchamp, Tom, with J. Childress 146, 146*n*
Benhabib, Seyla 37
Biswas-Diener, Robert, with E. Diener 5*n*, 78*t*
Black, Rufus 17
Boyle, Joseph, with G. Grisez and J. Finnis 17, 48*t*, 73, 291
Braybrooke, David 77*t*
Brentano, Franz 78*t*
Burdge, Rabel 218, 219, 220
Burki, A. A., with A. Ubaidullah 261

Carmen, Raff 129
Chambers, Robert 62, 78*t*, 151, 222, 223
Chenery, Hollis *et al* 19
Chevalier, Maurice 116
Childress, James, with T. Beauchamp 146, 146*n*
Clark, Samuel 47*n*
Cornia, G. Andrea 146*n*
Crocker, David 12, 55, 158*n*
Crutchfield, Richard S., with N. Livson and D. Krech 80*t*
Cummins, Robert 26, 66–8, 73, 75*t*, 76, 78*t*

Davitt, T. E. 78*t*
Devarajan, Shanta 212*n*
Dewey, John 149
Diener, Ed 82*t*
  with R. Biswas-Diener 5*n*, 78*t*
  with D. G. Myers 80*t*
Doyal, Len 69*t*, 75*t*, 78*t*
  with I. Gough 27, 68–9, 74, 158, 164–5
Drèze, Jean 92, 95
  with A. K. Sen 86, 89, 131, 169, 173, 176, 178, 187*t*
Dupuit, J. 206
Durdag, Mete, with L. Squire and I. M. D. Little 213

Dutch, Raymond M., with M. A. Taylor 70
Dworkin, Ronald 94

Eiselen, W. W. M. 142*n*
Ellerman, David 148–50
Finnis, John 3, 15–18, 20, 21, 27, 32, 39, 40, 43–59, 60, 61, 63, 67, 71, 72, 73–6, 78*t*, 85, 105–13, 123, 131*n*, 138, 144, 201, 288, 290–1
  with J. Boyle and G. Grisez 17, 48*t*, 73, 291
Freire, Paolo 149, 256
Fromm, Erich 79*t*

Galtung, Johan 79*t*
Geertz, Clifford 53, 139
Ghai, Dharam 125
Glover, Jonathan, with M. C. Nussbaum 13, 87
Gough, Ian
  with L. Doyal 27, 68–9, 69*t*, 74, 75*t*, 78*t*, 158, 164–5
  with T. Thomas 167
Goulet, Denis 79*t*, 163
Griffin, James 49, 71, 79*t*
Grisez, Germain, with J. Finnis and J. Boyle 17, 48*t*, 73, 291
Grotius, Hugo 47*n*

Harberger, Arnold C. 212
Hayek, Friedrich 100
Hicks, John 88–9, 119
Hirschman, Albert O. 149
Hobsbawm, Eric 155
Hopkins, M., with G. Sheehan 174
Hume, David 47*n*

Inglehart, Ronald 69–71
Insham, Jonathan, with D. Narayan and L. Pritchett 228

Jain, Pankaj 222

Kant, Immanuel 100, 149
Kautilya 90
Keynes, John N. 39–40, 57
Khan, Akhtar Hamid 234–5
Khan, Shoaib Sultan 235
Kierkegaard, S. A. 149
Krech, David, with R. S. Crutchfield and N. Livson 80*t*

Index of Names

Lane, Robert E. 80*t*
Lasswell, Harold D. 80*t*
Leach, M. 222
Lewin, Shira B. 39–40, 54, 57–8
Lisska, Anthony J. 16*n*
Little, I. M. D.
  with M. Durdag and L. Squire 213
  with J. A. Mirrlees 206, 209, 211, 215
Livson, Norman, with D. Krech and R. S. Crutchfield 80*t*

McGregor, Douglas 149,
MacIntyre, Alasdair 139, 139*n*
McKinley, Terry 188, 189
Marglin, Stephen 180
  with F. Apffel-Marglin 125
Marx, Karl 6, 95, 103
Maslow, Abraham H. 80*t*
Max-Neef, Manfred 25, 26, 60–1, 62*t*, 75*t*, 76, 80*t*, 164, 224
Menger, Carl 100
Mihaljeck, Dubravko, with G. Pohl 208
Mill, John S. 95, 103–4, 108
Mirrlees, J. A., with I. M. D. Little 206, 209, 211, 215
Murray, H. A. 80*t*
Musonius Rufus 48*t*
Myers, David G., with E. Diener 80*t*

Narayan, Deepa 26, 61–3, 64*t*, 71, 75*t*, 81*t*
  with L. Pritchett and J. Insham 228
Nawaz, Safia Ali 43–4, 53, 126, 272, 275
Nielsen, Kai 81*t*
North, Douglass 138
Nozick, Richard 94
Nussbaum, Martha C. 4, 12, 17, 21, 26, 28, 29, 32–43, 44, 44*n*, 46, 52, 54–60, 72, 74, 75*t*, 81*t*, 111*n*, 165
  with J. Glover 13, 87

Orshansky, Mollie 156

Packard, Vance 81*t*
Pattanaik, Prasanta 188, 189
Petesch, Patti 62
Petit, Philip 98*n*
Plato 108
Pohl, Gerhard, with D. Mihaljeck 208
Posner, Richard 199
Pritchett, Lant, with J. Insham and D. Narayan 228
Psacharopoulos, George 261, 262
Putnam, Hilary 108*n*
Putnam, Robert D. 204

Qizilbash, Mozaffar 12–13, 28, 71–2, 74, 75*t*, 76, 81*t*
Qureshi, Saeed 211

Ramsay, Maureen 68, 73, 75*t*, 76, 81*t*
Rawls, John 5, 29*n*, 33, 34, 41, 47, 54, 81–2*t*, 94, 110*t*, 111*n*, 170

Ricardo, David 95
Robbins, Lionel 14, 38, 85, 89–90, 112, 114, 133, 287
Rogers, Carl 149
Rokeach, Milton 64, 66, 82*t*
Rosenweig, Mark R. 214
Rowntree, B. Seebohm 185*n*
Ryff, Carol D. 82*t*

Salmen, Larry 221*n*, 222, 292*n*
Samuelson, Paul 7, 96, 97
Sandel, Michael 141
Schumacher, E. F. 149
Schumpeter, Joseph A. 125
Schwartz, Shalom H. 63–6, 75*t*, 82*t*, 83*t*
Scitovsky, Tibor 136
Sen, Amartya K. 6–11, 25, 28–32, 50, 52, 53, 55, 83*t*, 87–8, 90–1, 102–5, 134–5, 140–1, 142, 156, 161–2, 187*t*, 292, 297–8
  with S. Anand 10*n*, 83*t*, 182–3, 187*t*
  with J. Drèze 86, 89, 131, 169, 173, 176, 178, 187*t*
Shabnam 233
Shah, Meera K. 62
Sheehan, G., with M. Hopkins 174
Sidgwick, Henry 50
Smith, Adam 100, 185, 185*n*
Socrates 92, 136
Spitz, René 68*n*
Squire, Lyn
  with I. M. D. Little and M. Durdag 213
  with H. G. van der Tak 212, 216
Stewart, Frances 11–12, 27, 168, 171*n*
Stiglitz, Joseph E. 210
Streeten, Paul 15, 154, 167–8, 174
Sugden, Robert 11, 119
Sunstein, Cass 31–2, 93

Taja, Dadi 1–2, 5, 9, 25, 43, 86, 131, 138, 233
Taylor, C. N. 220
Taylor, Michael A., with R. M. Dutch 70
Thomas, Theo, with I. Gough 167
Townsend, Peter 156, 185, 185*n*
Trump, Thomas M. 70

Ubaidullah, A., with A. A. Burki 261

van der Tak, H. G., with L. Squire 212, 216

Walras, Marie Esprit Léon 90
Watson, John 39
Weber, Max 40
Wiggins, David 25, 85, 158, 159, 160–1, 162, 163, 186, 193
Williams, Bernard 12, 156
Wilson, W. 83*t*
Withey, Stephen B., with F. M. Andrews 77*t*

Zaid, Hakim 233

Index of Subjects

Note: Page numbers followed by '*n*' refer to footnotes and those followed by '*t*' refer to tables.

absolute needs, and basic needs 158–60
absolute poverty 155–8
　basic human needs approach 169
abstractions, disagreement over and general concrete functionings 31
accomplishment, prudential values for development 72*t*
achieved functioning 6
　indicators of capabilities 182–3, 184*t*
　see also functionings
achievement
　functions 50–1
　universal human values 66*t*
action, and practical reason 45–6
aesthetic experience
　basic reasons for action 48*t*
　sample comments on impact 279
affection 61, 74
affiliation, human capabilities 35*t*, 42
Aga Khan Rural Support Programme (AKRSP) 235
agency
　and achievement 129
　and freedom 6, 6*n*, 9, 19, 118*t*, 129–30
　intrinsic value 130–1
　and participation 127, 130–1
　and well-being 129–30
　see also empowerment
Agenda 21, dimensions of development 77*t*
aggregative considerations 103
agreements, incompletely theorized agreements 31–2, 93
American Economic Association 92
Aquinas (Finnis) 58
Arabsolangi *see* rose cultivation initiative
arbitrary preferences, principles of practical reasonableness 110*t*
Aristotelian Society 95
art
　Khoj literacy initiative 271*t*
　sample comments on impact 279
Asia Foundation, The 231–2
Asian values 141
assertive incompleteness 10, 10*n*, 104
　see also incompleteness
assessment *see* evaluation
autonomy
　autonomy-compatible models 148–50
　as basic human need 68

　see also informed consent
avoidance, method of 54
axiological categories 60–1, 75*t*, 80*t*

basic capabilities 33, 105, 165–6
　absolute poverty 155–8
　achieved functioning 182–3
　and basic needs 154–95
　basic and non-basic capabilities, example 178–80
　categories of 26–7
　cultural progress 189
　DAC indicators' failure to reflect participation/coercion 193–4
　definition 162–3
　evaluation of 11–13, 223–32
　and functionings 25
　indicators 181–94, 184*t*
　operational interpretations 174–6
　see also capability approach
basic human values *see* values
basic judgements 133–5
basic needs approach (BNA) 11–12, 14–15, 19, 122, 156, 166, 167*n*, 169
　see also needs
Basic Needs in Developing Countries (Stewart) 168
basic reasons for action 45–6, 51, 54, 84*n*
　assessment of Finnis' set 73–6
　dimensions of functioning 52–3
　intelligibility of other cultures 56
　poverty reduction 52
　see also dimensions of human functioning
being 60, 61*t*
　and doing 5
　study of nature of 45
beneficiary assessment 221, 221*n*
benevolence, universal human values 66*t*
Bergson–Samuelson Welfare Theorem 13
Best–Practice Participation 201*n*
bodily life, basic reasons for action 48*t*
bodily well-being 64*t*
　and central human functional capabilities 35*t*
capability approach (CA) 4, 288
　and basic human needs approach 166–70, 292
　capability expansion 205
　　case studies 280–7
　　evaluation 291–2
　　goat-raising initiative 248
　capability rights 99

capability approach (cont.)
　capability sets 8, 11, 27, 43, 95, 180–2, 184, 191, 194–5, 281, 285, 292
　　capability set analysis 218–32
　　central human capabilities, Nussbaum's approach 32–43, 35t, 59–60, 75t, 81t
　　criticism, valuation of capabilities 11–13
　　discussion of term 18–19
　　evaluation 87–8
　　freedom 6–8
　　functionings 5–6, 25, 170–6, 195
　　human capabilities, definition 32
　　incompleteness 10–11
　　need to attend to full menu 180–1
　　operational considerations 115–24
　　participation 294–5
　　pluralism 8–10
　　see also basic capabilities
'Capability and Well-Being' (Sen) 160
case studies see goat-raising initiative; literacy and community development initiative; rose cultivation initiative
central human capabilities
　Nussbaum's approach 32–43, 35t, 59–60, 75t, 81t
　see also basic capabilities; capability approach
China, one-child family policy 101
choice 18, 112
　assertive incompleteness 104
　collective choice, institutional frameworks 117–18
　and competence 176–7
　freedom 6–8, 283
　and growth 125
　human development 19
　identity shaped by choices 138
　information-gathering 120
　resource constraints 123–4
　underdetermined free choice 20, 127
　value 131
　see also coercion; freedom; participation; revealed preference
class, consensus 42
climate, health-care 183
coercion
　functionings and capabilities 175–6
　see also choice; decision-making; freedom; participation
Collective Choice and Social Welfare (Sen) 117
colours, as metaphor for values 52
combined capabilities 33
commitments
　characteristics of dimensions 51
　principles of practical reasonableness 110t
commodities
　basic human needs 166, 167n, 168
　and well-being 6

Commodities and Capabilities (Sen) 52, 297–8
common good, principles of practical reasonableness 110t
communication, difficulties and informed consent 295
community development and literacy initiative, case study 255–71
Community Guide to Social Impact Assessment (Burdge) 220
community-based organizations (CBOs) 128
competence, and choice 176–7, 295
concern clusters, dimensions of human development 77t
concrete functionings 31–2
conformity, universal human values 66t
conscience, principles of practical reasonableness 110t
consensus
　general concrete functionings 31
　international 33
　method of avoidance 54
　modifying lists 73
　Nussbaum's approach to central human capabilities 40–1
　ordering of options 3
consequences
　unintended but predictable 100–1
　see also evaluation
consequential analysis 102
consequentialism 90, 98
　definition 98n
consistency, revealed preference 97
consumption, savings 211–12
control
　central human functional capabilities 35t
　empowerment 8
　freedom from 7
cost-benefit analysis (CBA) 93, 199, 202–3, 206–18
　applicability to small NGO activities 207–9
　case studies, comparisons between 279–81
　changing attitudes towards 206–7
　distributive weighting 212–13
　efficiency CBA and social CBA 212
　evaluating change 232
　functionings, changes in 282
　goat-raising initiative, case study 236–46
　　benefits, income 238t
　　financial flows 237t
　Khoj literacy initiative 259–65, 260t
　limitations 234
　numeraire 211
　prices 209–10
　rose cultivation initiative 273–7
　savings/investment 211–12
　shadow wages 213–16
　social benefits 208–9
　social discount rates 210–11

Index of Subjects

weighting objectives 216–18
  see also evaluation
creation 61*t*
creativity 113, 188
critical reflection 92
Crying Out for Change (Narayan *et al*) 62–3
  see also Voices of the Poor
cultural anthropology, dimensions of development 53
culture
  absolute poverty 186
  and basic needs 294–6
  comparison of capabilities of different cultural groups 181–94
  consensus 42
  cross-cultural study, poor people 62
  cultural practice 139
  cultural value systems, and knowledge 135–6
  and development 141–3
  dimensions of human flourishing 54
  and identities 140–1
  indicators of 187–90
  intelligibility of different cultures 56
  multinationals 178
  possible Western bias of lists 72
  reasons for action 45–6
  relativity of basic needs 161
  see also tradition
data availability 183–4
data requirements 181
decision-making 13, 130
  see also choice; coercion; participation
decisions, public decisions, accountability 93
democracy
  democratic social choice 9, 23
  and famines 132
  value clarification 137
  see also choice; coercion; freedom; participation
'Democracy as a Universal Value' (Sen) 137
deprivation 78*t*, 156
  see also poverty
desire-fulfilment 5
detachment 110*t*
development 2
  anti-development critique 180
  development ethics, proceduralism 87–8
  development strategies, ends 92–3
  economic development, freedom-expanding assistance 146–8
  equality and expansion of capabilities 177–81
  introduction of novel practices 140
  values questions 14–15
  see also human development
Development Assistance Committee (DAC) 15, 181
  indicators of poverty 190–4, 192*t*

  see also Organization for Economic Cooperation and Development
Development as Freedom (Sen) 18, 22, 26, 31, 128, 137, 142
dialogue 56–8
discount rates, social discount rates 210–11
distributive weighting 206, 206*n*, 207, 207*n*, 212–13, 232
  goat-raising initiative 243
doing 60, 61*t*
  and being 5
domains of life satisfaction 66–8, 75*t*, 78*t*
dominance partial ordering 30, 31
Dominating Knowledge (Apffel-Marglin and Marglin) 180
drama, and cultural differences 189
drug addiction 259

economics
  DAC indicators 192*t*
  economic analysis 202–3
  economic rationality, and ethical rationality 90–1
  economic security, world values survey 71*t*
  and ethics 133
  microeconomic initiatives 3, 38
  policies and society 25
  theories 88–9
education
  DAC indicators 192*t*, 193
  and equality 173
  Pari Hari girls' education programme 178–80
  see also information; knowledge; literacy
efficiency
  and equality 103
  goat-raising initiative 246–7
  participation 132
  practical reasonableness, principles of 110*t*
  principle of 109, 112
emotions, and central human functional capabilities 35*t*
empirical data, substantiating sets of dimensions 56–7
empowerment 131*n*
  changes in functionings, case studies compared 282*t*
  cost-benefit analysis 208, 209
    weighting of objectives 217
  goat-raising initiative 247, 251*t*, 252
  informed consent 295–6
  Khoj literacy initiative 266, 267*t*, 269*t*
  participation 130–1
ends
  capability approach 205
  development strategies 92–3
  inaccurately reflected in revealed preference 98
  revealed preference theory 96

engineering rationality 90–1, 110t
  and ethical rationality 109, 112
enjoyment, prudential values for
        development 72t
entrenched needs 159, 159n
environment
  changes in functionings, case studies
        compared 282t
  environmental externalities 207
  environmental impact assessments (EIAs) 219
  environmental sustainability, DAC
        indicators 192t
  sample comments on impact 278
epistemology
  epistemological decentralization 120
  issue of and generation of capabilities lists 36
  Nussbaum's approach to central human
        capabilities 38–41
equality
  distribution of primary goods 183
  and efficiency 103
  functionings 173
  meeting basic needs 195
ethical rationality 106
  democratic discussion 92
  economic science 113–15
  and engineering rationality 109, 112
  poverty reduction 89–94
  principle pluralism 287–8
  see also practical reason; rationality
ethics
  development ethics, proceduralism 87–8
  and economics 133
evaluation
  beneficiary assessment 221, 221n
  capability changes 203–6, 291–3
  comparison of case studies 277–87
  cost-benefit analysis 202–3, 206–18
  multidimensionality 87–8
  participatory poverty assessments
        (PPAs) 223
  participatory social assessment 221–3
  qualitative ranking 229–30, 230t
  situated evaluation 100
  Social Assessment (SA) 221n
  social impact assessment 218–21
  valuing change in functionings and capabilities
        223–32
  see also cost-benefit analysis; goat-raising
        initiative; impacts; literacy and community
        development initiative; rankings; rose
        cultivation initiative
evil, Nussbaum's normative accounts of human
        development 55
expense, informational requirements of capability
        approach 120–2
external assistance, and participation 144–51
externalities 205

fairness 109n, 286
family planning 101, 176
famines, and democracy 132
fasting 171
feasible basic indicators 184
feminism, and problem of consensus 40
fertility rates, public discussion 133
finance see loans
flexibility
  dimensions of development 53–4
  and specificity 37–8
flourishing
  and basic human needs 165
  and functioning 52
  see also functionings
free choice 112–13
  underdetermined free choice 20, 127
  see also choice
free speech 111n
freedom 9, 12–13, 61t, 83t
  and capability, discussion of terms 19
  capability approach 6–8
  Finnis on 16–17
  freedom-expanding assistance 146–8
  and participation 127, 128
  prudential values for development 72t
  well-being 64t
  see also choice; democracy;
        participation
friendship
  basic reasons for action 48t
  and practical reasonableness 107
fulfilment, practical reason 45
full life 27
functionings
  achieved functioning 6, 182–3, 184t
  achievement 51
  capability approach 5–6, 25, 170–6, 195
  categories of 36
  changes in, case studies 281–2, 284
  definition 18
  dimensions of human functioning 26, 27, 28,
        59, 76
    adding and removing 73–6
    characteristics 49–51, 74t
    cultural anthropology 53
    identification of 45–8
    and needs 69
    rose cultivation initiative 43–4
    and space 52
  values 49–50, 76, 88, 292–4
  and ends 205
  flourishing 52
  general functionings approach 30–2, 37, 53,
        161
  human development 51–5
  multiple realizability 37
  practical reasoning 46

Index of Subjects

value 12, 30
see also flourishing
Fundamentals of Ethics (Finnis) 17, 109n

gender
   equality, DAC indicators 192*t*
   Khoj literacy initiative 262, 280
   literacy 172
   qualitative ranking, women's participation 229–30, 230*t*
   rose cultivation initiative in Pakistan 45
   see also goat-raising initiative; literacy and community development initiative; rose cultivation initiative
general functionings approach 30, 53, 161
   general concrete functionings 31–2
   and Nussbaum's multiple realizability 37
   see also functionings
globalization 101
goals
   goal rights system, definition 99*n*
   and indicators 189
goat-raising initiative 213
   case study 235–55
   changes in functionings 281*n*, 282*t*
   cost-benefit analysis 236–46, 279–80
   efficiency 246–7
   impacts 248–54
   income 236, 238, 238*t*, 239*t*, 240*t*, 241*t*, 281*n*
   market viability 247–8
   participation 284*t*
   qualitative grading 229
'Good as Discipline, Good as Freedom' (Nussbaum) 58
'Goods and People' (Sen) 166
governance, voice in consensus of central human capabilities 43
gross domestic product (GDP), India and Pakistan compared 234
gross national product (GNP) 14
   per capita, and definition of poverty 19
growth 19, 125
   see also development
Handbook on Economic Analysis of Investment Operations (World Bank) 207, 216, 264, 286
happiness 5
   avowed happiness 83*t*
   characteristics of dimensions 51
   goat-raising initiative, impact 251*t*
harmony 48*t*, 63
having 60, 61*t*
health 64*t*
   autonomy-compatible poverty reduction 150–1
   basic human needs 68
   as basic value 55
   central human capabilities 35*t*, 60

   changes in functionings, case studies compared 282*t*
   climate 183
   DAC indicators 192*t*, 193
   functionings and capabilities 175
   goat-raising initiative, impact 251*t*, 252
   health clinics 170–1, 173
   intermediate needs 69*t*
   life expectancy 68, 95, 158, 169, 182–3, 192*t*
   medicine and freedom-expanding assistance 146–7
   mortality rates 182, 192*t*
   Pari Hari project 179
   prudential values for development 72*t*
   social cost-benefit analysis 204
hedonism, universal human values 66*t*
helper-doer models *see* autonomy-compatible models
hierarchy, characteristics of dimensions 51
household welfare function 214–15
human capabilities
   definition 32
   see also capability approach
human capital 204
   Khoj literacy initiative 261
human development 201
   dimensions of human development 51–4, 75*t*, 77–83*t*, 187*t*, 290–4
   and economic development 19
   Finnis' approach 15–18, 43–59
   human development index (HDI) 98, 234
   India and Pakistan compared 234
   integral directiveness 106–8
   see also development
Human Development Reports 19, 87, 98, 177, 182
human goods
   acting for, morality 108
   and integral directiveness 107, 108, 109
   thick and vague conceptions 44, 44*n*
human impact 205–6
human nature 29, 39–40
human needs *see* needs
human poverty index (HPI) 187*t*
human rights 111*n*
   and obligations 99–102
identities 61*t*, 137–43
   and culture 140–1
ill-being, and well-being, cross-cultural study 62–3
imagination, and central human functional capabilities 35*t*
immoral choice 105*n*
impacts 205
   goat-raising initiative 248–54
   human impact 205–6
   impact assessment 22, 43, 228, 289, 294, 296

Index of Subjects

impacts (*cont.*)
  Khoj literacy initiative 258, 266–71
  rose cultivation initiative 277
  sample comments on 278–9
  social impact assessment (SIA) 218–21
  see also evaluation; rankings
imperfect obligations 100
imperialism, and culture 188
implementation 15
Impossibility Theorem 94, 127
income
  assessment of initiatives 1–2
  distributional weights, goat-raising initiative 243
  goat-raising initiative 236, 238, 238*t*, 239*t*, 240*t*, 241*t*
  income generation 1, 2, 8, 22, 43, 126, 144, 200–1, 217, 234, 252, 256–7, 261, 264, 272, 284, 291, 295–6
  income per capita 5
    and human development index 98
  indicator of capabilities 182–3
  Khoj literacy initiative 262–5
  literacy initiative 257
  rose cultivation initiative 8, 274–5, 276–7, 276*t*
  see also loans; wages
incommensurability 36, 50, 50*n*, 108
  non-existence of objective aggregate 95–6
incompletely theorized agreements 31–2, 93
incompleteness 10–11, 104, 289–90
  see also partial orderings
India
  basic capabilities 173
  compared to Pakistan 234
  property rights 41
  tradition 141
'Indian Traditions and the Western Imagination' (Sen) 141
indicators, basic capabilities 181–94
individual advantage 9
inequality 155
Inequality Reexamined (Sen) 4, 10, 29, 103, 113, 181
information
  asymmetric technical information and asymmetric values information 144
  choice 116, 117–19, 118*t*
  ethical rationality 115
  goat-raising initiative, benefits 255
  information-gathering 120–2
  participatory social assessment 221–3
  value changes 133
  value formation 133–6
  see also education; knowledge; literacy
informational pluralism 94–102
  human rights and obligations 99–102
  revealed preference 95–8

situated evaluation 100
unintended but predictable consequences 100–2
work of J. Finnis 16
informed consent
  autonomy-compatible poverty reduction 150–1
  empowerment 295–6
  freedom-expanding assistance 146–8
  see also autonomy
inner peace
  changes in functionings, case studies compared 282*t*
  goat-raising initiative 251
  Khoj literacy initiative 266, 268*t*, 270–1*t*
  rose cultivation initiative 1, 8, 9, 26
  sample comments on impact 278
  see also religion; spirituality
instrumental mode of conduct 66
insurance, goat-raising initiative 246–7
integral directiveness 106–8
integral human flourishing 52
interacting 60, 61*t*
intermediate needs 69*t*, 75*t*, 78*t*
internal capabilities 33
international consensus, capability approach 32–4
International Labour Organization (ILO), World Employment Conference 169
interpersonal comparisons 38, 87, 114*n*, 127
intransitive effects 152
  culture 140–3
  identity 137–43
  practices 138–40
introspection
  human nature 39–40
  introspective analysis 39–40, 57–8, 60
invisible hand 100
irreducibility, criteria for dimensions of human flourishing 74*t*
iterative questioning 54, 55

joy, dimensions of human development 77*t*
justice 4, 30, 34, 85, 87, 94, 104–5, 108, 111*t*, 133*n*, 158*n*, 177–8

Kerala, family planning 173, 176
Khoj literacy and community development initiative 200, 229, 255–71, 280, 282*t*, 284*t*, 286, 295
knowledge 63
  basic reasons for action 48*t*
  changes in functionings, case studies compared 282*t*
  and cultural value systems 135–6
  goat-raising initiative, impact 250*t*, 252
  indicator of capabilities 182
  Khoj literacy initiative 266, 267*t*, 270*t*
  and power 57–8
  prudential values for development 72*t*

Index of Subjects

qualitative ranking 229
and reasons for action 45–6
sample comments on impact 278
social cost-benefit analysis 204
as value 49
see also education; information; literacy
Komila Integrated Rural Development Project 235
law, criticism of concept of value-free law 15–16

learning, value formation 135
leisure 61*t*
  goat-raising initiative 253
  shadow wages 214–15
liberalism 34, 37, 58
Liberalism and Natural Law Theory (Finnis) 48t
life
  basic reasons for action 48*t*
  central human functional capabilities 35*t*
  changes in functionings, case studies compared 282*t*
  goat-raising initiative, impact 251*t*, 252
  Khoj literacy initiative 268*t*, 270*t*
  value of 55–6
life domains 78*t*
life expectancy 68, 95, 158, 169, 182–3, 192*t*
  see also health
literacy
  and gender in Pakistan 172
  literacy and community development initiative, case study 255–71, 280, 282*t*, 284*t*, 286, 295
  prudential values for development 72*t*
  see also education
'Living Standard, The' (Sen) 9, 181
loans
  goat-raising initiative 237*t*, 238
  see also income; wages
Mahabharata, and situated evaluation 100
many-one problem 168
market
  market failures, cost-benefit analysis 206
  market viability, goat-raising initiative 247–8
  role of 13
marriage, basic reasons for action 48*t*
material well-being 64*t*
materialism, modernization survey 70–1, 71*t*
Mavi Women's Organization 272
maximization 105, 105*n*
means of freedom 12
medicine, and freedom-expanding assistance 146–7
metaphysical views
  and list of central human capabilities 34, 34*n*
  reasons for action 47, 47*n*
  see also religion
methodology
  identifying valuable capabilities 3

participation 128
microeconomic initiatives 3, 38
migrant labour, shadow wages 214–15
modernization, and value priorities 69–71
Modernization and PostModernization (Inglehart) 70
morality
  acting for human goods 108
  integral directiveness 106
  moral judgements 45
  practical reasonableness 49, 108
  and rationality 106–8, 123
mortality rates
  DAC indicators 192*t*
  indicator of capabilities 182
  see also health
motives 80*t*
multidimensionality, evaluation 86–8
multinationals, and culture 178
multiple realizability, pluralism in Nussbaum's central human capabilities approach 37

National Environmental Policy Act (1969) (USA) 219
natural law 16*n*, 17
'Natural Law and Legal Reasoning' (Finnis) 109*n*
Natural Law and Natural Rights (Finnis) 15–16, 17, 45, 48*t*, 58
'Nature and classes of Prescriptive Judgements, The' (Sen) 133
Nature and Significance of Economic Science, The (Robbins) 114
needs 26, 75*t*, 79*t*, 80*t*, 81*t*
  absolute needs 158–60
  absolute poverty, basic human needs 169
  basic capabilities 154–95
  basic human needs, Doyal and Gough 68–9
  basic needs approach 11–12, 14–15, 19, 122, 156, 166, 167*n*, 169
  Braybrooke 77*t*
  Brentano 78*t*
  capability approach 166–70, 292
  criteria for generating classification of 62*t*
  and culture 294–6
  definition 15, 163–5
  and dimensions 69
  informing political behaviour 80*t*
  instinctive and universal needs 80*t*
  intermediate needs, Doyal and Gough 69*t*
  Max-Neef's axiological categories 60–1
  Packard's hidden needs 81*t*
  relativity of 160–2
  understanding, need for 61*t*
net present values (NPV) 211
Nicomachean Ethics (Aristotle) 18, 29
non-compulsive judgements (NJ) 134, 134*n*
non-governmental organizations (NGOs) 28
  activities, multidimensionality 86–7
  NGO Resource Center (NGORC) 126

normative approach
  Nussbaum's functionings 54–6
  Pattanaik and McKinley on indicators of culture 189–90
  universal 32
nourishment
  basic needs 163
  indicator of capabilities 183, 183n
nuclear family, modernization survey 70
numeraire 211

objectives
  development strategies 92–3
  human development 50
  see also ends
objectivity 135
  objective aggregate, non-existence of 95–6
obligations, and human rights 99–102
operational considerations, capability approach 115–24
opportunity costs 206
  goat-raising initiative 242, 243
  Khoj literacy initiative 261, 262
  shadow wages 213–14
Orangi Pilot Project 235
Organization for Economic Cooperation and Development (OECD) Development Assistance Committee (DAC) 15, 181, 190–4, 192t
  indicators of poverty 190–4
  poverty reduction 26
outcomes, and participation 127
overlapping consensus 33, 34, 36, 37, 41, 42, 73
Oxfam
  Annual Report (1995–6) 2
  budgetary constraints 199
  choosing between alternatives of efficiency and empowerment 287
  cost-benefit analysis, weighting of objectives 217
  culture and basic needs 294
  evaluation of change 231–2
  initiatives, cost-benefit analysis 212
  Oxfam Handbook, cultural and ethical disagreements 140
  participation 125–6, 129n, 154
  see also goat-raising initiative; literacy and community development initiative; rose cultivation initiative
Pakistan
  compared to India 234
  see also goat-raising initiative; literacy and community development initiative; rose cultivation initiative
Pareto-optimality 90, 94, 116
Pari Hari, girls' education programme 178–80
partial orderings 3, 17, 104, 127

dominance partial ordering 30, 31
  see also incompleteness
participation 15, 61t, 125–9, 234
  agency freedom 131
  autonomy-compatible models 148–51
  as basic need 174
  case studies compared 283–4, 284t
  constructive effects 133–7
  culture and basic needs 294–5
  effect 228
  and external assistance 144–51
  goat-raising initiative, impact 251t
  indicators of participation 173, 296
  information-gathering and choice 120
  intransitive effects 137–43
  intrinsic value 130–1
  participatory social assessment 221–3
  practical reason and principle pluralism 288–9
  qualitative ranking, participation 229–31, 230t
  rose cultivation initiative 125–6, 154, 273
  sample comments on impact 279
  subsidiarity 143–4
  transitive effects 132–3
  weakness of DAC indicators 193–4
  see also choice; decision-making; democracy; freedom; revealed preference
participatory poverty assessments (PPAs) 223
participatory rural appraisal (PRA) 205, 222, 224
participatory social assessment 221–3
particularity see concrete
passivity, basic human needs approach 169
paternalism 58
phonetics, literacy initiative 256
phronimos 108
physical security, world values survey 71t
plan of life, principles of practical reasonableness 110t
play
  basic reasons for action 48t
  and central human functional capabilities 35t
pluralism
  capability approach 8–10
  Nussbaum's central human capabilities 37–8
  work of J. Finnis 16
  see also principle pluralism
political liberalism 37
poor, well-being according to 64t
'Poor, Relatively Speaking' (Sen) 157
Portraits Questionnaire (PQ) 65n
'Possibility of Social Choice, The' (Sen) 38
postmaterialism, modernization survey 70–1, 71t
poverty
  absolute poverty 155–8, 163, 165–6, 168, 176, 185–6
  DAC indicators of 190–4, 192t
  definition 19–20
  international indicators 186–7
  relative and absolute 185n

relativity of basic needs 161–2
secondary poverty 185n
and social pathology 61
see also deprivation
Poverty and Famines (Sen) 155
poverty reduction 84
  autonomy-compatible models 150–1
  basic reasons for action 52, 53
  ethical rationality 89–94
  and tradition, conflict 128
power
  and consensus of central human
    capabilities 41–3
  decision-making 36
  and knowledge 57–8
  universal human values 66t
Practical Principles, Moral Truth and Ultimate
  Ends (Grisez, Boyle and Finnis) 48t, 73
practical reason 13, 16, 17, 28, 29n, 35
  and basic values of human existence 45–7
  and consensus 41
  identifying human capabilities 42, 43–59
  and morality 49
  Nussbaum 37
  and plural principles 287–90
  principles of 13, 45, 45n, 66, 71, 105n, 108–9,
    110–11t, 288, 290
  structure 20
  see also ethical rationality; rationality
practical reasonableness 63
  basic reasons for action 48t
  and friendship 107
  principle pluralism 108–9, 110–11t
'Practical Truths, Principles, and Ultimate Ends'
  (Finnis, Boyle and Grisez) 17
practice 138–40
pre-morality, dimensions of human
  functioning 49
prescriptivity issue, issue of and generation of
  capabilities lists 36
prices, sets of 209–10
'Prima Mangiare, Poi Filosofare' (Carmen) 129
primary goods 30, 34, 81–2t, 158n
principle pluralism 18, 95
  Finnis 105–13
    integral directiveness 106–8
    practical reasonableness 108–9, 109–10t
    and practical reason 287–90
  Sen 102–5
Prisoners' Dilemma 97
proceduralism 87
process, and consequences 87
productive resources, allocation 13
productivity, social capital 204–5
profit-sharing, rose cultivation initiative 276, 276t
property rights, Nussbaum's approach to central
  human capabilities 41
protection 61

prudential values 71–2, 75t, 79t, 81t
psychology 5
  psychological well-being 64t
  universal psychological needs 68
public decisions, accountability 93
public income, premium on 212n
purdah 262

qualitative data, participatory approaches 128
qualitative ranking 229–30, 230t
  see also evaluation
quality of life domains 66–8, 75t, 78t
quality of life index, value-based 82t

rankings
  goat-raising initiative 253t, 254
  see also evaluation; impacts
rationality 3
  ethical rationality, poverty reduction 89–94
  Finnis 17–18
  and morality 106–8, 123
  rational choice theory 85–6
  see also ethical rationality; practical reason
Ravat Goth 248
re-estimated rates of return (RERR) 208
reasonable doctrine, and values 29n
reasonableness, practical reasonableness, principle
  pluralism 108–9
reasons for action *see* basic reasons for action;
  dimensions of human functioning
redistribution, and growth 19
reflective equilibrium 33, 42
reflexive goods 165n
relationships
  changes in functionings, case studies
    compared 282t
  goat-raising initiative, impact 250t, 253
  Khoj literacy initiative 268t, 270t
  sample comments on impact 278–9
relative poverty 156
relative weighting 29, 96, 143, 188, 228, 230
religion
  basic reasons for action 48t
  changes in functionings, case studies compared
    282t
  goat-raising initiative, impact 250t, 253
  impact, sample comments on 278
  Khoj literacy initiative 269t, 271t
  modernization survey 70
  Pari Hari project 179
  and reasons for action 47, 47n
  see also inner peace; metaphysical truths;
    spirituality
reputation, reasons for action 57
resources, constraints, and choice 123–4
respect, and principles of practical reasonableness 110t
revealed preference 7–8, 10, 15, 38
  informational pluralism 95–8

revealed preference (*cont.*)
  and introspection 40
  see also choice
rights *see* human rights
rose cultivation initiative 1–2, 5, 8, 9, 53, 200–1
  assessment of activity 36
  case study 271–7
  changes in functioning 282*t*
  cost-benefit analysis 273–7, 280
  feasibility considerations 119–20
  identity 137–8
  impact assessment 43–4
  multidimensionality 86
  participation 125–6, 154, 273, 284*t*
  subsidiarity 143
  transitive effects 132
Rural Women's Welfare Organization (RWWO) 200, 229, 235, 236, 295
  costs, goat-raising initiative 240, 241*t*, 242, 244–6*t*, 249*t*
  see also goat-raising initiative
satisfaction 5
savings
  and consumption 211–12
  Pari Hari project 179
  savings premium 211–12, 215
Scandanavian welfare study 77*t*
security
  universal human values 66*t*
  well-being 64*t*
self-determination
  free choice 113
  see also choice
self-direction
  participation 130–1
  universal human values 66*t*
self-esteem 9
self-evidence 50, 50*n*, 106
self-expression
  basic reasons for action 48*t*
  world values survey 71*t*
self-integration 63
  basic reasons for action 48*t*
  see also inner peace
self-interest 50, 91, 100
self-respect, prudential values for development 72*t*
senses, and central human functional capabilities 35*t*
sexual ethics, J. Finnis 17
sexual permissiveness, modernization survey 70
shadow prices
  cost-benefit analysis 208–9
  goat-raising initiative 242
  labour, goat-raising initiative 240, 242
shadow wages, cost-benefit analysis 213–16

shame, as indicator of capability deprivation 185–6
situated evaluation 100
skilful performance, basic reasons for action 48*t*
sociability 107
  basic reasons for action 48*t*
Social Assessment (SA) 221*n*
social benefits, cost-benefit analysis 208–9
social capital, productivity 204–5
social choice theory 128
social cost-benefit analysis (SCBA) 202, 204, 206
social discount rates 210–11
social impact assessment (SIA) 218–21, 289
social organization 236
social pathology, and poverty 61
social rationality 107
social well-being 64*t*
society, and economic policies 25
space 4
  and dimensions 52
  and pluralism 9
specificity, and flexibility, pluralism in Nussbaum's central human capabilities approach 37–8, 76
spirituality
  goat-raising initiative, impact 250*t*
  modernization survey 70
  see also inner peace; religion
Standard of Living, The (Sen) 12
  see also Tanner Lectures
state, as protector 58
stimulation, universal human values 66*t*
structural adjustment 101, 145
structure, work of J. Finnis 16
subjective well-being 27, 66, 80*t*
subsidiarity 143–4, 152–3
subsistence 61
substantive goods 165*n*
substantive and valuational judgements (SVJ) 88
sum-ranking 90
surplus labour, shadow wages 214–15
sustainability 10*n*

Tanner Lectures 12, 18
  see also Standard of Living, The (Sen)
taxonomy 67, 68, 73, 76
technical rationality *see* engineering rationality
terminal mode of conduct 66
terminal values 82*t*
terminology 205
theoretical reflections, substantiating sets of dimensions 56–7
theory, and participation 128
Theory of Justice (Rawls) 170
thick and vague conceptions of human good 44, 44*n*

Index of Subjects

thought, and central human functional capabilities 35*t*
time, relativity of basic needs 161, 162
trade, choosing set of prices 209–10
trade-offs, and democratic discussion 92
tradition
 and poverty reduction, conflict 128
 universal human values 66*t*
 see also culture
transcendence, basic reasons for action 48*t*
transitive effects, participation 132–3, 152
truth, and consensus 40

ultimate principles 104
understanding, human need for 61*t*
unintended consequences 100–1
United Nations
 Human Development Reports 19, 87, 98, 177, 182
 poverty reduction 19–20
 United Nations Development Programme (UNDP) 182
 United Nations Educational, Scientific and Cultural Organization (UNESCO) 181
 World Culture Report 187–90
 United Nations Industrial Development Organization (UNIDO) 204, 211, 217, 227
unity, Pari Hari project 179
universal psychological needs 68
universal values 34, 50, 54*n*, 59–60, 63–6, 66*t*
utilitarianism 5, 7, 105
 revealed preferences 98
 welfare economics 30, 38
utility, and commodities 5–6

valuable capabilities 3, 3*n*, 25–32, 53
 see also capability approach
values
 asymmetric values information 144–5
 creation of 172–3
 definition 63
 and dimensions 49–50, 76, 88, 292–4
 freedom 6–7
 and human development 290–1
 human values 27, 45, 45*n*, 63–6, 66*t*, 75*t*, 78*t*, 80*t*, 83*t*
 information and value changes 133
 prudential values 71–2, 72*t*
 and reasonable doctrine 29*n*
 sought by all, Goulet 79*t*
 valuational function 52
 value areas 78*t*
 value conflicts 11–12
 value formation 133–7

value judgements 3, 3*n*, 11, 14, 16, 17, 20, 21, 22, 30, 93, 117, 134, 137, 156, 195, 205, 212, 216–17, 265
 selecting capabilities to focus on 8–9
 and value of life 55–6
value-free law, criticism of concept 15–16
values questions, welfare economics and development 14
world values survey, Inglehart 69–71
 see also basic human values; universal human values
variolation 150
verstehen 40
voice, identifying human capabilities 41–3
Voices of the Poor (Commissioned by the World Bank) (Narayan *et al*) 20, 62, 63, 179, 223

wages
 goat-raising initiative, assessment of benefits 238, 240, 241*t*, 242
 Khoj literacy initiative 259, 260*t*, 261
 see also income; loans
weighting
 impacts 226–7
 literacy initiative 256
 objectives, cost-benefit analysis 216–18
welfare 5
welfare economics 13
 theories, information pluralism 94–5
 utilitarianism 30, 38, 90
 values questions 14
welfare function 214–15
well-being 5, 39–40, 52
 and agency 129–30
 dimensions of 26, 61–3, 64*t*, 72, 75*t*, 81*t*, 82*t*
 domains of subjective well-being 66–8
 and ill-being, cross-cultural study 62–3
 Narayan 26, 61–3, 64*t*, 71, 75*t*, 81*t*
 and participation 127
 relativity of basic needs 160
 well-being achievement 129
 well-being freedom 129
 wellness, dimensions of 82*t*
Western bias, lists 72
Women, Culture, and Development (Nussbaum and Glover) 37, 87
Women and Human Development (Nussbaum) 32–3, 41–2
work 63
 changes in functionings, case studies compared 282*t*
 goat-raising initiative, impact 251*t*
 Khoj literacy initiative 267*t*, 270*t*
 sample comments on impact 279

World Bank 98
    cost-benefit analysis 206, 207, 212, 216
    Handbook on Economic Analysis of Investment
        Operations 207, 216, 264, 286
    identifying capable changes in poverty
        alleviation 27
    participation 125
    participatory social assessment 221
    poverty reduction 20
    Poverty Reduction Group 61–3
    re-estimated rates of return (RERR) 208
    World Development Reports 15, 27
World Culture Report (UNESCO) 187–90
World Development Reports
    (World Bank) 15, 27
world values survey, Inglehart 69–71